the Unofficial Guide® to Outlook® 2007

Marc Orchant

Wiley Publishing, Inc.

W9-BON-321

Unofficial Guide® to Outlook® 2007

Published by
Wiley Publishing, Inc.
111 River Street
Hoboken, NJ 07030-5774
www.wiley.com

For general information on our other products and services or to obtain technical support please contact our Customer Care Department within the U.S. at (800) 762-2974, outside the U.S. at (317) 572-3993 or fax (317) 572-4002.

Wiley also publishes its books in a variety of electronic formats. Some content that appears in print may not be available in electronic books. For more information about Wiley products, please visit our web site at www.wiley.com.

Library of Congress Control Number: 2006939439

ISBN: 978-0-470-04596-1

Manufactured in the United States of America

10 9 8 7 6 5 4 3 2 1

Page creation by Wiley Publishing, Inc. Composition Services

To my wife Sue, who inspires me daily with her creative works and brilliant smile.
To my daughter Rebecca, whose writing is a constant source of pride and joy.
To my son Jason, who shares my passion for cool toys and bright shiny objects.
To my mom Glenda, for teaching me the single most important life lesson—do what you love and everything else takes care of itself.
To my dad Norman, for showing me how to be a great husband, father, and friend.

Acknowledgements

I'm so thankful for the support, assistance, and encouragement of many people without whose help this book could not have been written. I'd like to extend special thanks to: Jeff P. Van Dyke and the great group of people at VanDyke Software, Richard Lusk, Oliver Starr, Michael Sampson, and the rest of the team at Foldera, Neil Salkind, Jeremy Wright, James Kendrick, Kevin Tofel, Ed Bott, Eric Mack, David Allen, Michael Linenberger, Hobart Swan, Dan Farber, and Sarah Waffle. Special thanks to everyone on the Wiley team and especially Cricket Krengel for guidance, support, and understanding when "real life" sometimes got in the way of book writing.

Credits

Acquisitions Editor
Jody Lefevere

Project Editor
Cricket Krengel

Technical Editor
Mark H. Walker

Copy Editors
Gwenette Gaddis Goshert
Lee Y. Miao

Editorial Manager
Robyn Siesky

Business Manager
Amy Knies

Vice President & Group Executive Publisher
Richard Swadley

Vice President & Publisher
Barry Pruett

Project Coordinator
Erin Smith

Graphics and Production Specialists
Sean Decker
Carrie A. Foster
Denny Hager
Jennifer Mayberry
Melanee Prendergast

Quality Control Technicians
Cynthia Fields
Brian H. Walls

Proofreading and Indexing
Potomac Indexing, LLC
Jennifer Stanley

Book Interior Design
Lissa Auciello-Brogan
Elizabeth Brooks

Special Help
Jenny Watson

Wiley Bicentennial Logo
Richard J. Pacifico

About the Author

Marc Orchant has been building, testing, and sometimes breaking hardware and software for 25 years. A recovering graphic designer, Marc is currently the VP of Marketing at Foldera, Inc., a prolific blogger, co-host of On The Run With Tablet PCs, a weekly podcast, and a self-admitted "productivity maven, gadget freak and software addict." Marc was named a Microsoft MVP (Windows — Tablet PC) in January, 2006 and is the co-author (with Jeremy Wright) of two personal productivity training programs for Microsoft, a contributor to the Office Online Community Expert Zone, and contributed an essay titled "Work is Broken" to the *More Space* project.

Before joining Foldera, Marc was Storyteller at VanDyke Software, a developer and publisher of Secure Shell (SSH) client and server software for Windows and UNIX. During the dot-com days Marc led the development and implementation of a Web-based digital asset management system used by a number of major motion picture and television studios in Hollywood. He traveled the country as a Market Development Manager for Agfa Digital Printing Systems and has spoken at a number of conferences and seminars including Seybold San Francisco and XPlor International and contributed articles to a wide range of print and online outlets.

Marc was a pioneer in the digital graphics industry. He helped establish the largest high-end digital graphics studio and imaging center in New Mexico where he played with a lot of really cool stuff. Marc is currently involved in the New Mexico Information Technology and Software Association and co-chairs its Workforce Education Alliance, a partnership between the IT industry, public education, and government that is working to integrate information technology standards and well-defined career pathways into the curriculum of New Mexico high schools.

Contents

If you are reading this book, it's a safe bet that you either have a shiny new copy of 2007 Microsoft Office Outlook or are trying to decide whether an upgrade is a good idea. Outlook 2007 is part of the 2007 Microsoft Office system — the most radically redesigned version of the suite in years. Some, myself included, have said that Office 2007 is the biggest gamble Microsoft has ever made. The Office suite is one of the company's core products and much of its revenue comes from new license sales and upgrades to this collection of productivity applications. To make the kind of substantial changes to a cash cow like Office, there must have been some very powerful reasons.

The fact of the matter is that Microsoft doesn't have much external competition in the office productivity application space. Sure, there is OpenOffice, an open-source suite and its commercial cousin StarOffice, which is sold by Sun Microsystems. These suites offer the basics — word processing, spreadsheet, and presentation tools. Corel, a company best known for graphics applications, has been gamely trying to keep WordPerfect, once the reigning champion in the word processing world, relevant after acquiring the application from Novell a few years ago. But even when people get a copy of Corel WordPerfect preinstalled on a new PC, the odds are that a copy of Microsoft Word, as part of the Office suite, is going to be installed. Even on the Mac platform, Microsoft Office:Mac is the clear leader.

So what would prompt Microsoft to roll the dice and introduce radical changes to such an important part of their product line? Well, from my perspective, the only product Office really competes with is the previous version

xix

of Office. Microsoft has continually added new features to the suite to convince users to upgrade to the newest version and that has become a harder and harder proposition to sell. Most people don't need more features — in fact many complain about bloat in recent versions of Office and an inability to find the features and tools they want to use.

To address those concerns, something had to change. And Microsoft has responded with a bold attempt to redefine the Office experience that, in most respects is a qualified success. Although this is actually the twelfth major release of Office (the codename for this release during testing was Office 12), it's almost like a version 1.0 release in many respects.

The core applications in the Office suite — Word, Excel, PowerPoint, and Outlook — have seen the biggest change in the user interface (UI) area with the introduction of the new Ribbon that replaces the menus and toolbars you've all become accustomed to using. Unlike the first three applications, the Office team has taken a hybrid approach to implementing the Ribbon in Outlook 2007, employing it in the content forms used to create and edit individual items while keeping the main Outlook views in more conventional menus and toolbars mode. Even in the main views, there are plenty of new features and enhancements to add a shiny new look to Outlook.

What's new in Outlook 2007?

The interface changes to Outlook fall into two main categories: the changes made to the main views interface and the new look of the content forms which is consistent with the changes made in the other core Office suite applications. But Outlook 2007 offers more than just a cosmetic makeover. There have been substantial changes to functionality as well.

Chapter 1 covers the new features and capabilities in Outlook 2007 in detail but here is a quick overview of the major enhancements and new features in this release.

New tools

- **To-Do Bar.** Outlook 2007 provides a new pane that displays the Date Navigator thumbnail calendar, a list of upcoming appointments, and an improved version of the Task Pad tasks list that was previously only available in the Calendar view. The To-Do Bar can be viewed in two modes — full view or minimized view or hidden completely. In minimized view, screen real estate is maximized but all of the information on the To-Do Bar can still be accessed with a click of the mouse.

- **Improved Navigation Pane.** Like the To-Do Bar, the Navigation Pane can now be minimized to provide more room on the screen to view content in the main window area. All content on the Navigation Pane can be accessed with a mouse click when in minimized view. These collapsible areas are a great help for those who use small screen devices like compact laptops, Tablet PCs, and UMPCs (Ultra Mobile PC).

- **Improved Calendar display.** The Calendar, in day and week views, now provides the option of displaying tasks for that day or week directly below the calendar grid. Having all of your commitments visible in one place is a terrific improvement to the Calendar and Task.

- **Integrated RSS.** Outlook 2007 can mnage subscriptions to RSS (Really Simple Syndication) feeds from Web sites, blogs, and other sources. Chapter 6 details how RSS works in Outlook 2007, Internet Explorer 7, and Windows Vista.

- **Instant Search.** Outlook uses the Windows Desktop Search engine in Windows XP and Vista's built-in indexing and search engine to provide powerful and lightning-fast search tools. Results appear immediately and as you type, Outlook filters the results to narrow the list of found items down. Instant Search also provides an advanced Query Builder interface that allows you to construct powerful search formulas tat can be saved as Search Folders. See Chapter 16 for more information about Instant Search.

Interface enhancements

The big change in how Outlook 2007 looks is the use of the new Ribbon in the content forms used to create and edit individual information objects like e-mail messages, calendar items, and tasks in Outlook. Chapter 5 documents the sweeping changes fond in these forms. Here are a few of my favorite features of the all-new Office 2007 Ribbon UI:

- **Live Preview.** When authoring or editing content, Outlook displays the effect of each font, style, color, or other formatting option in real time on the text or object you have selected. If you have ever made repeat trips to a formatting dialog box trying to get things to look the way you'd like, this feature will save you a substantil amount of time and open up your creative potential.

- **MiniBar.** When you select text in any of the content forms, a small toolbar that contains the most commonly used foratting options appears beneath the cursor, saving you a trip to the top of the window to access the ribbon. This MiniBar can be invoked at any time with a right-click.

- **Quick Access Toolbar.** The Quick Access Toolbar is a customizable bar where you can install any command you want immediate access to. The Quick Access Toolbar sites above the ribbon by default but can be displayed as a full-length toobar elow the ribbon if you prefer.

Integration with other Microsoft products

Microsoft has made a serious effort in Outlook 2007 to provide greater integration with other applications in the suite and with other products and services. For example, Outlook uses Word as its editor (the only choice in the new version), can display Office documents attached to e-mail messages, and supports editing of content stored on SharePoint servers. Integration with Office OneNote 2007 is significantly enhanced and you can now create and manage tasks that remain fully synchronized between the two environments.

The new Office Live Essentials and Premium subscription services can be connected to using Outlook 2007 to access the e-mail account and application services provided. For small business owners and sales professionals, the Business Contact Manager add-in for Outlook included in some versions of the Office 2007 suite can connect to Microsoft Small Business Accounting, which Microsoft now offers free of charge, to provide a set of customer relationship management, sales automation, and billing tools. This may be the most integrated and connected version of Outlook ever.

Putting it all in perspective

I said two things at the beginning of this introduction — that Office 2007 was a lot like a version 1.0 release and that it was a qualified success. For most people, I think Outlook 2007 is a significant upgrade with enough compelling new features and usability enhancements to justify the expense in time and money to make the switch. But there is still room for improvement.

There's an old saying amongst long-time users of Microsoft products that you should wait for version 3.0 before taking any new release from the company seriously. Others are of the opinion that it's crazy to install any major upgrade from Microsoft until the first Service Pack has been released. I can say with confidence that neither of those bits of conventional wisdom apply to this release. I've been working with Microsoft products for more than twenty years and have been actively testing their new wares for nearly ten. I have never seen a beta test with as large of a community of engaged, vocal, and passionate testers as this one.

Office 2007 has been given an unprecedented shakeout by this community and it's ready to be used on a daily basis. I have no doubt that additional features and functionality will continue to be added in the future. The architecture of the new suite and Outlook in particular is designed to allow extensions and enhancements to be added both by Microsoft and a thriving community of third-party developers.

There is a lot to like in Outlook 2007. I think it is the most capable version of the application yet and provides a unique platform for managing the ever-increasing amount of information we're all juggling. The emphasis on making the application easier and more enjoyable to use benefits power users and newcomers alike. I hope you find this guide useful as your exploration begins and a useful reference as integrate Outlook into your work and your play.

I've written at least one hundred blog posts about Outlook over the past four years, documenting how I use the application and sharing tips and tricks about how to fine-tune the interface and create productive workflows. I've incorporated a number of these ideas into this book. The best advice I can give to you is to go beyond the out-of-the-box default installation of Outlook and reshape this application to meet your unique needs. It's not as hard as you might think and the payback on your investment of time can be extraordinary.

Special features

Every book in the Unofficial Guide series offers the following four special sidebars that are devised to help you get things done cheaply, efficiently, and smartly.

1. **Hack:** Tips and shortcuts that increase productivity.

2. **Watch Out!:** Cautions and warnings to help you avoid common pitfalls.

3. **Bright Idea:** Smart or innovative ways to do something; in many cases, this will be a way that you can save time or hassle.

4. **Inside Scoop:** Useful knowledge gleaned by the author that can help you become more efficient.

We also recognize your need to have quick information at your fingertips, and have provided the following comprehensive sections at the back of the book:

1. **Glossary:** Definitions of complicated terminology and jargon.

2. **Recommended Reading:** Outlook can be used as the dashboard or central hub of your information management strategy. In Appendix B, I have provided a list of titles by some of the leading thinkers in the personal productivity space.

3. **Online Resources:** The Web offers a wealth of resources to help you get the most out of Outlook 2007. Appendix C provides a list of the sites I have found most useful for Outlook users.

4. **Index**

How Can I Use Outlook and What Is New?

GET THE SCOOP ON...
How Outlook processes information ▪ New features in
Outlook 2007 ▪ Ribbons, dialog boxes, toolbars, and
more ▪ New to Outlook 2007

Outlook Is More Than an E-Mail Program

If you're like most people who use Outlook, chances are you think of it as an e-mail program that also happens to include some other features that you've looked at and maybe used occasionally. If Outlook is the program installed for you on your office PC and you work in an Exchange Server environment, you may also think of it as a calendar and meeting management application. I have a different idea about what Outlook is. Outlook is an *information processor*. More specifically, Outlook is a *personal* information processor.

What do I mean by that? Think about the other applications included with Microsoft Office, which is how most people come to have Outlook installed on their PCs. Microsoft Word is a word processor. Microsoft Excel is a number and data processor. Microsoft PowerPoint is an idea processor. That's what PCs are used for — processing "stuff" and turning it into, well, other stuff. Word is used to turn thoughts, interactions, and conversations into documents like letters, reports, and books. Excel converts numbers and other data into charts, reports, balance sheets, and forecasts. PowerPoint, when used well, can distill ideas into compelling presentations, and so on.

Outlook processes information that is personally meaningful to you into actions and commitments. It helps you organize, store, retrieve, and share that information.

3

Outlook provides tools for creating, organizing, and using information, which include:

- E-mail
- Contacts
- Calendar
- Tasks
- Notes
- Activities

To be sure, there are any number of applications you can use that touch one or more of these information areas. But there are only a few applications that address all of them, and none enjoy the advantage of being included in the world's most widely installed productivity suite. Microsoft has designed Outlook to be an essential and tightly integrated piece of the Office environment. With this newest version of Outlook, even if you've been using Outlook for a while already, you are going to be amazed at the new look and features. This chapter is designed to take you on a short tour of the new look and feel and let you know what's new and what's improved.

E-mail

E-mail is the most frequently used and best understood of Outlook's capabilities. No matter what kind of e-mail environment you work in, Outlook provides a powerful set of features for working with your messages. You may use Outlook to connect directly to your Internet Service Provider (ISP) to send and receive your e-mail. This is commonly referred to as Internet Mail mode. This book assumes you use Outlook in this way.

One of the great new features in Outlook 2007 is the account creation tool that can figure out most of the settings for you when you set up a new e-mail account (see Figure 1.1). All you need to provide is the e-mail address and your account ID and password, and Outlook fills in the rest of the information required to get your account set up.

There are four common protocols used to send and receive e-mail. Outlook supports them all.

Add New E-mail Account

Internet E-mail Settings
Each of these settings are required to get your e-mail account working.

User Information

Your Name: `John Doe`

E-mail Address: `john.doe@bigco.com`

Server Information

Account Type: `POP3`

Incoming mail server: `mail.bigco.com`

Outgoing mail server (SMTP): `smtp.bigco.com`

Logon Information

User Name: `john.doe`

Password: `******`

☑ Remember password

☐ Require logon using Secure Password Authentication (SPA)

Test Account Settings

After filling out the information on this screen, we recommend you test your account by clicking the button below. (Requires network connection)

[Test Account Settings ...]

[More Settings ...]

[< Back] [Next >] [Cancel]

Figure 1.1. The Add New E-mail Account dialog box in Outlook 2007 is used to set up Internet e-mail accounts.

Exchange Server

Outlook can also connect to a Microsoft Exchange Server to send and receive information. Microsoft Exchange Server provides organizations with the ability to serve up e-mail, calendar, and contact management services to its employees and provides great tools for sharing information, managing meetings, delegating tasks, providing Web access to your Outlook information, and integrating messaging (voice mail, fax, instant messaging, and Internet news).

Setting up an Exchange Server account works a bit differently than setting up an Internet mail account because the server administrator has a lot of control over what information resources your account is permitted to view and access.

Hack

While this is not an Exchange guide, most of the information in this book is every bit as applicable to an Exchange user as it is to folks using Outlook in Internet Mail mode.

POP3

POP3 is the most common type of e-mail account offered by ISPs. The important thing to know about POP3 e-mail is that when you receive e-mail from the server, it is typically delivered to your PC and deleted from the server. You can change this behavior, but many ISPs place limits on how much e-mail you can leave on their servers and for how long. Figure 1.2 shows the Internet E-mail Settings dialog box's Advanced tab where you can modify these preferences. You access the Internet E-mail

Figure 1.2. Outlook's default settings for POP3 accounts are set to retrieve mail to your PC.

Settings dialog box by clicking the More Settings button in the Add New E-mail Account dialog box pictured in Figure 1.1.

IMAP

Internet Mail Access Protocol (IMAP) differs from POP3 and works more like Exchange Server in that e-mail resides on the server and is synchronized to your PC. The primary advantage of IMAP is that your e-mail is stored on the server and can be accessed from more than one PC.

HTTP

You probably recognize HTTP from your Web browsing experiences. The acronym stands for HyperText Transport Protocol. In Outlook, the HTTP protocol option is used to connect to Web-based e-mail services like Microsoft's HotMail.

Contacts

Outlook is a powerful contact manager. You can associate contacts with both calendar and task items and use the Outlook Journal to track your interactions with each contact in your list. Outlook can also access Microsoft MapPoint or online services to generate a map to a contact's location, dial the contact's phone, and more, as pictured in Figure 1.3.

Figure 1.3. Outlook makes it easy to initiate a wide range of actions for any contact in your list.

In the previous release of Microsoft Office (2003), Outlook received a thorough makeover in terms of general navigation and e-mail reading. In Outlook 2007, there are even more changes. You explore these changes later in this chapter, but it's worth noting right here that no view in this version of Outlook has had more work done to it than the calendar. That's welcome news actually because this view was most in need of a thorough redesign.

The new calendar finally shows not only the appointments you have set for each day but also the tasks you've assigned a due date that falls on that day or in that week, as shown in Figure 1.4. While earlier versions of Outlook provided the Task Pad as an option in the calendar view, it required significant adjustment to be really useful. With each day's tasks now displayed directly below the day's events, getting a handle on your commitments for each day has never been easier.

Figure 1.4. Outlook 2007 features a completely redesigned calendar, with an integrated task list for each day, improved navigation, and a much more attractive and easy to read display.

Tasks

The Tasks view in Outlook has also been refreshed for Outlook 2007 and uses the same color categories as the Calendar. What's more important is that Outlook 2007 puts your tasks front and center in every view with the addition of the new To-Do Bar, which you can see in Figure 1.5. The To-Do Bar is now accessible in all Outlook views and can be conveniently collapsed to the right edge of the screen when you don't need it using the Show/Hide button at the top of the bar. The Navigation Pane on the left side of the main Outlook Window can be displayed or hidden the same way. By default, the To-Do Bar contains the current month's calendar, the day's tasks, and the Task Input Panel (called the Task Pad in previous versions of Outlook), which displays upcoming tasks and provides an area where you can instantly create a new task item. Chapter 14 describes how the To-Do Bar can be customized to present task information in the way you find most useful.

Figure 1.5. The new To-Do Bar.

Notes

If ever there was a feature in Outlook that screamed for attention, it's the Notes tool. About the best thing I can say is that it hasn't gotten any worse in this release. If you need to capture a quick note — the kind of thing you might scribble on a sticky note — then the Notes feature works just fine. Otherwise, there are far better places in Outlook to capture information.

Other applications, such as Microsoft Office OneNote can integrate nicely with Outlook and provide a much better environment for note-taking and information management. Integration with other Office applications and third-party programs is discussed in Chapter 17.

Journal

Outlook's Journal has gotten a bum rap in my opinion. I regularly encounter people who have a vague sense that there's something bad about Journal — some reason that's hard to articulate as to why they shouldn't be using it. I think I know why. If you use Journal to track your interactions with every contact in your list, Outlook's data files can grow to an enormous size. If, on the other hand, you use Journal to track your interactions with your most important contacts (your boss, your direct reports, your customers, your family), you will have an amazingly detailed record of every interaction — e-mail, meeting, phone call, and task — available at the click of a mouse button (see Figure 1.6). Chapter 11 discusses in depth just how useful the Outlook Journal can be.

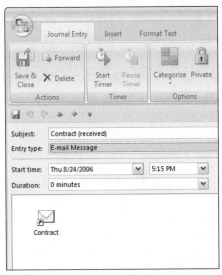

Figure 1.6. Outlook's Journal can automatically track every interaction with key contacts. You can also manually create Journal items to track specific calls or other activities with any contact.

What's new in Outlook 2007?

Microsoft Office 2007 may very well be the most ambitious redesign of the productivity suite ever. This new edition introduces sweeping user interface (UI) changes in the core Office System applications (Word, Excel, PowerPoint, Access, and Outlook), a new graphics engine, and a new XML-based file format for Office documents. In Office 2003, Outlook was the bright, shiny object of upgrade attention. In Office 2007, it might appear that Outlook has taken a backseat to the other core Office applications.

Not so, although there is a bit of UI multiple personality syndrome at work. If you're already familiar with Outlook, the changes to the main display views will be apparent, but at first glance these views do not appear substantially different from previous versions (see Figure 1.7). Spend a few minutes exploring Outlook 2007, and you soon discover that there are a number of significant improvements and enhancements, even in these standard views. Jensen Harris, a member of Microsoft's Office development team who has blogged extensively about the UI redesign in Office 2007, has written that there are more than 40 unique application experiences in Outlook and that it is the program most often used to read, write, and edit content in the Office suite.

The radical changes in Outlook's UI appear in the windows used to create and edit items like e-mail messages, appointments, and tasks. The shell — the main interface used to view your Inbox, calendar, and task list — has been updated but retains the familiar look of Office 2003.

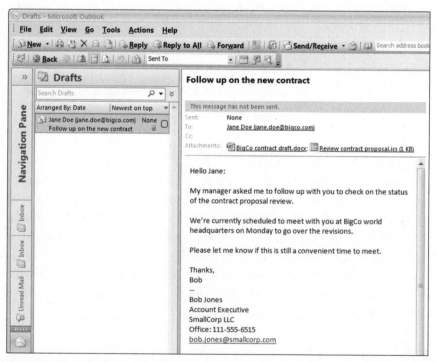

Figure 1.7. The main Mail view in Outlook 2007 uses the now familiar three-pane view introduced in Outlook 2003, freshened up with a new color scheme and a few additions like the search box.

The first reaction nearly everyone has when they see the new Office UI is "what were they thinking?" It's that different. A number of members of the Office design team have been interviewed about the new UI design, and they all point to a few common themes:

- The standard File, Edit, View, Help menu paradigm has been around for a long time and has become the standard way applications present their features.

- Usability testing prior to beginning the new design revealed that most users of Office applications spend a lot of time looking for less frequently used features. This is called the "I know it's in here somewhere" quandary.

- In these usability interviews, many Office users said that they know they use only a fraction of the power and capability in Office applications.

The radical new look of Office 2007 applications

Office 2007 is Microsoft's attempt to almost completely reinvent how you interact with Office applications. I say almost because not every menu has been eliminated and not all Office applications have undergone this makeover. The Office product line (now called the Office System) has expanded considerably over the years and now includes a number of specialized applications that many users of the core Office suite may have never used. A good example is Microsoft Office Visio, an application for generating structured diagrams, architectural and engineering drawings, and advanced charts. Another is Microsoft Office Project, a powerful tool for managing complex projects. Neither of these applications has adopted the new look used in the core Office suite.

The programs that do get the new user interface are Word, Excel, PowerPoint, Outlook (except for the shell), and Access.

These are the programs that people use the most, and the design team really wanted to concentrate on making the document authoring experience better, so they started with the programs most centered on document creation.

Inside Scoop

Office 12 was the prerelease code name for Office 2007. Microsoft, like many software companies, uses temporary names while software is being developed and tested. Windows Vista, the newest version of the Windows operating system, was known as Longhorn while it was being built. The next version of Windows already has a code name — Vienna.

Armed with this information, the design team set out to reinvent how Office applications would manifest themselves to the user.

While the content creation interface in Outlook has undergone a radical transformation, the main views in the application have been enhanced in more subtle fashion. The overall effect of these changes is a more colorful and customizable application for managing all of your personal information. Unlike Word or Excel, where you work in a single application interface, Outlook provides a number of different views that are dependent on the type of information you're working with. Each of these main views is supported by a content form for creating new items and editing and reviewing existing items.

The Mail view, for example, presents a main view that allows you to perform the following activities:

■ View the contents of your Inbox as a list.

■ View the contents of individual e-mail messages in the Reading Pane.

■ Organize mail by creating and using folders.

■ Tag e-mail messages with category labels and action flags.

■ Delete already read and unwanted e-mail.

■ Convert e-mail messages into calendar appointments or tasks — one of Outlook's coolest tricks that is covered in Chapter 12.

When you need to create a new e-mail message, you invoke one of Outlook's content forms — in this case the New Mail form, shown in Figure 1.8. It is in these forms that Microsoft has made the decision to implement the new Office UI.

Watch Out!

In previous Outlook versions, you could choose Word or Outlook as your e-mail editor. In Outlook 2007, Word is the only option. The transition may be challenging for those who have used Outlook's editor in the past.

Figure 1.8. The New Mail dialog box in Outlook 2007 uses the new Office 2007 UI.

Other important changes to be aware of are to keyboard shortcuts. Some of the key combinations have changed but adapting to the new shortcuts is not terribly hard. Fortunately, Ctrl key shortcuts, such as Ctrl+B for bold, remain exactly the same. The Alt key accelerators have changed, but Office 2007 provides a visual overlay that displays all of the available accelerators when you press the Alt key, as shown in Figure 1.9.

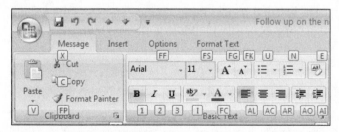

Figure 1.9. The Alt key accelerators.

Common elements of the new UI

The most striking aspect of the new Office user interface is the near total absence of the menus and toolbars you've become accustomed to using. These familiar interface components have given way to a set of visual devices that look nothing like any previous version of Office.

The Ribbon

The first thing you see in the composition forms is something Microsoft calls the Ribbon. Figure 1.8 shows a portion of the Message Ribbon in the New Mail message window. Stretching across the top of this and every content form in Outlook is a horizontal bar containing the Office button used to access file commands, a series of tabs labeled with common functions like Write and Insert, and a colorful display of commands and options appropriate to that function featuring a number of large, intuitive icons.

The Ribbon can be minimized so that only the tab names are displayed to provide a document-only window to work in. This is especially helpful when you are working on a laptop or Tablet PC with a smaller screen. With the Ribbon visible, double-click any of the Ribbon's tabs to minimize it. Double-click any of the tabs again and it is restored. You can also set a preference to have the Ribbon appear in a minimized state by default in all new documents.

Contextual tools and the MiniBar

One of the important design goals Microsoft set for Office 2007 was to move frequently accessed commands closer to where you are currently working. Your mouse logs many miles traveling up to the menus or toolbar and back to the spot in the document you are working in every day. Windows has tried to cut down on all that mousing around by displaying a context menu that appears with a click of the right mouse button.

Most PC users have learned to use these context menus. Office 2007 takes the concept to an entirely new level. When you select text in any of the

---

Hack

Office 2007 provides a much-improved environment for Tablet PC users. Tapping on the Ribbon controls is significantly easier than navigating menus with the pen. The Tablet pen button can be used to produce a right click, which provides access to a complete set of formatting options for composing or editing content.

content creation forms in Outlook, a new command palette called the MiniBar, shown in Figure 1.10, appears ghosted above the text you selected. If you move your cursor closer to the MiniBar, it darkens and becomes a miniature toolbar you can use to apply Bold, Italic, Font Size, Color, and other common formatting commands. Move the cursor away from the edge of the MiniBar, and it fades away. This is particularly helpful when you are working on an e-mail message, appointment, or task item and have switched to the Insert tab on the Ribbon. The MiniBar puts commonly used formatting options right at the tip of the cursor rather than forcing you to switch tabs, make your formatting changes, and then switch back.

Right-clicking on a selection of text opens a context menu as in previous versions of Outlook but adds the MiniBar as well to make quick formatting changes a snap.

Figure 1.10. Mouse over a selection of text and the MiniBar fades into view.

Dialog boxes and dialog launchers

With all of these sweeping changes to the primary interface you use when authoring or editing documents, you may be wondering just how deeply these changes go. The good news is that the dialog boxes you've become accustomed to using for making compound changes to a document or selection of text haven't changed very much. But, because the Ribbon has replaced the menus formerly used to access those dialog boxes, how you access them has changed.

Take a closer look at the Ribbon; you can see that some of the groups have a small arrow in the lower-right corner. This is a visual clue that there are additional commands available for that group of commands. When you mouse over one of these arrow icons, you see a Super Tooltip — a small window appears that explains what clicking on the arrow does. Figure 1.11 shows a preview of the Clipboard Pane that appears when you mouse over the Clipboard button's arrow icon in the Ribbon. If you click the arrow, the Clipboard Pane opens on the right edge of the composition area.

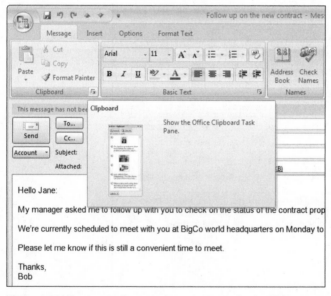

Figure 1.11. Mouse over the arrow icon on a group in the Ribbon to get a preview of the dialog box or pane it opens. Click the arrow to make it happen.

Quick Access toolbar

One of the ways Outlook users have enhanced their use of the program in the past is by customizing the toolbars in the main views and content forms. Customizing the toolbars in the main views is done exactly as in previous versions. I show you how to remove toolbar items you don't need and enhance or add the ones you do use in Chapter 14.

The new UI provides a different way of creating your own custom toolbar. The Quick Access toolbar (QAT) can be displayed in the Ribbon itself or as a new, window-wide strip directly below the Ribbon. You can add and remove commands using the down-arrow icon at the right end of the QAT. By default, the QAT appears above and to the right of the Office button in the upper-left corner of the window in what is called small mode. Figure 1.12 shows the QAT in this default position. Figure 1.13 shows the QAT displayed in large mode as a window-wide toolbar below the Ribbon. I have added a number of commands I commonly use to the QAT in this figure.

Quick Access toolbar - small mode

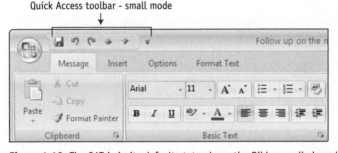

Figure 1.12. The QAT is in its default state above the Ribbon, called small mode.

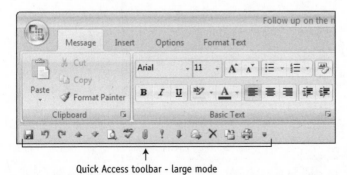

Quick Access toolbar - large mode

Figure 1.13. The QAT is in large mode below the Ribbon with custom commands added.

The new Office button

The sole drop-down menu in the new Office UI is a new version of the File menu that is accessed from the Office button in the upper-left corner of the content window. All of the commands that relate to document usage and sharing reside on this menu. The Ribbon is focused on creating, editing, and using content. The new File menu contains application-wide commands for saving, sharing, and sending documents. In Outlook 2007, the File menu provides a quick way to create a new Outlook item, send a message, or print the current item. Figure 1.14 shows the new File menu. If you look carefully, you can see an option labeled Editor Options in the lower-right corner of the menu. This is another way to access the Application Settings dialog box in addition to the link on the QAT menu.

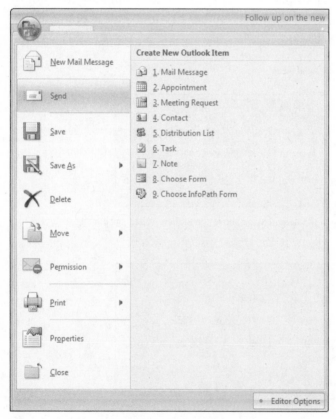

Figure 1.14. The new File menu in Outlook 2007.

Live preview

Outlook 2007 generates a real-time preview when you scroll through formatting options. If you are trying to decide on a font or color scheme to apply to a new e-mail you are composing or formatting a table or diagram you have inserted, Outlook now updates the message for you as you mouse over each option in the font or style menu. This is an extraordinary time-saver compared to the old method of selecting the font menu, scrolling to a particular typeface, and clicking to select that choice. Live previews allow you to see exactly what your message looks like instantly and provides the ability to experiment with a variety of formatting options.

Outlook 2007 exclusive

Above and beyond the common, sweeping UI changes to the Office authoring environments, Outlook 2007 has been enhanced in a number of ways specific to managing and interacting with your personal information. These changes make it easier to deal with the ever-increasing number of e-mail messages, appointments, and tasks in your busy life. By design, Outlook presents a lot of information on the screen no matter which view you happen to be using. If you've used previous versions of the application, you'll immediately notice that Outlook 2007 has a cleaner, more organized presentation that puts more information at your fingertips without creating additional visual clutter.

The To-Do Bar

In previous versions of Outlook, you were disconnected from your calendar and task list when you were working with e-mail. I have always found this to be a serious problem because e-mail is where requests for new appointments and actions that require attention often originate. When you receive an e-mail from a customer or coworker asking if you can attend a meeting, previous versions of Outlook forced you to switch views, determine your availability, and then switch back to respond.

In Outlook, incoming e-mail can be instantly converted into calendar events or tasks. This capability is one of Outlook's greatest strengths and is discussed in detail in Chapter 12. In Outlook 2007, you can, for the first time, see your calendar and tasks at the same time you are processing newly arrived e-mail. This saves time and allows you to make better decisions about these incoming requests. The new To-Do Bar, pictured in Figure 1.15, puts all of this information at your immediate disposal.

The To-Do Bar can be collapsed to a thin strip at the right edge of your screen by clicking the chevron (>>) at the top of the bar. When collapsed, the To-Do Bar displays your next appointment running vertically down its length. You can opt to open a quick view of the To-Do Bar by clicking anywhere on the collapsed strip. It disappears again as soon as you click anywhere else on the screen. Chapter 14 shows you how to customize what is displayed on the To-Do Bar and its Task Input Panel.

The To-Do Bar is off by default in the Calendar — but its visibility persists on a per module basis, so you can have it on in Mail view but off everywhere else if you want. The To-Do Bar's visibility is controlled using the To-Do Bar command found on the View menu.

Figure 1.15. The To-Do Bar makes your calendar and tasks accessible without switching views.

Improved Calendar views

Most Outlook users agree that reading e-mail was the biggest area of improvement in Outlook 2003 with the introduction of the Reading Pane. In Outlook 2007, that distinction goes to the Calendar, which has been thoroughly redesigned and improved. In much the same way that the To-Do Bar provides a more integrated view of your calendar and tasks when working in other views (especially e-mail), the Calendar view has been enhanced to incorporate the task items due on each day into its presentation. Other enhancements include a better way to view your personal calendar alongside a shared calendar, a new task entry field in the Day view, and quick access tabs at the edge of the Day view calendar to jump to your next and previously scheduled appointments, pictured in Figure 1.16.

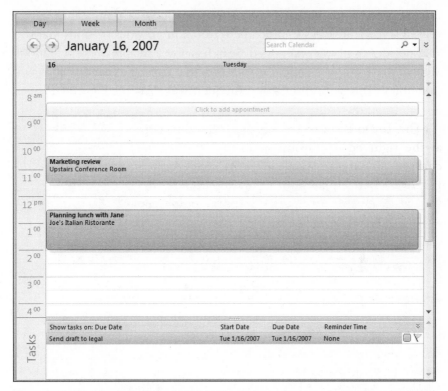

Figure 1.16. The Calendar in Outlook 2007 has been given a fresh new look, with an integrated task view and improved navigation.

Instant Search

One of the greatest frustrations faced by Outlook users is finding information once it has been filed away. While Outlook has offered search capabilities in previous versions, the truth is, they did not work very well. The interface was difficult to use, and the results from a simple search were too large to be very useful. You literally had to search through the search results to find what you were looking for. In fact, this same issue has vexed Windows users on a more general level as well.

These search deficiencies lead to the development of a number of third-party solutions including Google, Yahoo!, Copernic, and others. Microsoft's MSN division even jumped into the game with their own desktop search utility. All of these general Windows solutions, as well as Outlook-specific organizational add-in programs, are discussed in Chapter 16.

The good news is that Outlook 2007 includes a significantly better search feature. It works so much better than in previous versions that you may decide it's all you really need. Search is now available in every Outlook view in the form of a simple search box that can be expanded to reveal additional criteria for more powerful queries as shown in Figure 1.17.

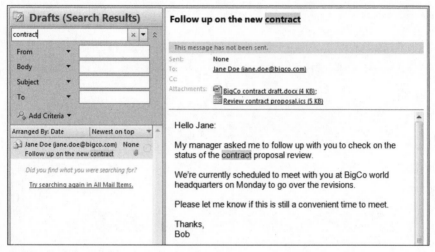

Figure 1.17. Outlook 2007 provides a powerful search tool in every view of the program. An e-mail search is pictured here. Note how matching terms are highlighted.

RSS subscriptions

The rapid growth in the popularity of blogs and Web sites offering RSS (Really Simple Syndication) feeds has been nothing short of phenomenal. There are millions of blogs and Web sites you can subscribe to so that the newest information available is delivered directly to you. In addition to Web-based services that allow you to subscribe to and read RSS-delivered content, a relatively new type of application called an RSS aggregator has become popular to manage these functions on your PC. This new approach to acquiring news and other interesting content has largely taken place since the last version of Outlook was released, and a third-party add-in like NewsGator has been required if you wanted to subscribe to and read information delivered via RSS directly into Outlook.

Outlook 2007 provides a basic set of features to allow you to subscribe to RSS feeds without the need to use additional software. While not as powerful as some third-party products, the addition of RSS to Outlook is

Bright Idea

RSS feeds can often replace e-mail newsletter subscriptions. Many newsletter publishers now offer RSS feeds that allow you to subscribe to specific categories of information you are interested in. These feeds are more immediate than newsletters and arrive as soon as new content is published.

a welcome addition. Chapter 6 explains how to use Outlook to aggregate and read RSS feeds.

Improved Categories

Outlook Categories can assist you in filtering and searching for tasks, appointments, and contacts. In previous versions of Outlook, viewing Categories was not a part of the out-of-the-box experience and required some customization to views to make them useful. Categories are much more visible in Outlook 2007, and they're colorful too. Each category in Outlook can now have a color associated with it, which affects the display of calendar and task list items. Prior to Outlook 2007, the only way to color code items was using labels that only applied to calendar items. In Outlook 2007, tasks and e-mail messages can now use the color coding associated with categories to make visual searching much faster. Figure 1.18 shows the Color Categories dialog box where you can create, edit, color code, and assign categories to any of these items in Outlook.

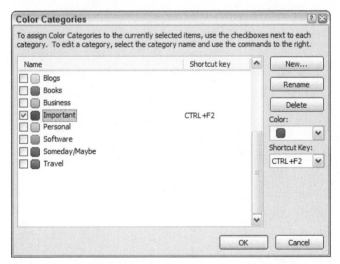

Figure 1.18. Outlook 2007's improved Color Categories dialog box makes extensive use of color to help you tag and visually identify related items.

Just the facts

- Outlook is much more than just an e-mail client and provides a unique and powerful environment to manage all of your personal information.

- The new user interface in Outlook 2007's content forms and other core Office applications eliminates conventional menus and toolbars and puts all of the commands and features you need right in front of you.

- Unlike other Office 2007 applications which use the new Ribbon exclusively, Outlook 2007 retains conventional menus and toolbars in its main views.

- In the new Ribbon, the Quick Access Toolbar allows you to keep the commands you use most often in a single, easily accessed place.

- The new To-Do Bar keeps your appointments and tasks available in every view.

- Outlook 2007 provides powerful new built-in searching.

- Outlook 2007 eliminates the need for additional software to subscribe to RSS feeds.

GET THE SCOOP ON...
Outlook in different environments ▪ Pulling off
the perfect upgrade ▪ Mixing and matching Office
versions ▪ Migrating your existing Outlook data

Read This First

O ne of the things that makes Outlook such a versatile
information processor is the range of environments
it can be used in. Chapter 3 discusses how to install
Outlook 2007 or upgrade from a previously installed version. Before you begin either process, having an understanding of the kind of environment you'll be using
Outlook in will help you plan your installation or upgrade
properly. Once installed, Outlook looks and behaves the
same way, regardless of whether you are working in an
Exchanger Server environment or you use Outlook as a
stand-alone e-mail and information management application at home, in the office, or on the road. Some specific
installation issues are related to each environment, and the
first part of this chapter provides you with the information
you need to have a trouble-free installation experience.

If you have purchased a separate copy of Outlook 2007,
rather than the entire Office 2007 suite, there are important considerations you need to be aware of when using a
mix of old and new Office components. If you have been
using Outlook prior to getting your copy of Outlook 2007,
you probably have data you would like to import into your
new installation. If you have been using a different application for e-mail prior to installing Outlook 2007, your
import options and technique depend on which application you used. The second part of this chapter discusses
the process of importing your existing information into
Outlook 2007.

How (and where) will you use Outlook?

As I mentioned in the introduction to this chapter, Outlook can be used in a variety of environments. If you use Outlook as a stand-alone application and connect to an Internet Service Provider (ISP) for your e-mail, it's probable that you are responsible for installing and maintaining Outlook yourself. If you work in an Exchange or SharePoint Server networked environment, you are more likely to have an IT support person or department who can assist you with installation, configuration, and maintenance. And, if you're a sales professional who uses the Business Contact Manager add-on for Outlook, there are additional considerations you need to take into account when using Outlook as a Customer Relationship Management (CRM) application.

No matter which of these profiles best describes how you use Outlook, understanding the options available to you when installing and configuring Outlook can save you a lot of time and aggravation down the road and make your initial experience with Outlook 2007 a lot more productive and enjoyable.

Outlook for personal use (Internet only)

If you use Outlook as a stand-alone application at home or work, as opposed to an office environment with an Exchange Server, a number of considerations need to be well understood. All of your information will reside on your PC, and you will be responsible for making sure that your Outlook installation is up-to-date and adequately protected from technical and security problems that may occur. Not to worry — this book assumes that you are using Outlook this way and will provide the information you need to address issues related to the security, maintenance, and backup of your data.

This book shows you how to take advantage of the integration Outlook 2007 provides for managing all of your personal and work-related information. Many of the new features described in Chapter 1 make this easier than ever before and provide you with a significantly improved range of options for displaying all of the information you need to access right in front of you at all times.

Don't be concerned about missing capabilities provided in the Exchange Server and SharePoint Services collaborative environments. The Hotmail Premium (covered in Chapter 23) and new Office Live (covered in Chapter 24) subscription services extend Outlook beyond your desktop.

Outlook in an Exchange Server environment

The Exchange Server Outlook experience differs from desktop use (or home use). Exchange Server sits between your PC and the outside world and, unlike Internet-only mode, the server handles connecting to the Internet, fetching, and sending mail. In an Exchange Server environment, your local copy of Outlook is referred to as an Exchange client.

In an Exchange Server networked environment, all your information resides on the Exchange Server, which backs it up on a regular basis and usually scans it to prevent virus and other malware infections. Unfortunately, if your connection to the network fails, you won't have access to your data. Check with your Exchange Server administrator or IT department to see if you can use Cached Exchange mode, especially if you use a notebook or Tablet PC to work at home or while traveling. Cached Exchange mode maintains an up-to-date, synchronized copy of all of your information on your PC and provides the ability to work with your information even when you are not connected to the office network.

If your organization uses an Exchange Server, you should check with your network administrator or IT department before installing or upgrading to Outlook 2007. Most Exchange-based organizations prefer that end users do not install or upgrade Outlook themselves as there are a number of considerations, configurations, and settings that you will not have at hand to perform the installation or upgrade successfully. Exchange Server is often configured to push your account settings from the server to your PC. In this kind of business environment, you probably do not have the appropriate permissions necessary to install software on your PC without the assistance of an administrator.

Exchange Server provides other benefits, including Web-based access to e-mail and other information in addition to calendar, contact, and file sharing with your coworkers. Figure 2.1 shows the Outlook Web Access interface provided by Exchange Server that allows you to access your Exchange account from any PC connected to the Internet using a Web browser. Chapter 2 provides an in-depth look at these and other features you can use in an Exchange Server environment.

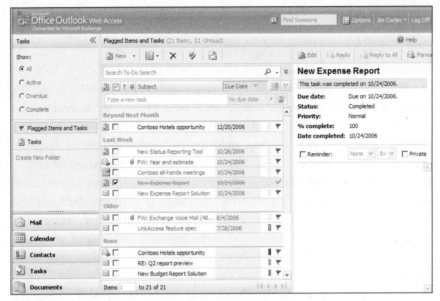

Figure 2.1. Exchange Server provides Outlook Web Access, a Web-based portal to your e-mail and other information.

While Exchange Server has traditionally been used by larger organizations with the IT staff, infrastructure, and budgets to support it, Microsoft now offers a subscription service called Office Live Essentials that provides a hosted Exchange environment at prices low enough to make Exchange affordable for organizations with only a few employees. Chapter 23 provides an overview of the Office Live subscription offerings.

Outlook used to access SharePoint Services

Microsoft SharePoint Server provides a Web-based collaboration space and has traditionally been found in corporate environments. With the introduction of Microsoft Live Office in early 2006, however, small businesses and other kinds of organizations that do not have the IT

Inside Scoop

Microsoft Office Live, contrary to what the name implies, is not an online version of the applications found in the productivity suite. Office Live is a set of subscription services to provide a domain name (yourcompany.com), e-mail addresses, and Web-based application services to smaller organizations. The Office Live Basics service is free.

infrastructure, technical expertise, or budget to operate their own SharePoint Services now have a cost-effective way to take advantage of SharePoint. The availability of Live Office completely redefines the economics of using a SharePoint Services collaboration site.

A SharePoint Services site allows team members to view a shared calendar, contact list, task list, and documents using a standard Web browser or Outlook as shown in Figure 2.2. When you access a SharePoint site using Outlook, the information on the site is synchronized with a local copy on your PC, and the information you are able to view in Outlook is only as current as the last time you connected to the SharePoint site. SharePoint allows administrators to apply specific permission sets to different members of the team, and you may be granted permission only to read, add, and modify files on the site. Outlook 2007 adds the ability to directly edit items on the SharePoint Server from within the program — a huge time-saver over Outlook 2003 that forced you to switch to a browser to edit content.

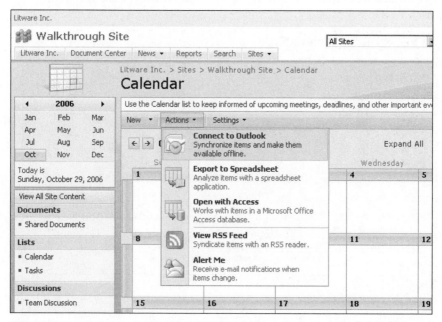

Figure 2.2. A typical view of a SharePoint Services collaboration site is shown from Outlook 2007.

Outlook with Business Contact Manager

Business Contact Manager is a lightweight Customer Relationship Management add-on for Outlook first introduced with Outlook 2003. It is designed for use by individuals or small businesses, unlike more robust (and expensive) server-based CRM solutions, and is designed to extend Outlook's core information management capabilities with tools to track interactions with prospects and customers. Business Contact Manager adds new menus, toolbars, forms, and features to Outlook to assist with generating correspondence, tracking meetings and calls, managing opportunities, and other sales-related concerns. Examples of these new controls are pictured in Figure 2.3. Chapter 19 takes a more in-depth look at the features provided by Business Contact Manager, which is included in the following business versions of Microsoft Office 2007:

- Microsoft Office Professional 2007
- Microsoft Office Small Business 2007
- Microsoft Office Outlook 2007 with Business Contact Manager

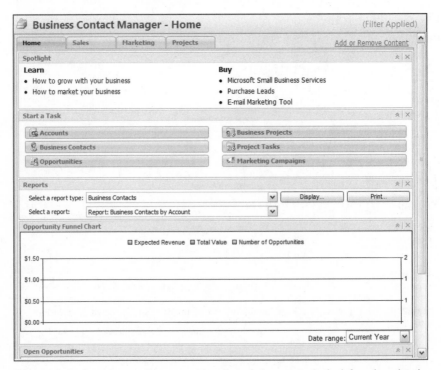

Figure 2.3. Business Contact Managers add toolbars and menus to Outlook for sales-related activities.

Inside Scoop

It is not possible to have two different versions of Outlook installed on a single PC, even one with multiple ser accounts. Outlook is so deeply embedded into Windows that you will run into trouble if you try to do this.

Upgrading from earlier versions of Outlook

Upgrading Outlook isn't difficult if you get yourself organized first. The steps needed to gather the required information and files depends on the version of Outlook you are currently using. If you are upgrading from Outlook 2003 or Outlook 2002 (XP), the process is straightforward. If you are using an older version of Outlook like 2000, you need to keep in mind some special considerations as you upgrade.

Make your upgrade experience a happy one

When upgrading from a previous version of Outlook, you can run the installer for Microsoft Office 2007 and let it import your existing Outlook settings and data as part of the overall installation process. If you are upgrading from Outlook 2000, you may need to re-import your data after completing the basic installation of Outlook 2007. Outlook 2000 (and earlier) employed something Microsoft called Internet Mail Only (IMO) mode that used the Windows Address Book (WAB) rather than the Personal Storage File (PST) to store contact information. Upgrading directly may cause some of your WAB data to disappear. Should this problem occur, you can restore your missing information by manually importing the WAB data into Outlook 2007 — but you should back up this data before beginning the installation. The Windows Address Book usually can be found at C:\Windows \ Application Data \ Microsoft \ Address Book with the extension ".wab"

There is no better insurance policy to guard against potential upgrade problems than ensuring you have backed up your valuable information and settings. There are few things worse than the panic and

Watch Out!

It's difficult to predict whether an upgrade process will proceed smoothly or create problems. There are many variables that can affect the upgrade process. Be safe and back up all of your Outlook data before you begin an upgrade.

dread you experience after an installation process goes badly, and you realize that irreplaceable information has been corrupted or deleted.

To import your WAB file into Outlook 2007 following an upgrade from Windows 2000 IMO or an earlier IMO version, follow these steps:

1. Choose File ⇨ Import and Export. The Import and Export Wizard shown in Figure 2.4 is displayed.

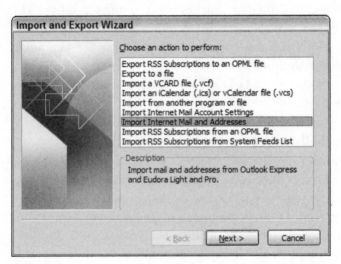

Figure 2.4. The Import and Export Wizard dialog box is the first step in the process and provides a range of data types you can import into Outlook 2007.

2. From the list of actions displayed, select Import Internet Mail and Addresses and click Next. The Outlook Import Tool shown in Figure 2.5 is displayed.

3. Select the Outlook Express 4.x, 5.x, 6.x radio button. Make sure that only the Import Address book check box is selected and click Next. The Import Addresses dialog box is displayed.

4. Choose one of the options pictured in Figure 2.6 to tell Outlook how you prefer to handle duplicate contact records and click Finish. The wizard asks you to locate your WAB file and imports your address book into Outlook 2007.

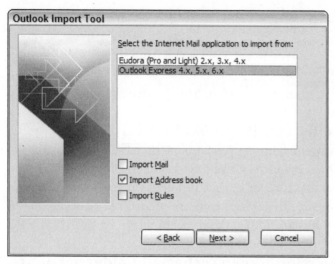

Figure 2.5. The Outlook Import Tool dialog box is the second step in the Import process and allows you to select the application you will be importing from.

Figure 2.6. The Import Addresses screen lets you decide how to handle duplicate records.

Hack

A temporary workaround, if you have a powerful enough PC, is to run a second instance of Windows on your PC in a Virtual PC machine, but this is a rather expensive proposition as you need an additional Windows XP or Windows Vista license to install on the virtual machine.

There can be only one (Outlook, that is)

Unlike the other applications in Microsoft Office, it is not possible to have more than one instance of Outlook installed on your PC. If you need to keep Outlook 2003 or earlier installed on your system due to compatibility issues with third-party software or another reason, you will not be able to use Outlook 2007 on that machine.

Mixed Office version issues (especially older versions of Word)

As I mentioned in Chapter 1, a big change in Outlook 2007 is that Word is the e-mail editor — you do not have the choice, as in previous versions, to use an internal editor for composing your messages. If you install Outlook as a stand-alone product, the application includes enough of Word 2007 code to provide you with the editing environment. If you have Office 2007, I strongly recommend that you install, at minimum, both Outlook and Word and that you uninstall any previous version of Word. While an older version of Word can coexist on your system with either stand-alone Outlook 2007 or a full or partial Office suite installation, you have less potential for conflicts if you stick with the latest versions of both. Other Office applications present no problems coexisting with Outlook 2007, so if you have a copy of Microsoft Office Publisher 2003 or Vision 2003 that you want to continue using, you can easily do so.

Importing data from other programs

Upgrading to Outlook 2007 is a straightforward process. If you have been using a different application for e-mail, you should know that Outlook directly supports importing data from the following e-mail applications:

- Outlook Express 4.x, 5.x, and 6.x
- Eudora Pro and Eudora Light 2.x, 3.x, 4.x, and 5.x

- MSN Explorer 8
- Schedule+ 7.x, SC2

Data from these applications can be imported directly into Outlook 2007. If you are using another e-mail application not listed above, I recommend you consult the documentation, help file, or online support for that program to see if specific information about what export formats are supported is available. Contact, calendar, and task information can be imported into Outlook from a standard comma separated value (CSV) or tab-delimited text (TXT) file.

Just the facts

- Outlook can be used in a number of different environments, including as a stand-alone e-mail and personal information manager and as a client in an Exchange Server environment.

- Outlook Live is a subscription option that allows you to access your e-mail and personal information using a standard Web browser when you are away from your PC.

- Microsoft Office Live includes a variety of subscription services to provide smaller organizations with domain names, Web sites, e-mail addresses, and Exchange Server or SharePoint Services collaborative environments at no or low cost.

- Business Contact Manager, a lightweight CRM add-on for Outlook, provides extra features to support sales professionals and is included in certain versions of Microsoft Office 2007 and with a stand-alone copy of Outlook.

- Preparation before beginning an upgrade can save you from a lot of extra work or even loss of data if something goes wrong.

- If you are upgrading from Outlook 2000 or earlier and your contact information is stored in a Windows Address book file format (.wab), you can manually import the information should some of your contact records fail to appear in Outlook after upgrading.

- Outlook can directly import information from Outlook Express, Eudora, and other e-mail applications you might have used prior to installing Outlook 2007.

GET THE SCOOP ON...
Get prepared before you install ▪ Repair and back up your
existing data files ▪ Make the right installation decision ▪
E-mail account setup is easier than ever ▪ Understand
where Outlook stores your information

Installing Outlook 2007

Installing Outlook 2007 or upgrading from an older version is usually a trouble-free experience and Microsoft has gone to great lengths to make the process even easier in the latest version. There is always the chance that something might not go as intended — Murphy's Law certainly applies to computers from time to time — and being prepared for problems is the best way to make sure they don't ruin your day. The first part of this chapter shows you how to make sure you have a clean backup copy of all of your important information and the account information you need to get Outlook 2007 set up properly. The second half of this chapter discusses how to create additional e-mail accounts, change where Outlook 2007 stores your information, and how to maintain and repair your personal data files.

Upgrade checklist for Outlook — before you begin

"Be prepared" is the Boy Scout motto. That sentiment is just as applicable to installing software as it is to getting ready for a hike in the wilderness. To make sure you are completely prepared for a trouble-free upgrade experience, I recommend the following steps to get everything ready:

Chapter 3

1. Scan and repair your existing Outlook Personal Storage file(s) (PST).

2. Back up your current PST file(s).

3. Prepare an account information profile for each e-mail account you use.

If you are installing Outlook for the first time, feel free to jump ahead to the next section.

Scanning and repairing your existing Outlook PST files

When you upgrade from a previous version of Outlook, all of your account information, e-mail, contacts, appointments, and tasks are copied into the new Outlook environment for you. You can improve the odds that this takes place with no errors and no loss of data by checking the integrity of your existing PST files and repairing any errors in that file before you begin the upgrade. Fortunately, the Microsoft Personal Folders Scan/Repair Utility (SCANPST.exe) is already installed on your PC to help you do just that. This utility is invaluable, not only for preparing your PST files for an upgrade but also for maintaining the health of your Outlook information on an ongoing basis to reduce the likelihood of serious problems. Chapter 25 discusses how to maintain your Outlook environment in greater depth.

The default location for SCANPST.exe is the following folder on your PC: C:\Program Files\Common Files\System\MSMAPI\1033.

I suggest you add the SCANPST application to your Start menu so it is easier to use as part of your regular ongoing maintenance in the future. You can do this by dragging the application's icon to your Start menu button. This "pins" a shortcut to the utility in the top left section of the Start menu where you can access it easily in the future. If you have recently run SCANPST.exe and it appears in the list of recently opened applications in the left pane of the Start Menu, you can right-click the utility's icon and choose Pin to Start Menu from the context menu.

To scan your PST file(s), first make sure you have exited from Outlook on your PC. Launch SCANPST and use the Browse button to locate the PST file you want to scan and, if needed, repair. When you have selected the PST file, you should see a long path name in the text entry field as shown in Figure 3.1. The default location for Outlook data files, where "username" is the name of the Windows account, is C:\Documents and Settings\user name\Local Settings\Application Data\Microsoft\Outlook.

Click the Start button. Depending on the size of your PST file, the scan can take anywhere from a few seconds to several minutes. After the scan is complete, the utility presents a report dialog box, such as the one pictured in Figure 3.2. If no errors were found, click OK. Repeat the process for any other PST files in your Outlook configuration.

If errors exist in your PST file, you see a dialog box, such as the one pictured in Figure 3.3. Don't panic. It is not at all unusual to find errors in PST files, especially if you have never used the SCANPST utility in the past. Most PST errors can be resolved using this utility and if your existing Outlook installation has been operating without incident, the likelihood that there is anything seriously wrong is very low. Notice that there is not a lot of detail, and clicking the Details button at the bottom of the dialog box rarely provides any useful information.

Before you click the Repair button, be sure to select the Make

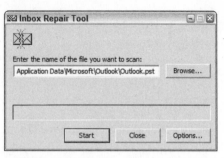

Figure 3.1. The SCANPST utility Inbox Repair Tool dialog box with a .pst selected.

Figure 3.2. SCANPST found no errors in this file.

Figure 3.3. SCANPST found errors in this .pst file. Note the Backup option check box has been selected.

Inside Scoop

You may have noticed that I repeatedly reference the possibility that you have more than one PST file. Some people prefer to use a separate PST file for each e-mail account they use or to separate information related to a specific period of time.

backup of scanned file before repairing check box. This is cheap insurance should something go wrong when the utility attempts to repair the file. By using this option, you have a backup copy to work from using more advanced and involved techniques should they become necessary. SCANPST suggests a filename, usually Outlook.bak if your PST file has the default name Outlook.pst. You can rename the file or change the location of the backup file if you like by editing the path statement in the text field or by using the Browse button.When you click Repair, the utility attempts to fix the errors it has found, but you see no visible indication of what is happening. As is the case with the scan of the PST file, the time required to repair the file varies but rarely takes more than a minute. A simple success or failure confirmation dialog box displays when the process has completed. When you click OK, SCANPST closes.

Assuming the repair was successful, you should probably perform one more scan on the PST file to make sure no additional repairs are necessary. I have seen, in rare cases, files that required two or three passes with the SCANPST utility to completely repair the damage. If the repair was not successful, refer to Chapter 25 to learn about some more advanced techniques for salvaging as much information as possible from a badly damaged PST file.

Backing up your current Outlook PST files

Now that you have successfully verified and, if necessary, repaired your PST file(s), the next step in preparing for your upgrade to Outlook 2007 is to make a backup copy of the files. This is more of that cheap insurance I keep mentioning. You can back up your files to another location on your hard drive, to a second drive on your PC or network, or to a removable medium like a CD, DVD, or USB flash drive. I prefer the last method. Although writing to an optical disk or USB drive is a bit slower than simply copying the file on your hard drive, you gain an extra measure of protection for your valuable information in the event your PC suffers a hardware problem.

There are two approaches you can take to backing up your existing Outlook data and settings before proceeding with the upgrade — the hard way and the easy way. The hard way is to manually locate and copy your existing Outlook data files and write down all of your account settings or create screen captures of each account setting screen. This is a laborious and often frustrating process. The easy way, if you are using Outlook 2002 (XP) or 2003, is to use an excellent utility called OutSource-XP from TotalIdea Software.

OutSource-XP provides one-click backup of your Outlook data files, application settings, and e-mail account configuration. The backed-up files can be stored on your PC, an external drive, a USB thumb drive, or permanently archived to a CD or DVD. This tool is invaluable not only when performing an upgrade, but also as a maintenance tool for regular backup of your Outlook data, which is covered in Chapter 25. Consider that the backup process takes minutes and the cost of a blank CD is less than a dollar. This is cheap insurance. A commercial version of OutSource-XP is available that adds the ability to compress the backed-up files. Should something go awry with your upgrade, you can use OutSource-XP to restore your data and settings from your backup.

To back up using OutSource-XP, download a copy of the software from the TotalIdea Web site and run the installer. The first time you run OutSource-XP, you are asked to choose what version of Outlook you have installed on your PC.

When the main OutSource-XP window, pictured in Figure 3.4, is displayed, click the tab labeled Backup and select the Outlook files and settings you want to back up. I recommend you select your Outlook.pst file (or whatever your main PST file is named) and any other PST files you use on your PC, such as your Signatures and Dictionary, and that you select the two check boxes in the upper-right corner for your e-mail account and registry settings. Specify where you want the backup stored and click the Create Backup Now button. That's it. You have successfully created a backup of all of the necessary files to restore your Outlook configuration.

There's no harm in selecting everything in the Backup options. The backup file becomes larger but unless you have modified templates, installed macros, or modified your Outlook installation extensively, most of the other backup options are not necessary. When the backup is complete, burn a copy onto a CD or DVD and store it in a safe place.

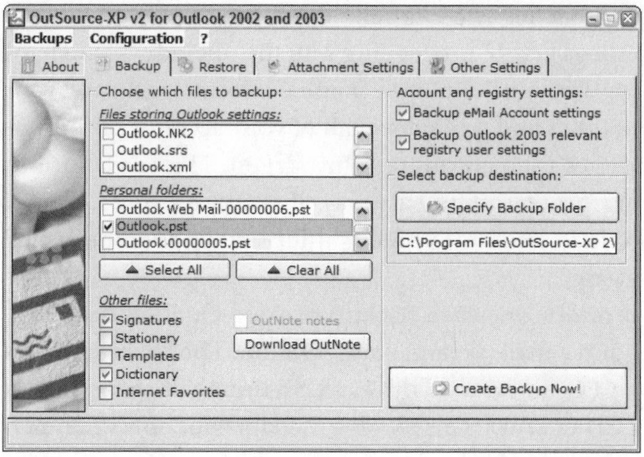

Figure 3.4. Backup screen in OutSource-XP from TotalIdea Software.

If you are using Outlook 2000 or earlier, you have to manually back up your data files the hard way. Unless you specified an alternate location for your data files or moved them, you can find them in the following location on your PC, where "username" is the name of your Windows account: C:\Documents and Settings\username\Local Settings\Application Data\Microsoft\Outlook.

I recommend you back up all of the files in this folder. If you have created e-mail signatures, I recommend you copy them to a text file or Word document.

You can access your e-mail signatures by choosing the Options command from the Tools menu, selecting the Mail Format tab, and clicking the Signatures button. You can copy each signature you have set up by selecting it, clicking the Edit button, and copying it from the edit field in the dialog box as shown in Figure 3.5. Chapter 6 explains how to create e-mail signatures and how to optionally select which signature is used by default in each e-mail account you use.

Figure 3.5. Edit Signature dialog box.

Hack

You can use a USB thumb drive to create a portable copy of your entire Outlook environment that you can use to synchronize information between two PCs. Be sure to check with your company's IT policy to make sure this is permitted if you plan to bring your Office information to your home PC.

Capturing your current e-mail account settings

The last vital piece of information you need to have available before you begin your installation or upgrade is your e-mail account settings. When you signed up with your ISP, acquired a new Web mail account, or were provided an e-mail account by your company, you received information about how to connect to the mail server for that account. You need to know the following basic information about each e-mail account you want to access in Outlook:

■ Account name (usually the portion of your e-mail address to the left of the "@" symbol)

■ Account password

■ Incoming mail server (usually something like `mail.isp.com` where "isp" is the name of your e-mail provider)

■ Outgoing mail server (usually `smtp.isp.com`)

You may need additional information depending on how your ISP or other mail provider sets up accounts. When in doubt, contact your ISP, network manager, or the support desk at your e-mail provider to make sure you have the correct settings. Most ISPs make this information available on their Web sites or in the user manual they provided when you established your account.

If Outlook is currently installed on your PC, you can get all of this information, except passwords, from the E-mail Accounts dialog box (shown in Figure 3.6). To find this information, choose Tools ⇨ E-mail Accounts; in the dialog box displayed, select View or Change existing e-mail accounts and click Next. In the next dialog box, select the e-mail account whose settings you want to review and click the Change button (or simply double-click the account in the list).

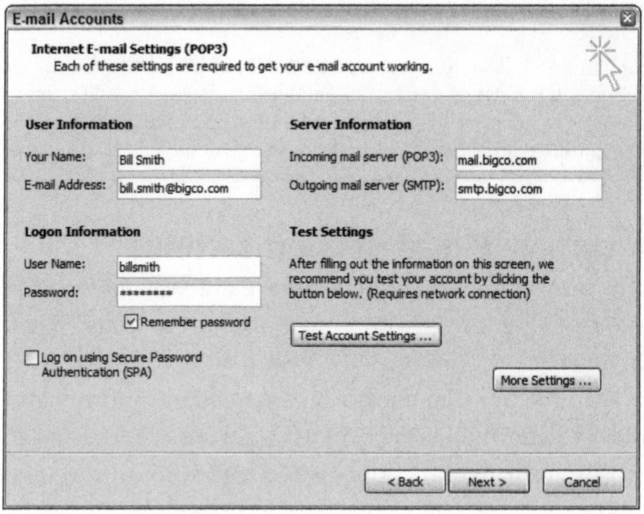

Figure 3.6. The E-mail Accounts dialog box contains some of the information you need to re-create the account.

The More Settings button opens a secondary account information dialog box, the Internet E-mail Settings, where advanced settings can be made. Open the dialog box and examine each tab for any information you may have added when you first set up that account. The most common changes are on the General tab pictured in Figure 3.7 where you can add an account name (this is where the name of your PST file comes from), your company name (if applicable), and the e-mail address you want to have replies sent to.

There are two common options for capturing this information. You can write it down manually on a note pad or in a text file on your PC, or you can capture a screen shot of each screen. Of the two, I prefer to use screen captures because it is faster

Figure 3.7. The Internet E-mail Settings dialog box is most commonly used to name your account and set reply options.

Watch Out!

You are not able to retrieve your e-mail account password from this dialog box. Passwords are masked to prevent someone from gaining access to your account. If you have forgotten your account password, you need to contact your e-mail provider or network manager to recover or reset it.

and it helps me remember exactly where each bit of information needs to be entered if I need to re-create one of my accounts. I print the screen captures out and store them in a folder in my filing cabinet for easy reference.

Install and configure Outlook 2007

If you've recently acquired a new PC with Office preinstalled or work at a company where an IT staff sets up your machine for you, the first part of this section doesn't really apply to you. If you are setting up your own PC and installing a new copy of Office 2007 or Outlook 2007 as a stand-alone product, you'll be happy to know that the process is usually very simple. In a typical install or upgrade, Outlook does all the heavy lifting. All you probably need to do is provide your product key, which is a lengthy sequence of numbers and letters that is usually provided on a sticker inside the installer disk case.

What are you installing?

Your installation choices are dictated in large measure by whether you are installing a stand-alone copy of Outlook or you are installing the entire Office 2007 suite. If you are installing just Outlook, you should have already made the decision as to whether you are upgrading or installing a brand new copy of the software. The Outlook installer scans your system for a previously installed version and offers to upgrade it for you. As mentioned earlier in this chapter, this is the fastest way to perform an upgrade and you should accept this option.

If you are installing a copy of the entire Office 2007 suite, the same holds true if you have an older version of Outlook already installed on your system. The big difference when you install the entire suite is that you have the option of selecting only those applications you want by choosing the custom installation option. Unlike previous versions of Office, you no longer have the "Install on first run" option, so if you plan to do a customized installation of Office 2007, it's better to install every-thing you think you may need right from the start.

The new Office installer – what's changed?

The Outlook/Office installer looks a little different, but the changes are cosmetic until the end of the installation. Beginning with Office 2003, Microsoft has been working to create connections between Office and the Internet beginning with the online help and research pane features added in that version. In Office 2007, this trend continues, and you now have the option to register for online services provided by the Office Online Web site as part of the installation process. When the local soft-ware installation is complete, you are presented with the success screen pictured in Figure 3.8. Clicking the Register for Online Services button launches your Web browser and provides you with an opportunity to reg-ister for Office Online.

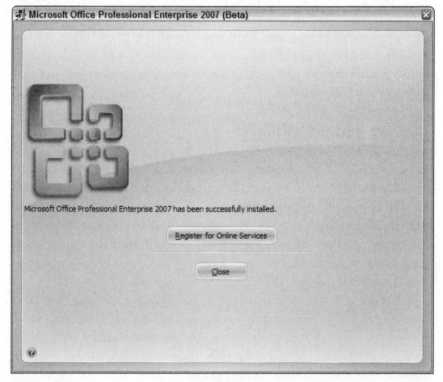

Figure 3.8. You can opt to register for online services from Office Online after your installation has completed.

The newly designed Office Online Web site offers a wealth of on-demand training courses, templates, clip art, and updates for Office 2007. Appendix C includes links to a selection of online training exercises that are particularly well aligned with the topics in this book.

Setting up your e-mail accounts

It's increasingly common for people to have two or more e-mail addresses. In most business settings, you have at least one e-mail address, more if you are in a public-facing position. Your ISP includes an e-mail address in your account. You may have taken advantage of a free, Web-based e-mail account from a provider like Hotmail, now known as Windows Live Mail. Using Outlook 2007, you can have all of your mail from these disparate sources brought into a single, unified environment where you can read, respond, organize, and file this ever-increasing amount of incoming information.

Before you add an e-mail account to your Outlook environment, you should understand that you have options that affect where the information from each e-mail account is stored and how you access it. If you are adding a POP3 e-mail account (the most common type), you can choose to have all your POP3 e-mail arrive in the Inbox in your personal folder. The advantage to this approach is that you have a single Inbox. That is also the drawback to this approach. If you bring all of your e-mail into a single Inbox, things can get a bit overwhelming, especially if you receive a lot of e-mail.

You do have the option to create a new PST file for each POP3 e-mail account. This provides some important benefits that can make managing your e-mail and maintaining Outlook quite a bit easier. Setting up a separate PST file for each account allows you to use separate backup and archiving schemes for each account. This approach also keeps each PST file smaller than using a single file for all of your accounts, and Outlook is definitely happier when it works with smaller PST files.

If you have an e-mail provider who uses IMAP, you have no choice — all of your mail for that account will be received into a separate PST file that is dedicated to that account.

Outlook 2007 is a lot smarter

Microsoft's Outlook team put a lot of work into making the process of adding an e-mail account a simple matter of providing a few bits of information. If you ever added an account in a previous version of Outlook, you will appreciate the result of all of that hard work. To set up most accounts in Outlook 2007, you only need to provide three pieces of information, and Outlook takes care of the rest for you. The process for adding an account begins by choosing Tools ⇨ Account Settings. The dialog box shown in Figure 3.9 displays.

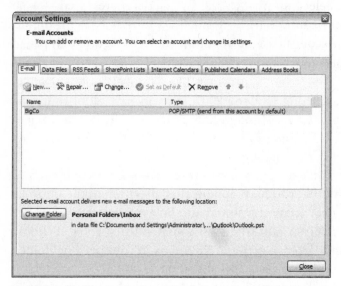

Figure 3.9. The Account Settings dialog box provides a management dashboard in Outlook 2007.

This dialog box is the management dashboard for all of your e-mail accounts, RSS subscriptions, SharePoint subscriptions, shared calendars, and address books. There are tabs across the top of the display field that allow you to select which information source you want to manage. The first tab provides access to a variety of tools for managing your e-mail accounts and is a significant improvement over the interface used in Outlook 2003 and earlier.

Just below the tabs is a row of buttons for creating a new account, repairing an existing account's settings, editing an account's settings, choosing which account will be the default for sending mail, removing accounts from your Outlook environment, and scrolling through your accounts. Below this row of controls is a list of your current e-mail accounts. Below that list is a button labeled Change Folder that provides a new capability that has been sorely missing in Outlook — the ability to select where new incoming mail from each account will be delivered by defining either an Inbox folder or a creating a new PST file.

Setting up Internet e-mail accounts

To add a new e-mail account to Outlook 2007, begin by clicking the New button which displays the Add New E-mail Account dialog box pictured in Figure 3.10. Select the first of the two options presented — a new Exchange Server or Internet e-mail account and click Next. In the next dialog box, the Account Basics dialog box shown in Figure 3.11, provide the following information:

- Your name
- Your e-mail account (`yourname@isp.com`)
- Your password (you need to enter it twice)

When you click the Next button, Outlook tries to connect to the mail server at the domain your e-mail account is hosted at (the isp.com portion of your e-mail address) and if successful, configures the rest of your account setup for you. This may not sound like a big deal, but it is a terrific time-saver and can prevent a lot of frustration. Outlook displays its progress in contacting and negotiating with your e-mail server and finishes things off by generating a test message sent back to your own e-mail account to verify that everything is working properly.

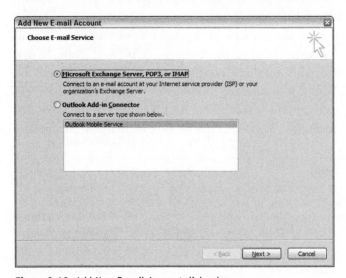

Figure 3.10. Add New E-mail Account dialog box.

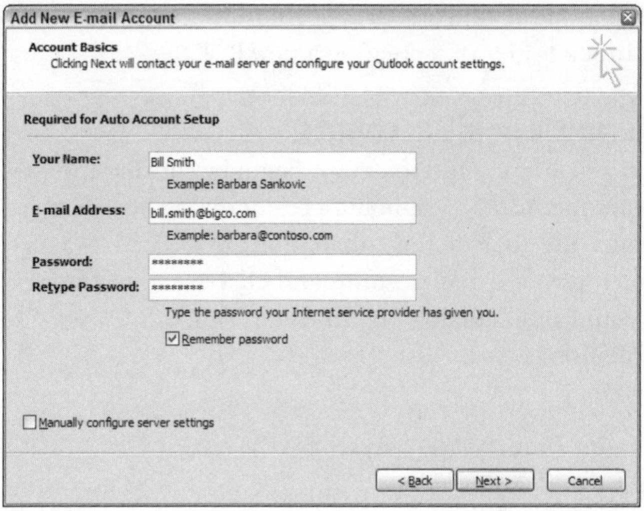

Figure 3.11. Outlook 2007 only needs three bits of data to set up an e-mail account for you.

If the automatic account creation was successful, you see the success dialog box pictured in Figure 3.12. If Outlook encounters a problem creating the account using the basic information you have supplied, you have the option to go back to the New Account dialog box where you can manually configure your account. I have tested Outlook 2007 against a number of e-mail servers and Web services, and I have yet to find an e-mail service it cannot auto-configure.

Of course, you have the option to manually configure your e-mail accounts as in previous versions of Outlook. The Add New E-mail Account dialog box has a Manually configure server settings check box in the lower-left corner. If you select that check box and click the Next button, you see the manual version of the Add New E-mail Account dialog box pictured in Figure 3.13. This dialog box is identical to the one

---

Inside Scoop

The Account Basics dialog box allows you to have Outlook remember your password. This can save time but you can add an extra security layer by deselecting this option. If you share a PC with others or use a laptop, you may want to require that your account password be manually entered before mail can be sent or retrieved.

used in Outlook 2003 and provides fields for entering the incoming and outgoing mail server addresses associated with your account. Should the automatic account detection fail, you are presented with this dialog box so you can manually configure the server addresses and other settings.

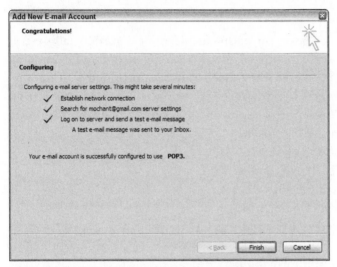

Figure 3.12. The portion of the Add New E-mail Account dialog box confirming your e-mail account was successfully configured.

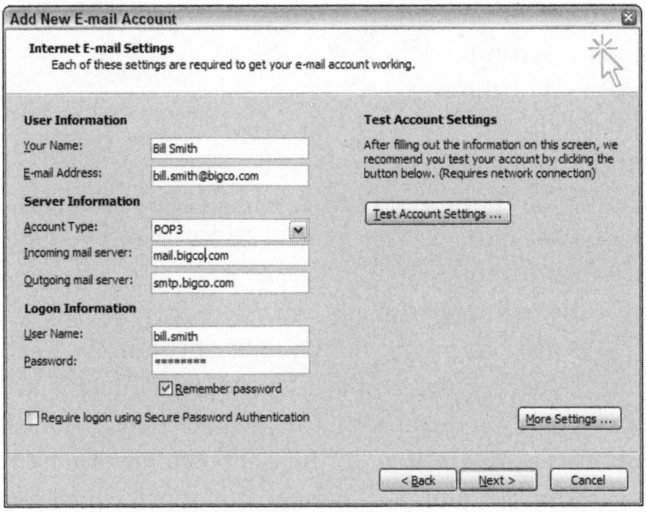

Figure 3.13. Add New E-mail Account dialog box in manual mode.

Inside Scoop

If you regularly have a need to access your e-mail account from computers other than your primary PC, the option to Leave a copy of messages on the server can come in quite handy. I recommend you also select the Remove from server when deleted from 'Deleted Items' option if you do elect to leave mail on the server.

The most likely reason for automatic account detection failure is if your e-mail provider uses non-standard ports for incoming or outgoing e-mail. If this is the case, it is very likely you were provided with the specific ports being used when you received your account information from your provider. These port settings are accessed by clicking the More Settings button in the lower-right corner of the Add New E-mail Account dialog box that opens the Internet E-mail Settings dialog box pictured in Figure 3.14. Click the Advanced tab to modify the port settings to match those in the account information you received from your e-mail provider. Then click OK and use the Test Account Settings button in the Add New E-mail Account dialog box to verify that the account is properly configured.

In the Advanced tab, you can also adjust the behavior of your e-mail account to control how e-mail on the server is handled in

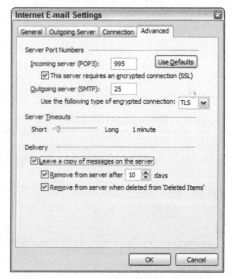

Figure 3.14. The Internet E-mail Settings dialog box allows you to fine-tune your account settings.

the Delivery section at the bottom of the tab. You can make these adjustments for any Internet e-mail account in your Outlook environment once the account has been created, regardless of whether the account was automatically configured or set up manually. The default state for new accounts in Outlook is to leave all three of the options under Delivery unchecked. Most ISPs enforce a quota — a limit on how much e-mail you are allowed to keep on the server — so be sure to check what your quota is before deciding to keep e-mail on the server after you have received it into your local PST file.

Setting up Exchange Server accounts

If your organization uses an Exchange Server, *always* check with your IT staff or network administrator before attempting to establish an account on the server. Your administrator may prefer to set up the account for you. If you use a laptop or Tablet PC and work in an Exchange Server environment, ask your administrator about using Cached Exchange mode. This feature, first introduced in Outlook 2003 and improved in Outlook 2007, creates a copy of your Exchange account on your local PC that allows you to work very effectively even when you are not connected to the office network. Whenever you are connected to the network, your local cached copy is synchronized to the server.

Setting up how (and when) you connect

Outlook is preconfigured to send and receive e-mail automatically from the account(s) you set up when you installed or first ran the application. But you have the power to control whether each account uses automatic or manual send/receive and can organize these accounts into different groups. The Send/Receive Groups dialog box, pictured in Figure 3.15, can be accessed from the Tools menu, from the Send/Receive button on the Standard toolbar, or by pressing Ctrl+Alt+S.

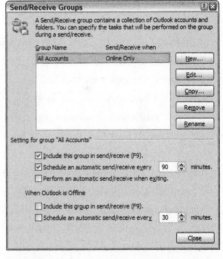

Figure 3.15. The Send/Receive Groups dialog box is used to configure how and when Outlook automatically performs a send and/or receive operation.

Working offline in Outlook

If you are like most users, you generally work online with Outlook and your mail server delivers new e-mail as it arrives and sends your outgoing e-mail immediately. However, there are times when working online is not practical or even possible. There may be times when a network connection is not available at your location or you're traveling. And, depending on the ISP you use and the connection quotas and fees associated with your plan, there may be times when you'd prefer not to connect even if you can.

In an Exchange Server environment, your messages are saved in your server's mailbox. When you are connected to the server, all of Outlook's features, such as opening, moving, and deleting items are available to you. When you work offline, you lose access to all of the items on the server. Offline folder files (OST) stored on your computer provide a way to make your information available even when you're not connected. An OST file is a local copy of your Exchange Server mailbox. When you are online, this file is automatically synchronized with the server.

If you use an Exchange Server e-mail account, check with your Exchange administrator to see if they support Cached Exchange mode. When you use Cached Exchange mode, the absence of a network connection is almost completely transparent and you can continue to work in Outlook as if you were connected.

If you use Outlook in Internet mode and use a POP3 or IMAP account from your ISP or an HTTP (Web mail) account like Hotmail, things work differently. When you are online and are connected to the mail server, Outlook sends and receives messages immediately. For POP3 e-mail accounts, messages are sent immediately if the Send immediately when connected check box is selected on the Mail Setup tab in the Options dialog box. When you are working offline, all accounts use the schedule in the Send/Receive Groups dialog box. IMAP accounts work less well since folders on the server are not available when you work offline. If you use an IMAP account, only your personal folders are available. You can compose and save draft e-mails, but you are not be able to queue messages to be sent later as you can with POP3.

Bright Idea

If you use a cell phone as a modem via USB or Bluetooth, set up a Send/ Receive group called Mobile that only downloads the headers of new messages and prevents attachments from downloading. This can save connection time and fees but still allow you to check the subject lines of new mail and decide what to download on a per message basis.

Outlook has a group named All Accounts set up by default. In the lower portion of the Send/Receive Groups dialog box are options that control whether a selected group is included when you click the Send/Receive button in the toolbar or use the keyboard shortcut F9. You can choose whether or not you want a group included in a Send/Receive operation, how often Outlook automatically performs a Send/Receive operation for that group, and whether Outlook should perform a Send/Receive operation for that group when you exit the application. The settings at the bottom of the dialog box control how Outlook behaves when you are working in Offline mode (see the preceding sidebar Working offline in Outlook for more information about working in Outlook when you are not connected to the network or Internet).

Select the All Accounts group and click the Edit button to access the Send/Receive Settings dialog box as shown in Figure 3.16. In this dialog box you can select which of your e-mail accounts you want to include in the selected group, where incoming e-mail is delivered (the default is the Inbox in your Personal Folders), and how much of each e-mail message is downloaded. This last setting can be very helpful if you are trying to download new e-mail on a slow connection. While many people work exclusively in a high-speed Internet-connected environment, there are still many situations where a broadband connection is not available. Whether you find yourself in an environment where only dial-up connectivity is available or you are using a cell phone to connect to the Internet via USB or Bluetooth, having a Send/Receive group that limits the amount of each e-mail message that is downloaded and ignores attachments can be a lifesaver.

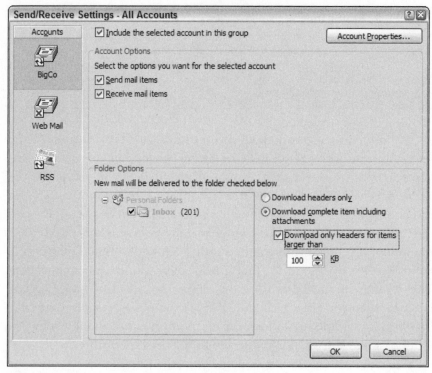

Figure 3.16. The Send/Receive Settings dialog box allows you to select which accounts are included in a named group.

Where Outlook stores your stuff

In Outlook 2003, working with your Personal Storage Files meant choosing Tools ⇨ Options, clicking the Mail Setup tab in the Options dialog box, and then clicking the Data Files button to get to the Outlook Data Files dialog box. An alternative method was to use the Control Panel's Mail icon to access your data files. Outlook 2007 streamlines this marathon of clicking by providing a tab right inside the Account Settings dialog box. Clicking the Data Files tab provides you with direct access to your PST file(s) as Figure 3.17 illustrates. The functionality is essentially the same as that provided in the previous version, but integrating these tools directly into the Account Settings dialog box provides one place to look for everything related to your accounts and your data. It's a smart change.

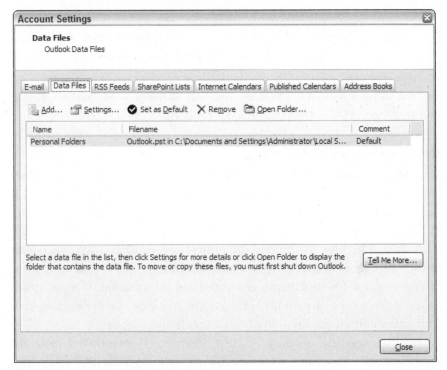

Figure 3.17. The Account Settings dialog box has a tab to take you directly to your Data Files options.

Discovering where your PST files live

By default, Outlook stores your PST files in a deeply nested folder inside the Documents and Settings folder on your hard drive. The easiest way to access this folder is to choose Tools ⇨ Account Options in Outlook. In the Account Options dialog box, select the Data Files tab, highlight your PST file, and click the Open Folder button on the command bar above the file list. The folder containing the PST file you selected opens on the desktop.

This folder is set to be hidden by default so if you want to access your PST files manually, you first need to modify your Windows Explorer settings so that hidden folders are visible.

1. In a Windows Explorer window (any window will do), Choose Tools ⇨ Folder Options.

2. Select the View tab and look for Hidden files and folders in the list under Advanced Settings.

3. Click Show hidden files and folders.

4. Click OK. Even after they have been made visible, hidden folders appear dimmed to indicate they are not typical folders.

Now that you can actually see the folders, you can navigate your way to the following folder: C: \ Documents and Settings \ username \ Local Settings\Application Data\Microsoft\Outlook.

Backing up your PST files

Now that you know where your PST files are located and how to get to them, backing up these critical data files can be done in any number of ways. If you prefer the manual approach, simply copy the files on a regular basis to another folder, another hard drive, or to a CD, DVD, or USB flash drive. I highly recommend the optical disk or flash drive approach. Offline storage on a semi-permanent medium is the safest and most cost-effective option for backing up any important information. If you choose to use a flash drive, I strongly recommend you lock the drive using the physical switch on the drive to prevent accidental erasure.

In the upgrade section of this chapter, I introduced you to OutSource-XP. You can use this utility to back up your PST files and other important Outlook settings and files with a couple of mouse clicks, then burn a copy of the resulting backup to a CD or DVD. It's a fast and comprehensive way to make sure you have a current backup of your critical data.

How frequently you should back up is a topic that has been written about frequently and, as the saying goes, your mileage may vary. My rule of thumb is that you should back up your Outlook data once a week if you can, especially if you use a POP3 account. If your e-mail provider uses IMAP, your e-mail messages are being backed up on the server side. And if you work in an Exchange Server environment, all of your account data, including your contacts, appointments, and task list are being backed up from the server.

Bright Idea

Consider using a CD-RW or DVD-RW rewritable disc for your weekly backups if you prefer not to have an ever-growing pile of discs accumulating. While they are a bit more expensive, these discs can be reused hundreds of times.

Moving Outlook Personal Folders files

You might decide that you'd prefer Outlook's data files were stored in another location on your computer — possibly a location you can get to quickly, such as a folder inside your My Documents folder. Frankly, there aren't any compelling reasons I can think of why you'd want to do this since Outlook 2007 makes it easy enough to open the default folder, buried though it may be. Nevertheless, if you have the urge to do this, here's how to do it:

1. In Outlook, select Account Options from the Tools menu.

2. Click the Data Files tab and highlight your PST file.

3. Click the Open Folder button on the command bar.

4. Exit Outlook (you cannot move a PST file if Outlook is using it).

5. Use Windows Explorer to move each PST file from the default location to another folder on your computer.

6. In Control Panel, click User Accounts, and then click Mail. If you are using the Classic view in Control Panel, double-click Mail.

7. Click Show Profiles and then select the profile that contains the PST file.

8. Click Properties and then click Data Files.

9. Select the data file from the list and then click Settings.

10. When a message appears notifying you that the data file cannot be found at the old location, click OK.

11. Browse to the new folder location, select the data file, and then click Open.

12. Click OK and then click Close twice.

13. Click OK.

14. Restart Outlook.

Repairing Outlook PST files

In the upgrade section of this chapter, I showed you how to use SCANPST to verify and, if necessary, repair your PST files. I recommend you use this utility to verify the integrity of your PST files before you perform each backup. The scan and repair usually takes only a few minutes, and you can be sure the data you are backing up is free from corruption or errors.

SCANPST lives in a different location in Outlook 2007. The new version locates the utility in the following folder: C:\Program Files\Microsoft Office\OFFICE12.

Just the facts

- Make sure you have backed up all of your Outlook data and settings to a CD or DVD before you launch the installer.

- Scan and repair your Outlook PST files and perform any repairs if errors are found before you back up your files.

- Make sure you have an accessible copy of the account information related to each of your e-mail accounts stored somewhere you can easily find it — either in a text file or Word document or on paper.

- Outlook supports POP3, IMAP, and HTTP (Web mail) accounts and can also be used as a client on an Exchange Server network.

- Outlook 2007 features a new, intelligent e-mail account setup agent that can configure a new e-mail account using three pieces of information: your name, account user name, and password.

- If you work in an Exchange Server environment, always check with your Exchange administrator or IT staff before you attempt to set up an account yourself.

- Send/Receive Groups allow you to precisely control when and how Outlook fetches and sends e-mail from each of your accounts when you are working online or in offline mode.

- Having a well-defined backup strategy is an important part of maintaining your Outlook environment properly and can be a lifesaver should something go wrong with your installed copy of the application.

Put Outlook to Work

GET THE SCOOP ON...
Outlook as the all-day application in Office ▪ The
Navigation Pane – your Office GPS ▪ The different
Outlook views

PART II

Moving Around in Outlook 2007

Chapter 4

When Office 2003 was released, almost everyone agreed that Outlook was the most improved application in the suite. The addition of the Reading Pane, Search Folders, and other features made Outlook a much easier program to use and a more pleasant and productive place to spend time. This was a smart move on Microsoft's part because usage studies repeatedly show that Outlook is the Office application most likely to be running on PCs for hours at a time each day. You might only open Word when you have a document to write or edit or PowerPoint if you are preparing a presentation. But Outlook manages information you need to access all day long.

Recognizing this, the Office team has continued to improve Outlook in Office 2007. Chapter 1 discusses some of the sweeping changes to the user interface that impact all of the core applications in Office 2007 as well as some of the enhancements specific to Outlook. This chapter shows you how many of these changes have been integrated into the Outlook interface in both small and big ways. Outlook is unique among the core Office suite applications because it can be used to manage different types of information, and it presents a unique view for each. Outlook's main views include:

- Mail
- Contacts
- Calendar
- Tasks
- Notes
- Journal
- Folders

In addition to these main views, Outlook presents content creation and editing forms for each information type it manages. These forms are where the new Office 2007 user interface appears.

The Navigation Pane

The Navigation Pane, which appears at the left edge of Outlook's main window, was first introduced in Outlook 2003 replacing the older, less functional Outlook Bar. The Navigation Pane is something of a chameleon in that it changes dynamically, depending on which of the main views you are working in. Like a GPS system in your car, the Navigation Pane is a handy guide to help you find your way that updates as you enter different information "neighborhoods." Chapter 14 shows how each of these Navigation Pane views can be customized in a number of ways to present exactly the information you prefer to see. These customization capabilities allow you to make Outlook even more useful. Outlook's default views, including how the Navigation Pane initially presents itself, have been designed to work well for a variety of different users but are not really optimized for any particular usage scenario.

Navigation buttons

Outlook provides a set of large buttons and smaller icons at the bottom of the Navigation Pane that allow you to switch from one view to another.

Inside Scoop

If you have learned the keyboard shortcuts for navigating around Outlook, you will be happy to know that they remain unchanged from those in Outlook 2003. A list of commonly used keyboard shortcuts appears in a sidebar later in this chapter.

If you prefer to use the keyboard, Outlook also provides shortcuts for switching views. Views can also be selected from the Go menu. This is a common characteristic of Office applications — there is often more than one way to perform an operation.

You may notice that in its default configuration, the Navigation Pane displays the most commonly used views in Outlook — Mail, Contacts, Calendar, and Tasks — as large buttons. Below these four buttons there is a fifth button area displaying a series of smaller icons as pictured in Figure 4.1. In the default configuration, three of these small icons are displayed for accessing the Notes, Folder List, and Shortcuts. There is a fourth icon for accessing the Navigation Pane menu that is indicated with a small triangle icon. Keep in mind this is only the default setup — you can change the order and display to suit your preferences quite easily.

Click for additional icons

Figure 4.1. Outlook's Navigation Pane in its default state.

Customizing the Navigation Pane

The Navigation Pane can be customized in four ways. You can:

- Reduce the large buttons and add them to the row of small icons displayed at the bottom of the button bar.

- Control which buttons or icons are visible (hidden items can always be accessed from the Navigation Pane menu icon).

- Rearrange the display order of buttons and icons.

- Collapse the Navigation Pane to save space.

Bright Idea

Maximize your Outlook application window and drag the sizing handle up as far as it will go. Then use the Restore Down button (the middle button in the upper-right corner of the title bar between Minimize and Close) to shrink the Outlook window. Notice how Outlook dynamically reduces large buttons to icons for you.

Using button or icon mode

To reduce the amount of space the navigation buttons take up on the pane, you can reduce them to
the small icon state by simply clicking and holding
the mouse button down on the sizing bar above the
first button (Mail in the default state) and dragging
down. As you drag the bar down, each large button
will, in turn, disappear and be replaced by an icon
on the bottom bar. Drag all the way down and you
will see only a single row of icons. As your folder
hierarchy inevitably grows, the ability to create more
room to see the folder display by minimizing these
large buttons to icons comes in very handy.
Figure 4.2 shows the Navigation Pane with all of
the buttons reduced to icons.

Figure 4.2. Outlook's Navigation Pane with all buttons reduced to icons.

You can also use the Navigation Pane menu to collapse or expand the button display by selecting the
Show More Buttons or Show Fewer Buttons commands on the menu that is shown in Figure 4.3. As
I said previously, Office applications often provide
more than one way to perform a task. I personally
find it much faster to simply drag
the sizing handle up or down and
generally leave all of the buttons in
their small icon state. The number
of large buttons you can display is
directly related to the resolution of
your monitor and whether your
Outlook application is maximized
(full screen) or floating.

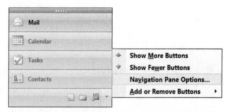

Figure 4.3. The Navigation Pane menu provides commands for customizing the state, order, and visibility of buttons.

Rearranging Navigation button visibility and display order

The Navigation Pane menu also allows you to control the visibility and
select the order in which the buttons and icons are displayed. Click on the
triangle icon to show the Navigation Pane menu and select the Navigation
Pane Options command that will display the dialog box shown in Figure
4.4. You can choose which views will be displayed by selecting or deselecting the check box next to each view. You can control the order in which

the view icons appear by selecting an item and using the Move Up or Move Down buttons to change its spot in the display order.

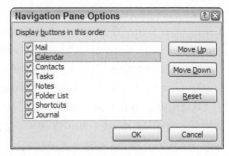

You can also control the visibility of view icons directly from the Navigation Pane menu. As shown in Figure 4.5, if you select Add or Remove Buttons on the menu, a submenu appears listing all of the view icons. Click on a highlighted icon to hide it or click on an unhighlighted icon to show it.

Figure 4.4. The Navigation Pane Options dialog box allows you to control the visibility and display order of the Navigation Pane icons.

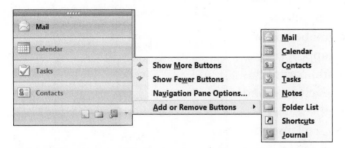

Figure 4.5. You can quickly show or hide any view icon from the Add or Remove Buttons menu.

Controlling the visibility of the Navigation Pane

A particularly useful new feature in Outlook 2007 is the addition of a way to change the visibility of the Navigation Pane. In Outlook 2003, you were limited to hiding or showing the Navigation Pane using the Alt+F1 keyboard shortcut or the View Menu command. Outlook 2007 adds the ability to collapse the Navigation Pane to a thin strip at the left edge of the application window. In this collapsed state, the Navigation Pane remains onscreen but takes up much less screen real estate while still providing access to folders, views, buttons, icons, and the Navigation Pane menu.

As you can see in Figure 4.6, the Navigation Pane in its collapsed state displays any view buttons you have set to display in large mode as icons in a vertical strip. Any view buttons displayed in icon mode and the Navigation Pane menu can be accessed by clicking the arrow icon at the bottom of the collapsed pane. Clicking any of the icons or making a selection from the menu switches views instantly. Depending on the vertical size of your Outlook application window, the collapsed Navigation Pane also displays one or more of the folders in your Favorite Folders list and a button labeled Navigation Pane.

In Figure 4.6, you can see a pop-up display of the folder list that allows you to quickly navigate from one folder to another without having to expand the Navigation Pane from its collapsed state. This is the pop-up display for the Mail view. Each of Outlook's other views provides a different display that allows you to select from a number of preconfigured layouts appropriate to that view. The second part of this chapter examines each view and these preconfigured layouts.

This ability to collapse the Navigation Pane is, in my opinion, a rather brilliant bit of interface design that provides all of the features you need to move around in Outlook while using as little of your screen as possible. In combination with the new To-Do Bar, which can be collapsed and expanded in similar fashion, Outlook 2007 provides more control over how screen space is used

Figure 4.6. Outlook's Navigation Pane is in its collapsed state with the folder list pop-up menu displayed.

than any previous version — an important thing considering how much information Outlook's views are designed to present.

Navigating with the keyboard

As in previous versions of Outlook, you can quickly switch views directly from the keyboard or by selecting a view from the Go menu pictured in Figure 4.7. Each view has an associated Ctrl+number shortcut. If you've used a previous version of Outlook and have learned these shortcuts, you'll be happy to know that they remain unchanged. See Table 4-1 for a complete list of these shortcuts.

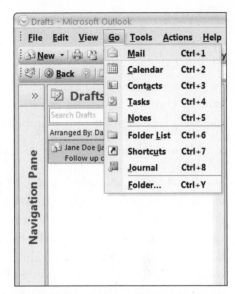

Figure 4.7. The Go menu provides yet another way to switch between Outlook's main views.

Table 4-1: Navigation Keyboard Shortcuts			
View	**Keyboard Shortcut**	**View**	**Keyboard Shortcut**
Mail	Ctrl+1	Folder List	Ctrl+6
Calendar	Ctrl+2	Shortcuts	Ctrl+7
Contacts	Ctrl+3	Journal	Ctrl+8
Tasks	Ctrl+4	Folder	Ctrl+Y
Notes	Ctrl+5		

Different views for different uses

Outlook has six main views, each of which provides a number of layouts that allow you to view your information in different ways depending on what it is you've set out to accomplish. The six main views are:

- Mail
- Contacts
- Calendar

- Tasks
- Notes
- Journal

In Outlook 2003, the Mail view was the recipient of most of the attention. In Outlook 2007, the enhancements are spread out more evenly and every view benefits with a freshened look and new features.

Mail view

Despite its ability to manage many types of information, Outlook is best known and most frequently used as an e-mail client. The main Mail view, pictured in Figure 4.8 includes, from left to right, the Navigation Pane, the Message List — a vertical pane displaying the contents of the selected mail folder (in this case Drafts) that includes the new Search tool at the top, and the Reading Pane in vertical format. This Reading Pane, introduced in Outlook 2003, can also be viewed horizontally. The orientation of the Reading Pane can be changed on the View menu.

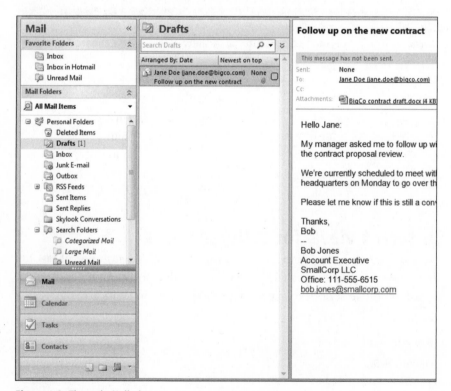

Figure 4.8. The main Mail view.

You can choose to turn the Reading Pane off if you want to see an expanded list of the selected folders contents that can be very helpful when you are performing file management activities, such as selecting a group of e-mail messages to copy, move, or delete. The Reading Pane can be turned off by choosing View ⇨ Read Pane ⇨ Off or by clicking the Reading Pane button on the Advanced toolbar.

As I mentioned earlier, the Navigation Pane display is dynamic, and its contents change depending on which view you are working in. In Mail view, the Navigation Pane includes two sections, Favorite Folders and Mail Folders.

Favorite Folders

Favorite Folders is an area you can customize to make it easy to get to the folders you access most often. To add a folder to the Favorite Folders list, navigate to the folder in the All Mail Items section — immediately below the Favorite Folders section in the Navigation Pane — and drag the folder up to the Favorite Folders list.

Outlook displays three favorites by default — Inbox, Unread Mail, and Sent Items. You are not stuck with these defaults. You can remove any folder from the favorites list by right-clicking it and selecting Remove from Favorite Folders on the context menu.

All Mail Items

As its name implies, All Mail Items shows you a hierarchical tree of all your mail folders. A folder with nested subfolders has a plus sign icon next to it. You can display the subfolders by clicking the plus sign and hide them by clicking a second time. A number of other folders are automatically created in your Personal Folders list, including Deleted Items, Drafts, Junk E-mail, Outbox, RSS Subscriptions, Sent Items, and Search Folders.

By default, Outlook organizes all of your mail under the top-level icon labeled Personal Folders. If you add additional POP3 e-mail accounts, all incoming mail will be delivered to the Inbox in your Personal Folders

Bright Idea

Add a Favorite Folders item for each of your Inboxes to build a quick list of folders most likely to contain new, unread mail. You can also add folders related to the hot projects you're currently working on and remove them when the project is completed.

Inside Scoop

Both Internet Explorer 7 and Windows Vista, the new version of the operating system, have RSS functionality built in so that you will be able to subscribe to or read any RSS feed in either Outlook or your browser using a centrally managed subscription list.

unless you specify a different destination folder in the Account Options dialog box or use a separate PST file for that account. If you add an IMAP e-mail account to Outlook it always uses a separate PST file and presents its own set of folders that are actually stored on the IMAP mail server.

RSS Subscriptions folders

RSS (Really Simple Syndication) subscriptions deliver the newest information from blogs and Web sites directly to you. Prior to Outlook 2007, you needed to use an application or Web-based service called an RSS aggregator to manage and read these subscriptions (or feeds) on your PC. Because Outlook is a perfect place to receive, read, and store information, a few enterprising third-party developers like NewsGator and Attensa created add-ins for Outlook to provide RSS aggregation features directly into the program.

Outlook 2007 provides a basic set of features to allow you to subscribe to RSS feeds without the need for additional software. While not as powerful as these third-party products, the addition of RSS to Outlook is welcome and indicative of Microsoft's larger strategy to make RSS an information standard in Windows. RSS feed items appear in much the same way an e-mail message does in Outlook, but in the Reading Pane you are provided with a link that allows you to either go directly to the blog or Web site or attempt to render the page directly in Outlook. Depending on how a particular RSS feed has been configured, this local rendering option will not always work. More on subscribing and reading RSS feeds can be found in Chapter 6.

A brief look at Outlook Search Folders

Search Folders were first introduced in Outlook 2003. In Outlook 2007, Search Folders become even more powerful and useful thanks to the new application-wide Search indexing and interface tools added in this version. A Search Folder isn't actually a discrete storage unit like the other folders you can create to organize e-mail messages. A Search Folder is actually a set of criteria you define to find messages that have one or more attributes in common.

Outlook's default installation provides a few example Search Folders including Unread Mail and Large Mail. As those labels imply, Unread Mail searches across all of your Outlook mail folders and finds all messages that have yet to be marked read. You can view all of these messages in the Search Folder, mark them as read, move them into other folders, or delete them. But if you delete a Search Folder, the only thing you delete is the query, not the actual messages. Chapter 13 is devoted to Outlook's Search Folders and new built-in search tools.

Contacts view

Outlook's Contacts view is much more than just an address book. Contacts can be used to create new e-mail messages, meeting requests, task assignments, or Journal entries. The integration of Contacts into everything you do in Outlook is one of the application's great strengths, and Chapter 7 explores how you can accomplish all of these tasks and more.

Outlook 2007's Contacts view, pictured in Figure 4.9, adds a new view type — the business card — to the standard layouts offered in previous versions. Figure 4.9 shows the results of a search, conducted directly in Contacts view by typing a search term into the new Search box at the top of the main display area, with the result displayed as a business card.

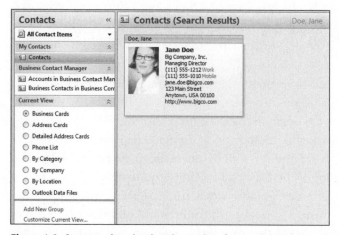

Figure 4.9. Contacts view showing the results of a search in Business Card layout.

The Contacts view presents a different look in the Navigation Pane than the one used by the Mail view and contains the following sections:

- My Contacts
- Current View
- Contacts Links
- Contacts List

My Contacts

This section displays the contact list or lists you are currently viewing. In stand-alone mode, you generally use a single contact list but can create additional lists if you prefer to keep work and personal contacts separate. If you work in an Exchange Server or SharePoint environment, shared Group Contact lists you have open will also be listed here.

Current View

This view allows you to select from a number of built-in layouts. As I mentioned earlier, the Business Card layout is new in Outlook 2007. The remaining layouts are carried over from previous versions and allow you to filter and sort contacts based on different attributes. Any of these standard layouts can be fine-tuned to your specific needs. This customization potential is covered in Chapter 14.

Contact Links

This section provides one-click links to create a New Group (only useful when connected to Exchange Server or SharePoint Services) or quickly access the Customize Current View dialog box.

Calendar view

Next to e-mail, Outlook is mainly used to manage time and tasks. The Calendar view is where the time element of this juggling act is practiced. The Calendar view has been upgraded significantly in this release, featuring a much more colorful, modern look, better integration with the task list, and other enhancements, which can be seen in Figure 4.10. The Calendar view layout of the Navigation Pane is quite distinct from how it is used in the Mail or Contacts views. In this view, the top of the Navigation Pane displays a two-month thumbnail Calendar at the top of the Navigation Pane. Below the thumbnail Calendar are the Groups area (similar to the one in the Contacts view Navigation Pane) and a set of Calendar links that allow you to take advantage of the significantly improved Calendar sharing options in Outlook 2007.

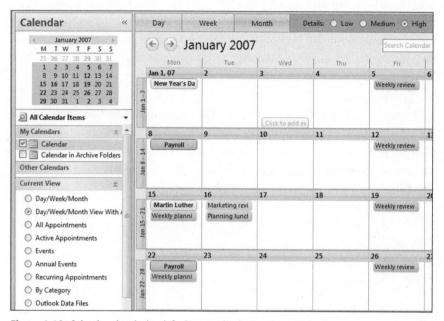

Figure 4.10. Calendar view in its default state displaying the month view.

You can use the first link to open a shared calendar on your local network or the Internet. Shared calendars are covered in Chapter 8. The second link invokes Outlook 2007's ability to send your calendar to others by e-mail. The third link is used to initiate the process of publishing your calendar to the Internet. The final link allows you to create a new group.

The Calendar area of the view has the new search box at the top. Immediately below are a set of controls to select which calendar layout you want to view — day, week, or month. Both the day and week modes now include a task list at the bottom of the calendar showing tasks assigned to each day being viewed. This makes time and task management a lot easier to accomplish because, for the first time, you have the ability to see all of the commitments you have made in one place. In week mode, you can select between a workweek and full week display. The month mode allows you to choose what priority level of appointment should be displayed (high, medium, or low) that can be helpful in simplifying the display of a busy calendar.

The task lists displayed in these modes are one of two ways Outlook 2007 provides a more integrated view of your time and task commitments. The new To-Do Bar described in Chapter 1 and covered in greater detail in Chapter 9 also interacts with the Calendar view in an interesting way. If you expand the To-Do Bar, the thumbnail Calendar no longer appears on the Navigation Pane and is now located on the To-Do Bar, along with a list of upcoming appointments and tasks as shown in Figure 4.11.

Unless you have a large monitor running at a high resolution, you will probably want to collapse either the Navigation Pane or the To-Do Bar. I have found the best arrangement for the Calendar view is to collapse the Navigation Bar and expand the To-Do Bar as Figure 4.11 illustrates. You can access the Navigation Pane options using the pop-up panel when you need them.

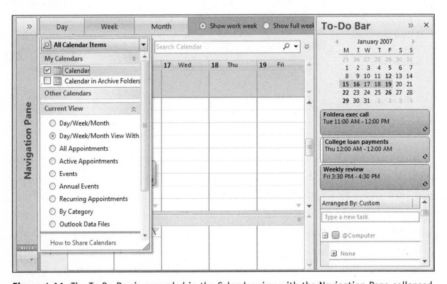

Figure 4.11. The To-Do Bar is expanded in the Calendar view with the Navigation Pane collapsed.

Task view

While the Task view in Outlook 2007 doesn't have quite the same dramatic changes you see in the Calendar view interface, some serious work has been done to improve how you manage your tasks in this new version. A new, predefined layout has been added, categories have been improved, and the flag feature introduced in Outlook 2003 has been almost completely redesigned. Figure 4.12 illustrates these improvements showing the new To-Do Bar Task List view, sorted by date.

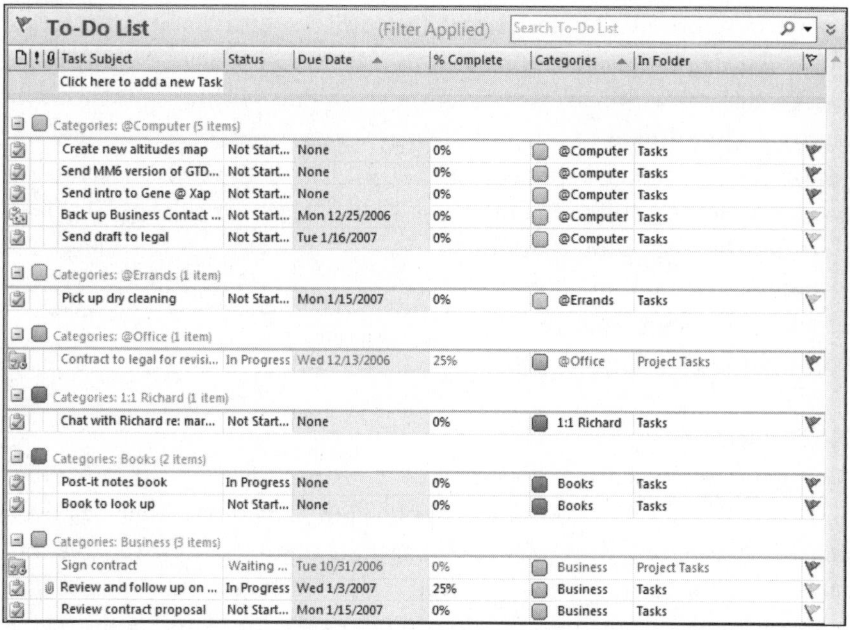

Task Subject	Status	Due Date	% Complete	Categories	In Folder
Click here to add a new Task					
Categories: @Computer (5 items)					
Create new altitudes map	Not Start...	None	0%	@Computer	Tasks
Send MM6 version of GTD...	Not Start...	None	0%	@Computer	Tasks
Send intro to Gene @ Xap	Not Start...	None	0%	@Computer	Tasks
Back up Business Contact ...	Not Start...	Mon 12/25/2006	0%	@Computer	Tasks
Send draft to legal	Not Start...	Tue 1/16/2007	0%	@Computer	Tasks
Categories: @Errands (1 item)					
Pick up dry cleaning	Not Start...	Mon 1/15/2007	0%	@Errands	Tasks
Categories: @Office (1 item)					
Contract to legal for revisi...	In Progress	Wed 12/13/2006	25%	@Office	Project Tasks
Categories: 1:1 Richard (1 item)					
Chat with Richard re: mar...	Not Start...	None	0%	1:1 Richard	Tasks
Categories: Books (2 items)					
Post-it notes book	In Progress	None	0%	Books	Tasks
Book to look up	Not Start...	None	0%	Books	Tasks
Categories: Business (3 items)					
Sign contract	Waiting ...	Tue 10/31/2006	0%	Business	Project Tasks
Review and follow up on ...	In Progress	Wed 1/3/2007	25%	Business	Tasks
Review contract proposal	Not Start...	Mon 1/15/2007	0%	Business	Tasks

Figure 4.12. Task view displaying the new To-Do Bar Task List view.

The layout of the Navigation Pane in the Task view is similar to the Contacts and Calendar views, displaying the currently available groups (by default Outlook 2007 shows My Tasks and the To-Do Bar Task List), and the Current View List that lists the redefined layouts you can select to view your tasks. At the bottom of the Navigation Pane are links to define a new group and to customize the current view.

The addition of the To-Do Task Bar fundamentally changes the role that tasks play in managing your commitments in Outlook by making them accessible in any view. The utility of the To-Do Task Bar is greatest in views other than the Task view, and the new To-Do Bar Task List view allows you to configure what displays on the To-Do Bar when you are working in these other views.

When follow-up flags were first introduced in Outlook 2003, they were a mildly useful way to tag an e-mail message for future attention.

But the initial implementation was difficult to customize and ended up being useful only for tagging and sorting mail messages for a handful of projects. Outlook 2007 adds a time element to these flags, which can now be attached to any information object in Outlook. Figure 4.13 shows the flag customization dialog box that allows you to associate a start and end date to any task, appointment, or e-mail message as well as setting up a reminder alert for when you want that item brought back to your attention. Chapter 9 describes the new, improved flags in greater detail.

Figure 4.13. Outlook's follow-up flags can be customized with date information and reminders.

Notes view

As I mention in Chapter 1, Outlook's Notes view is the least impressive and most limited function in the application. The Notes view has been paid scant attention by the Outlook design team in the 2007 version and, aside from inheriting the inherent value of Outlook's significantly improved color categories as illustrated in Figure 4.14, nothing has changed from the previous version. Notes do not use the new Office 2007 Ribbon UI and are best thought of as an electronic version of a sticky note — a good place to quickly jot down an idea or simple list. In general, it is much more useful to capture information that is related to a task or appointment in the notes field of that object or to create a new Journal entry for a contact-related event than to use Outlook's Notes view.

Journal view

Like the Notes view, the Journal view in Outlook 2007 is essentially unchanged from the previous version. Journal is discussed in depth in Chapter 11 and, as mentioned previously, remains the least understood part of Outlook by many users. Figure 4.15 shows the form used to create a new Journal entry. In the main Journal view, the Navigation Pane options are essentially the same as for the other, non-e-mail views listing the current Journal file (typically this is My Journal — the Journal component of the current PST file), a number of predefined layouts, and links to create a new group or to customize the currently selected layout.

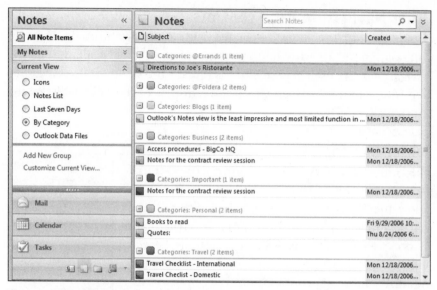

Figure 4.14. Outlook's Notes view in Notes List layout sorted by Outlook's new color categories.

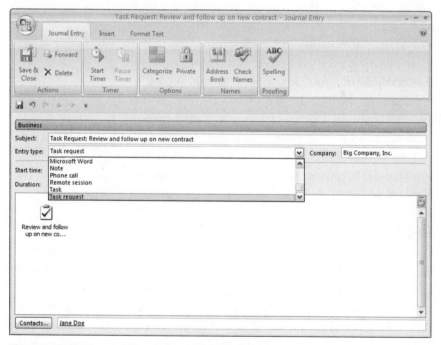

Figure 4.15. The form used to create or edit Journal entries.

Other Navigation Pane controls

In addition to the icons associated with each of the main views in Outlook, there are two buttons that affect what is displayed in the Navigation Pane itself. These buttons replace the standard display associated with each of the main views with a display of the Folder List or the Shortcuts List.

Folder List view

The Folder List view, shown in Figure 4.16, is, at first glance, identical to what is displayed in Mail view below the Favorite Folders list. The difference is that this view displays an icon for each of the main views as well as the Inbox, RSS Subscriptions, Search Folders, and any other folders you have created to organize your mail or subscriptions.

An advantage to the Folder List display in the Navigation Pane is that you can jump from a non-mail view — say the Calendar — directly to a specific Mail or RSS subscription folder.

If you do prefer the Folder List display to using the Navigation Pane icons, here's the secret to maintaining the persistence of this display: always use the icons in Folder List to navigate between Outlook's views. This persistence even survives an exit from Outlook. When you next launch the application, it remembers your Folder List display preference.

Figure 4.16. Outlook's Folder List panel in the Navigation Pane.

Shortcuts

Over time, your folder list can get a bit cumbersome as the number of mail folders you create and the number of RSS feeds you subscribe to grow. Outlook's Shortcuts display in the Navigation Pane works very much the same way putting a shortcut to a frequently accessed folder on your desktop does. Instead of opening My Documents, then opening Work Stuff, and then opening Reports (for example), you can access the Reports folder directly if you have a desktop shortcut that points to it.

The Shortcuts panel, shown in Figure 4.17, works in very much the same way. You can add any folder or view in Outlook to the list of shortcuts as well as links to folders or files on your PC and URLs for frequently visited Web pages. The order of shortcuts can be adjusted using the same technique as the one used for rearranging the buttons on the Navigation Pane. Simply right-click the shortcut you want to move up or down in the list and choose the appropriate command from the context menu.

To add an Outlook folder or view, click the Add New Shortcut link in the Navigation Pane. This opens a dialog box that displays every folder in Outlook in an expandable tree. Select the folder or view from the list and a shortcut is added.

To add a folder or file from a Windows Explorer window or your desktop, simply drag the file or folder to the bar at the top of the Shortcuts panel (where the word "Shortcuts" appears). Your cursor changes to an arrow with a plus sign. Release the mouse button, and a shortcut to the folder or file is added to the list. When you click a folder shortcut, the folder window opens. When you click a file shortcut, the application associated with that file type is launched, and the file is opened.

Figure 4.17. Outlook's Shortcut panel can provide one-click access to views and folders in Outlook, files and folders on your PC, and Web pages.

To add a Web page URL to the Shortcuts list, use your browser to navigate to the page you want to add to the list and drag and drop the URL from the browser address bar to the Shortcuts panel. When you click on a Web shortcut in the list, the page loads inside the main view area of Outlook. If you display the Web toolbar in Outlook, you have access to a simple set of browser controls — forward, back, refresh, and stop buttons along with an address bar you can manually enter URLs into.

Hack

Did you know Outlook can be used to browse the Web? Right-click in any empty area of the toolbar section of the main Outlook window and choose the Web Toolbar from the list. You now have a browser right in Outlook.

Just the facts

- The Navigation Pane helps you find your way and updates as you enter each new area.

- Customizing the layout of the Navigation Pane can provide more room to see your folder list in the Mail view.

- Collapse and expand the Navigation Pane to use your display space more effectively in every Outlook view.

- Keyboard shortcuts can make switching between Outlook's main views a lot more efficient.

- Outlook Search Folders are a powerful tool for collecting related information without moving information from the folders in which it resides.

- Add the Task lists to the daily and weekly Calendar views to more easily view all of your commitments for a specific day or week.

- The To-Do Bar provides access to upcoming appointments and tasks in any Outlook view and is particularly useful when working in Mail view.

- The Folder List view in the Navigation Pane provides an alternative to using the navigation icons that offers an enhanced ability to jump directly to a specific e-mail or RSS folder.

- Shortcuts provide the ability to access frequently used files and folders on your PC and Web sites directly from Outlook.

GET THE SCOOP ON...
The new look of Microsoft Office 2007 ▪ Find anything
faster and easier in Outlook 2007 ▪ The power of Word
2007 in Outlook ▪ The Office 2007 user interface

The Bold New Office 2007 User Interface

Chapter 5

Microsoft has often been described as a company that is better at replicating and mass-producing someone else's ideas than it is at innovating itself. Office 2007 should put that claim to rest once and for all. The design and architecture of the new Office System is revolutionary and utterly redefines the way productivity software is used. Combining a new user interface, a powerful new graphics engine, and enhanced integration between applications, the new Office is unlike anything that has come before it.

Outlook 2007 puts all of these features to work to make it easier than ever for you to manage your messages, contacts, appointments, and tasks. The completely new user interface is employed in the windows you use to create and edit information items in Outlook. In this chapter, I show you the interface elements that are common to all of Outlook's composition windows and main views.

The new Search box

One of the biggest challenges facing e-mail users is finding messages after they have been filed away in a folder. Many people end up leaving a lot of e-mail in their Inboxes in a vain attempt to avoid losing potentially important messages. The Search feature in previous versions of Outlook simply did not provide the speed or the results most users were looking for.

This led Microsoft to develop a search tool that indexed the contents of Outlook and the file system on your PC to make the kind of search results you have come to expect from the Web available on your local PC. This Outlook-specific tool was called Lookout and proved to be immensely popular with Outlook users.

Lookout was so popular that Microsoft bought the company and hired its developer, Mike Belshe, to work in its MSN division on the Windows Desktop Search (WDS) product. WDS and other desktop search tools work so well because they index the information on your hard drive or network shares and scan that index very quickly when you initiate a search. Outlook 2007 now has this kind of indexing and search capability built into the application, and search is now available in every view in the program.

Simple Search

In the Mail view, the Search box appears directly above the message list. To perform a keyword search, you simply enter a word or phrase into the Search box. As you type, Outlook begins searching against the e-mail messages in the currently selected message folder and begins displaying results almost instantly. The more you type, the more filtered and accurate the results. The message list is replaced with a list of matches, and the keyword or phrase you entered in the Search box is highlighted in each message in the results.

Searches are view-specific. That is, when you enter a search word or phrase while in the Mail view, you are searching through your mail messages. When you search in the Calendar view, you are searching through your appointments.

Inside Scoop

This dynamic presentation of search results as you type is sometimes called "word wheeling" and is available in the Windows Desktop Search tool as well. Vista, the next generation version of Microsoft Windows, has an index-and-search engine built in and provides word wheeling as well.

Compound Search

The Search box can be used to assemble a more advanced, compound search. If you click on the icon next to the Search box text entry field (it looks like two arrows pointing down) you can add another criterion to your search, as illustrated in Figure 5.1. Outlook defaults to Category as the default for this next search criterion, but you can use the drop-down menu to select from an extensive list of message attributes.

Figure 5.1. The Search box is available in all Outlook views and provides a simple keyword or phrase search. You can easily add additional criteria to refine your search.

Recent Searches

You can access a list of your most recent searches, expand your search temporarily to include all mail items, change search options, and get help on searching from the drop-down menu at the right end of the search entry field, as pictured in Figure 5.2.

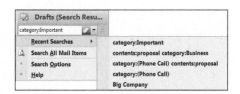

Figure 5.2. The Search box menu allows you to access recent searches and change options.

Search Options

The Search Options dialog box, shown in Figure 5.3, provides you with control over:

- Which PST files are indexed for a search

- Searching as you type (on or off)

- Keyword match highlighting (on or off and color high-lighted)

- Whether deleted items for the current folder are searched

- Whether search is on a per folder or All Mail Items basis by default when searching e-mail

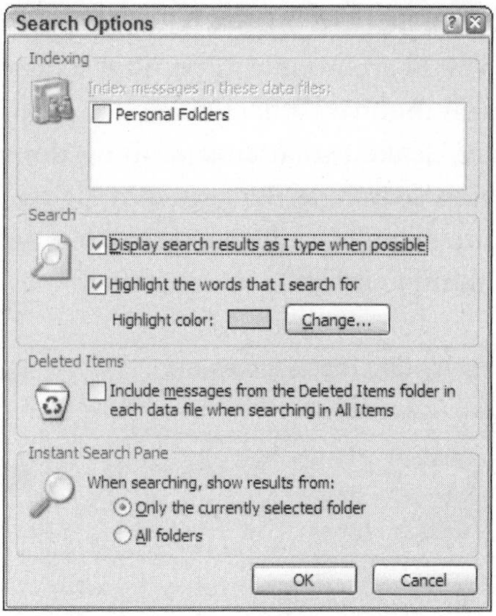

Search Options

Indexing

Index messages in these data files:
☐ Personal Folders

Search

☑ Display search results as I type when possible
☑ Highlight the words that I search for
Highlight color: ☐ Change...

Deleted Items
☐ Include messages from the Deleted Items folder in each data file when searching in All Items

Instant Search Pane
When searching, show results from:
◉ Only the currently selected folder
○ All folders

[OK] [Cancel]

Figure 5.3. The Search Options dialog box lets you define what files are indexed and how a search operates.

Composing new Outlook items

To this point, you have seen a number of impressive improvements in how Outlook helps you work. Now enter into a completely different dimension — one where things look very different than anything you have seen before. I don't think it is an overstatement when I say that the Office interface designers have set a goal to redefine how productivity software looks and works on our PCs.

The new Office interface is such a radical departure from anything you have ever seen in so-called "serious" software that your first reaction might be very much like the one I had in the spring of 2005 when I first saw the direction the Office interface was headed. As I recall, the first words out of my mouth were, "What are you thinking?"

After about twenty minutes, I was grinning like Alice's Cheshire cat. I'll admit it right here — I am a huge fan of the new look and feel of Office 2007. Once you get comfortable with this new way of creating and editing content, you will find yourself getting more done in less time. What's more important is that the end product — in this case, your e-mail correspondence — looks better and communicates your thoughts more effectively and with greater impact.

Where Outlook 2007 uses the new user interface

As I pointed out in Chapter 1, Outlook is something of a hybrid in how it uses the new Office UI. The main views do not easily lend themselves to the new UI treatment. Content creation and editing do, so you see the new Ribbon-driven interface manifest itself in the forms you use for creating and editing e-mail messages, contacts, appointments, tasks, and Journal entries.

I admit that switching between the conventional menu and toolbars UI in the main views and the new Ribbon-based UI in the content windows was a little disconcerting the first few times I opened composition windows. After working in Outlook 2007 for a few days, I became accustomed to the mix of old and new interfaces. While I appreciate and enjoy the way the Ribbon works when I'm composing and editing content, I have come to agree with the Office UI team that it is a difficult proposition thinking about how a Ribbon-based UI would work in the main views as well as the menu and toolbars UI does. It is entirely possible, though, that a future version of Outlook will adopt the new user interface even in the main views.

Word 2007 is your editor

In versions prior to Outlook 2007, you had the option to use an internal editor or Microsoft Word to compose your e-mail messages. That option is no longer present — Word is the editor for e-mail in Outlook 2007. If you have upgraded your entire Office installation to the new version, you will find that many of the e-mail composition tools you use are identical to those found in Word. Figure 5.4 illustrates the Editor Options dialog box, accessible from the new Office button in the composition window, where you can set preferences for how the Word engine works inside Outlook. In this figure, the Advanced options are displayed.

There are three screens of options available in this dialog box.

■ **Popular.** This group allows you to choose global options that control the appearance of the Mini toolbar formatting tool and tool tips, Live Preview of formatting changes, and your name and initials which are used in Review cycles. You can also select the language you work in and which theme you want applied to Outlook (Luna or Obsidian).

- **Proofing.** This group provides options for Auto-Correct and spelling and grammar checking.

- **Advanced.** This group (shown in Figure 5.4) provides a diverse set of controls that affect editing, displaying, printing, and sharing features.

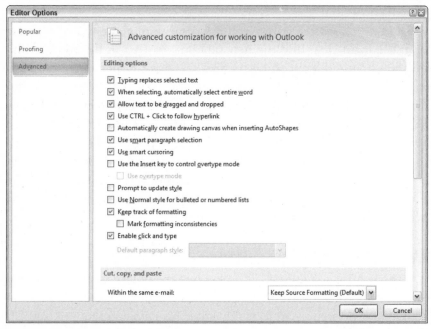

Figure 5.4. The Editor Options dialog box on the Office button menu provides access to settings for the Word-based editor in Outlook 2007.

The new item composition Ribbon

Outlook's message composition Ribbon provides a set of tabs that switch between groups of associated commands and features. In addition to the tabs, the new Office UI uses a single menu to provide file-related commands. For example, the tabs in the e-mail composition window include:

- Message (shown in Figure 5.5)
- Insert
- Options
- Format Text

Figure 5.5. The new Ribbon UI replaces the toolbars used in previous versions of Outlook in composition windows.

You also see tabs appear temporarily to provide additional commands appropriate to the content you currently have selected — such as a picture or graphic, a table, or other objects you can insert into your e-mail messages and other information objects. These are called contextual tabs and they are another way the Office UI designers have tried to make the right commands accessible when you need them.

Working with the Ribbon UI does require some adjustment to the way you have become accustomed to working in Outlook and other Windows applications. While the Ribbon appears, at first glance, to be an interface designed specifically for the mouse or Tablet PC stylus, you can access the vast majority of the Ribbon using your keyboard as well. When you press the Alt key, a set of small tool tip icons appears indicating the letter key required to access that command. Secondary commands can then be accessed by pressing the appropriate letter.

For example, with the Message tab displayed in a new Mail message window, you can access the font list by holding down the Alt key, pressing the B key, then the F key. Using the down arrow key, you can then traverse the font list to select the font you want to apply to the selected text, followed by the Enter key. It's actually a lot simpler in practice than it sounds. And the key sequences for commands you use regularly will undoubtedly become second nature.

The Office menu

The large round button in the upper-left corner of the new Office UI is called the Office menu. It provides access to a two-pane menu with file-related commands in the left pane and options to create a new Outlook item in the right pane, as shown in Figure 5.6. At the top of the Office menu, a new item menu appropriate to the type of document you are currently working on is displayed. The Office menu in a mail window also displays the Send command. You can access the Office menu using the keyboard shortcut Alt+F — the same keyboard shortcut used in previous versions of Office to access the File menu. As with the Ribbon commands, pressing the Alt key after the menu is displayed shows the appropriate letter to press to access any of the commands on the menu.

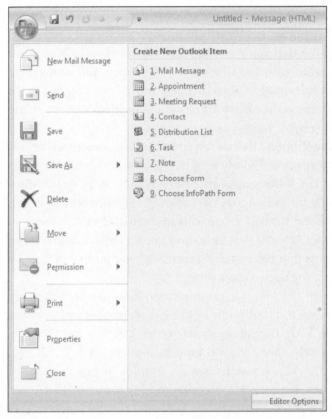

Figure 5.6. The Office menu provides the functionality of the File menu and also allows you to create a new Outlook document.

 Inside Scoop

In addition to these key sequences, all of the Ctrl key shortcuts you learned to use in previous versions of Outlook are still available, like Ctrl+S for Save or Ctrl+B for Bold.

The Message tab

The Message tab is the default view when you open a new window to create an e-mail message, contact, appointment, task, or Journal entry. The Message tab is also the default display when you open an existing e-mail "reply to" or "forward it" or when you open other Outlook information objects to review or edit them. The Ribbon in the Message tab contains specific tools and controls for the type of object you are composing or editing. As with every tab on the Ribbon, these controls have been organized into groups based on the extensive usability feedback Microsoft has received from users. The Ribbon UI can display a new, more informative Super Tooltip, as Figure 5.7 shows for the Calendar button. These Super Tooltips display helpful information about the function of each button in the Ribbon.

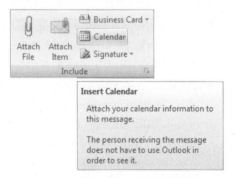

Figure 5.7. Hovering over a control in the Ribbon, such as the Calendar button, shows a Super Tooltip.

The Insert tab

The Insert tab, shown in Figure 5.8, is identical in all of Outlook 2007's composition windows. The command groups on this Ribbon provide access to a variety of objects which can be inserted into any of Outlook's information objects. Office 2007 includes a brilliant new graphics engine that is shared across all of the core applications called SmartArt. This engine provides a rich set of tools for creating structured diagrams, including organization charts and Venn diagrams, and inserting them into an Office document. You must have an active insertion point in the message body for most of these tools to be available. If you are composing a plain text message, many of these tools will be inactive.

Inside Scoop

How does Microsoft collect this usability data? When you first install Office, you are asked if you want to participate in the Customer Experience Improvement Program. If you agree to participate, Outlook sends information about what commands you use to Microsoft. No personal information is ever sent.

Figure 5.8. The Insert tab on Outlook's Ribbon provides groups of controls for inserting a variety of objects and information into your mail messages.

■ **Include.** The Include group contains commands allowing you to attach a file or an Outlook item such as a business card, a task, or a calendar appointment to a message.

■ **Tables.** The Tables group also contains a single command, but don't let this apparent simplicity fool you. The drop-down menu on the Table button provides a grid that allows you to define the number of columns and rows you'd like in the table as well as access to a series of Table-related commands, as shown in Figure 5.9.

■ **Illustrations.** The Illustrations group provides tools to insert a Picture (from a file, scanner, or camera), a SmartArt diagram graphic, a chart, or a shape. Shapes can be combined to produce a wide variety of diagrams, flow charts, and process diagrams. SmartArt graphics are converted into a non-editable

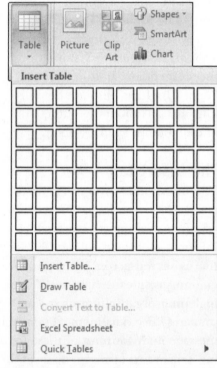

Figure 5.9. Inserting a table into a mail message is as simple as dragging across the number of rows and columns in the table drop-down menu.

raster or bitmap graphic when the Outlook object (e-mail message, appointment, or task) is saved or sent. Shapes, on the other hand, retain their "object-ness" and can be edited, re-colored, and rearranged after the message has been sent or saved. An example of a SmartArt graphic is shown in Figure 5.10.

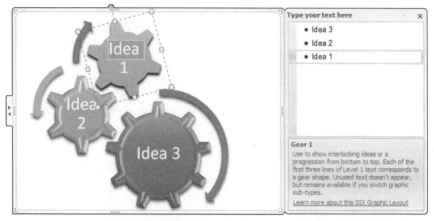

Figure 5.10. A SmartArt graphic illustrating a series of ideas is an example of the kind of structured diagrams you can create with just a few clicks of the mouse.

- **Links.** The Links group includes buttons that allow you to create a Hyperlink or a Bookmark. Hyperlinks can point to Web pages, documents on your PC or a network share, or an e-mail address. Bookmarks are internal to your message and allow you to embed navigational links in long messages. Bookmarks are generally more helpful in Word documents than e-mail messages.

- **Text.** The items in the Text group include tools for adding a text box (useful for calling out text in a sidebar or adding emphasis), Quick Parts, which draw from a library of reusable text elements you can create, WordArt, Drop Caps, Date and Time (either as a dynamic field or static text), or an Object. If you have used previous versions of Office, most of these tools are probably quite familiar. Depending on the complexity of your e-mail message, you may find some of these tools useful. Objects, in particular, are a powerful tool

 Watch Out!

Once you save a draft or send an e-mail message containing a SmartArt diagram, it cannot be edited or changed. If you need to reuse a SmartArt graphic, you should build it in Word or PowerPoint 2007 and drag a copy from that document into your Outlook message window.

that allows you to embed information created in other applications directly into the body of your e-mail message. Figure 5.11 shows a Word object embedded in an Outlook e-mail. As the illustration shows, Outlook treats this object as a picture, but it is actually linked to the source document and can be edited in Word by double-clicking on the object.

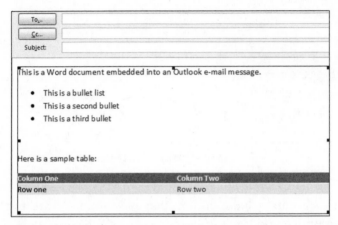

Figure 5.11. Outlook treats this embedded Word object as a picture, as shown in the Ribbon. The object contents can be edited in Word by double-clicking.

■ **Symbols.** The Symbols group provides access to the Office Equation Editor and Symbol library. This group also includes a tool for inserting a horizontal rule into your message.

Creating tables

The table tools in Outlook 2007 should be quite familiar to Microsoft Word users. While these tools have been available to Outlook 2003 users who set Word to be their e-mail editor, the enhancements in Office 2007 make tables easier to create and format than ever before. As with all inserted objects, when you select a table element in an Outlook e-mail message, the Ribbon displays a contextual tab with relevant command groups for formatting the table. Tables are a great way to present any structured data — both textual and numerical — and can add significant information value to your messages.

You have the option of inserting either a native table or using Excel spreadsheet information in your messages. To insert a table into a message, switch to the Insert tab and click on the Table button. The drop-down menu pictured in Figure 5.12 is displayed. The quickest way to insert a table is to drag across the grid to select the numbers of rows and columns you require. You also have the option to use the Insert Table command to open the standard Insert Table dialog box, or the Draw Table command, which are identical to the ones found in Office 2003.

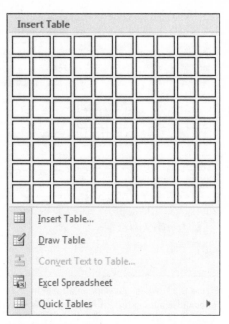

Figure 5.12. The Table menu on the Insert tab of the Ribbon lets you quickly create a table in a number of ways.

After the table has been inserted into the message body and a cell or range of cells is selected, the Table tabs are dynamically displayed on the Ribbon. The Design tab contains controls related to the look of your table, and the Gallery drop-down menu, pictured in Figure 5.13, provides one-click access to a variety of built-in styles. These Table styles use the same settings as the themes you can apply to your entire message on the Message Options tab, and your table will update itself automatically if you decide to switch themes after creating the table but before sending the message.

The Layout tab, shown in Figure 5.14, contains formatting tools related to the structure of your table and allows you to add or remove rows and columns, adjust the alignment of cell text, and perform simple data operations in the table. Building a table that contains rows of figures and performs simple calculations is entirely possible using nothing more than the built-in table tools in Outlook.

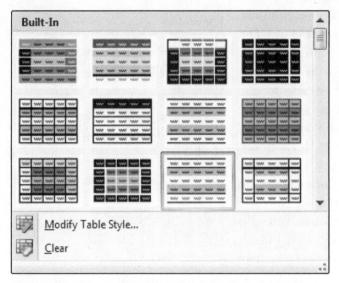

Figure 5.13. When you work on a table in an Outlook message, the Ribbon displays contextual Table tabs. The Gallery menu provides a selection of pre-defined styles.

Figure 5.14. The Layout tab contains tools for changing the structure and data operations in your table.

There may be occasions when you need more calculating power than the simple formulas and functions provided by the Word-based editor. When you need to pull out the heavy artillery, Outlook can insert an Excel spreadsheet into the message body. Choose Excel Spreadsheet from the Table menu and an instance of the Excel application is launched, inserting a new spreadsheet object into your message. Of course, Excel must be installed to use this option. Figure 5.15 shows an active Excel spreadsheet in the e-mail message body with Excel's Ribbon displayed.

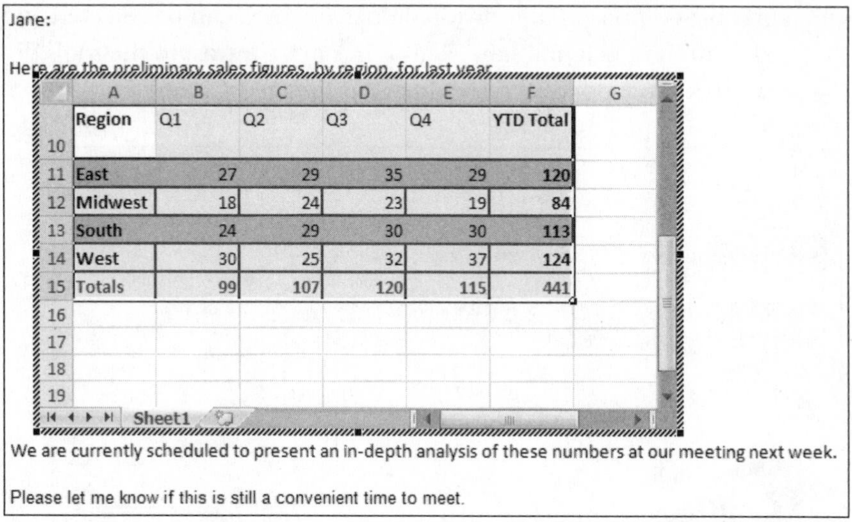

Jane:

Here are the preliminary sales figures by region for last year.

	A	B	C	D	E	F	G
	Region	Q1	Q2	Q3	Q4	YTD Total	
10							
11	East	27	29	35	29	120	
12	Midwest	18	24	23	19	84	
13	South	24	29	30	30	113	
14	West	30	25	32	37	124	
15	Totals	99	107	120	115	441	
16							
17							
18							
19							

Sheet1

We are currently scheduled to present an in-depth analysis of these numbers at our meeting next week.

Please let me know if this is still a convenient time to meet.

Figure 5.15. An active Excel spreadsheet can be inserted into your e-mail message and is edited and formatted using all of Excel's advanced features.

Inserting illustrations

The old saying that a picture is worth a thousand words can certainly apply to e-mail, and Outlook 2007 contains a wide array of tools for importing and creating graphics. Earlier in this chapter, I describe the new SmartArt graphics engine shared by all Office 2007 applications. In addition to the professional graphics you can generate with this tool, Outlook has a few additional new tricks up its sleeve with the ability to generate charts or use shapes to construct diagrams right in the message body. The ability to import photos and other graphic elements from your hard drive, digital camera, or scanner that were available in Outlook 2003 are carried forward as well, and all graphics operations benefit from the dynamic Picture tab displayed on the Ribbon when a graphic object is selected.

The dynamic nature of these contextual tabs when working with graphics really demonstrates how deep a transformation the architecture of the Office suite has undergone. Depending on the type of graphic element you insert, a set of tools optimized for that type of image is displayed. Figure 5.16 shows the Picture Tools tab that is displayed when an object-oriented or vector graphic like a Windows Metafile (.wmf) is selected. The tools on this Ribbon tab are all oriented toward working with a graphic composed of individual objects which can be selected and changed from their original state. This is in stark contrast to the tools displayed when a bitmapped or raster image is selected (.bmp).

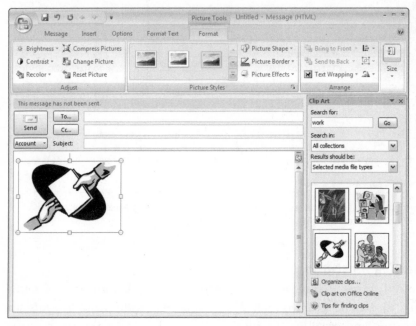

Figure 5.16. The Picture Tools tab contains controls for working with object-oriented graphics.

Artwork is available from many sources including CD and DVD stock art collections, digital cameras and video recorders, and scanners. There are many online sources of both royalty-free and commercially licensed artwork in both vector and raster formats as well. Office includes some clip art that is installed directly onto your PC with the suite and the Office Online Web site offers a large library of additional images that can be searched from the Clip Art task pane in Outlook.

If you insert a photographic image, the Picture Tools tab, shown in Figure 5.17, is displayed. The tools on this tab are nothing short of extraordinary and produce stunning visual effects that previously required expensive and complicated software and a significant level of expertise. Note in particular the large Picture Styles group in the center of the tab which drops down to provide a nice selection of advanced image treatments. These styles incorporate perspective, shadow, and edge effects and can be applied with a single click. If one of the presets doesn't meet your needs, you can use the individual effects controls to

Inside Scoop

There are two primary types of graphics — vector and raster. Vector graphics are resizable with no loss of resolution, can be edited at a discrete level, and use little disk space. Raster graphics are composed of pixels and lose quality as they are enlarged. They are edited using pixel-based painting tools and can be extremely large in file size.

the right of the Picture Styles drop-down menu to create your own styles, which can be saved for future use.

Figure 5.17. The Picture Tools tab provides Picture Styles that can produce stunning effects with a single click.

Office 2007's new SmartArt graphics, described earlier in this chapter, provide a broad range of templates for structured graphics like process models, Venn diagrams, and organization charts. These vector graphics can be resized and shared among Office documents. As I mentioned earlier, Outlook renders these graphics as bitmaps when the message they are contained in is saved or sent. If you need to use a SmartArt graphic in multiple documents, it is advisable to create them in a Word or PowerPoint document and copy them into your e-mail message.

When you insert a SmartArt graphic into a mail message, two contextual tabs are displayed. The Design tab, shown in Figure 5.18, provides a drop-down menu that lists the SmartArt graphic types, styles, and color schemes. The Format tab provides editing tools, only some of which are appropriate to SmartArt graphics. Others, like the WordArt Quick Styles, are used with other graphic formats.

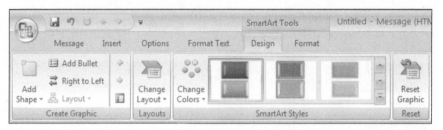

Figure 5.18. A SmartArt graphic can be quickly formatted using the menus and commands on the contextual Design tab.

Inserting a chart into an Outlook e-mail message works similarly to inserting an Excel spreadsheet as an instance of Excel is launched to define the data to be used to generate the chart. When you select the Insert Chart command on the Ribbon, a gallery of chart types, pictured in Figure 5.19, is displayed. When you select the chart type you want to generate, an Excel sheet opens. Enter the data for the chart, and it appears in the e-mail message. Once the chart has been generated, you can refine the formatting of the chart on the contextual Chart Tools tabs, shown in Figure 5.20 (Design) and 5.21 (Layout), that appear on the Ribbon when you select the chart object.

Shapes, like SmartArt graphics, are new to Office 2007. When you chose to insert a shape into your e-mail message, a drawing panel is created that is framed by black bars. This drawing panel can be enlarged or reduced in size as needed by dragging on these bars. To add a shape to your drawing, simply select an object from the Shapes gallery in the Insert Shapes group of the contextual Drawing Tools tab pictured in Figure 5.22. You can add additional shapes and apply styles, shadows, and other effects from the controls on this tab. Some objects can act as text containers, and the Mini toolbar is available to make text format changes once you have added text to the object by selecting the text you want to format and hovering the cursor over the selection.

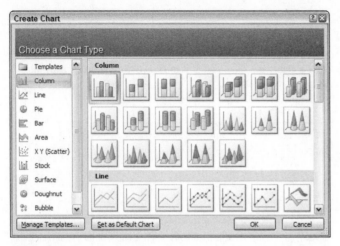

Figure 5.19. You can select any of these Excel chart types to insert into an Outlook information object.

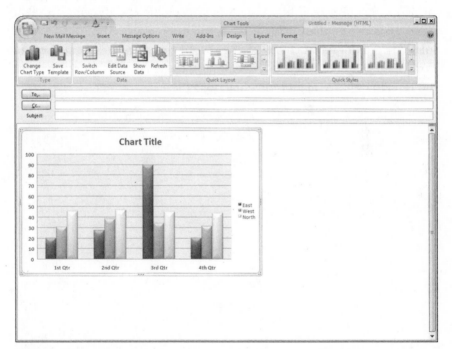

Figure 5.20. The Chart Tools Design contextual tab appears when a chart object is selected and provides access to the chart data and a gallery of chart types and styles.

Watch Out!
As with SmartArt graphics, once you save or send an e-mail message or other Outlook object containing a chart, it cannot be edited or changed. If you need to reuse a chart, you should build it in Excel 2007 and drag a copy into your Outlook message window.

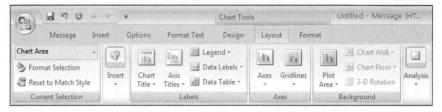

Figure 5.21. The Chart Tools Layout contextual tab appears when a chart object is selected and provides options for how the chart is displayed.

Unlike SmartArt graphics, drawings using shapes are completely free form. You begin with a blank slate and assemble the drawing to meet your needs rather than using a predefined template. Also, unlike both SmartArt graphics and charts, shapes-based drawings do not convert to bitmapped graphics when the e-mail message is saved as a draft or sent and remain editable at an individual object level.

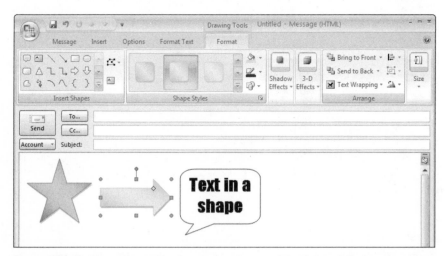

Figure 5.22. Shapes can be combined to produce structured drawings and diagrams in your e-mail messages.

Inserting hyperlinks and bookmarks

Hyperlinks and bookmarks are unchanged from previous versions of Office. Hyperlinks are text-based links that act like the Uniform Resource Locators (URL) you see displayed on Web pages. When you click a hyperlink, it opens the referenced Web page or document. The Insert Hyperlink dialog box, pictured in Figure 5.23, includes controls for adding a link to your e-mail message that can point to:

- ▪ An existing file or Web page
- ▪ A place in the current document (useful only in a long e-mail message)
- ▪ A new document you can create from the dialog box
- ▪ A "mailto" link that opens a new, preaddressed e-mail message in your recipient's default e-mail application with the address and (optional) subject line already entered.

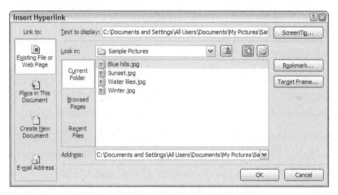

Figure 5.23. The Insert Hyperlink dialog box allows you to embed links to Web pages or documents in your e-mail message.

As shown in Figure 5.23, if you insert a hyperlink to an existing file or Web page, you have the option to browse for a file on your PC or a network share and pick from a list of recently browsed Web pages or a list of

Watch Out!

If you choose to share a file on your PC or a network share, be sure your recipient has access rights or the link does not function properly. Sharing files from your PC can be a security risk. Linking to a file on an Exchange, SharePoint, or file server is usually a safer alternative.

recently opened files. You can also open a browser window to navigate to a specific Web page by clicking the Web button above the pick list. This dialog box provides extensive built-in help that can be accessed by clicking the Help button (question mark) in the title bar.

Text enhancements

Text enhancements should be familiar if you have used Microsoft Word in the past and can make your e-mail message more document-like. They are available in Outlook because Word is the editor for your mail messages. Many of these enhancements are more appropriate for documents than they are for e-mail, and they should be used sparingly, especially if you are unsure whether your recipients also use Outlook.

- **Text Box.** If you want to create a sidebar or set some text apart from the body of your e-mail messages, inserting a text box allows you to format the border, fill color, and text color to call attention to the text inside. Once you have established these format choices, you can save the text box to a Text Box Gallery from the drop-down menu for reuse in future e-mail messages.

- **Quick Parts.** The Quick Parts drop-down menu allows you to insert fields and page numbers. These parts are rarely useful in an e-mail message and if you are like most Outlook e-mail authors, you can probably find little or no use for these elements in your messages.

- **WordArt.** WordArt is an engine used to create fancy text effects that are far more useful in fliers, brochures, reports, and other word processing documents than in e-mail messages. If you use Outlook e-mail for marketing purposes or to compose a newsletter, you may find WordArt useful. My advice, as a recovering graphic designer, is that you should use these text effects sparingly.

- **Drop Cap.** Creating an initial capital letter can be useful to signify the beginning of a new thought or topic. A drop cap can be useful in a longer e-mail message but, like most of these text enhancements, is more appropriate for a word processing document than an e-mail message.

- **Date & Time.** A number of formats for time and date stamps can be selected from this control's dialog box. If you want the inserted text to always display the current date or time, select the Update Automatically check box in the lower-right corner of the dialog box.

■ **Insert Object.** This control allows you to embed an object from another application into your e-mail message. You can embed an existing file or create a new one. As an example, you can embed a PowerPoint slide into your e-mail message using this control. I recommend you use file attachments rather than embedding objects as a general practice unless it is critical that the information contained in the embedded object be seen in context to the text in your e-mail message. Your e-mail message is smaller in size and more compatible with other e-mail programs if you attach files rather than embed objects.

Symbols

The Symbols group on the Insert tab contains controls for inserting equations, text symbols, and horizontal lines into your messages. Of these three controls, only the Equation control warrants much discussion as it is based on the new Equation Editor 3.0 included in Office 2007. The Equation Tools contextual tab, shown in Figure 5.24, appears when you click the Equation button or select Insert New Equation from the control's drop-down menu. I'm no math wizard and have very little need for adding sophisticated equations into my e-mail messages, but this has proved to be a very exciting tool for some of the cryptographers and software developers I work with and is very useful if you are involved in mathematics, science, economics, or other endeavors where, to paraphrase, an equation is worth a thousand words. Equations can be saved for reuse from the control's drop-down menu.

The Symbols control provides access to a small gallery of commonly used text symbols for trademarks, currency, and simple logic statements (equals, greater than, etc.). A More Symbols link below the gallery opens the standard Symbol dialog box that is unchanged from Office 2003.

The Horizontal Line control inserts a line object into your message at the active insertion point when clicked. Once the line has been inserted, it can be formatted by right-clicking the rule that opens the Format Horizontal Line dialog box. The width can be adjusted either as an absolute value in inches or as a percent of the message window width. Outlook's theme colors are available and the line width and alignment can also be adjusted.

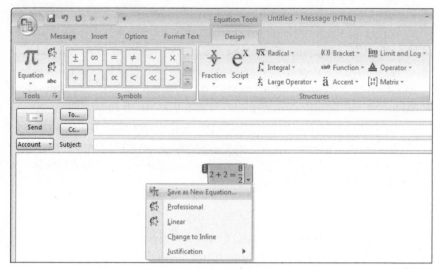

Figure 5.24. The Equation Tools tab is based on the new Equation Editor utility in Office 2007.

The Options tab

The Options tab contains groups that affect the format, overall appearance of text in your e-mail message, and its functionality. The Options tab is shown in Figure 5.25. The Options tab contains the following groups of controls:

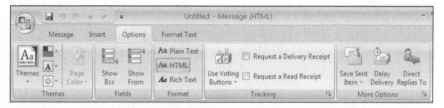

Figure 5.25. The Options tab contains controls that affect the overall format, appearance, and functionality of the current message.

- **Themes.** Themes are predefined styles that affect the color scheme and font families used in your message. Outlook 2007 includes a gallery of prebuilt themes and you can easily create themes that match your organization's graphic identity or that suit your personal tastes.

- **Fields.** The Fields group provides controls to show the Bcc and From fields in the message window. Bcc stands for Blind carbon copy — any recipients added to this field are not seen in copies of the message received by recipients whose addresses are entered in the To or Cc fields. Toggling the From field allows you to send a message on behalf of someone else. Be aware that this is a cosmetic change — the header information contained in all e-mail messages still identifies the actual e-mail account the message was sent from. Outlook actually decodes this discrepancy and labels messages sent in this fashion accordingly in the From column in the Message List.

- **Format.** This control sets the file format for the current message. In general, you should restrict your choices to either HTML or Plain Text. Rich Text is an Outlook-specific format that can cause readability issues for recipients who use another e-mail program.

- **Tracking.** The Tracking group includes three sets of controls. Voting buttons allows you to ask recipients to provide a response by selecting one of a set of answers you configure for a question posed in the message. Outlook provides a few prebuilt sets and you can easily configure your own response set as well. The two remaining controls request a receipt confirming that a message has been delivered or read. Not all e-mail applications support these receipt requests and in those, like Outlook, that do the ultimate control over responding to these requests is in the hands of the recipient. The dialog box icons in the lower-right corner of the Tracking control group and in the More Options control group described in the next bullet point both open the Message Options dialog shown in Figure 5.26, which provides additional settings related to the current message.

- **More Options.** This group contains an assortment of controls related to how the current message can be marked in terms of priority and sensitivity, where the message is saved after sending, and to what address replies are sent. As mentioned in the previous bullet point, clicking the dialog box icon in the lower-right corner of the control group opens the Message Options dialog box.

Message Options

Message settings

Importance: Normal

Sensitivity: Normal

Security

Change security settings for this message.

Security Settings...

Voting and Tracking options

☐ Use voting buttons:

☐ Request a delivery receipt for this message

☐ Request a read receipt for this message

Delivery options

☐ Have replies sent to: Select Names...

☐ Do not deliver before: None   12:00 AM

☐ Expires after: None   12:00 AM

Attachment format: Default

Encoding: Auto-Select

Contacts...

Categories ▼ None

Close

Figure 5.26. The Message options dialog box.

The Format Text tab

The Format Text tab, like the Insert tab, is identical in all of Outlook's composition windows and contains groups that control the appearance of text in your e-mail message and is very similar to the Formatting toolbar in Outlook 2003. The Format Text tab is shown in Figure 5.27.

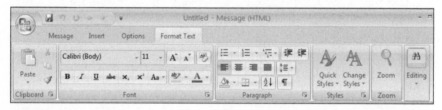

Figure 5.27. The Format Text tab contains many of the tools found on the Formatting toolbar in previous versions of Outlook.

- **Clipboard.** The Clipboard group is identical to the one displayed on the Message tab.

Hack

Any Ribbon tool can be added to the Quick Access Toolbar (QAT) by right-clicking its icon on the Ribbon. In its default position next to the Office menu button, you can scroll through the icons on the QAT. When placed below the Ribbon, you get a full-width toolbar.

▪ **Font.** The Font group provides access to basic font formatting options like font family and styles, size, and color. A Clear Formatting button in the upper-right corner of this group lets you quickly strip all formatting from selected text. The Font group controls provide a Live Preview as you hover over options like Font, Color, or Style. The arrow in the lower-right corner provides one-click access to the standard Font dialog box, which is unchanged from Outlook 2003.

▪ **Paragraph.** The Paragraph group contains controls that affect the active paragraph or a selected range of text containing more than one paragraph. You can create bulleted, numbered, or multilevel numbered lists; control paragraph indents; alphabetically sort a selection of paragraphs; show and hide nonprinting characters; adjust alignment and line spacing; and apply a background color and border to one or more paragraphs. The small arrow in the lower-right corner opens the Paragraph dialog box, which is also unchanged from Outlook 2003.

▪ **Styles.** The Styles group includes two controls that can apply a preset style on a paragraph-by-paragraph basis. The Quick Styles control, like the theme control on the Message Options tab, applies a predefined look to the paragraph that includes font, color, size, and line style. The Change Styles button displays a menu with predefined styles like Traditional or Modern. These changes can be applied and removed with a single click. The Change Styles menu also provides access to a dialog box where you can create your own Quick Styles and select the Default style for new messages.

▪ **Zoom.** The Zoom group contains a single button that opens the Zoom dialog box where you can select from preset or custom zoom levels.

- **Editing.** The Editing group contains controls that access the Find, Replace, and Select commands. On the Select control, you can select all text in the current message that matches the currently selected text — a fast way to make changes throughout the message body.

Just the facts

- Use the new Search feature in Outlook to find e-mail messages and to reduce or eliminate the need for a dedicated search application.

- Outlook uses conventional menus and toolbars in the main views and the new Office 2007 user interface in information object windows used to create or view items, including e-mail messages, contacts, appointments, tasks, and Journal entries.

- The editor in Outlook 2007 is a subset of Office Word 2007 and offers many of the same writing, editing, formatting, and proofing tools in the full version of that application.

- Related commands are grouped together in the Ribbon and organized on a series of tabs that can be accessed with the mouse or keyboard.

- You can easily show or hide the Ribbon and can access any command on the Ribbon using Alt key combinations.

- The Office menu in the new composition windows replaces the File menu and contains commands for sending or saving messages and for creating new Outlook information objects.

- The Insert and Format Text tabs are identical throughout Outlook's new composition windows.

- SmartArt graphics and Excel charts are converted to bitmap graphics when the object they have been inserted into is saved or sent. Shapes retain their "object-ness" and can be edited after they have been saved.

- Live preview effects are available for most of the elements you insert into information objects, allowing you to preview the changes that will be applied to the element before making a selection.

GET THE SCOOP ON...
The new look of the main Mail view ▪ A whole new
way to compose e-mail in Outlook ▪ Two ways to read
e-mail ▪ Juggling more than one e-mail account ▪
Outlook is now an RSS aggregator

Outlook Is an E-Mail Manager

Chapter 6

The vast majority of people who use Outlook use it primarily, if not exclusively, to send, receive, and manage their e-mail messages. In Chapter 4, you saw the different environments Outlook provides to manage various types of information. To one degree or another, the 200 million plus users of Outlook take advantage of these personal information management features. But rare is the individual who uses Outlook to manage his or her personal information exclusive of e-mail. This chapter introduces you to the features and capabilities Outlook provides for reading, composing, sending, and receiving e-mail messages. The user interface changes in Office 2007 provide a wealth of options that can assist you in making your e-mail more useful, delivering information with greater impact and effect than ever before.

Getting familiar with the e-mail view

The main Mail view in Outlook 2007, aside from the cosmetics of the new Office themes and the greater flexibility to expand and collapse the Navigation Pane and To-Do Bar, has not changed all that much from Outlook 2003. As I said in Chapter 1, Outlook was the beneficiary of the greatest attention from the design team in Office 2003, and this new version builds on the foundation established in that release.

The three-pane view

Outlook 2003 introduced the Reading Pane, which dramatically improved the experience of viewing e-mail messages. Prior to the 2003 version, Outlook was not much better for reading e-mail than the confusingly named Outlook Express e-mail application included in Windows. While seemingly a simple idea, the ability to read e-mail messages in a pane that was taller than it was wide made a dramatic improvement in the quality of the reading experience. In Chapter 4, you saw the default layout of the Mail view that is divided into three sections or panes.

Elements of the three-pane view

The idea of dividing the screen into panes is not unique. A number of e-mail programs use a similar structure. The three panes in Outlook's Mail view, as shown in Figure 6.1, are the folder list, the message list, and the Reading Pane. If you compare the default layouts of Outlook 2003 and Outlook 2007, the biggest visual difference between the two is the new Search box that appears at the top of the message list.

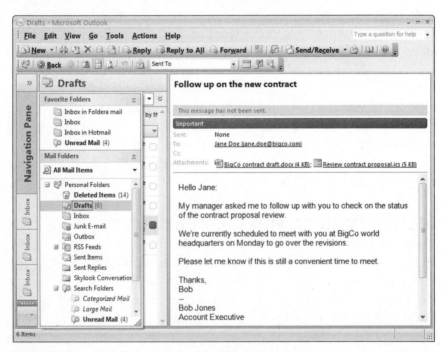

Figure 6.1. The main Mail view in Outlook is divided into three panes.

The folder list includes a number of default folders including the Inbox, Sent Items, Drafts, and Deleted Items folders. You can easily create new folders to store e-mail messages you want to keep after reading them. There are many schools of thought about how to manage the ever-increasing volume of e-mail received. E-mail has become one of the primary mediums for correspondence for business and personal communications because it is immediate, inexpensive, and easy to share with others. In Appendix B — Recommended Reading, I suggest a number of books that have different approaches to creating an effective e-mail organization structure. The one constant in all of these texts is that your Inbox, like your postal mailbox, is a place where new mail arrives. It should not be a place for you to store mail.

Customizing the three-pane view

Almost every view in Outlook can be extensively customized, and the message list in the main Mail view is no exception. Chapter 14 provides an in-depth look at how to customize Outlook views. These customizations allow you to define how information is displayed and sorted in list views like the message list in the Mail view. In addition to these list view customizations, there are changes you can make that affect the overall appearance of the Mail view.

- **The Reading Pane.** You can choose among three states for the Reading Pane — Off, Right, and Below. You can toggle the Reading Pane on and off from the Advanced toolbar by clicking on the Reading Pane icon. To switch between Right or Below alignment, select Reading Pane on the View menu and choose the position you prefer on the submenu that is displayed.

- **The Navigation Pane.** There are three possible states for the Navigation Pane as well, as discussed in Chapter 4. You can show or hide the Navigation Pane using the Alt+F1 keyboard command. You can choose between these two states or collapse the Navigation Pane from the View menu. And, you can collapse or expand the Navigation Pane using your mouse by clicking the chevron (>>) icon at the top of the Navigation Pane itself.

The exploding inbox

I have been counseling, teaching, and writing about e-mail management for a number of years. The single most common complaint I hear from people is how overwhelmed they are by the amount of e-mail they receive. I've met people who regularly receive hundreds of e-mail messages every day and who keep hundreds or even thousands of messages in their Inboxes. It's no wonder they complain that they can't find anything!

A question I often pose to the audience in the seminars and speeches I deliver is why they treat e-mail so differently from postal mail. I ask them to consider how they deal with postal mail.

If you're like most people, you go to the mailbox, pull out the day's mail, and head back inside. On the way from your mailbox to your door, you likely start to filter the new mail into three piles: stuff you have to deal with (bills), stuff you want to deal with (letters from friends and family, magazines, etc.), and stuff you neither need nor want (junk). Depending on the length of the walk back to your front door and how much mail you receive, you may have completed the filtering process before you get there.

The stuff you have to deal with goes into a specified place. The stuff you want to deal with goes on the kitchen table or the coffee table where you can read it at leisure. The stuff you neither need nor want goes right into the trash can. While there may be some variation, I'm confident this pretty accurately describes what you do six days a week.

Now ask yourself the following question:

Do you open and read a number of newly arrived pieces of mail, put them back in their envelopes, and take them back outside to place them back in your mailbox?

Think about it for a moment in terms of how you interact with your e-mail. If you're like the majority of people I work with on managing information overload, you do this all the time with your e-mail.

Imagine going to your mailbox at home and digging through dozens or hundreds of pieces of mail every time you went out to check for new mail or needed to find something important.

E-mail is not snail mail! Develop new habits for dealing with a new medium and get your Inbox empty on a regular basis.

■ **Default Views.** Outlook installs a number of predefined layouts for
each main view in the application. In the other views, these layouts
are listed in the Navigation Pane where you can switch between
them by selecting a radio button next to each. Because Mail uses the
Navigation Pane to display the folder list, you must access the predefined layouts for the Mail view by choosing Current View from the
View menu. Figure 6.2 shows the Timeline layout that replaces the
message list with a time-based display showing what day messages
arrived horizontally and in the order received during the day vertically. You can combine this timeline with the Reading Pane as
shown, if desired.

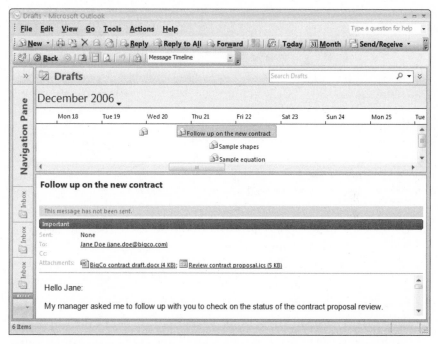

Figure 6.2. The main Mail view in Outlook displaying the Timeline view with the Reading
Pane below.

Do you ever need to open an e-mail message?

Maybe not. Since the introduction of the Reading Pane in Outlook 2003, I
have found the need to actually open e-mail messages in a new window has
diminished appreciably. With the addition of the collapsible Navigation

Pane in Outlook 2007, I open even fewer messages. The two most significant advantages are that I can review e-mail faster, and the Windows Task Bar isn't cluttered with as many Outlook windows.

The Message tab

The Message tab, pictured in Figure 6.3, is the default view when you open a new e-mail message or reply to or forward an existing message. Immediately below the Ribbon are buttons to the left of the address fields to send the current message and to select the account from which the message will be sent.

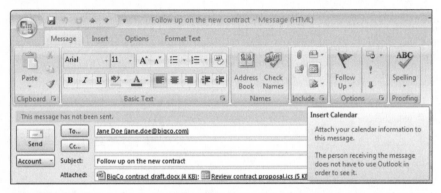

Figure 6.3. The Message tab in the Mail message composition form contains commands related to composing and addressing messages. The Calendar button shows a Super Tooltip.

- **Clipboard.** The Clipboard group provides access to the Cut, Copy, Paste, and Format Painter commands. The Paste button is the most commonly used and is therefore the largest button in this group. A drop-down menu allows you to choose Paste options (normal Paste or Paste Special that allows you to strip formatting from the Clipboard contents). The small arrow in the lower-right corner of the Clipboard group opens the Office Clipboard Task Pane at the right edge of the composition area. This feature stores all the content you copy or cut in all Office applications, allowing you to create a cross-application store of frequently used text and graphics clippings.

- **Basic Text.** The Basic Text group provides access to the most commonly used text formatting options, including font style, font size, bullets, numbering, indent and outdent (hanging indent), font formats (bold, italic, and underline), font color, highlight color, alignment, and the Clear Formatting tool. The small arrow in the lower-right corner opens the standard Font dialog box that is identical to the one in Outlook 2003.

■ **Names.** The Names group provides one-click access to the Address Book and Check Names features. The Address book is a floating window that displays your Outlook Contacts as well as any Contacts lists you have opened from an Exchange Server or SharePoint site. Check Names looks up the entries in the address fields (To, Cc, and Bcc) and completes the entries by matching the name you have typed with its corresponding Contact record. If a name doesn't match a Contact record, Outlook displays a warning message. You can also invoke the Check Names commands with the Crtl+K keyboard shortcut.

■ **Include.** The Include group allows you to attach one or more files, an Outlook Business Card, Calendar information, or a signature block to the e-mail message. The Business Card and Calendar options are new in Outlook 2007. Clicking on Business Card attaches your card to the message. The drop-down menu allows you to select another Contact's card. The Calendar button allows you to select a date range and copies information from your Outlook Calendar into the message body. As shown in Figure 6.4, you can select how much detail is included in the information and whether attachments to calendar items are also included. The information can be included in either a Daily Schedule or List View format and is pasted into the body of the e-mail and attached as an Outlook Calendar file (.ics) as shown in Figure 6.5. This figure also illustrates one of the contextual tabs the Ribbon displays when an inserted object, in this case a table, is selected. This Ribbon is only displayed when a table item is selected and provides access to a full set of tools for formatting the selected object.

Figure 6.4. The Send a Calendar via E-mail dialog box allows you to select a date range, layout, and detail level for calendar information that is included in the body of an e-mail message.

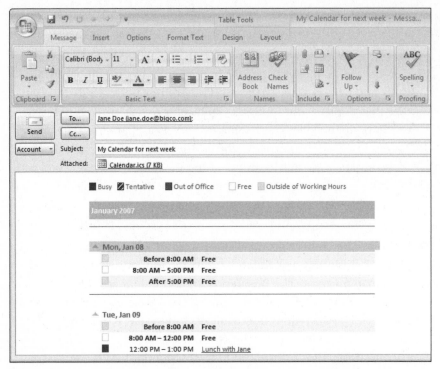

Figure 6.5. Outlook inserts the calendar information into the body of the e-mail message as a formatted table and also attaches an Outlook Calendar file (.ics) to the message. Note the Table Ribbon that is displayed when the table is selected in the message body.

■ **Options.** The Options group provides tools to assign a Follow Up Flag, permissions, and priority to a message and options to digitally sign and encrypt the message. Follow Up Flags are new in Outlook 2007 and allow you to set a follow-up reminder for a message from the Follow Up drop-down menu. Choose from a selection of predefined dates including Today, Tomorrow, This Week, Next Week, or Custom. If you select Custom, the dialog box shown in Figure 6.6 is displayed. You can set a Follow Up Flag and

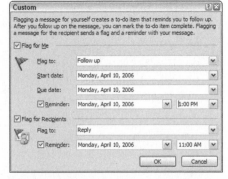

Figure 6.6. Custom Follow Up Flags allow you to automatically create a task in your To-Do list and set reminder alarms for yourself and/or the recipients of your message.

add a reminder alarm both for yourself and for recipients. Setting a Follow Up Flag automatically creates a task item and, when you clear the flag, the task item is marked as complete. A summary of the flag and the options you have chosen are displayed in a hard-to-ignore orange box above the address fields in the message window. Follow Up Flags, which can be assigned to both e-mail messages and tasks, are covered in greater detail in Chapter 9.

The Message Options tab

The Message Options tab, shown in Figure 6.7, provides access to a variety of different controls that affect how your e-mail message is formatted and delivered. At first glance, the inclusion of the Themes group might seem a bit incongruous as it is the only group on this tab that addresses formatting. It makes perfect sense when you consider that the controls in the Themes group affect your entire message.

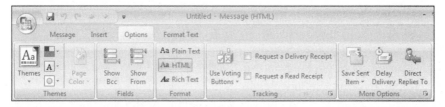

Figure 6.7. The Message Options tab.

- **Themes.** The Themes group provides access to a variety of visual styles that give you the ability to instantly change the color scheme and fonts used in your document — in this case, an e-mail message. The Live Preview feature in Office 2007 allows you to move your mouse cursor over each of the themes in the drop-down Gallery menu, shown in Figure 6.8, and see the actual content of your message reformatted on the fly. Select the theme you want to apply, and your message is reformatted. The Colors, Fonts, Effects, and Page Color buttons provide you with a more granular level of control if you want to override a component of a theme or want to design your own.

- **Fields.** The Fields group contains buttons to show or hide the Bcc and From fields in the message header.

- **Format.** The Format group provides options for Plain Text, HTML, or Rich Text formats for your message. If you switch from HTML or Rich Text to Plain Text, Outlook displays a warning dialog box that explains what formatting you will lose prior to converting the format.

- **Tracking.** The Tracking Group allows you to request a vote from recipients using built-in choices like "Yes, No, Maybe" or a custom set you define, and request a receipt when the message is delivered and/or read. You can access the Message Options dialog box by clicking on the small arrow in the lower-right

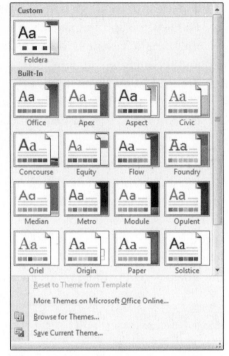

Figure 6.8. This Gallery menu is displayed when you click on the Themes control.

corner of the Tracking Group where many of the options on this tab can be set along with security controls and category tags.

- **More Options.** The More Options group is a grab bag of message-related options that control where a message is saved after being sent, how the message is encoded, whether delivery should be delayed until a specific time in the future, and to whom replies should be directed. These options can all be accessed in the Message Options dialog box as well.

Creating a new e-mail message

Creating a new e-mail message begins with opening a new Mail Message window. This can be done from the toolbar in any Outlook view. In the Mail view, a single click on the New button opens a new message window. In any other view, you can click and hold the mouse button down on the down-arrow icon to the right of the New button to display a menu showing the option to create a new e-mail message as well as other Outlook information objects.

Inside Scoop

Outlook 2007 uses the same keyboard shortcuts as previous versions. In Mail view, Ctrl+N opens a new message. In other views, Ctrl+Shift+M creates a new message.

E-mail formats (Message Options tab)

Outlook can send and receive messages in HTML, Outlook Rich Text, and Plain Text formats:

- **HTML format.** This is the default format in Outlook 2007 and is used by most popular e-mail applications. HTML supports all of the features available in Outlook 2007, including mixed fonts, character-level formatting, numbering, bullets, alignment, horizontal lines, pictures (including backgrounds), HTML styles, stationery, signatures, and linking to Web pages. Because most popular e-mail applications use HTML, I recommend you use this format for Internet e-mail messages.

- **Rich Text format (RTF).** This is a Microsoft-only format that the following e-mail applications support: Microsoft Office Outlook 2007; Microsoft Office Outlook 2003; Microsoft Outlook 97, 98, 2000, and 2002; and Microsoft Exchange Client Versions 5.0 and 4.0.

  Even if you work in an Exchange Server environment, I still recommend that you use the HTML format. Some organization policies enforce use of RTF because the messages tend to be smaller in size. RTF format supports text formatting, including bullets, alignment, and linked objects. Outlook automatically converts RTF formatted messages to HTML by default when you send them to an Internet recipient, so that message formatting is maintained and attachments are received.

- **Plain text.** This is supported by all e-mail applications. As its name implies, plain text doesn't support bold, italic, colored fonts, or other text formatting. It also doesn't support the display of images directly in the message body, although you can include the images as attachments.

  When you reply to a message, Outlook preserves the format of the original message. You can override this by selecting a format for the reply. If you change the format of a message you have received, any reply to that message is formatted with the new display format you selected.

In most cases, you don't need to change the message format. When you send an HTML message to a recipient whose e-mail application doesn't support HTML, the recipient's e-mail application automatically displays a plain-text version in the message body.

Pros and cons of HTML-formatted e-mail

Depending on the environment and industry in which you work, the use of HTML-formatted e-mail may be a generally accepted practice or considered a major breach of etiquette. There are both technical and emotional reasons behind the latter attitude, and it's most common to find this preference expressed by long-time Internet users and people focused on information security. The reasons are complex and outside the scope of this book, but the short version is that when you open an HTML-formatted message, you are essentially opening a Web page. While many HTML messages simply take advantage of the formatting capabilities the format provides, others call images and content that is fetched from a server somewhere on the Internet. This means that the same potential vulnerabilities exist when you open an HTML e-mail message as when you visit an unfamiliar Web site.

The best way to set these concerns to rest is to make sure your PC is adequately protected by antivirus and anti-spyware utilities, you have a firewall running on your PC that monitors inbound and outbound traffic, and you keep current with system updates from Microsoft. Outlook itself adds additional protections, which are discussed in Chapter 27.

The other reason some prefer plain text messages is that they are significantly smaller in size and can be read on a wider variety of devices. On a dial-up connection to the Internet when you are downloading mail messages, the difference can be quite noticeable. It's increasingly common to find people using a mobile phone, PDA, or converged device like a Windows Mobile Smartphone, Treo, or Blackberry to read e-mail, and plain text is much faster to download and easier to read on these devices' small screens.

Watch Out!

The firewall included in Windows XP Service Pack 2 only monitors outgoing activity. Other free and commercial firewall utilities watch incoming traffic as well. Windows Vista has a bidirectional firewall built in, but if you are running Windows XP SP2, you may want to install a more capable firewall.

Composing the message text

With a powerful word processing engine at its disposal, Outlook 2007 provides many options for formatting your e-mail messages. You can use any of the fonts installed on your PC, a variety of color and layout options, and images and graphics to enhance your communications. As a recovering graphic designer and the recipient of an average 400 to 500 e-mail messages every day, let me advise you that more is definitely not always better. Exercising some design restraint makes your messages easier and more enjoyable to read.

The Office design team has done an excellent job building some very tasteful and effective templates and styles into Outlook 2007 to get you started. Depending on your communication style and needs, these may be all that you ever need. If you have a desire to create your own templates and styles, Outlook 2007 makes it easier than ever to add your own unique look to your e-mail messages.

Composing an e-mail message works very much as in previous versions of Outlook or any other popular e-mail program. Click in the message area of a new e-mail message window and begin typing. As you type, Outlook, by default, checks your spelling and indicates misspelled or unrecognized words by underling them with a red squiggly underline. If you've used Word in the past, this is very familiar behavior.

Formatting message text

Formatting the text in your message is done using standard word processing techniques. Select some text and make changes to the font, size, color, or alignment. In Outlook 2007, these changes can be made in a number of ways. The Message tab on the Ribbon includes a group labeled Basic Text, shown in Figure 6.9, which allows you to apply many common format changes to your message text.

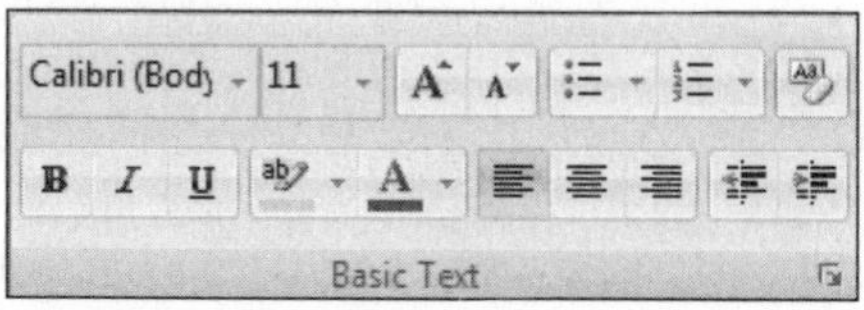

For more advanced formatting options, the Format Text tab,

Figure 6. 9. The Basic Text group on the Message tab of an e-mail message window provides access to the most commonly used formatting tools.

shown in Figure 6.10, provides a complete set of formatting tools that include everything in the Basic Text group and a broad range of additional options, including access to Styles and Proofing Tools. And, as mentioned earlier in this chapter, the Message Options tab includes the Themes group which can instantly change the look of an entire message.

Figure 6.10. The Format Text tab.

My favorite technique for quickly adjusting the format of message text is to use Outlook's new MiniBar. One of the complaints levied against the new Ribbon interface is the amount of mouse travel required to return to the top of the message window to access commands and the added step required to switch tabs on the Ribbon to access a desired control. Much of this mousing around can be easily avoided by using the keyboard shortcuts and accelerators built into Outlook and by adding frequently used commands to the Quick Access Toolbar that maintains a constant display regardless of which tab on the Ribbon is currently active. Customizing the QAT is discussed in Chapter 5.

But the MiniBar, pictured in Figure 6.11, is an ideal solution because it places the most commonly used formatting commands exactly where you would most like to find them — under the cursor. To access the MiniBar, select some text and leave the cursor on top of the selection. The MiniBar appears in ghostly fashion and becomes active as you move the cursor directly onto it. To hide the MiniBar, simply move the cursor away, and it fades out of view.

Figure 6.11. The MiniBar puts the most frequently used formatting commands directly at your cursor when you select a range of text.

Bright Idea

One of the tools on the MiniBar is the Format Painter — a tool overlooked by many Office users. To use the Format Painter, select text with the formatting you want to copy. Click the Format Painter tool icon and apply it to another selection of text by clicking and dragging the cursor over the text you want to "paint."

Checking your spelling and grammar

Outlook allows you to choose how you prefer to proof your writing. You can set a preference to have spelling checked as you type, only when you send a message, or not at all. This preference is set in the Editor Options dialog box. The simplest way to open this dialog box is to choose Tools ⇨ Options. And then in the Options dialog box, click the Mail Format tab.

To manually proof your text while composing a message, select Spelling and Grammar from the Proofing button on the Write tab. Grammar checking can be invoked by clicking the Check Grammar box in the Spelling and Grammar dialog box. If you like the assistance this tool provides, you can elect to have Outlook check your grammar as you type by selecting that option in the Editor Options dialog box. You can also force an immediate grammar check of the document at any time from this location by clicking the button labeled Recheck Document. Like Word, Outlook displays any grammatical errors with a squiggly underline — green in this case.

Attaching a file to your message

It is often helpful when sending an e-mail message, meeting invitation, or task assignment, to attach a file or Outlook information object. Files and Outlook items can be attached to a message by clicking on either the

Attach File or Attach Item button on the Message tab, shown in Figure 6.12. If you want to attach a file located on your PC or a network share, a standard file dialog box opens that allows you to navigate to the folder where the file is located. Clicking the Attach Item control opens a dialog box that allows you to select the Outlook item you want to attach.

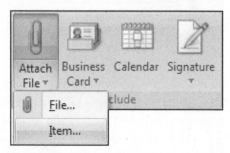

Figure 6.12. Use the Attach File or Attach Item control to send a file or Outlook item in your message.

If you want to attach an Outlook information object to your e-mail, follow these steps:

1. Click Attach Item. The Insert Item dialog box, shown in Figure 6.13, appears.

2. Select the Outlook folder that contains the information object you want to attach. A list of items appears in the field at the bottom of the dialog box.

3. Choose to insert the item as Text only or Attachment by clicking a radio button. The Text only option inserts the item's text into the body of the e-mail message at the current insertion point. This is the best option if you are sending the information to non-Outlook users. The Attachment option creates a file attachment which can be opened by the recipient and added to his or her Outlook environment.

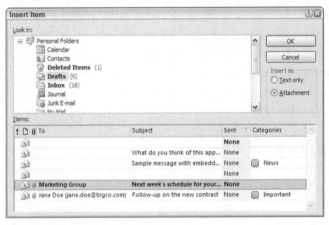

Figure 6.13. The Insert Item dialog box allows you to add an Outlook object as either an attachment (default) or text in the body of the message.

If you are attaching large documents or a number of different documents to an e-mail message, you may want to consider using a compression utility to reduce the file size. This has the benefit of making the file faster to send and receive, and it takes up less space on both PCs — yours and your recipient's. WinZip is the standard tool for compressing (or archiving as it is often called) ZIP files, but a wealth of choices are available ranging in price from free to around $40. What many people don't know is that Windows XP can create and open ZIP files without the need for any third-party software. Like a lot of what Microsoft builds into Windows, the functionality is very basic but if your needs are simple, you may not need any additional software.

Hack

To create a ZIP file in Windows XP, select the file(s) or folders you want to add, right-click one of them and select the Send To menu option. From the submenu, choose Compressed (zipped) folder. The ZIP file takes the name of the first file name (alphabetically) and adds the .zip extension.

Sending your message

After you have finished composing your e-mail message, you can either send it or save it as a draft. As I discussed earlier in the chapter, you can set options for when the message is sent on the Message Options tab. When you are ready to send your message, you have four options:

- Click the Send button on the Message tab.
- Select Send from the Office Button menu.
- With the Message tab visible, press Alt+S to select the Send group, then press S a second time to select the Send button.
- Press Alt+F to select the Office Button menu and then press E to select the Send command.

Saving a draft

If you want to save a draft copy of your message so that you can continue working on it or send it at a later time, you have the following options:

- Select Save from the Office Button menu.
- Press Alt+F to select the Office Button menu, then press S to select the Save command.
- Press Ctrl+S.

Your draft message is saved in the Drafts folder where you can access it when you are ready to continue editing or send the message. You can also use the Save As command on the Office Button menu to save the e-mail message to your PC file system, external from Outlook's PST file, in HTML, Outlook message (.msg), or plain text (.txt) formats.

Using e-mail signatures

E-mail signatures are predefined blocks of text you can automatically or manually append to your e-mail messages. Typically, an e-mail signature contains your contact information, but it can be defined to also include any text you routinely want to appear at the bottom of your e-mail messages, such as a privacy or confidentiality statement. Signatures are created and managed in the Signatures and Stationery dialog box. To access this dialog box, follow these steps:

1. Choose Tools ⇨ Options in any of Outlook's main views.

2. Select the Mail Format tab.

3. Click the Signatures button. The Signatures and Stationery dialog box, pictured in Figure 6.14, opens.

The Signatures and Stationery dialog box is a significant improvement over the Signatures dialog box in Office 2003 and older versions that was presented if you used the built-in Outlook editor. This new dialog box provides a rich text editor that allows you to apply fonts, size and color attributes, hyperlinks, and images to your signatures. These formatting options apply only to signatures in messages sent in Rich Text or HTML formats. Plain text messages strip the formatting options from your signature.

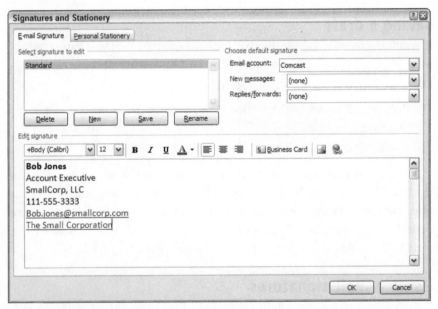

Figure 6.14. The Signatures and Stationery dialog box allows you to create and manage your e-mail signatures.

You can assign a default signature to each of your e-mail accounts and control whether a signature is automatically added to new e-mail messages, replies, and forwarded messages in this dialog box as well by using the controls in the upper-right corner of the dialog box.

Using Business Cards

Business Cards use a standard file format (.vcf) and can be attached to e-mail messages using the Business Card control on the Message tab. Business Card files can contain all of the information you can add to a Contact record and, when sent to another Outlook user, can be double-clicked to instantly add that contact to the recipient's Contact List. Other applications use Business Card files in a variety of ways, but virtually all popular e-mail and Personal Information Manager applications use the .vcf file format to import and export contact information. In the Signatures and Stationery dialog box, you can include your Business Card in your e-mail signature if you choose. Business Card files can also be saved as separate files on your PC and attached to e-mail messages as a file that can be especially useful if you are sending someone information about one of your contacts.

Reading and replying to e-mail

With the introduction of the Reading Pane in Outlook 2003, the need to open e-mail messages in a separate window was dramatically reduced. With the addition of the collapsible Navigation Pane in Outlook 2007, this need is even further reduced. Of course, the resolution and size of your display impacts this preference but given the increasing use of displays that are at least fifteen inches with resolutions of 1024 × 768 pixels or better, it is entirely possible to read all of your e-mail without ever needing to open a separate window.

Using the Reading Pane

Reading e-mail in the Reading Pane can be made a lot more convenient by turning on the Single Key Reading option. This feature allows you to scroll through an e-mail message using the space bar on your keyboard, not unlike using the Page Down key with one important difference. When you reach the end of the current message, the next message is displayed when you press the space bar again. This feature can be accessed by following these steps:

1. Choose Tools ⇨ Options in any of Outlook's main views.

2. On the Other tab in the Options dialog box, click the Reading Pane button in the Outlook Panes section of the tab. The Reading Pane dialog box, shown in Figure 6.15, appears.

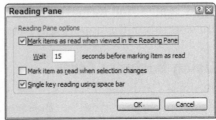

Figure 6.15. The Reading Pane dialog box provides options for reading and marking the read state of e-mail messages.

You can also set a preference for the waiting period after a message is selected in the Message List before marking the item as having been read and whether an item is marked as read when you select another item in the list. The combination of these Reading Pane features can be combined to provide a very efficient method of working your way through an Inbox full of e-mail messages or a folder containing content delivered via RSS from a blog or Web site.

Of course you can always open an e-mail message in its own window. While the Single Key Reading trick does not work in an e-mail message window, you can scroll through a message using the message window's scroll bar or the arrow and Page Up and Page Down keys on your keyboard. To move to the next or previous message in the Message List when reading in window mode, you can use the up and down arrows on the Quick Access Toolbar.

Replying to e-mail messages

Replying to e-mail messages can be done either from the Reading Pane or an open message window. There are, as you might have guessed, a few different ways to initiate a reply action.

Inside Scoop

If you use a Tablet PC, Outlook 2007 offers another way to scroll using the stylus. Click the Pan icon in the upper-right corner of a message window, and the cursor changes from a selection tool to a scroll tool. You can then scroll the message by dragging the stylus.

To create a reply when reading in the main Mail view in the Reading Pane, you can:

- Press Ctrl+R.

- Press Alt, then press R in the main Mail view, which selects the Reply button on the toolbar.

- Click the Reply button on the toolbar.

To create a reply when reading e-mail in a separate message window, you can:

- Press Ctrl+R.

- Click the Reply button in the Respond group on the Ribbon.

- Press Alt to switch into keyboard command mode, then press E to select the Respond group, and then press R to select the Reply button.

In either mode, you can also use keyboard shortcuts to Reply to All (Ctrl+Shift+R), Forward a message (Ctrl+F), or Forward a message as an attachment (Ctrl+Shift+F).

A note about e-mail etiquette

One of the truly curious things about e-mail is that everyone uses it, but very few people have ever actually been taught how to use it effectively or courteously.

The following ideas may or may not work in your organization or your personal life, but I offer them as food for thought about how you and the people you correspond with might be able to reduce some e-mail frustration.

The very first thing to consider is how and why you use the To and Cc fields. Consider a standard approach to these fields that makes it understood by all that if your name appears on the To line, the e-mail is directly addressed to you. If your name appears on the Cc line, you are being copied on the message because you have an interest in the topic but are not directly impacted by the message.

Subject lines can quickly become cluttered with a string of "Re" and "Fw" tags which Outlook (and most other e-mail applications) inserts automatically when you reply to or forward a message. Trim all but one of these tags so your subject lines have greater readability in the Message List.

(continued)

(continued)

Taking the subject line one step further, consider adopting a set of tags to prefix the subject line of messages sent internally. These tags immediately let the recipient(s) know whether an action is requested and they make it easy to sort the contents of the Inbox to group new e-mails so that they can be processed effectively and appropriately.

A suggested list of tags I've used includes:

- RR: Reply Requested (usually the same day)
- RRAL: Reply Requested at Leisure (in the next day or two)
- URG: Urgent (this should only be used in truly urgent circumstances)
- RAL: Read at Leisure (no reply expected)
- NRN: No Reply Necessary (content is timely and should be read soon after receipt)
- FYI: For Your Information (purely informational)

There are many more tips and techniques for making e-mail more effective, but this topic is outside the scope of this book. I have provided a list of recommended reading in Appendix B that addresses this topic.

Working offline

There are times when you may not have access to a network or Internet connection. Even in today's world of broadly available access, it happens. Outlook can be set to work in Offline mode when you know you will be disconnected. The primary advantage to doing this is that Outlook's Send/Receive groups can be set to act differently when the application is in Offline mode, which can prevent connection error messages from popping open and interfering with your work. Send/Receive groups are discussed later in this chapter.

To set Outlook to work in Offline mode, choose File ⇨ Work Offline in any of Outlook's main views. To return to Online mode, repeat this menu selection. Outlook displays an Offline indicator in the lower-right

corner of the application window
when you are offline, as shown in
Figure 6.16.

There are special considerations for Exchange and IMAP
accounts when you work offline.
If you work in an Exchange
Server environment that supports
Cached Exchange mode, there is
no need to select the Work

Figure 6.16. Outlook displays an Offline icon
in the lower-right corner of the main window
when you are working offline.

Offline command or to change how you work in any way. Any e-mail messages you compose are saved as drafts and sent automatically as soon as
you reconnect to the network or Internet. Any e-mail or other data you
have stored in your Exchange Server account is replicated on your PC
and remains available, even when you are offline. Exchange Server and
working in offline mode is discussed in detail in Chapter 20.

This news is not so good for IMAP e-mail users unless you have set
your IMAP account folders to fully synchronize with your e-mail server.
IMAP synchronization works better in some environments than others,
and performance issues with some IMAP servers taking an inordinate
amount of time to synchronize are frequent enough that many IMAP
users prefer not to subscribe to more than a few folders or to turn off synchronization entirely. If you are unfamiliar with subscribing to IMAP
folders and how it might impact performance, check with your network
administrator to see what he or she recommends.

A good work-around for offline situations if you work in an IMAP
environment is to drag any e-mail messages you want to read and reply to
into the Inbox in your Personal Folders list. This Inbox, in contrast to the
Inbox in your IMAP account folder list, is stored on your PC and the messages in it can be read in their entirety, replied to, or forwarded while you
are working offline. These replies or forwarded messages will be saved as
drafts and can be sent when you are next connected.

Hack

IMAP folder synchronization is managed by right-clicking the top-level folder in
an IMAP account in the folder list and selecting the IMAP Folders command.
Select the folder you want to subscribe to and click the Subscribe button. Use
the Subscribed tab to see which folders you are currently subscribed to.

Managing multiple e-mail accounts

If you are using more than one e-mail account in Outlook, you have the option to send a new e-mail message or reply to a message you have received using any of your accounts. You can also use Outlook's Send/Receive Groups settings to control when and how frequently each account connects to the network or Internet to send and receive e-mail messages. In a multiple account configuration, Outlook makes a few assumptions:

- When you reply to a message or forward it, Outlook assumes you want to use the e-mail account the message was received in.

- When you create a new e-mail message, Outlook assumes you want to use your default e-mail account to send it.

You can override either of these assumptions for each message you send by selecting the account you want to use from the Accounts button on the Message tab in the e-mail message window. All of your accounts are listed on the drop-down menu this button presents when you click it. If you want to change which of your e-mail accounts is the default account, you can make that change by choosing Tools ⇨ Account Settings. Select the account you want to make the default and click the Set as Default button on the control bar above the account list, as shown in Figure 6.17.

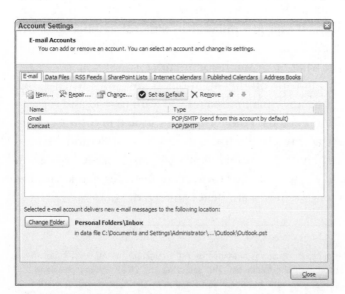

Figure 6.17. Select the account you want Outlook to use as your default and click the Set as Default button.

If you use a dial-up connection, it can be quite irritating to have your phone line tied up while checking all of your accounts. You may want to have some accounts checked frequently and others infrequently. Outlook's Send/Receive settings and groups provide you with as much control as you need over these connections. Send/Receive settings can also be used to control how much of a message is initially retrieved which can save you from wasting a lot of time waiting for an unwanted file attachment to download. If you are always connected using a broadband connection, a single Send/Receive group is probably all you need.

Using Outlook for RSS

RSS or Really Simple Syndication is a way for blogs and Web sites to provide a subscription link that you can use to get new content delivered to you, rather than surfing to the site and searching for the latest news or articles. Prior to the release of Outlook 2007, if you wanted to manage subscriptions and have content delivered to your Outlook environment, you needed to use a third-party add-in like NewsGator or Attensa. These and other add-ins are reviewed in Chapter 17.

With the releases of Outlook 2007, Internet Explorer 7, and the Windows Vista operating system, Microsoft has embraced RSS as a key technology for bringing content to your PC. Outlook is an ideal environment for aggregating, reading, and storing content delivered via RSS.

Adding RSS subscriptions

There are three ways to add RSS subscriptions to Outlook. If you are using Internet Explorer, the simplest method is to click the RSS icon on the browser's toolbar to add the site you are viewing to the system feeds list, which is a shared resource that can be used by both Outlook 2007 and Internet Explorer 7. This opens the dialog box shown in Figure 6.18.

If you use an alternate browser, you can add one feed at a time as you encounter a blog or Web site with content you want to subscribe to as described below. If you have

Figure 6.18. This Internet Explorer 7 dialog box adds an RSS subscription to the System Feeds list used by that browser and Outlook 2007.

been using another application or web service to read RSS, you can use a subscription list to import multiple RSS feeds into Outlook in a single operation. These subscription lists are called OPML (Outline Processor Markup Language) files.

One at a time

Adding a single RSS subscription is accomplished in three steps:

1. Copy the link to the RSS feed from the blog or Web site you want to subscribe to. These links are often displayed as an orange rectangular icon with the letters RSS or XML or as a text link labeled Syndicate this site. A standard icon to mark RSS feeds, pictured in Figure 6.19, has been adopted by Microsoft for use in Outlook 2007, Internet Explorer 7, and Windows Vista and is also used by Mozilla Firefox, a popular open source browser. As this standard icon is adopted by blogs and Web sites, it will be increasingly easy to find the link you need to subscribe.

Figure 6.19. This icon is being adopted as the standard indication that an RSS link is available on a blog or Web site.

2. Choose Tools ⇨ Account Settings and click on the RSS Feeds tab in the Account Settings dialog box that appears.

3. Click the New button on the control bar above the list box and paste the link you copied in step 1 into the New RSS Feed dialog box that opens. The RSS Feeds tab and New RSS Feed dialog box are shown in Figure 6.20.

Once you have created the RSS subscription, you can change the folder location where the RSS feed delivers new content by clicking the Change Folder button below the list. By default, Outlook creates a new folder for each RSS feed in Personal Folders\RSS Subscriptions\feed name.

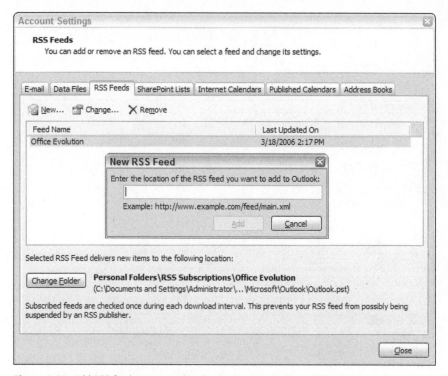

Figure 6.20. Add RSS feeds one at a time in the Account Settings dialog box.

Multiple feeds at the same time

To import an OPML file or the system feeds list:

1. Choose File ⇨ Import/Export. The Import and Export Wizard dialog box appears, as shown in Figure 6.21.

2. From the list of file types displayed in the Import and Export Wizard dialog box, select the appropriate file type and click Next.

3. Browse to find the OPML file on your PC or network share and click Next. The Import an OPML file dialog box appears.

4. Select the feed or feeds you want to subscribe to by clicking the check box next to each feed in the list, as pictured in Figure 6.22, and click Next.

5. The feeds are checked and an initial download of content takes place as soon as you tell the Import and Export Wizard to finish in the final screen of the wizard.

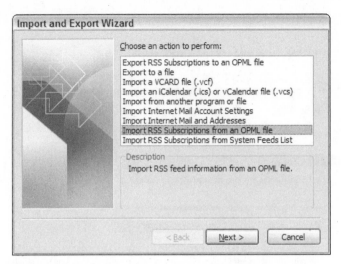

Figure 6.21. The Import and Export Wizard dialog box allows you to choose either an OPML file or systems feed list.

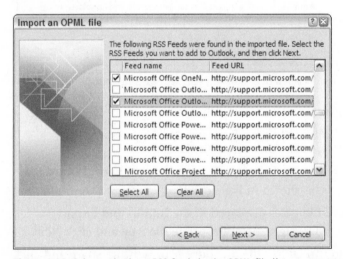

Figure 6.22. Select only those RSS feeds in the OPML file list you want to subscribe to.

Reading RSS subscriptions

Reading RSS in Outlook is identical to reading e-mail. If you click an RSS Feed folder in the Folder List, the Message List Pane shows all of the RSS articles in the folder. Just as is the case with e-mail, unread items have a bold subject line. Click the article or post you want to read, and it

Inside Scoop

RSS feeds come in two varieties. Some blogs and Web sites deliver a full feed containing the entire article. Others use a partial feed that shows the first few lines of text. All feeds display a link that opens the source blog or Web page in your browser.

is displayed in the Reading Pane. If you have enabled Single Key Reading, you can use the space bar to scroll through each post and jump to the next post in the list when you reach the bottom of the currently displayed post.

Unsubscribing from RSS subscriptions

Unsubscribing from RSS feeds in Outlook is at once simple and maddening. Simple because all you need to do to remove a subscription is

1. Choose Tools ⇨ Account Settings. The Account Settings dialog box appears.

2. Click on the RSS Feeds tab.

3. Highlight the RSS subscription(s) you want to delete.

4. Click the Delete button on the control bar above the subscription list.

You can also unsubscribe from a feed by selecting its folder in the Folder List in the Navigation Pane and pressing the Delete key or right-clicking the folder and choosing Delete from the context menu.

Using a Search Folder to create a river of news

Search Folders were first introduced in Outlook 2003 and remain essentially unchanged in the 2007 version. Many RSS aggregators provide a view that is often called a river of news that displays the most recent content from all RSS subscriptions in a list. If you are interested in scanning all of your new RSS feeds in a single view, an Outlook Search Folder can be configured to provide this capability very easily. To define this Search Folder, follow these steps:

1. Right-click the Search Folders icon in the Folder List and select the New Search Folder option on the context menu. The New Search Folder dialog box appears.

2. In the New Search Folder dialog box, scroll to the bottom of the list of predefined Search Folders and choose the very last item: Create a Custom Search Folder.

3. Click the Choose button located in the lower portion of the dialog box. This allows you to select the criteria for the new Search Folder by opening the Custom Search Folder dialog box.

4. Enter a name for the new Search Folder — something like "Unread News."

5. Click the Criteria button to establish your search parameters. The Search Folder Criteria dialog box opens.

6. In the Search Folder Criteria dialog box, pictured in Figure 6.23, click on the More Choices tab and select the first check box for Only items that are: and use the default criterion, which is unread.

7. Click OK to return to the Custom Search Folder dialog box.

Figure 6.23. Use the Search Folder Criteria dialog box settings to create a folder that lists all unread RSS feeds.

8. Click the Browse button to select the folders to include in the search. The Select Folder(s) dialog box appears.

9. Uncheck the Personal Folders check box and select RSS Subscriptions folder as pictured in Figure 6.24. Make sure the Search subfolders check box in the lower-left corner is checked, and then click OK.

10. Click OK twice to close all dialog boxes and return to the main Mail view. A new Search Folder appears with the name you provided in Step 3.

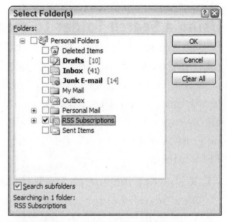

Figure 6.24. In the Select Folder(s) dialog box, deselect Personal Folders and select RSS Subscriptions to define what folders will be searched for the new river of news folder.

Clicking this Search Folder displays all new RSS feed content in the Message List. The default view for the Message List organizes the content by folder, but you can customize this view to present the new content by date and time received or other criteria if you prefer. Now, when you are ready to scroll though all newly received RSS content, you have a single folder that presents the information in river of news style. Search Folders are discussed in greater detail in Chapter 13, and customizing views in Outlook is covered in Chapter 14.

Just the facts

- Many people make the mistake of using their Inboxes as a place for important information and end up overwhelmed by the amount of information they have to search to find what they are looking for. Learn to work with e-mail in a similar fashion to how you handle postal mail.

- Composing e-mail in Outlook 2007 is a brand-new experience, offering a range of formatting options and graphics tools unlike anything previously available.

- Outlook supports HTML, Rich Text Format, and plain text formats for e-mail messages.

- Signatures and Business Cards make it easy to add personal contact information to your e-mail messages.

- Changing the way you use the address fields and subject line in your e-mail messages can help clarify who needs to do what action when your message is received.

- Outlook is an excellent manager of multiple e-mail accounts and provides a range of options for deciding when e-mail is sent and received and where it is stored.

- Working offline presents some interesting challenges for both Internet Mail and Exchange Server users. Configuring Outlook for offline work allows you to continue to be productive even when a network or Internet connection is unavailable.

- Outlook 2007 can now aggregate and manage information delivered via RSS subscriptions to Web sites and blogs without the need for third-party add-ins.

Chapter 7

GET THE SCOOP ON...
What's new in the main Contacts view ▪ The new Contact
dialog box ▪ Two ways to create new contacts ▪ Making
things happen from the Contacts view ▪ Using Contacts
and Outlook's Journal to maintain an activity history

Outlook Is a Contact Manager

Your Contacts list plays a powerful role in making Outlook your personal information manager. In addition to the generally understood use of the Contacts list as an address book for storing information about a person such as e-mail addresses, phone numbers, title, and company, the Contacts list also provides a kind of glue that can bind together all of the other information objects you create and manage in Outlook.

The first part of this chapter shows you how to navigate through the main Contacts view, create and manage contacts, and generate a variety of activities and communications from the Contacts list. The second part of this chapter shows you how to maximize the potential of linking your contacts to appointments and tasks and briefly explains the relationship between your contacts and Outlook's Journal, which is covered in detail in Chapter 11.

Getting familiar with the Contacts view

The main Contacts view in Outlook 2007 hasn't changed all that much from Outlook 2003. Two new elements have been added in this version of Outlook: a new Business Cards view and the Search box. If you are familiar with Outlook 2003, you should feel right at home in the Contacts view in Outlook 2007.

The main Contacts view is divided into two panes — the Navigation Pane on the left side of the application window and the Contacts list in the large area on the right side. The Navigation Pane contains a set of radio buttons that allow you to select different layouts for the Contacts list and a set of related links that appear differently depending on whether you are using Outlook in Internet Mail mode or are connected to an Exchange Server or SharePoint site. Outlook's Business Contact Manager, designed for small business use as a lightweight Customer Relationship Management (CRM) solution, also changes the Contacts view by adding additional fields of information, predefined views, and new menu options. Business Contact Manager is described in detail in Chapter 20.

You can select from the following predefined layouts to work with your Contacts list:

- **Business Cards View (new).** Each contact is viewed as if looking at that person's business card, complete with photograph.

- **Address Cards View.** Each contact's mailing address, phone numbers, and e-mail address is displayed in a more compact view.

- **Detailed Address Cards View.** Similar to the Address Cards view with more fields of information displayed for each contact.

- **Phone List View.** A compact, spreadsheet-style view listed in alphabetical order.

- **By Category.** Similar to Phone List View but grouped by category, which can be collapsed or expanded.

- **By Company.** Same as By Category but grouped by company.

- **By Location.** Same as By Category but grouped by location information like zip code or country.

- **By Follow Up Flag.** Contacts are grouped by the Follow Up Flag currently attached to each contact record. Although this view was introduced in Outlook 2003, it is far more useful in Outlook 2007 due to the improvements in the flags feature.

- **Outlook Data Files.** Displays contact records from all open Outlook data files that contain a Contacts folder. Most useful when connected to an Exchange Server with shared Contacts lists.

The new Business Cards view allows you to see each contact in your list in an electronic version of a business card binder. A series of alphabetical tabs runs down the right side of the display and, like an analog Rolodex, allows you to quickly skip to a particular part of the list. In this view, you can see a photo of your contacts if you have added them to your contact records as shown in Figure 7.1.

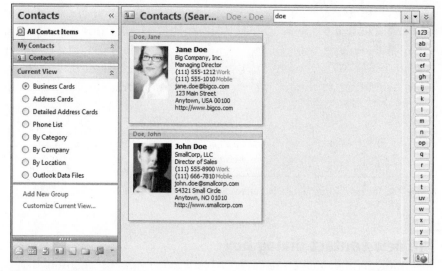

Figure 7.1. The Business Cards layout in the main Contacts view can show a contact's photo along with standard contact information.

A view that I have found to be particularly helpful is By Follow Up Flag. Flags have been dramatically improved in Outlook 2007 and now are tied to due dates for follow-up activities. When you view your Contacts list in Follow Up Flag layout, you see which contacts you have an appointment, task, or e-mail follow-up with and can sort that view by name, company, due date, or other criteria. It's a powerful, people-oriented way to leverage the capabilities of the flag feature.

The new Search box

Chapter 5 describes the new search capabilities in Outlook 2007. In the Contacts view, Search works in very much the same way it does in every other view in Outlook. The essential difference is that when you attach additional criteria to your search query, you are presented with a list of all available fields used in Contact records. Figure 7.2 shows a two-criteria search query using a contact's last name and company. Note that search results are displayed in the same view currently being used to view your contacts.

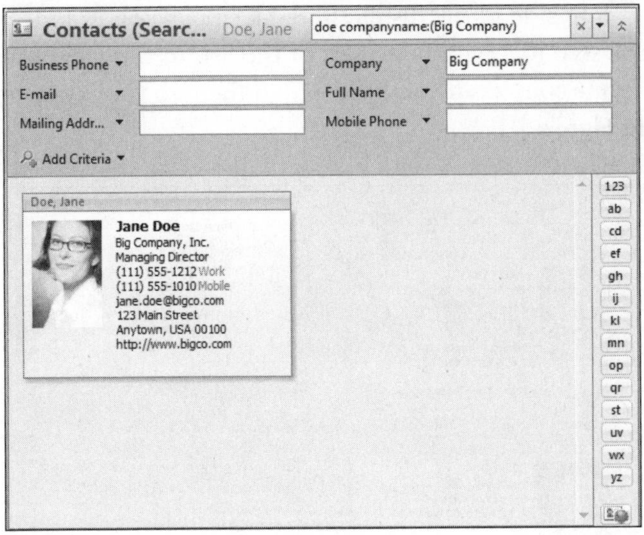

| Contacts (Searc...   Doe, Jane | doe companyname:(Big Company) | × ▼ ⌃ |

Business Phone ▼		Company ▼	Big Company
E-mail ▼		Full Name ▼	
Mailing Addr... ▼		Mobile Phone ▼	

🔍 Add Criteria ▼

Doe, Jane

Jane Doe
Big Company, Inc.
Managing Director
(111) 555-1212 Work
(111) 555-1010 Mobile
jane.doe@bigco.com
123 Main Street
Anytown, USA 00100
http://www.bigco.com

123
ab
cd
ef
gh
ij
kl
mn
op
qr
st
uv
wx
yz

Figure 7.2. The new search feature in Outlook applied in the Contacts view.

The new Contact dialog box

When you create a new contact record or want to view information about one of the contacts already in your list, you are presented with the new user interface version of Outlook's Contact dialog box. Like the Mail Message dialog box discussed in Chapter 6, the Contact dialog box pictured in Figure 7.3 has undergone an Office 2007 transformation and now uses a ribbon with tabs to provide access to all of the tools and controls used to create and interact with contacts.

If you are familiar with previous versions of Outlook, you may notice other new features in the Contact dialog box including the new Business Cards view in the lower-right corner of the dialog box that is identical to the layout presented for each contact in the Business Cards layout in the main Contacts view. Categories that are attached to the contact you are viewing or creating are displayed at the top of the Contact dialog box.

Inside Scoop

You can quickly add an additional category to a contact with at least one category already assigned by double-clicking the existing category marker. This will open the Color Categories dialog box that allows you to assign, edit, and create new categories.

In other respects, the Contact dialog box is essentially the same as the one used in Outlook 2003.

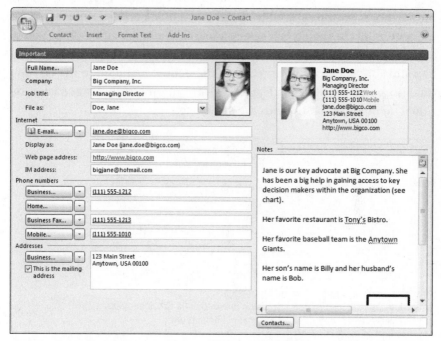

Figure 7.3. The new Contact dialog box now displays a Business Card and color categories.

The File menu

The new Office button displays the Office 2007 version of the File menu, as described in Chapter 5. In that description, I mentioned that the new File menu changes slightly depending on which composition dialog box you happen to be working in. As Figure 7.3 shows, the File menu displays the New command appropriate to the view you are currently working — in this case it displays New Contact. The Save As command provides an option to save a contact to disk as a VCF (Virtual Card Format) file which can be imported into a variety of other contact management applications.

Also on the right pane of the File menu is the Distribution List command. Creating a Distribution List is a handy way to send an e-mail message to or schedule an appointment with a group of contacts without having to individually select each contact every time. Distribution Lists might include all of the members of a project team, a department, or your family. When you select the Distribution List command, you are presented with the Distribution List dialog box shown in Figure 7.4. Clicking the Members button or double-clicking in a blank area of the list pane at the bottom of the dialog box opens a search dialog box that allows you to add contacts to the list. You can also create a new contact from this dialog box and add a descriptive note about the people included in the list. You can also assign a Follow Up Flag to a Distribution List that tags each individual member of the list with the same flag.

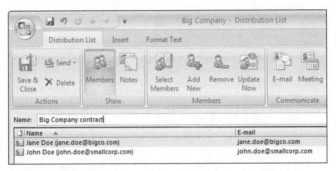

Figure 7.4. Use the Distribution List dialog box to build a list of contacts you frequently send e-mail to or schedule appointments with.

Using a Distribution List

Adding a Distribution List to an e-mail message or appointment request is essentially the same as adding a contact name. You can type part of the Distribution List name into the appropriate field in the New Mail Message dialog box (To, or CC) and press Ctrl+K to look up a matching record or click the button next to any of those fields to choose it from the Select Names dialog box. Outlook indicates a Distribution List by showing its name in bold and attaching a small plus sign icon to the list name as shown in Figure 7.5.

Hack

If you don't want everyone on your Distribution List to see the other members' names and addresses, you can send the message to yourself and put the Distribution List in the BCC field. Every member of the list only sees your name and their name in the message they receive.

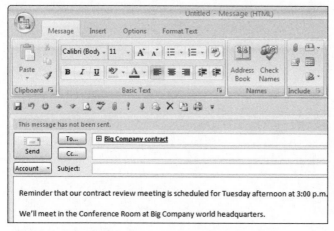

Figure 7.5. A Distribution List is shown in bold with a plus sign icon in the recipient fields of a new e-mail message.

Sending to part of a Distribution List

There may be times when you want to send a message to some of the members of a Distribution List but not to all of them. To edit the recipients for a specific message, click the plus sign icon next to the Distribution List name to expand the list. When you do this, Outlook displays the warning dialog box pictured in Figure 7.6.

This warning only applies to the list as it is being used in the message or invitation you are

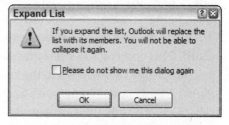

Figure 7.6. When you expand a Distribution List, Outlook displays this warning dialog box.

creating. After expanding the list to show the individual names and addresses, you can delete those you do not want to send the message to. You are not changing the list itself when you do this. To edit a Distribution List to permanently remove (or add) members, open it from the Contacts list.

The Contact tab

The Contact tab in the Contact dialog box, pictured in Figure 7.7, contains five groups of controls:

- Actions
- Show
- Communicate
- Options
- Proofing

Figure 7.7. The Contact tab in the Contact dialog box displays the principal controls used with people in your list.

Actions group

The Actions group includes standard Save & Close and Delete commands, present in the Actions group of all Outlook composition dialog boxes, along with Save & New and Send. Save & New, as the name implies, allows you to save the current contact record and open a new, blank record. This control also presents a second option when you click on the small drop-down arrow icon to the right of the icon as shown in Figure 7.8 labeled New Contact from Same Company. This command creates a new contact record with the Company name, address, and Web site information copied from the current contact but with the Name, E-mail, and Phone fields blank. The Send command allows you to attach the current contact record to a new e-mail message in one of three formats:

- **Send as Business Card.** Inserts an image of the card in the message body of the e-mail message and attaches a VCF file containing the contact's information.

- **Internet Format (vCard).** Attaches a VCF file to the new e-mail message.

- **Outlook Format.** Attaches a native Outlook contact file that can be double-clicked by a recipient to add that contact directly into the Outlook Contacts list.

Figure 7.8. The drop-down menu of the Save & New control displays a command to create a new contact from the same company as the currently displayed contact.

Show group

The Show group includes commands labeled General, Details, Activities, Certificates, and All Fields. General and Details are a pair and toggle between two views of the Contact form. The General view is the one that a contact record opens by default when you are creating a new record or viewing a contact in your list. The Details view, shown in Figure 7.9, contains fields for additional information about the contact. Activities is a specialized search view that scans your entire PST file and displays all tasks, events, e-mail messages, and Journal entries related to that person.

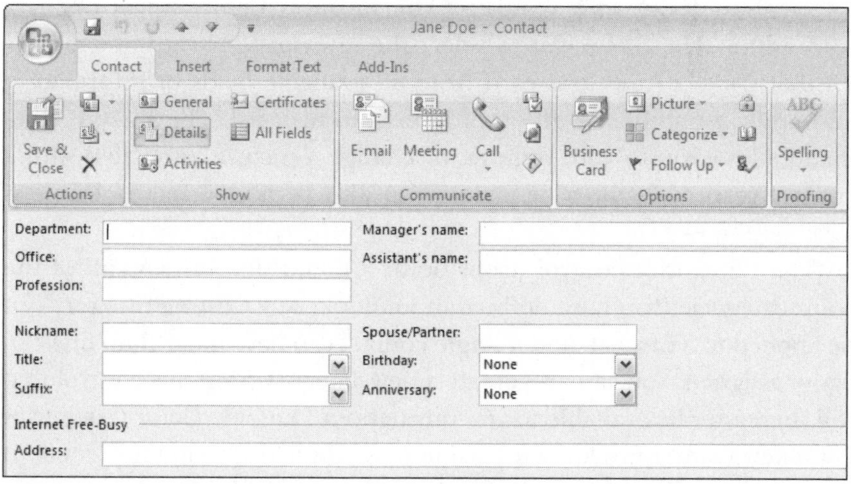

Figure 7.9. The Details view in a Contact record provides a number of additional fields to store information about that person.

Inside Scoop

If you prefer working in a spreadsheet-like format, you can select All Contact Fields from the drop-down menu in the All Fields view and use the form displayed to rapidly enter information about a new contact.

Certificates are used to import, manage, and apply digital certificates shared between you and that contact. These certificates are used to encrypt messages and, unless you work in a corporate or research environment, it is unlikely you will use them. The All Fields control displays a drop-down menu that provides access to every field of information available in Outlook organized into groups such as e-mail fields or phone fields.

Communicate group

The Communicate group includes controls to initiate new actions for the contact you are viewing. You can generate a new e-mail, schedule a meeting, begin a phone call, assign a task, view the contact's Web page, or generate a map showing his location.

Options group

The Options group collects a variety of controls together for adding information about your contacts. The Business Card control opens a card editor that allows you to select the information you want to view on that contact's business card from all available fields of information and apply a number of different layouts to his card. The Picture command allows you to add, remove, or change a picture associated with a contact record. Pictures or images can also be added in the Business Card editor.

The Categorize control drops down a menu that displays all of the color categories you have defined in Outlook. Any existing category can be applied to a contact, and a single contact can have more than one category assigned. You can also create a new category from this control that will thereafter be available to you throughout Outlook. Color Categories are a new feature in Outlook 2007 and are discussed in greater detail in Chapters 8 and 9 which deal with Outlook Calendar and Tasks.

The Follow Up control shows a drop-down menu displaying flags you can assign to a contact as shown in Figure 7.10. These flags, associated with relative dates like Today, Tomorrow, or This Week, create a new Task associated with the contact you assign the flag to. If you need to set a reminder to return a phone call, confirm a meeting date and time, or any other action associated with a specific contact, the new Follow Up Flags provide a fast and efficient means of capturing that action.

In addition to relative dates like Today and Tomorrow, you can assign a flag with a specific date or no date at all. You can also set a reminder alarm on a Follow Up Flag.

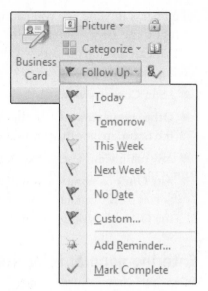

Figure 7.10. Follow Up Flags generate a task when applied to a contact.

Proofing group

The Proofing group provides access to the following tools:

- Spelling & Grammar
- Research
- Thesaurus
- Translate
- Translation Screen Tip
- Set Language (for translation)
- Word Count

Creating a new contact

There are two ways to create a new contact in Outlook. If you receive a message from someone not in your Contacts list, you can right-click on his or her e-mail address and select the Add to Outlook Contacts command. This opens a new Contact dialog box with the sender's name and e-mail address already entered. If you are unsure whether the sender of an e-mail is in your list, you can use the Look up Outlook Contact command on the same context menu to see if he is already in your list.

You can also create a new Contact from scratch using any of the following techniques:

- **Main Contacts view.** Click the New button on the Standard toolbar.

- **Other main views.** Click the down arrow next to the New button on the Standard toolbar and select Contact from the drop-down menu.

- **Any main view.** Use the keyboard command Ctrl+Shift+C.

- **Any Outlook composition dialog box using the new user interface.** Select New Contact from the File menu displayed when you click the Office button in the upper-left corner of the window.

Entering general information

When the New Contact dialog box is displayed, you are ready to begin entering information in the General view, which is pictured in Figure 7.3 earlier in this chapter. If you are familiar with previous versions of Outlook, especially Outlook 2003, this should be familiar territory.

If you are new to Outlook, note that the field descriptions in the Contact dialog box are actually buttons, and each is accompanied by a second button with a triangle icon pointing downward. Clicking the field description button opens a dialog box where you can enter information. The triangle icon button reveals a number of labels that can be applied to the information in each field.

In the phone fields, you can select one of nineteen descriptions for each of the numbers you enter. In the address field, you can select between a contact's business address and home address using the triangle icon and can establish which address is used for addressing correspondence and in mail merges for each contact by selecting the check box labeled This is the mailing address. You can associate up to three e-mail addresses with each contact using the triangle icon next to that field.

Entering detail information

The Details control switches the view to a second screen where you can enter additional professional and personal information about a contact including his or her manager's and assistants' names, birthday, spouse's name, and other data. The Detail view is shown in Figure 7.9 earlier in this chapter.

Bright Idea

Contact pictures do not need to be very large or high resolution. Most cell phone cameras are perfect for capturing an image of your contacts. Next time you collect a new business card, ask the person if he minds if you take a quick picture of him as well. Be aware that personal privacy concerns should always be respected and that some companies prohibit the use of cell phone cameras on their premises.

Adding a picture

If you have access to a picture of a contact, you can add it to his contact record by clicking on the Add Picture button pictured in Figure 7.11. A standard file dialog box will open that you can use to navigate to the folder or network share where the contact's picture resides. Once a picture has been added to a contact record, it is displayed in the Contact dialog box and in Business Cards view. A contact picture can be changed or removed by right-clicking on the image.

Figure 7.11. Click the Contact Picture button to add an image to a person's contact record.

Generating a map

Outlook 2003 required a separate program, Microsoft MapPoint, be installed on your PC to generate a map showing a contact's location. In Outlook 2007, mapping has moved to the Web and no additional software is required. If your contact record includes an address, you can generate a map of the location by clicking on the Map control. These maps are generated using the Windows Live Local service, pictured in Figure 7.12, on the Web, so you need to be connected to the Internet to access this feature. Windows Live Local not only displays a map of the contact's location, it can also generate driving directions from your location to the contact.

Windows Live Local is powered by a Microsoft service called Virtual Earth. For many locations, high resolution satellite imagery is available in addition to a standard map. Windows Live Local provides an alert when these images are available and allows you to view an aerial or bird's-eye view of the contact's location. Figure 7.13 shows a bird's-eye view of One Microsoft Way on the company's main campus in Redmond, Washington.

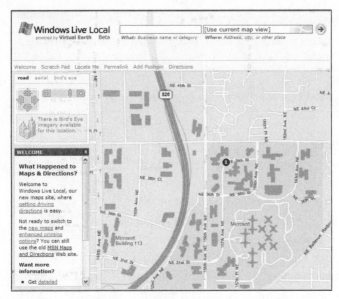

Figure 7.12. Clicking the Map control generates a map in Windows Live Local to the contact's location.

Figure 7.13. For many locations, Windows Live Local provides high resolution satellite images in addition to maps.

Adding notes and graphics

Outlook has provided a free text area for recording notes about a contact in its previous versions. This Notes field is even more useful in Outlook 2007 with the addition of the new SmartArt graphics and Word editing tools. Figure 7.14 shows text and an organizational chart, one of the many SmartArt objects available in Office 2007, added to a contact record. You can also add hyperlinks to Web pages or documents, images, charts, and drawings constructed using the Shapes tools. Images, graphics, and text from other applications can also be dragged and dropped into the Notes field.

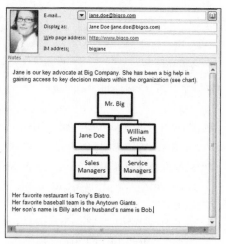

Figure 7.14. Text and graphics can be added to the Notes field in a Contact record.

I recommend the Notes field for information that is relatively time insensitive and that you use an appointment, task, or Journal entry linked to the contact to record time-sensitive information as all of those objects are time- and date-stamped. You can use the Activities control described earlier in this chapter to quickly collect all information related to a contact.

Assigning categories

Categories have undergone a major overhaul in Outlook 2007 as described in Chapter 1. In previous versions of Outlook, Categories, while useful, were essentially text markers used to filter items in list views. With the addition of color in Outlook 2007, they have become a much more visible way to tag related items with a visual, as well as text, marker. Categories can now be assigned to everything in Outlook as you will see in the next two chapters.

Working with Contacts list

The new Ribbon makes working from your Contacts list easier and more efficient than ever. All of the activities you can initiate from within

Outlook are available in the Communicate group on the Contact tab shown in Figure 7.15.

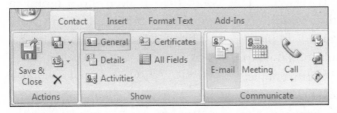

Figure 7.15. The Communicate group on the Contact tab in the Contact dialog box.

- **E-mail.** Click the E-mail control and a new message window is opened with the contact's name and address entered in the To field.
- **Meeting.** Click the Meeting control and a new appointment invitation window opens as pictured in Figure 7.16. You can select additional recipients of the meeting invitation, add text and graphics, and attach files. Appointments and invitations are covered in greater detail in Chapter 8.

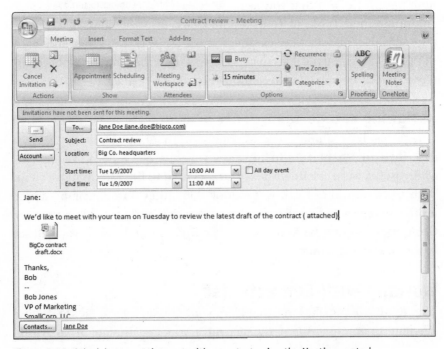

Figure 7.16. Schedule an appointment with a contact using the Meeting control.

■ **Call.** Click the down arrow at the bottom of the Call control to open a menu listing all of the contact's phone numbers. If you have a messaging application, such as Windows Live Messenger configured to initiate phone calls, the number you select is dialed.

■ **Assign Task.** Click the Assign Task control to create a new task item that can be assigned to the contact as shown in Figure 7.17. Tasks and assignments are covered in detail in Chapter 9.

■ **Web Page.** Click the Web Page control to open the Web page listed in the contact's record in your browser.

■ **Map.** Click the Map control to generate a map using Windows Live Local as described earlier in this chapter.

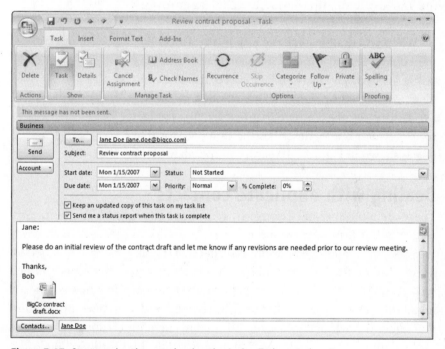

Figure 7.17. Create and assign a task using the Assign Task control.

Setting Follow Up Flags for contacts

Follow Up Flags are one of my favorite new features in Outlook 2007 for the simple reason that they provide a very visible and easy-to-use way to align upcoming actions and events with specific people in my Contacts list. While it has always been possible to create new tasks and reminders related to an action or event and link them to a person or group, Follow Up Flags are the most effective approach I've used.

Once applied, these flags can be viewed using the By Follow Up Flag layout in the main Contact view or in the Task list in the To-Do Bar, shown in Figure 7.18. Notice that the To-Do Bar has been designed to display a lot of information in a very small space. The contact name, action, reminder alarm (if set), color categories, and flag type are all included. If you hover the cursor over an item in the Task list, a tool tip window appears that provides the same information.

When you double-click the task in the To-Do Bar, the contact record window associated with that flag task is opened. The flag can be cleared, marked complete, or deleted by right-clicking the task in the To-Do Bar or in the orange banner in the contact record, which briefly describes the due date for that flag as shown in Figure 7.10 earlier in this chapter.

Figure 7.18. A Follow Up Flag task viewed in the To-Do Bar's Task list.

Dealing with duplicate contacts

There are a number of reasons why you might end up with duplicate contacts. One of the most common is that you add a contact from a newly received e-mail message and simply forget that you already have that person in your list. Outlook detects this when you attempt to save the new contact record and provides you with an opportunity to either add a new contact or update the existing contact record in your list with any new information that might be included in the record you are currently creating.

Like many of the dialog boxes and tools in Outlook 2007, the Duplicate Contact Detected dialog box has been significantly improved. Outlook displays the current record from your Contacts list, as shown in Figure 7.19, at the top of the dialog box and previews what the updated Business Card will look like in the lower left. In the lower right, Outlook highlights the specific fields that will be updated in the record.

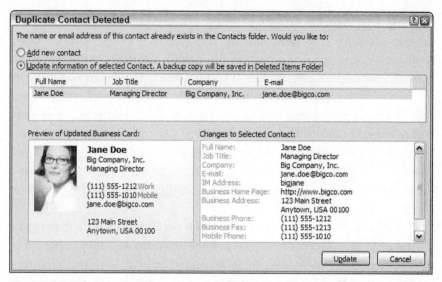

Figure 7.19. When you attempt to create a contact that already exists, the Duplicate Contact Detected dialog box is displayed.

You have three options when this dialog box is displayed. You can add a new contact, choose to update the existing contact record with new information, or click Cancel and leave everything as it was. If you do cancel out of the dialog box, you still have to close the New Contact dialog box and tell Outlook not to save changes.

The second most likely reason why you might end up with duplicate contacts is synchronization with mobile devices like PDAs and Smartphones. Should this occur, you either need to manually delete the duplications or use a third-party tool to clean up your Contacts list. There are a number of utilities that can tidy up your Contacts list. Appendix C includes a list of online resources where you can find these tools.

Inside Scoop

There are times when you might want to have two separate contact records for the same person. You might want, for example, to mark one private and share the second. I recommend you make an obvious change in one of the record's name fields to remind you which is which.

Using contacts effectively in Outlook

In this chapter, I've described a very contact-centric way of using Outlook — one where you generate e-mail messages, appointments, and tasks from the Contact view. If you tend to look at what you do from the perspective of who you are doing it with, this may work well for you. This is a natural approach for people involved in certain kinds of work and personal pursuits. In fact, the Business Contact Manager add-on for Outlook, which is discussed in Chapter 19, is a decidedly people-oriented approach designed for sales professionals and small business owners who often define everything they do in the context of the person or company they are engaging with.

For others, the perspective from which they approach their personal information management may be activity oriented and more aligned to their calendar or to-do list. As is discussed in the next two chapters, Outlook provides a means for linking your activities, whether they are time-based or task-based, to your contacts. Regardless of which perspective you approach your information from, creating these links between what you are doing and with whom you are doing it is critical to getting the most out of Outlook as a personal information manager.

When you are creating a new appointment or task, there is a button and field at the lower left of the dialog box labeled Contacts. If you've used Outlook in the past, you may be familiar with this control and information field. Or, like many longtime Outlook users, you may have looked at this field once and promptly ignored it because the value of entering contact information into an appointment or task wasn't clear to you.

Many Outlook users create a subject line in their appointments or tasks like "Meet with Jane" or "Send package to Bob" and feel that the connection between the action and person is adequate. It may be — depending on how many people named Jane or Bob they happen to deal with.

When you use the contact link features in Outlook though, you create connections between a specific contact and every message or action related to him or her that can provide an extraordinary benefit to you over time. You build a complete history of your interactions with every person you engage with that eliminates the need to try remembering when you last met, spoke on the phone, or assigned a task. The ability to reference this ongoing history is a powerful tool and one well worth developing new habits to take advantage of.

Bright Idea

Try to develop the good habit of always linking your appointments and tasks to the appropriate contacts in your list. Doing so gives you an easily accessed history of every interaction you've had with that person or group.

Search implications

One reason why contact linking can be a helpful habit to develop is the new search feature in Outlook 2007. If a contact is linked to a task or appointment, it adds a useful bit of data you can use as a search criterion when you are building a query. If, for example, you wanted to search for all tasks linked to Jane Doe that were completed in the first quarter of 2006, having a contact link to all of the tasks that were either assigned to Jane or listed her as a contact would generate a more accurate list. You also eliminate a lot of false positives in your search results by using the contact link rather than free text (keyword search), especially if some contacts have similar names.

Journal and Activities implications

Outlook's Journal is discussed in detail in Chapter 11. When you create a contact link in your appointments or tasks, Outlook uses that link to create a new entry in that contact's Journal record if you are tracking your interactions with that contact using the Journal. The Activities control in the Contact tab of the Ribbon, described earlier in this chapter, also relies on these contact links to generate its list of items related to a contact.

Just the facts

- The Contact view in Outlook adds a new Business Cards view and an enhanced By Follow Up Flag view.

- Outlook 2007 allows you to share contact information in a number of formats including Virtual Card Format, a standard file type that can be opened by people using other applications and operating systems.

- Distribution Lists are a handy tool that allows you to send the same e-mail message or appointment request to a group of people quickly.

- If you work in a contact-centric fashion, the new Ribbon controls make it easier than ever to initiate communications with people on your list from a single location.

- Follow Up Flags is a powerful new tool to create tasks and reminders for next actions related to a person you are working with.

- New contacts can be created from incoming e-mail messages by right-clicking the sender's name in the From field.

- Outlook 2007 uses the Windows Live Local online service to generate a map of your contact's location, including driving directions and, in many cases, high-resolution satellite imagery.

- SmartArt and other editing tools allow you to add reference information in the Notes field of a contact record.

- Color Categories allow you to visually associate a contact with projects or priorities.

- Outlook scans new contacts when you save them and warns you if it detects a duplicate contact.

GET THE SCOOP ON...
What's new in the main Calendar view ▪ The new
appointment dialog box ▪ Sharing your calendar by
e-mail ▪ Using drag-and-drop to create appointments ▪
Sharing your calendar with others

Chapter 8

Outlook Is a Time Manager

O utlook's Calendar is the place where you schedule and organize your day. The Calendar not only allows you to track your own activities — it also provides the ability to schedule meetings and view your own calendar side-by-side with calendars shared by coworkers, friends, and family. No component of Outlook has received more attention in this new version than the Calendar view.

There are three types of Calendar objects in Outlook: appointments, meetings, and events. Appointments are scheduled on the Calendar at a set time and for a specific duration. Meetings are like appointments but have other people involved, either by your invitation or your acceptance of someone else's invitation. Events are specific to a day or range of dates but have no specific time component.

The first part of this chapter introduces the new look of the main Calendar view and how the new user interface has changed the Appointment dialog box. The second part of this chapter focuses on using the Calendar to manage your own time, schedule and invite others to meetings, and share your calendar.

Getting familiar with the Calendar view

From an architectural perspective, the main Calendar view hasn't changed radically from Outlook 2003. The main view is divided into two panes in the same way as the

Contacts view with a Navigation Pane on the left side of the screen and the main viewing area to the right. But the appearance of the Calendar view, pictured in Figure 8.1, is dramatically different.

Appointments, meetings, and events are displayed using gradient shaded color based on their categories and are much easier to read than in Outlook 2003. The Navigation Pane shares all of the configurability described earlier in the book in terms of button and icon display and the ability to collapse or expand the pane to increase your viewing area. A task area has been added to the bottom of the Calendar in Day and Week view to provide a more complete look at your commitments and activities.

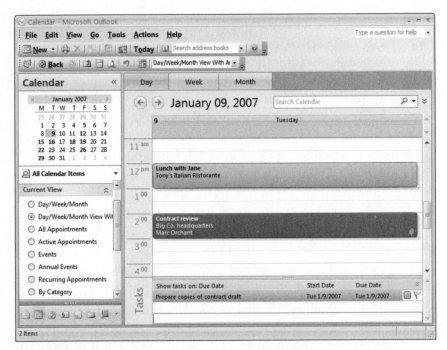

Figure 8.1. The main Calendar view in Day mode with the Navigation Pane expanded.

Inside Scoop
The Calendar Tasks list in Day and Week views can be collapsed or expanded by clicking the chevron icon at the right end of the divider bar between the time grid and the Tasks list. Dragging this divider bar resizes the Tasks list.

The Navigation Pane in Calendar view contains the Date Navigator, a thumbnail monthly calendar, a list of the Calendars you can view, and the standard Navigation Pane buttons and icons for switching between views in Outlook. The Date Navigator is more than just a miniature calendar. It displays dates in bold that have appointments, meetings, or events scheduled and, as its name implies, can be used to quickly navigate to any day in the Calendar. The bar at the top of the Date Navigator displays the month currently displayed with arrows to navigate to the previous (left) and next (right) month. Depending on the size of your window and the state of the navigation buttons and icons, you will see one or more months displayed.

Below the Date Navigator is a list of the calendars currently available to you. Select the check box next to a listed calendar to display it in the viewing area. If you select more than one calendar, they will be side by side.

Calendars can be added from sources including an Exchange Server, SharePoint Server, network share, or the new Office Online Web site. Adding calendars is discussed later in this chapter. Below the calendar selectors are links to browse calendars online, send a calendar via e-mail, and publish a calendar to your local network or the Internet.

Choosing your view

Outlook 2007 provides a new set of controls for switching between the different Calendar views. In previous versions, views were selected from the Standard toolbar. In Outlook 2007, view controls are presented as tabs on the Calendar at the top of the main view area. The currently selected tab is highlighted in orange. These tabs are much easier to use than the old toolbar, especially on smaller notebook screens and when using a Tablet PC pen. The following views are available:

- **Day view.** Shown in Figure 8.1, this view displays one day at a time with tasks due on that date displayed below the time grid.

- **Week view.** Shown in Figure 8.2, this view displays the Calendar one week at a time in either work week (Monday through Friday) or full week (seven days) mode. You can toggle between the two layouts using radio buttons at the top of the main viewing area to the right of the view tabs. Tasks for each day are displayed below the time.

Figure 8.2. Main Calendar in Week view.

- **Month view.** Shown in Figure 8.3, this view displays the Calendar one month at a time. This view offers three detail levels that can be selected using the radio buttons to the right of the view tabs at the top of the main viewing area. These detail levels control how much information is displayed in each cell on the Calendar grid. The Tasks list is not available in the month layout.

- **List view.** Calendar items can also be viewed as a list using the drop-down menu on the Advanced toolbar, as shown in Figure 8-4. A number of predefined layouts are included with Outlook. You can use the Define Views command on the menu to customize an existing layout or create a new layout. Customizing layouts is discussed in Chapter 14.

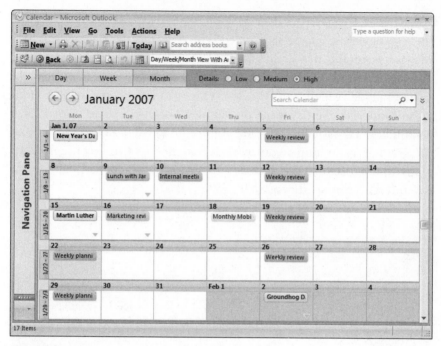

Figure 8.3. Main Calendar in Month view.

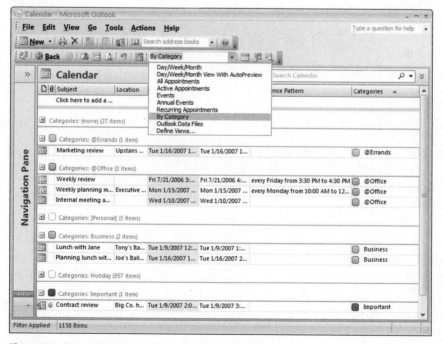

Figure 8.4. Main Calendar in List view filtered by category.

Using the Reading Pane with the Calendar

The Reading Pane can be used in conjunction with the Calendar to provide access to the detailed information included in an appointment, meeting, or event. Figure 8.5 shows the Reading Pane open to the right of the Calendar which is in Day view. This layout shows the appointment in the context of the day while providing all of the detailed information contained in the Notes field of the appointment itself. Keep in mind that the Reading Pane allows you to read, but not edit, the content of an appointment. To change any of the information contained in the appointment, you need to actually open the item.

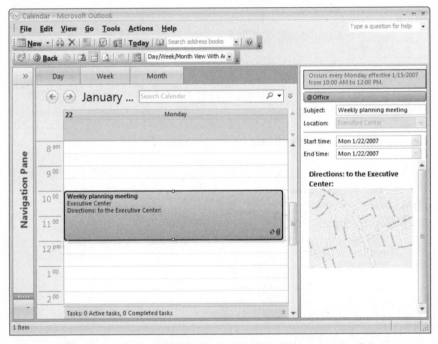

Figure 8.5. The Calendar in Day view with the Reading Pane displayed to the right.

This Reading Pane technique can also be used when looking at your Calendar in other modes. Figure 8.6 shows the Calendar in work week layout with the Reading Pane displayed at the bottom of the Outlook window. Arranging the screen like this allows you to look at your work week with the details of a particular appointment immediately below the Calendar. You can change the position of the Reading Pane on the View menu and can turn it on and off using either the View menu or the toolbar.

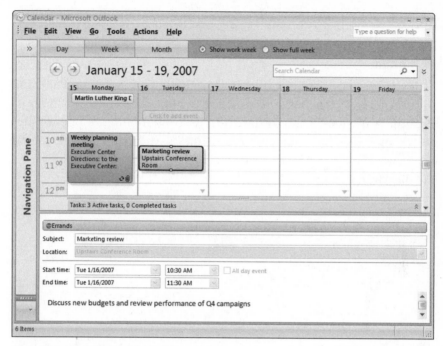

Figure 8.6. The main Calendar in full week view with the Reading Pane displayed below.

Using the To-Do Bar with the Calendar

The biggest change to Calendar view is the addition of the new To-Do Bar. It replaces the Task Pad used in previous versions of Outlook to integrate time and tasks. The To-Do Bar, used in conjunction with main Calendar view, provides the best time and task management user interface Outlook has ever offered.

The To-Do Bar, like the Navigation Pane, can be collapsed or expanded as needed. Figure 8.7 shows the Calendar in Week view with the To-Do Bar displayed to the right. The To-Do Bar contains, from top to bottom, the Date Navigator, the next scheduled appointments, and a Task list that can be organized based on:

■ Categories

■ Flag: Start Date

■ Flag: Due Date

■ Folder (Mail, Contacts, Task)

- Type (Mail, Contacts, Task)
- Importance (High, Normal, Low)
- Custom

If your display is large enough to have both the Navigation Pane and To-Do Bar open at the same time, notice that the Date Navigator "jumps" from the Navigation Pane to the To-Do Bar when both are open. I personally find very little reason to have the Navigation Pane expanded when I work in Calendar view and tend to use a layout very much like the one displayed in Figure 8.7.

Figure 8.7. The main Calendar view in Week view with the To-Do Bar expanded.

Hack

Remember that even when collapsed, you can access the controls in the Navigation Pane by clicking the vertical tab labeled Navigation Pane. You can also switch to any other main view by clicking on the arrow icon at the bottom of the Navigation Pane.

The Previous Appointment and Next Appointment tabs

Another very nice touch added to the Calendar in Outlook 2007 is the addition of Previous Appointment and Next Appointment tabs, which appear on the Day and Week views when the day or week you are currently viewing has no scheduled appointments, meetings, or events. These tabs, pictured in Figure 8.8, make it one-click simple to jump to the next day that has a scheduled item.

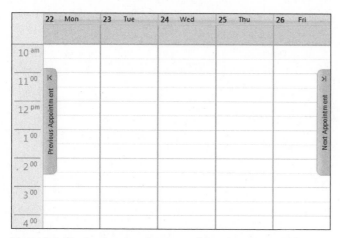

Figure 8.8. The Previous Appointment and Next Appointment tabs appear when no scheduled events are visible.

The new Appointment composition window

When you create a new calendar object or view existing information from your Calendar, the new Appointment composition window is displayed. Like the other composition forms in Outlook, the first tab contains the essential commands and controls needed to create, edit, or update appointments, meetings, and events. The Insert and Format Text tabs are identical to those in the Contact dialog box discussed in Chapter 7. The Add-ins tab only appears if you have installed third-party software which is discussed in Chapter 17.

The File menu

The File menu accessed from the Office button changes slightly when you are working in the Appointment window, as shown in Figure 8.9. The top command creates a New Appointment. A second command on the File menu that is related to the Calendar is a new Meeting Request that appears in the right pane. This command, like all of those listed in the right pane, is accessible from any of Outlook's composition windows. A Meeting Request is similar to a New Appointment but is sent via e-mail to the attendees you invite to join the meeting.

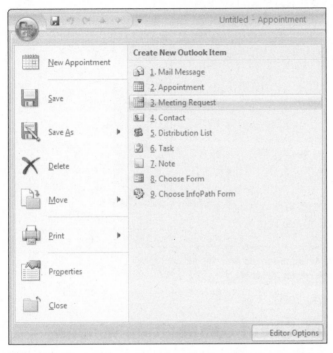

Figure 8.9. File menu as displayed from the Appointment composition window.

If you have used previous versions of Outlook, the Appointment composition window should look very familiar below the new Ribbon, which is shown in Figure 8.10. The Appointment window, pictured in Figure 8.11, includes fields labeled Subject, Location, Start time and date, and End time and date. Next to the time and date fields is a check box for marking a Calendar item as an All day event. Below these fields is a blank Notes field for entering information about the appointment and at the very bottom of the window is the Contact field discussed at the end of Chapter 7.

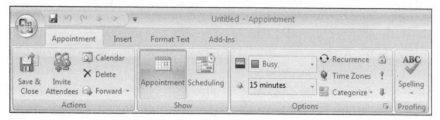

Figure 8.10. The Appointment tab in the Ribbon in Outlook 2007's Appointment composition window — same controls with a new look.

If you are creating an appointment that pertains to people in your Contacts list, adding their names in this Contact field in the lower-left corner of the window creates a contact link to their records. If you extend a meeting invitation to contacts in your list, their names are automatically added in the field when the invitation is sent.

The Appointment tab

The Appointment tab on the Ribbon in the Appointment window, pictured in Figure 8.11, contains four groups of controls:

- Actions
- Show
- Options
- Proofing

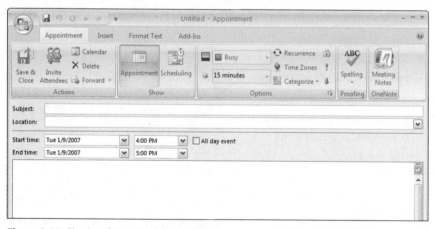

Figure 8.11. The Appointment tab in the Appointment composition window displays the principal controls used to add events to your calendar.

Actions

The Actions group includes standard Save & Close and Delete commands, present in the Actions group of all Outlook composition windows. Specific to the Appointment composition window Ribbon are controls to Invite Attendees (issue a New Meeting Request), open a shared Calendar for those invited, and Forward the meeting information to an e-mail recipient.

Invite Attendees adds a To field to the appointment and sends an invitation to people you want to invite without having to use the Scheduling control described below. The Forward control has a drop-down menu that provides two choices: Forward and Forward as iCalendar. Forward generates an e-mail message with the Calendar item attached as a native Outlook Calendar object and is designed to be sent to other Outlook users.

Show

The Show group contains the Appointment and Scheduling controls. Appointment is always selected by default when creating a new calendar item. Clicking Scheduling switches the window view to a time grid for adding people and resources to your meeting. Planning meetings and inviting others to attend is discussed later in this chapter.

Options

The Options group includes a variety of controls for adding additional information or qualities to your Calendar item.

- **Show As.** Labels the block of time as Free, Tentative, Busy, or Out of Office on your calendar. This labeling is visible to anyone you share your calendar with.

- **Reminder.** Allows you to set a reminder alarm in advance of the event.

- **Recurrence.** Opens a dialog box, pictured in Figure 8.12, which provides options for establishing a repeating entry on your calendar. You can set how frequently the recurring event takes place and for how long.

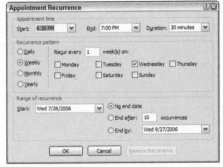

Figure 8.12. This dialog box is displayed when you click Recurrence in the Appointment composition window.

Watch Out!

When you double-click an instance of a recurring event in the Calendar, Outlook gives you the option to edit either that occurrence or the entire series. If you delete an instance of a recurring event from the Calendar, you delete only that instance. If you click the Delete control in the Appointment dialog box of an instance, the entire series is deleted.

- **Categorize.** Displays the same drop-down menu of Color Categories used in the Mail Message and Contact dialog boxes. As in those environments, you can assign one or more categories to a Calendar item.

- **Private.** Prevents those you have shared your calendar with from seeing any details about this appointment.

- **High Importance and Low Importance.** Assign a priority to this event which can be helpful when viewing your calendar in one of the List views described earlier in this chapter. All new appointments have Normal Importance by default.

Creating a new appointment

By now, it should come as no surprise when I tell you that there is more than one way to create a new appointment in Outlook 2007. You can create a new Calendar item from scratch using any of the following techniques:

- In the main Calendar view, click the New button on the Standard toolbar.

- In any other main view, click the down arrow next to the New button on the Standard toolbar and select Appointment from the drop-down menu.

- In any main view, press Ctrl+Shift+A.

- In any Outlook composition window that uses the new Office 2007 user interface, select New Appointment from the File menu displayed when you click the Office button in the upper-left corner of the window.

Adding basic information

Once the Appointment window is open, creating an appointment or event is very straightforward. The following fields are available:

- **Subject.** Text entered here appears in the Calendar and List views.

- **Location.** Text entered here is displayed in the Calendar. The Location field is persistent in the sense that it "remembers" previously entered locations. If you regularly have appointments in a certain location, click the down arrow at the right end of the Location field and you are able to select from recently entered locations.

- **Start date and time.** Clicking on the down arrow at the end of these fields drops down a thumbnail calendar and list of times respectively. If your appointment starts at a time other than the top of the hour or on the half hour, you need to manually enter that time.

- **End date and time.** This is similar to the fields above. By default, Outlook assumes that an appointment ends on the same date as it starts. Events that span more than one day on the calendar are presented as a banner that stretches across the days the event takes place. If you manually entered a time in the Start fields, Outlook adjusts the times listed in the End time field to be half-hour and full-hour increments from that starting time.

- **All day event.** Selecting this check box makes the appointment into an Event which, like the multiday Calendar items mentioned in the previous bullet, is presented as a banner at the top of the Calendar cell or cells of the event. Start and end time fields are removed when you select this check box.

- **Notes field.** As was the case with the Contact dialog box, you can add just about any type of information you'd like in the Notes field. Text can be entered or pasted from another source. Hyperlinks to Web sites and documents can be added and documents can even be inserted. You can paste in a map, picture, or graphic or add a table, Shapes drawing, or SmartArt object.

- **Contacts.** Type in the names of people associated with the event. Outlook automatically looks them up when you save the appointment and prompts you if a name you've entered doesn't match one of your contacts. You can also click the Contacts button to open a Contact Picker dialog box.

Scheduling appointments and inviting others to attend

Clicking the Scheduling control replaces the fields described above with the time grid that displays the schedules of invitees to the meeting, as shown in Figure 8.13. This timeline runs horizontally across the window. As you add people to the meeting, their schedules, if available, are added to the timeline to indicate when they are already committed to another event. If an attendee's schedule is not available, his or her timeline is marked with a series of diagonal lines.

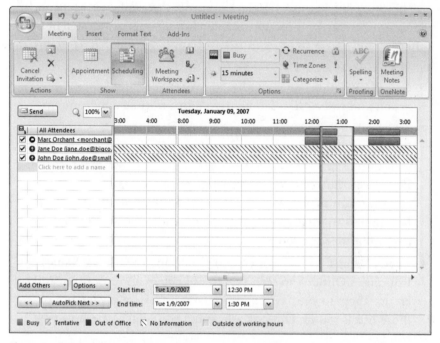

Figure 8.13. Scheduling view of the Appointment composition window.

To add a person to the schedule, click in the first empty cell in the first column below your name and type his or her name. If the person is in your Outlook Contacts list, that record links to the meeting, the name is underlined, and the e-mail address appended. If an invitation recipient is not yet in your Contacts list, you can add a new contact by using the Check Names control that appears when the dialog box changes into a meeting invitation. This change occurs as soon as the first invitee is added to the scheduling grid. This change can also be initiated by clicking on the Invite Attendees control in the Actions group. Either

Inside Scoop

Until recently, Microsoft offered a free service called Free/Busy Server that allowed you to post your schedule availability to assist in meeting management if you weren't working in an Exchange Server or SharePoint environment. That service has been discontinued and is replaced by a similar capability in Microsoft Office Online, which is discussed later in this chapter.

technique causes a number of changes to occur in the Appointment composition window.

The Save & Close and Delete controls are replaced by Send and Account controls like those found in a Mail Message window. The Invite Others group is replaced with an Invitation group that contains the following controls:

- **Cancel Invitation.** Clicking this control cancels the Scheduling action and reverts the Calendar item to a normal appointment.

- **Address Book.** This control opens the Select Attendees and Resources dialog box that lists all of your Outlook contacts from your own list and any servers or shared lists you may have opened. If you are connected to an Exchange or SharePoint Server, your administrator may have made a list of resources available as well. Resources can include meeting rooms, audio visual equipment, and other meeting tools.

- **Check Names.** As mentioned above, clicking the Check Names control causes Outlook to scan the list of invitees and resources and reference them to your available Contacts lists. If an invitee not on those lists is found, Outlook asks you if you want to create a new contact.

- **Forward.** This control works exactly the same way as in a normal appointment, allowing you to send a copy of the calendar item as an e-mail attachment in either native Outlook or iCalendar format. Forwarding a copy is not the same as sending an invitation. An invitation, when received via e-mail, requests that the invitee accept or reject the invitation. A forwarded copy simply provides a copy of the Calendar item which the recipient can choose to open and add to his or her Calendar or not.

- **Allow New Time Proposals.** Checking this box formats the invitation in such a way that recipients of your invitation cam reply to you and the other invitees with a proposal to meet at a different time.

- **Request Responses.** Checking this box adds a prompt to the invitation that, when opened by the recipient, requests that they respond to the invitation. This is similar to requesting a read receipt in an e-mail message.

Once you have added your invitees and resources to the scheduling grid, you can use the icon field next to the person or resources name to assign a status icon. You, as the initiator of the event, are automatically assigned the Meeting Organizer icon. Invitees are assigned a Required Attendee icon by default that appears as a red circle with an arrow pointing upwards. Click that icon and you can change a person's status to Option Attendee, which displays a blue circle with a lowercase letter "i." A resource can be given its own icon which displays a green circle with a building icon.

There are a few additional controls in the Scheduling view worth noting:

- **Zoom.** Located just above the scheduling grid, this control allows you to zoom the grid in and out in terms of the range of dates and times displayed. The default zoom level of 100% shows the date currently selected. The 50% zoom level shows the entire week surrounding the current date selected.

- **Add Others.** This button drops down a menu that allows you to choose either your Outlook Contacts or a Public Folder on a remote server containing a list of contacts or resources.

- **Options.** This button drops down a menu that lets you display only working hours, toggle the display of meeting details for existing items on your and your attendees' calendars, quickly select all or only required people and resources, and refresh the display of free and busy time for people and resources in your schedule.

- **Time selectors.** The two buttons at the bottom-left corner of the dialog box jump to the next earlier and later time when all of the people and resources you have added to the schedule are free. This can be particularly helpful when trying to set up a meeting with a larger group of people or a group of any size with very busy schedules.

Once the Scheduling tab has been completed, you can return to the Appointment view by clicking on the Appointment control in the Show group. Since the previous version of Outlook, a To field has been added that lists all of the invitees. An information banner is also added in the form of an orange box above the To field that shows the current status of the invitation. Until you actually send the meeting invitation, the field displays the text "Invitations have not been sent for this meeting." Once sent, the information banner displays the date and time the invitation was sent.

There is another method for creating a new meeting directly from the main Calendar view. On the Advanced toolbar there is a button labeled "Plan a Meeting." By default, it is located next to the List view menu at the right end of the toolbar. Clicking that button opens the Plan a Meeting dialog box, shown in Figure 8.14. This dialog box can also be accessed from the Actions menu in the main Calendar view.

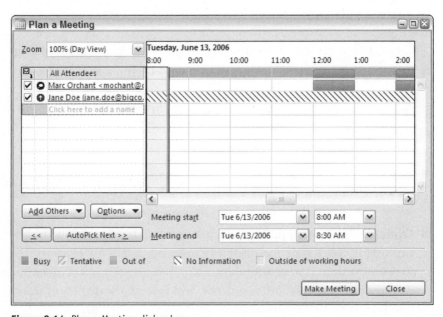

Figure 8.14. Plan a Meeting dialog box.

Most of these capabilities have been part of Outlook for some time. The difference is in how easy Outlook 2007 makes it to set up a new meeting and invite others.

Bright Idea

To make a meeting more effective, consider adding a proposed agenda and any documents that are to be discussed in the meeting. It can also be helpful to assign specific roles for the meeting, such as timekeeper and scribe.

Setting reminders

Outlook provides two ways to set reminders for Calendar items.

- **Default reminders.** In the Options dialog box accessed from the Tools menu you can set a default reminder for all new calendar items. This preference is illustrated in Figure 8.15. The default time for reminders is 15 minutes but it can be set for up to 2 weeks in advance.

- **Per-appointment reminders.** As you are creating a new Calendar event, use the Reminder control in the Options group to set a reminder for that appointment. You can, of course, set a reminder for any existing event as well.

Figure 8.15. Choose a default reminder for Calendar items in the Options dialog box.

Additional options for reminders can be set to control the display of reminder alerts and what sound is played when an alert is displayed. To access these options, select the Advanced Options button on the Other tab in the Options dialog box. In the Advanced Options dialog box, select the Reminder Options button at the bottom of the dialog box. You can use any WAV audio file to accompany your reminder alerts.

Setting general Calendar options

From the Options dialog box, accessed from the Tools menu, you can set general preferences for how the Calendar works in Outlook 2007. From the Preferences tab of the Options dialog box, select the Calendar Options button icon that opens the Calendar Options dialog box, pictured in Figure 8.16.

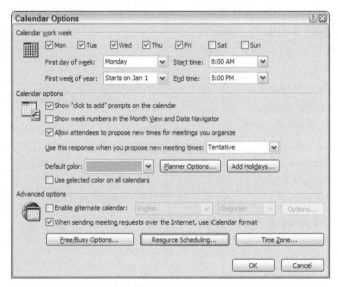

Figure 8.16. General preferences for Calendar view can be set in the Calendar Options dialog box.

Using Recurrence to create automatic appointments

If you have events that take place on a repeating basis in your work or life, using Outlook's ability to automatically create future instances of these appointments can be a great time-saver. You can create a recurring appointment by clicking the Recurrence control in the Options group on the Appointment tab. The Appointment Recurrence dialog box is shown in Figure 8.12 earlier in this chapter.

The first set of criteria relates to the appointment time. As you select the start and end times, Outlook automatically calculates the duration of the appointment. Alternatively, you can set the start or end time and specify the duration.

Depending on the frequency with which the recurring appointment takes place, the Appointment Recurrence dialog box displays different options to specify when future events appear on the Calendar. These options are illustrated in Figure 8.17.

The final section of the dialog box establishes how many future occurrences of the event will be generated, either by number or end date. Selecting no end date creates a permanently recurring appointment.

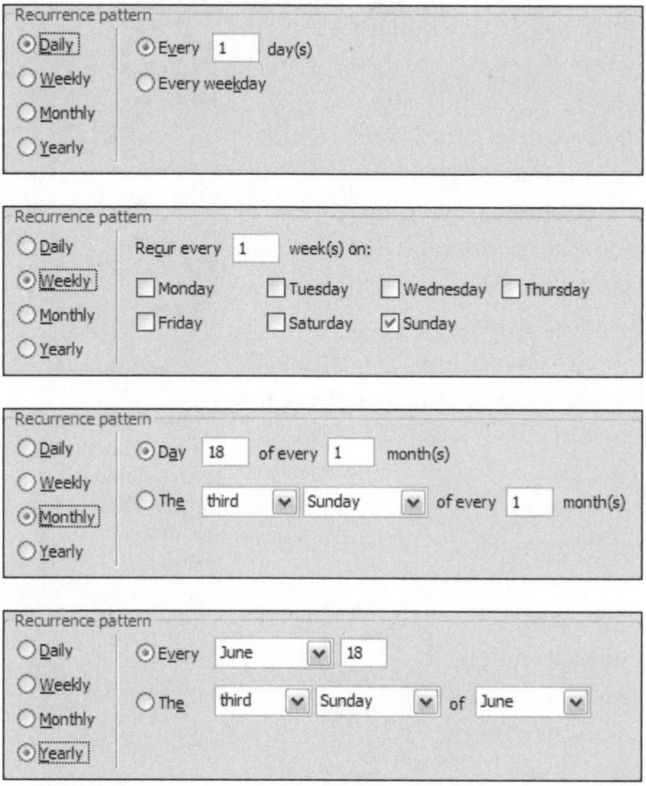

Figure 8.17. The options in the Recurrence pattern section of the Appointment Recurrence dialog box change depending on the frequency of recurrence.

Defining and using Color Categories

In previous versions of Outlook, only Calendar items could be color coded using a limited feature called Labels. Categories, shared across all Outlook objects, could also be applied but only from inside the Appointment dialog box or a specially constructed List view. Compounding these issues, only a limited number of Labels were available. It made for a cumbersome and not entirely useful system.

Outlook 2007 changes all that with the introduction of Color Categories that can be applied to all Outlook objects. Combining color and category tags makes great sense and adds significant utility to the idea of tagging related messages, events, tasks, and notes. In any of Outlook's List views, you can sort items by Category which can be a fast way to review all related items. Customizing List views is discussed in Chapter 14.

You can apply one or more Color Categories to a Calendar item using the Categorize control in the Options group on the Ribbon, as pictured in Figure 8.18. Outlook comes with a pre-built set of categories like Anniversary, Birthday, and Business as well as generic categories named for their color. The first time you apply one of these generic categories, Outlook asks you if you want to give the category a more useful name.

To manage your existing Color Categories or create new ones, select the All Categories command at the bottom of the Categorize control's drop-down menu that opens the Color Categories dialog box, shown in Figure 8.19. Shortcut keys can be assigned to categories in this dialog box, making it even easier and faster to apply them to Calendar items.

Figure 8.18. The Color Categories menu can be accessed from the Categorize control in the Appointment dialog box.

Sharing calendars in Outlook 2007

Sharing your calendar with coworkers, family, or friends makes scheduling faster and easier. Outlook 2007 provides two new ways to share your Calendar information with others, even if you do not have

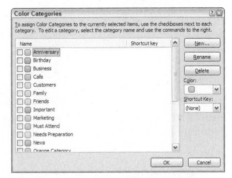

Figure 8.19. The Color Categories dialog box allows you to add, edit, and delete categories and add keyboard shortcuts to categories.

access to an Exchange or SharePoint Server. You can send your Calendar in an e-mail message as formatted HTML and an ICS file attachment and you can publish your Calendar using the free Office Online service.

In general, I recommend using the e-mail method to share a small amount of Calendar data — a day or two, maybe a week — with someone you are trying to set a meeting or date with. Using the e-mail method allows you to control how much information you share and the period of time you are sharing information about. Publishing a calendar on Office Online does provide access controls, but if you grant someone access to your shared Calendar, they see everything you have chosen to publish.

Sharing your Calendar via e-mail

To send a recipient information from your Calendar, click the link on the Navigation Pane that reads Send a Calendar via E-mail. The dialog box shown in Figure 8.20 displays. Select which Calendar to extract the data from, the Date Range — Today is the default selection — and Detail level you want to share with the recipient.

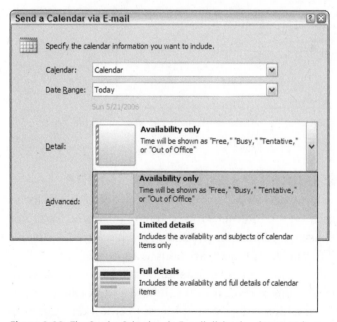

Figure 8.20. The Send a Calendar via E-mail dialog box lets you choose the date range and detail level to share.

After you have set your preferences, Outlook scans your Calendar, extracts the scheduled appointments, and formats an e-mail message with your Calendar presented in HTML and attached as an ICS file as shown in Figure 8.21. Enter the recipient's name in the To field, add some message text, and send it on its way.

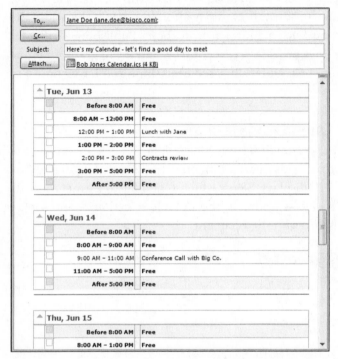

Figure 8.21. Calendar information formatted in HTML and attached as an ICS file.

Sharing your Calendar using Office Online

One of the features provided by the Office Online service is the ability to publish your Calendar on the Internet. Once you have registered for Office Online you can publish your Calendar and share it with selected recipients or make it generally available with no restrictions as appropriate.

If you are sharing your personal calendar, you probably want to restrict access only to family and friends. If you have a work calendar you want to share, you probably want to restrict access to coworkers and business partners. On the other hand, if you are publishing a calendar for your neighborhood association or civic group, you might decide that publishing that calendar with full public access is more desirable.

The first step in publishing your calendar is to click the link in the Navigation Pane labeled Publish My Calendar. The Publish calendar to Microsoft Office Online dialog box appears, shown in Figure 8.22. You must register on the Office Online Web site to use this service. If you attempt to publish a calendar and have not registered, you are first asked to sign up and then are allowed to proceed as described here. In this dialog box, which is similar to the one displayed when sending your calendar by e-mail, you can select which calendar you want to publish, the level of detail you want to make visible, and whether you prefer to restrict access to those you specifically invite or make the calendar accessible to anyone. Figure 8.23 illustrates the three levels of visibility you can select from.

Figure 8.22. Publish calendar to Microsoft Office Online dialog box.

Figure 8.23. Select the level of detail you want to make visible in your published calendar.

You can upload your calendar as a static version or choose to have your local changes synchronized with the online version. Once your calendar data has been uploaded to Office Online, you are provided with the opportunity to send an e-mail message inviting others to view your calendar. The recipients receive an e-mail message containing a link that opens your calendar in their Web browser. If they are Outlook users, they can subscribe to your calendar which downloads a copy to their local Outlook installation. If you chose to dynamically update your online calendar, their

Inside Scoop

When you publish a calendar to Office Online service, information is updated and synchronizes based on the date range you have selected. Because these are relative dates like 30 days prior or Next 60 days, the information remains current over time.

local copy also updates on a regular basis as changes are synchronized.
When someone viewing your cal-
endar online clicks the subscription link, their local copy of
Outlook opens or launches and
the dialog box shown in Figure
8.24 asks them to confirm they
want to download your calendar
and add it to their list of calendars.

Figure 8.24. The calendar subscription confirmation dialog box.

Adding a calendar to Outlook

Outlook 2007 has the ability to manage any number of calendars. You
can create multiple calendars in your local copy of Outlook as discussed
earlier for different sets of event information related to the different
areas in your life. You can also access group calendars from Exchange
Servers and SharePoint sites or subscribe to online calendars published
by others or offered on Office Online.

If you work in an Exchange Server or SharePoint environment, your
administrator can provide you with the information required to access
the group calendars available from those servers. To access a calendar
online, whether published by an individual or organization or from
Office Online, navigate to the Web site that hosts the calendar you want
to add to Outlook and click the link to the calendar.

Using Office Online as an example, follow these steps to add a new
calendar to your local Outlook installation.

1. Open a Web browser and go to Microsoft Office Online
   (http://office.online.com).

2. Look for the link that reads Internet Calendars for Microsoft Office
   Outlook 2007. Find a calendar that you would like to add from the
   list of available options.

3. Click the link for the calendar you want to add. The dialog box shown in Figure 8.25
   appears.

Figure 8.25. This dialog box is displayed to
confirm you want to add an Internet calendar
to Outlook.

4. Click Yes. The calendar downloads and installs into your local Outlook. The newly added calendar appears in the Navigation Pane under the heading Other Calendars.

Viewing multiple calendars

In previous versions of Outlook, you had the ability to view more than one calendar at a time in side-by-side mode as pictured in Figure 8.26. To enable side-by-side mode, select the check box next to the additional calendar you want to view. In this viewing mode, the calendars are linked and as you scroll up or down in the time grid or forward and back between dates, the two calendars move in parallel. Switching between Day, Week, and Month views is similarly linked. While comparing calendars in this fashion makes it possible to view your personal calendar alongside a group or Internet calendar, it can be cumbersome on smaller displays, even with the Navigation Pane minimized. This is especially true in Week and Month views.

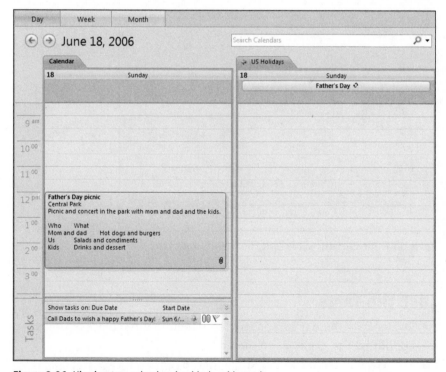

Figure 8.26. Viewing two calendars in side-by-side mode.

Outlook 2007 provides a new way to view two calendars by overlaying one calendar over another as shown in Figure 8.27. To enable this overlay mode, click on the small arrow in the top-left corner of the second calendar. The two calendars can now be viewed together. Click either calendar's tab to bring it to the front. Any new appointment you create is added to whichever calendar is on top.

This capability becomes even more useful as you add additional calendars to your view. In a work scenario, you could, for example, look at your personal, work group, and project milestone calendars in similar fashion. This enhanced method of working with multiple calendars is another way the Outlook 2007 calendar system has been greatly improved.

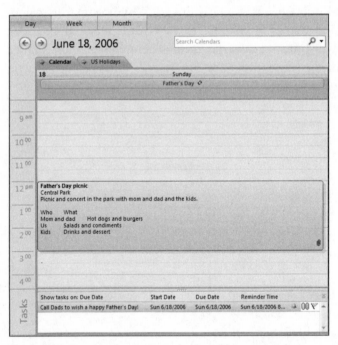

Figure 8.27. Two calendars in the same view with separate tabs.

Just the facts

- Outlook's Calendar can be used to schedule three types of items: appointments, events, and meetings.
- The Date Navigator in the Navigation Pane can be used to check your monthly schedule at a glance.

- The Reading Pane can be used to display an appointment's details side by side with the calendar.

- Calendar items can be enhanced with text, hyperlinks, embedded documents, tables, SmartArt objects, and Shapes-based drawings.

- Meetings can be planned in the Appointment dialog box or from the main Calendar view using the Plan A Meeting toolbar button or Actions menu item.

- The Recurrence control lets you set up repeating appointments at specific intervals over a defined period of time.

- Color Categories can be used to tag Calendar items as well as contacts, messages, tasks, and notes, enabling faster system-wide search and organization of your information.

- Outlook 2007 enables sharing of your calendar via e-mail and the free Office Online service.

- You can add additional calendars to your local Outlook environment from a range of sources including Exchange and SharePoint Servers, Web sites, and Office Online.

- Outlook allows you to view two or more calendars side by side or in the new overlay mode.

GET THE SCOOP ON...
What's new in the main Tasks view ■ The new Task dialog
box ■ Connecting tasks with contacts ■ Assigning and
accepting tasks ■ The all-new To-Do Bar ■ Customizing
Tasks lists

Outlook Is a Task Manager

Maintaining a list of things to do is something most of us have tried as a way of keeping track of our commitments with varying degrees of success. There are books, seminars, and even stores in your local mall devoted to the art and science of keeping track of the things you need and want to do. Outlook 2007 introduces a number of new enhancements to its Tasks view that make managing these commitments easier and faster.

The integration between tasks, calendar items, e-mail messages, and contacts has been dramatically improved in Outlook 2007 with the introduction of three new features:

■ Follow Up Flags make any of these Outlook items actionable by allowing you to tag the item with a reminder to perform an action on a specific date or with a general reminder that something needs to be done (the No Date Flag).

■ Color Categories allow you to tag all related items with a category label and color that makes it easy to sort your list views to group together related events, messages, tasks, or people.

■ The always-accessible To-Do Bar and new integrated task lists in the Calendar's Day and Week views keep your task accessible no matter where you happen to be working in Outlook.

195

The first part of this chapter introduces the new look of the main Tasks view and how the new Office 2007 user interface has changed the Task dialog box. The second part of this chapter focuses on using Tasks to manage your to-do list and assigning tasks to others.

Getting familiar with the Tasks view

At first glance, the main Tasks view hasn't changed radically from Outlook 2003. The main view is divided into two panes in the same way as the Contacts and Calendar views, with a Navigation Pane on the left side of the screen and the main viewing area to the right, as pictured in Figure 9.1. The most significant changes to the main Tasks view are the addition of the new To-Do Bar and a generally improved display of information in the list layouts in Outlook 2007.

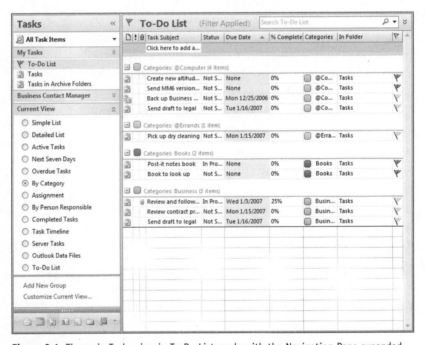

Figure 9.1. The main Tasks view in To-Do List mode with the Navigation Pane expanded.

The ability to collapse and expand both the Navigation Pane and To-Do Bar in Outlook 2007 provides a number of screen layout configurations for the main Tasks view that can really enhance your ability to manage your to-do list and develop an efficient work style.

Bright Idea

Clicking on the All Task Items bar itself changes the main display area into a Search All Task Items layout. Enter a keyword or two and press Enter to search through all of your available tasks. You can, as with all searches in Outlook 2007, add additional criteria to your search to narrow the results.

The Navigation Pane

The Navigation Pane in the Tasks view is similar to what you see in Contacts view. At the top of the Navigation Pane is an All Task Items bar with a drop-down menu that allows you to select the sources from which your task list is composed. The contents of this list vary, depending on whether you are connected to an Exchange Server or SharePoint site, but includes, at minimum, Personal Folders and Archive Folders. If you have subscribed to any Internet Calendars (as discussed in Chapter 8) that choice also appears on the Tasks menu.

Directly below the All Task Items bar is a section labeled My Tasks with three options listed: To-Do List, Tasks, and Tasks in Archive Folders. Each of these options filters your tasks to include only those items with a Follow Up Flag attached (To-Do List), items in your PST file (Tasks), and items you have archived. Outlook remembers the layout you have applied to each of these filters so that as you select each option, the items matching that filter use the display preference you have established.

Choosing your view

These display preferences are set in the next section of the Tasks Navigation Pane. Under Current View, Outlook provides the following layout options to arrange and present your tasks:

- Simple List
- Detailed List
- Active Tasks
- Next Seven Days
- Overdue Tasks
- By Category
- Assignment
- By Person Responsible
- Completed Tasks

- Task Timeline
- Server Tasks (new)
- To-Do List (new)

The interaction between the layout options in Current View and the filters in My Tasks can produce some interesting, and potentially confusing, results. The To-Do List filter in My Tasks, for example, selects only those task items that have a Follow Up Flag attached. The To-Do List under Current View accomplishes essentially the same thing.

Additional customizations to how information is displayed can be accomplished by sorting any view by clicking on the column headers in the list. If you sort your task list by Category, for example, the display of your tasks is grouped by that tag. These changes are persistent. That is, when you make a change to the sort order of items in a particular view, Outlook remembers that change and presents items sorted in that order whenever you switch to that view.

It is well worth spending a bit of time exploring which layouts and sort orders work best to define the optimum views for the way you work. How you end up choosing to filter and sort your task list is purely a matter of personal preference and may change depending on what information you are most interested in at a particular time. I regularly use the Overdue Tasks view, for example, to do a quick check of things that have been slipping when I'm doing a review of my progress on personal and work projects. I also use the Next Seven Days layout when I need to get a handle on what the coming week looks like.

You can alter the layout of the Task List in the following ways:

- Select a layout from the Navigation Pane in either expanded or collapsed view.
- Select Current View from the View menu and make a selection from the submenu displayed.

Hack

You can show or hide any of Outlook's toolbars in the main views by right-clicking a toolbar or empty region in the toolbar area. The display of toolbars is global — if you choose to show a toolbar while in Tasks view, it is visible in all main views.

- Select a layout from the Current View control on the Advanced toolbar if you have it visible.

Using the Reading Pane with the Tasks List

The Reading Pane can be used in Tasks view to provide an in-depth look at the contents of the currently selected task in the list as pictured in Figure 9.2. By default, the To-Do List view is configured to show the selected task's information in the Reading Pane to the right. If you prefer the Reading Pane on the bottom of the screen, you can change its position using the Reading Pane commands on the View menu.

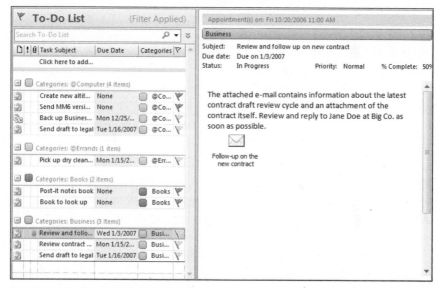

Figure 9.2. The Reading Pane can be used to display the contents of a task item.

The new Task dialog box

When you create a new task object or view existing information from your Tasks list, the new Task dialog box is displayed. Like the other composition forms in Outlook, the first tab, Tasks in this case, contains the essential commands and controls needed to create, edit, or update the item appropriate for the main view you are working in. The Insert and Write tabs are identical to those in all Outlook composition dialog boxes as described in Chapter 7.

The File menu

The File menu accessed from the Office button changes slightly when you are working in the Task dialog box, as shown in Figure 9.3. The top command creates a new task. This command, like all of those listed in the right pane, is accessible from any of Outlook's composition windows.

The Task dialog box, pictured in Figure 9.4, is essentially the same as in previous versions of Outlook below the new Ribbon. Fields are labeled Subject, Start

Figure 9.3. File menu as displayed from the Task dialog box.

date, Due date, Status, Priority, and % Complete. A Reminder can be set for a task by selecting the Reminder check box and choosing a date and time. You can have Outlook play a sound by clicking on the small speaker button.

Next to the Reminder controls is a field labeled Owner which should have your name listed. This field is not directly editable but displays someone else's name if you have assigned the task you are viewing to another person. When you are viewing a task assigned to someone else, you can view, but not edit, the item's information.

Below these fields is a blank Notes field for entering information about the task. At the very bottom of the window is the Contact field discussed at the end of Chapter 7.

If you are creating a task that pertains to one or more people in your contact list, adding their names in this field creates a contact link to their records. If you assign a task to a contact in your list, the recipient's name is automatically added in the field when the assignment is sent.

Watch Out!

Task assignments only work if the person you are sending the assignment to also uses Outlook. Managing tasks with non-Outlook users is better handled using e-mail or other tools.

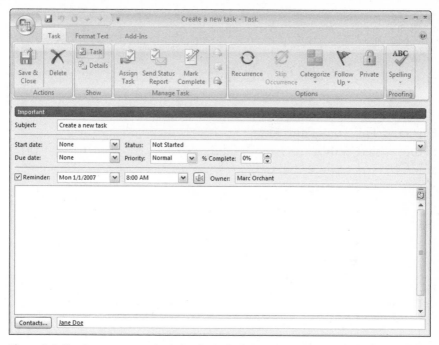

Figure 9.4. The Create a new task window in Outlook 2007 — same controls with a new look.

The Task tab

The Task tab, pictured in Figures 9.4 and 9.5, contains five groups of controls:

- Actions
- Show
- Manage Task
- Options
- Proofing

The Actions group includes standard Save & Close and Delete commands, present in the Actions group of all Outlook composition windows.

The Show group contains the Task and Details controls. Task is always selected by default when creating a new task item. Clicking on Details switches the dialog box view to a layout, pictured in Figure 9.5, where you can capture additional information related to the task.

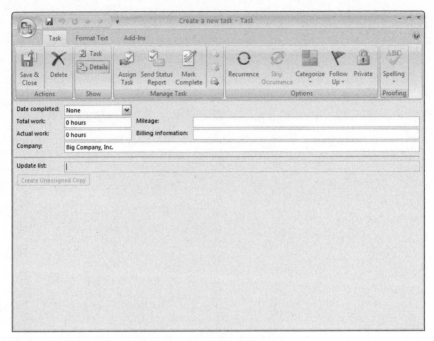

Figure 9.5. Details view in the Create a new task window.

The Manage Task group contains the following controls related to assigning and managing tasks:

■ Assign Task

■ Send Status Report

■ Mark Complete

■ Reply, Reply to All, and Forward

Assigning tasks to others is described in detail later in this chapter.

The Options group includes a variety of controls for adding additional information or qualities to your task item.

■ **Recurrence.** This allows you to define a task item for actions that need to be done on a repeating basis.

■ **Skip Occurrence.** This allows you to skip one instance in a recurring task series.

■ **Categorize.** This allows you to apply one or more Color Categories to the current task and is identical to the control in the Contact and Appointment dialog boxes discussed in Chapters 7 and 8.

- **Follow Up.** This attaches a flag to the current task and is also identical to the control in other Outlook item composition dialog boxes.

- **Private.** This marks the tasks that cannot be viewed if you share your Task list with others in an Exchange Server or SharePoint environment.

The Proofing group contains a single control for Spelling. Clicking the down arrow at the bottom of the control provides access to other Proofing tools and the Office Research Pane.

Creating a new task

As is the case with other information items, there is more than one way to create a new task in Outlook 2007. You can create a new Task item using any of the following techniques:

- In the main Tasks view, click the New button on the Standard toolbar.

- In any other main view, click the down arrow next to the New button on the Standard toolbar and select Task from the drop-down menu.

- In any main view, press Ctrl+Shift+K.

- In any Outlook composition dialog box that uses the new user interface, select New Task from the File menu displayed when you click the Office button in the upper-left corner of the window.

- Add a new task directly to the Tasks list in the main view by entering text in the field labeled Type a New Task.

- Add a new task directly to the Tasks list in the To-Do Bar by entering text in the field labeled Type a New Task in the task list at the bottom of the bar.

- Tasks can also be created in Microsoft Office OneNote and synchronized with your Outlook Tasks list. Using Outlook and OneNote together is discussed in Chapter 17.

Adding basic information

Once the Create a new task window is open, the process is very straightforward. The following fields are available:

- **Subject.** Enter text that should appear in the Tasks list views.

- **Start date.** Click the down arrow at the end of this field, which drops down a thumbnail calendar.

- **End date.** Click the down arrow, similar to the field above. By default, Outlook assumes that a task will end on the same date as it starts.

- **Status.** Select from one of three values — Not Started, In Progress, or Complete.

- **Priority.** Select between Low, Normal, or High. Outlook defaults to Normal for all new tasks you create. Low priority tasks are marked with a blue down-arrow icon in list views. High priority tasks display a red exclamation point icon.

- **% Complete.** Change this value using the up and down controls that provide built-in values of 25%, 50%, and 100%. Changing the % Complete value to anything above 0% automatically changes the status field to In Progress. Setting the % Complete value to 100% changes the Status field to Complete and cancels a pending Reminder or clears a Follow Up Flag if one has been set.

- **Notes.** Add just about any type of information you'd like in the Notes field. Text can be entered or pasted from another source. Hyperlinks to Web sites and documents can be added, and documents can even be inserted. You can paste in a map, picture, or graphic, or add a table, Shapes drawing, or SmartArt object.

- **Contacts.** Type in the names of people associated with the event. Outlook automatically looks them up when you save the appointment (or when you press Ctrl+K, the keyboard shortcut) and prompt you if a name you've entered doesn't match one of your contacts. You can also click the Contacts button to open a contact picker dialog box.

Assigning tasks

Task assignment is designed to be used between Outlook users. Assigning a task to another person is accomplished by clicking on the Assign Task control in the Manage Task group. When you click this control, Outlook adds a To field above the Subject field and two check box options in the space used for setting a Reminder in a personal task, as shown in Figure 9.6. These two options allow you to track the progress of an assigned task by updating your local copy of the task as its status is changed and to receive a report when the task is marked complete. The Actions group in the Ribbon is replaced with a Send group that contains the Send and Accounts controls used in the Mail Message dialog box.

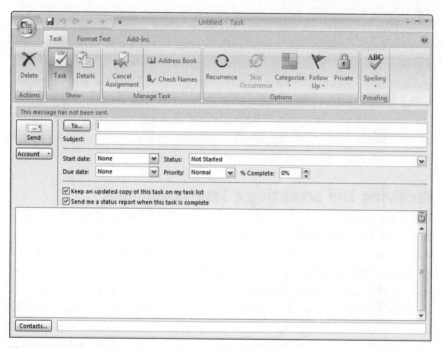

Figure 9.6. Once a Task has been assigned in Outlook, the Task window adds new controls to the Manage Task group.

After you have filled in the appropriate information and added a recipient, clicking the Send control sends a specially formatted e-mail as a task request to the contact. The person you send the task request to becomes the temporary owner of the task if he accepts the assignment. Recipients can decline the task, accept the task, or assign the task to someone else. If the task is declined, it is returned to you.

Watch Out!

Even though a declined task is returned to you, the task is still owned by the recipient until you return it to your own Tasks list. You can do this by clicking the Cancel Assignment control within the Manage Task group in the Ribbon.

When a recipient accepts a task assignment from you, that person becomes its new owner. If that person assigns the task to someone else, ownership transfers to that new recipient. Only a task owner can make changes to the task — it is a read-only record in the local Tasks lists of the previous owners. When the current owner updates a task, Outlook updates all copies of the task — the copy in your Tasks list and all copies in the lists of other prior owners of the task if that option was selected when the task was assigned. When the task is marked complete, Outlook automatically sends a status report to all previous owners of the task if that option was selected when the task was assigned.

Receiving and accepting a Task assignment

Task assignments arrive in Outlook as a specially formatted e-mail message displaying controls to Accept or Reject the assignment. Assuming that you accept the assignment, Outlook may send updates on your progress that are automatically generated if the sender has selected that option when making the task assignment. You can also generate an update on your progress on the task at any time by opening the task and clicking on the Send Status Report control. All previous owners of the task are sent an update that synchronizes their local copy of the task to its current status.

Recurring tasks

There are certain tasks in your lives that you need to perform on a regular basis. Outlook provides controls for defining recurring tasks, pictured in Figure 9.7, that are very similar to those provided for creating recurring appointments in the Calendar. Recurring tasks have one important difference. Using the Regenerate new

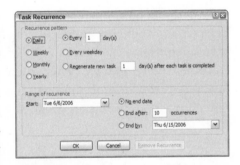

Figure 9.7. The Task Recurrence dialog box in Daily mode.

task option, you can set up a recurring task so that it automatically generates the next instance of that task when the current iteration is marked complete.

This is a great feature — one of my favorite little-known tricks in Outlook — because it keeps the Tasks list from looking like a never-ending repetition of the same thing over and over again. I much prefer seeing only a single instance of a task like "RSVP for monthly user group meeting" in my list, confident that when I have accomplished that task for the current month, a new instance is automatically generated. In every other respect, the Recurrence options are identical to those provided for Calendar items, as shown in Chapter 8.

The new To-Do Bar

The new feature in Outlook 2007 that changes the way the application works more than any other has to be the new To-Do Bar, shown in Figure 9.8. This addition to the display options in Outlook brings tasks front-and-center in every view in the application and allows you to instantly see how many current commitments and activities you have at a glance. In the months that I have been testing and using Outlook 2007, I have configured every main view to show the To-Do Bar, and I have never felt more in control of what is going on in my day. The To-Do Bar includes the following elements:

Figure 9.8. The new To-Do Bar displaying two months in the Date Navigator.

▪ **Date Navigator.** The Date Navigator, as described in Chapter 8, is a thumbnail calendar display that shows one or more months, depending on the width of the To-Do Bar. The current date is highlighted in an orange box, and all dates that have

Inside Scoop

You can use the Back and Forward controls on the Advanced toolbar to assist you in navigating between Outlook views in much the same way these controls work in a Web browser. After clicking a day in the Date Navigator in the To-Do Bar, use the Back button to return to the previous view you were working in.

at least one appointment, event, or meeting scheduled appear in bold. Clicking on a date switches you to the Calendar with that day displayed in Day view.

- **Next Appointments.** The To-Do Bar displays the next three scheduled items on your calendar below the Date Navigator in colored blocks based on the Color Category assigned to the event. The item's subject line, time, and location are shown. In the lower-right corner of each item, icons representing recurrence, attachments, and additional categories are also shown, as appropriate.

- **Task List.** At the bottom of the To-Do Bar is a display of your Tasks list. The Outlook team put a lot of work into making this miniature version of the Tasks list more informative and easier to configure than the Task Pad in previous versions of the program.

Configuring the To-Do Bar

Outlook 2007 provides three sets of controls for configuring and customizing the information display in the To-Do Bar. Right-click the To-Do Bar's title bar, and the menu shown in Figure 9.9 is displayed. From this menu, you can expand (Normal), collapse (Minimized), or hide (Off) the To-Do Bar and select which information components are displayed.

Selecting the Options command at the bottom of this menu opens the To-Do Bar Options dialog box shown in Figure 9.10. In this dialog box you can choose how many rows of thumbnail calendars are displayed in the Date Navigator, how many appointments are shown, and whether the Tasks list is visible.

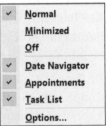

Figure 9.9. To-Do Bar configuration menu.

Figure 9.10. Configure the display options for the To-Do Bar in this dialog box.

As an example of how these controls can optimize the To-Do Bar's display, examine the variation picture in Figure 9.11. I have set the number of Date Navigator rows to two, reduced the number of appointments displayed to one, and narrowed the width of the To-Do Bar to use as little screen space as possible. This arrangement is ideal on lower resolution displays or when working in portrait mode on a Tablet PC.

The third set of controls for adjusting how information is displayed in the To-Do Bar can be accessed by right-clicking the sort bar at the top of the Tasks list in the To-Do Bar. The menu pictured in Figure 9.12 is displayed and allows you to sort the Tasks list by Categories, Start Date, Due Date, or other criteria. The Show in Groups command adds a separator bar with the name of each grouping of items that allows individual groups to be collapsed or expanded.

The Custom command on this menu opens Outlook's standard Customize View: To-Do Task List dialog box, which is shown in Figure 9.13. Customizing list views in discussed in depth in Chapter 14.

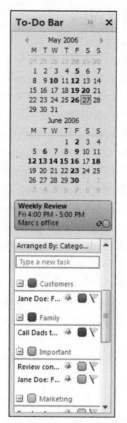

Figure 9.11. A To-Do Bar setup optimized to use as little width as possible.

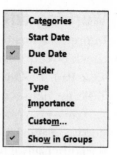

Figure 9.12. Sort the display of the To-Do Bar's Tasks List from this menu.

Figure 9.13. The Customize View: To-Do Task List dialog box for the To-Do Bar.

Working with Tasks

In previous versions of Outlook, the list views in the Tasks list displayed a check box for marking a task complete, in both the main view and the Task Pad. In Outlook 2007, this control is not included by default in Tasks list views although it can easily be added.

While I have not been able to find a public statement as to why this decision was made, I applaud it. I have lost count of how many times I have inadvertently clicked on the Complete check box and had an active task disappear from my list. Restoring a task that has been accidentally marked complete to active status requires quite a few mouse clicks and, depending on the length of your Tasks list, a lot of scrolling or sorting.

In Outlook 2007, the UI has been configured so that applying actions to tasks is accomplished primarily by right-clicking a task in the list or by opening the item and working with it in the Task dialog box. If you right-click a task in a list view, the menu pictured in Figure 9.14 is displayed, allowing you to perform a number of actions on the task including marking it complete.

Figure 9.14. Right-click a task item to display this menu of actions.

Customizing the Tasks lists

If you really miss having the check box component in your Tasks list, adding it is a simple matter. Customizing Outlook's List views is a dense topic that is discussed in detail in Chapter 14 but, since I am focused on Tasks in this chapter, I explain how to add the Complete check box to your lists here.

One of the tools provided to perform these customizations is a dialog box called the Field Chooser. This control displays all of the available fields that can be displayed in the list you are currently viewing and makes it a simple matter of dragging and dropping field names onto or off of the list to change its appearance.

To add the Complete check box to the main view of the Tasks list, right-click the column header bar at the top of the Tasks list which opens the context menu shown in Figure 9.15. Select the Field Chooser command that opens the Field Chooser dialog box

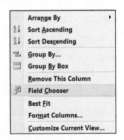

Figure 9.15. Right-click the column header bar to show this menu.

shown in Figure 9.16. The Field Chooser is a floating dialog box that sits above all open Outlook windows. Figure 9.16 shows the Complete field selected.

Drag the Complete field from the Field Chooser dialog box to the column header bar. As you move along the bar, red arrow icons display where the new field will be added and shown in Figure 9.17. When the field is positioned where you would like it, release the mouse button and the field is added. As long as the Field Chooser dialog box remains open, you can drag any field in the column header bar to any position you prefer. To remove a column, drag it off the bar. When the field icon shows a large black X, release the mouse button and it is removed. Figure 9.18 shows the Tasks list with the newly added Complete check box.

Figure 9.16. Field Chooser dialog box.

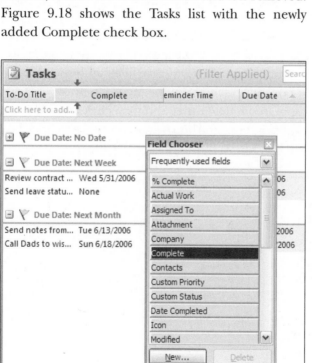

Figure 9.17. Drag the new field to the desired location using the arrow icons as a guide.

Inside Scoop

The Field Chooser can also be shown or hidden using the Field Chooser button on the Advanced Toolbar. If your current toolbar configuration does not include this button, you can learn how to add and remove toolbar buttons in Chapter 14.

Adding a Complete check box to the Tasks list in the To-Do Bar works differently. To add the field to the To-Do Bar, right-click the category header bar at the top of the Tasks list in the To-Do Bar and choose the Custom command. The Customize View: To-Do Task List dialog box shown earlier in the chapter in Figure 9.13 opens.

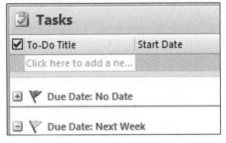

Figure 9.18. The Tasks list with the Complete check box added to the left of the To-Do Title.

Click the Fields button to display the Show Fields dialog box pictured in Figure 9.19. Click the Complete field in the left list box and then the Add button in the center column. Once the Complete field has been added to the list in the right list box, select it and use the Move Up or Move Down button to the desired spot in the field order and then click OK. Click OK in the Customize View dialog box, and you see the Complete check box added to the To-Do Bar Task List as shown in Figure 9.20.

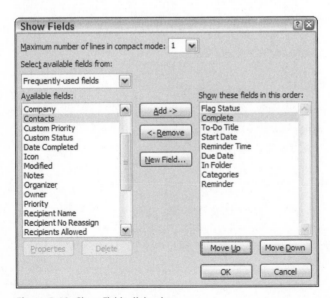

Figure 9.19. Show Fields dialog box.

Outlook 2007 has raised the bar in terms of visibility, accessibility, and usefulness of Tasks. Creating tasks using drag-and-drop techniques and converting Outlook items from one form to another can substantially improve your ability to use tasks effectively. These topics are discussed in detail in Chapter 12.

Figure 9.20. The To-Do Bar Tasks list with the Complete check box added immediately following the task description.

Just the facts

■ Outlook 2007 introduces the new To-Do Bar to keep your Tasks and next appointments accessible in all views.

■ The Navigation Pane contains filters and layouts that allow you to view your Tasks list in a variety of ways.

■ Changes made to each layout of the Tasks list are persistent.

■ You can use the Reading Pane to view the information (read-only) contained in a Task while working with your Tasks list.

■ There are a variety of ways to create a new Task including toolbar buttons, the Office menu, task input fields in both the main Tasks list and the To-Do Bar Tasks list, and the Ctrl+Shift+K keyboard shortcut.

■ Assigning tasks is only available when working with other Outlook users. When you assign a task to someone else, he becomes the task owner.

■ Recurring tasks work very much like recurring appointments with the additional ability to automatically generate the next instance of the task when you mark the current instance complete.

■ The To-Do Bar provides a variety of options to customize its display of Tasks and Calendar information.

■ Working with Tasks in Outlook 2007 is predominantly done by right-clicking a task or opening the Task dialog box.

■ The Complete check box is not displayed, by default, in Outlook 2007 Tasks list views, but it can be easily added.

19

GET THE SCOOP ON...
Making good use of Outlook Notes ▪ When it's time
to use another application ▪ Setting Outlook Notes
preferences

Outlook Is a Notes Manager

The Notes feature has been paid scant attention in Outlook 2007 and remains essentially unchanged from previous versions. Notes are useful if there is information you want to capture and have available while working in Outlook and you are simply unable to decide where else to put it. If you think about Outlook Notes the way you think about using sticky notes in the paper world, you will have a good understanding of how they are best used.

In the "paper world," you often need to jot down a quick idea or create a quick list. You scribble something on a sticky note, slap it onto the side of your PC monitor, and figure out what to do with that information at a later time. Outlook Notes can be used in essentially the same way.

If you use Outlook Notes with an understanding of their limitations, you may find them useful. Trying to do too much with Notes can lead to a lot of frustration. This chapter describes how Notes can be a useful accessory.

The Notes feature has inherited two welcome new features in Outlook 2007. In previous versions, Notes were limited to one of five colors which were purely cosmetic. Unless you mentally made an association between green notes and financial information, for example, coloring a note green had no real value. In Outlook 2007, Notes can have Color Categories applied in the same way you can add a Color Category tag to an e-mail, contact, calendar item, or task. This ability to categorize Notes makes them easier to organize and sort in a meaningful way. The second Outlook feature that makes Notes more useful is the addition of a Search box to the main Notes view. All Outlook Notes are indexed and fully searchable.

Getting familiar with the Notes view

The Notes view uses the same two-pane layout as the Contacts and Tasks views, as shown in Figure 10.1. At the top of the Navigation Pane is an All Note Items bar with a drop-down menu that allows you to select the sources your Notes list is composed from. The contents of this list includes, at minimum, Personal Folders and Archive Folders.

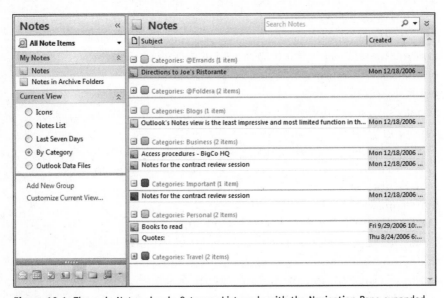

Figure 10.1. The main Notes view in Category List mode with the Navigation Pane expanded.

Choosing your view

The next section of the Navigation Pane, the Current View, provides the following layout options to arrange and present your Notes:

- Icons
- Notes List
- Last Seven Days

- By Category
- Outlook Data Files (new)

If you select the Icons layout option, you can right-click anywhere in the main view and choose the icon size that works best for your display. I have found the By Category view most useful as I have developed the habit of adding a Color Category tag to just about every object I create in Outlook 2007, including my Notes.

Anatomy of a Note

Outlook Notes look very much like the sticky note you use on your paper world desk. They don't look much like any other object you work with in

Outlook. Notes do not have scroll bars, title bars, or any visible controls aside from the close box in the upper-right corner of the window and the window-sizing handle in the lower-right corner. A Note can optionally display the time and date it was last modified in the small status bar area at the bottom of the window. If you click the small icon in the top left corner of a Note, you can access the Notes menu, as pictured in Figure 10.2.

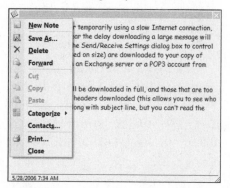

Figure 10.2. An Outlook Note with the Notes menu displayed.

The Notes menu

The Notes menu offers three commands that warrant a brief explanation.

- **Forward.** This command allows you to attach a Note to a new e-mail message in native Outlook Note format. You can also use the Save

Inside Scoop

Lacking a scroll bar, Outlook Notes can be navigated using the Page Up and Page Down or arrow keys on your keyboard. You can also drag the Note window to make it larger to see more of the text and deal with sometimes awkward line wrapping issues.

As command to save a Note in either Rich Text Format (.rtf) or as a plain text file (.txt).

■ **Categorize.** Categorize provides access to Outlook Color Categories. You can apply more than one category to a Note. The Note appears in the color of the last category applied. Applying Color Categories to Notes makes sorting and organizing much easier and more effective.

■ **Contacts.** This command opens a simple dialog box with a single field and button labeled Contacts. I recommend you click the Contacts button and find the Outlook Contact record you want to associate with the current Note. There is no visible indication that a contact association has been established when viewing the note, and it does not show up in the contact's Activities list when you are working in the Contacts view.

When you right-click a Note in List view in the main view, you are presented with an abbreviated version of the Notes menu, as pictured in Figure 10.3. The Quick Print option sends the Note directly to your default printer without showing a dialog box.

Figure 10.3.
Abbreviated Notes menu.

Creating a new Note

You can create a new Note using any of the following techniques:

■ In the main Notes view, click the New button on the Standard toolbar or press Ctrl+N.

■ Select the New Note command from the Notes menu in an open Note.

■ In any other main view, click the down arrow next to the New button on the Standard toolbar and select Note from the drop-down menu.

■ In any main view, press Ctrl+Shift+N.

■ In any Outlook composition dialog box that uses the new user interface, select New Note from the File menu displayed when you click the Office button in the upper-left corner of the window.

Hack

You can use Outlook Notes on your PC desktop. Open a Note and drag its window to your desktop. It remains on the desktop even if Outlook is minimized, and you can copy or drag text into the Note window from another application.

Search your Notes

You can use Outlook 2007 search features to find a specific Note in much the same way as in other views. You can either use the simple, one-box search method by typing a term into the Search box in the upper-right corner of the main view or use an Advanced Search, shown in Figure 10.4, which displays a number of available criteria at once. As in other Outlook views, you have the ability to construct a search query by adding criteria one at a time.

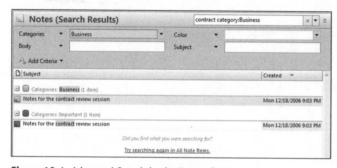

Figure 10.4. Advanced Search in the Notes view.

Setting Notes preferences

Preferences for the Notes view are accessed in two locations in the Options dialog box accessed from the Tools menu. From the default Preferences tab of the Options dialog box, click the Notes options button in the Contacts and Notes section to access the Notes Options dialog box, shown in Figure 10.5. In this dialog box, you can set the default color for all new Notes, the window size that new Notes open in, and the font that is used in all

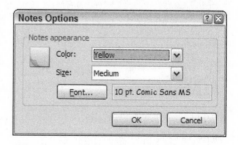

Figure 10.5. The Notes Options dialog box.

Notes, existing and new. The default color you select in this Notes Options dialog box is associated with Notes that have no category assigned to them.

To enable or disable the date and time stamp at the bottom of each Notes window, choose Tools ⇨ Options and click the Other tab in the Options dialog box. In the Other tab, click the Appearance button. The Advanced Options dialog box appears as shown in Figure 10.6. In the Appearance options section in the middle of the dialog box there is a single check box for turning this option on and off.

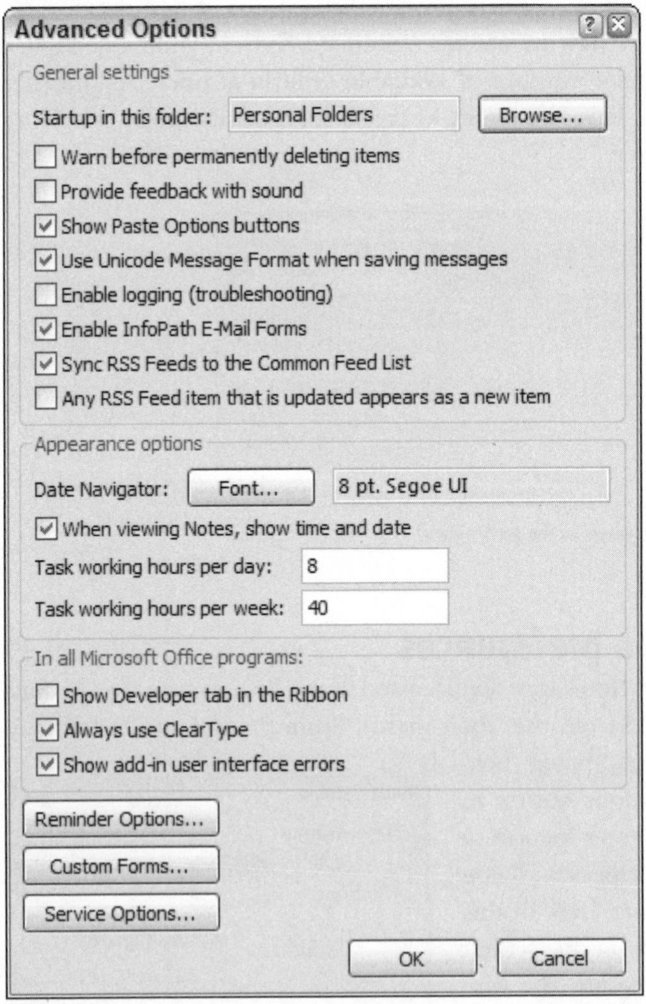

Figure 10.6. To view the time and date stamp of a Note, check this option in the Advanced Options dialog box, accessed from the Other tab in Outlook's Options dialog box.

When it's time to use another application

When you need more than the very simple text capture capabilities Outlook Notes provides, you have many options available for information capture, organization, and sharing. Windows XP and Vista include both NotePad and WordPad, and either is a much more powerful environment for working with text and, in the case of WordPad, graphics. You can use Outlook's ability to insert a document into a Contact, Calendar, or Task item to link the note file to that object or use the Shortcuts view in the Navigation Pane to link to the file.

A wealth of third-party applications are also available, a few of which are discussed in Chapter 17. But it is worth mentioning in the context of Notes in Outlook that Microsoft Office OneNote 2007, which is included in some versions of Microsoft Office 2007, has been updated with Outlook integration in mind. OneNote 2007 can create and synchronize meeting notes, use Follow Up Flags, and install a Send to OneNote button in Outlook's Standard toolbar.

Outlook Notes are handy, in much the same way a pad of sticky notes can be. You wouldn't use a sticky note to write anything of particularly great length, and any important information you capture using this tool often ends up in a more permanent location. You can use Outlook Notes as a quick and easily accessed container for information as you encounter it — just don't plan on writing the Great American Novel using this feature.

Just the facts

- Notes in Outlook 2007 are the electronic equivalent of the sticky notes you use in the paper world.
- Notes can now be tagged with Outlook 2007 Color Categories.
- An Outlook Note can be associated with one or more of your Outlook Contacts.
- The Notes menu, accessed by clicking the icon in the upper-left corner of a Note window, contains commands for acting on Notes.
- As long as Outlook is running, you can have Notes windows open on your desktop to copy or drag information into from other applications — even when the main Outlook window is minimized.

- Notes are best used for brief amounts of text, and you might consider using NotePad, WordPad, or another application for more extensive text capture, editing, and organization.

- For advanced note-taking and information capture, Microsoft Office OneNote 2007 offers excellent integration with Outlook 2007 and can synchronize notes and Follow Up Flags between the two programs.

GET THE SCOOP ON...
What the Journal does ▪ Why you should (or shouldn't)
use the Journal ▪ Viewing activities in the Journal ▪
Configuring the Journal

Outlook Is an Activity Tracker

Chapter 11

The Journal may be the most misunderstood and least appreciated feature in Outlook. It gets so little respect (in a Rodney Dangerfield sort of way) that when you first attempt to open the Journal view in Outlook, the application presents the dialog box shown in Figure 11.1 that asks you if you really want to do that. The warning message suggests that you might be better off tracking your interactions with your contacts by using the Activities control in the Contact dialog box.

As I mention in Chapter 1, one of the primary reasons the Journal has such a bad reputation is that, configured improperly, it can swell the size of your Personal Folders (PST) file which can make your Outlook environment unstable. The program defaults have long since been altered to make that unlikely, but it's hard to shake a bad reputation once it has been earned. The Journal, as it manifests itself in Outlook 2007, can be a great tool for people who want or need to view their work in terms of activities. It can be especially powerful if you bill your time by the hour.

In the most basic terms, you can think of the Journal as a database that automatically records every interaction you have with those contacts you choose to track. The Journal works behind the scenes most of the time, silently recording every e-mail, meeting request, and task assignment you send to designated contacts. It also creates a record of every Outlook item in which you create a contact link.

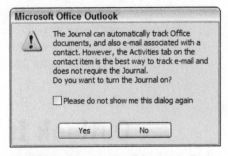

Figure 11.1. This warning dialog box is displayed the first time you open the Journal.

When you open the Journal, you are presented with a timeline view that allows you to view all of your tracked activities and documents in a variety of layouts that organize the information by different criteria like contacts and categories. In this chapter, I show you how the Journal can be used to view and annotate these interactions with your contacts, provide some advice about whether the Journal is right for you, and show you how to configure the Journal.

Should you use the Journal?

In Chapter 7, I mention that creating contact links has implications that relate to the Journal and describe the Activities control that generates a list view showing all of the Outlook-based interactions you have had with that contact. On a one-contact-at-a-time basis, this is a powerful tool that encapsulates all of your interactions with one person, as shown in Figure 11.2.

If all you really need is a way to track your interactions with individual contacts one at a time, you probably don't need to use the Journal. If, on the other hand, you think it would be valuable to be able to see everything you did in Outlook as it relates to specific groups of contacts in the contexts of activity type, time frame, or category, keep reading. This is what the Journal was designed to do.

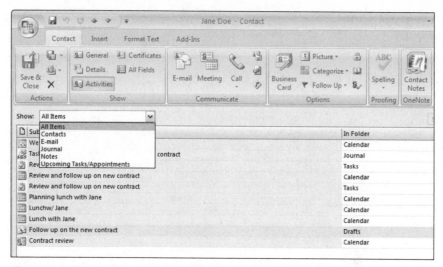

Figure 11.2. The Activities control in the Contact dialog box generates a list of interactions with that person.

Getting familiar with the Journal view

The Journal view uses the now-familiar two-pane layout, as shown in Figure 11.3. At the top of the Navigation Pane is an All Journal Items bar with a drop-down menu that allows you to select the sources from which your Journal view is composed. The contents of this list includes, at minimum, Personal Folders and Archive Folders.

Choosing your view

The next section of the Navigation Pane, the Current View, provides the following layout options to arrange and present your Journal entries:

- By Type
- By Contact
- By Category
- Entry List
- Last Seven Days
- Phone Calls
- Outlook Data Files (new)

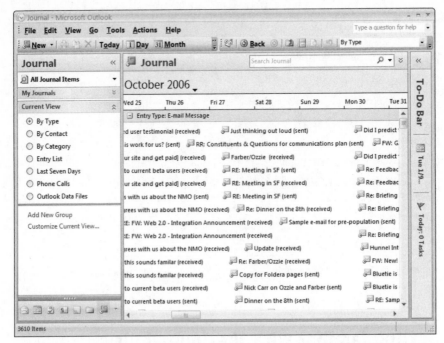

Figure 11.3. The main Journal view in Category List mode with the Navigation Pane expanded.

The top of the Journal's main viewing area shows a timeline which you can scroll forward and back to find a specific date. You can change the level of detail in the timeline using the Day, Week, and Month toolbar buttons in the Standard toolbar, and you can access a Date Navigator thumbnail calendar by clicking the small triangle next to the name of the month in the timeline to jump to any specific date.

If you have read this far and have decided that the Journal is a feature that can add value to your Outlook setup, you probably should add a button for Journal to the Navigation Pane, as pictured in Figure 11.4. Complete instructions for adding and arranging buttons and icons on the Navigation Pane appear in Chapter 4, but here's a quick summary of the steps you need to take to add the Journal button to the Navigation Pane:

1. Click the menu icon at the right end of the Navigation Pane button bar and select Navigation Pane Options from the menu.

Figure 11.4. The Navigation Pane with the Journal button added.

2. Select the Journal button in the Options dialog box.

3. Use the Move Up and Move Down buttons as needed to position the Journal button where you would like it to appear.

4. Click OK.

The new Journal composition window

When you manually create a new Journal entry or view an existing, automatically generated entry, the Journal composition window is displayed. The Journal Entry tab contains the essential commands and controls needed to create, edit, or update Journal entries. The Insert and Format Text tabs are identical to those in other Outlook composition dialog boxes.

The File menu

The File menu accessed from the Office button changes slightly when you are working in the Journal Entry composition window, as shown in Figure 11.5. The top command creates a new Journal entry.

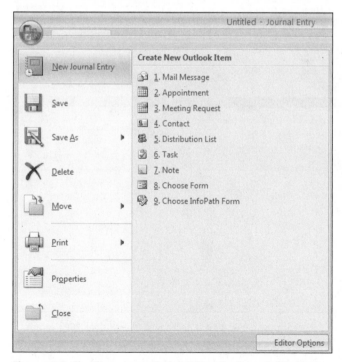

Figure 11.5. The File menu as displayed from the Journal dialog box.

The Journal Entry composition window, pictured in Figure 11.6, is essentially the same as in previous versions of Outlook below the new Ribbon. Fields are displayed labeled Subject, Entry type, Company, Start date and time, and Duration. An icon representing a clock face is also displayed which is animated when you are using the Journal timer feature.

The Journal Entry tab

The Journal Entry tab in the Journal Entry composition window, pictured in Figure 11.6, contains four groups of controls:

- Actions
- Timer
- Options
- Names
- Proofing

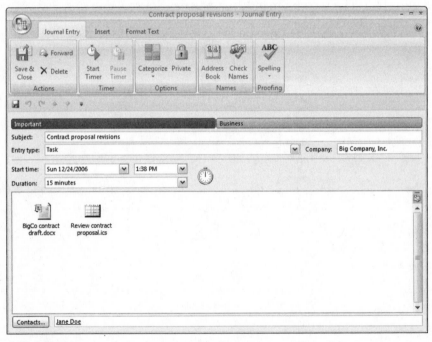

Figure 11.6. The Journal Entry composition window is unchanged from Outlook 2003 except for the new Ribbon UI.

Actions group

The Actions group includes standard Save & Close and Delete commands, present in the Actions group of all Outlook composition windows, along with a Forward command that sends a copy of the Journal entry in native Outlook format as an attachment to an e-mail message. You can use the Save As command on the Office Button menu to save a Journal entry as a Rich Text Format (.rtf) or plain text (.txt) document if you want to share the details of an entry with someone who does not use Outlook.

Timer group

The Timer group contains the Start Timer and Pause Timer controls. The Timer feature is very helpful when you are tracking the time a phone call, meeting, or other activity requires for billing or reporting purposes in a manually created entry.

Options group

The Options group includes two controls:

- Categorize is identical to the control in other Outlook composition dialog boxes and allows you to apply one or more Color Categories to the current Journal entry.

- Private marks the Journal entry so that it cannot be viewed by others.

Names group

The Names group includes two controls. The first opens the Address Book to choose contacts to associate with the Journal entry. The Check Names control performs a lookup if you have manually typed contact names into the form.

Proofing group

The Proofing group contains a single control for Spelling. Clicking on the down arrow at the bottom of the control provides access to other Proofing tools and the Office Research Pane.

Journal tracking options

You can select what kinds of information are tracked in the Journal from the Journal Options dialog box. This dialog box can be accessed by selecting Options on the Tools menu in Outlook's main view. The Journal

Options button is located in the Contacts and Notes section in the middle of the Preferences tab in that dialog box, as shown in Figure 11.7. In the Journal Options dialog box, shown in Figure 11.8, select what Outlook information you want to record for selected contacts. This dialog box also provides tracking for other Office documents. To keep the size of your Journal database as compact as possible, I suggest you limit tracking to those individuals with whom you interact most or customers to whom you need to present documentation for billing purposes.

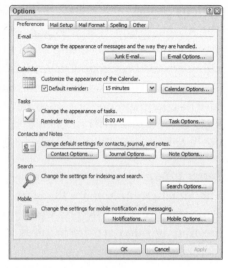

Figure 11.7. The Journal Options button in the Options dialog box provides access to the Journal Options dialog box.

In the lower-right corner of the Journal Options dialog box is a button labeled AutoArchive Journal Entries. If you plan to use the Journal feature, I recommend you change the default auto archive settings so that Journal entries are archived on a more frequent basis than the rest of your Outlook data. You might even consider creating a separate archive file just for these archived Journal entries.

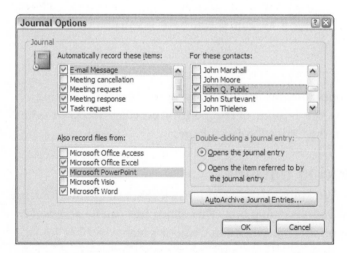

Figure 11.8. The Journal Options dialog box allows you to select what Outlook information will be tracked in the Journal.

Watch Out!
The Journal Options dialog box is one-size-fits-all in the sense that you cannot choose different tracking options for each individual contact. The more items you track and the larger the set of contacts you select, the larger your Journal data becomes.

Archiving these items will help you control the size of your primary (PST) file. You give up nothing by doing this — your archived Journal items can easily be accessed both in the Journal view and through Outlook Search. Chapter 26 covers archiving and other maintenance techniques in depth.

Manually creating a new Journal entry

Although the Journal automatically creates entries based on the options you have selected, there are times when manually creating a new entry can be useful. If, for example, you are starting a consulting phone call or are meeting with a client, you can manually create a new entry, start the Timer, and record meeting notes in the Notes field in the entry itself. Make sure that you create a Contact Link by entering the person's name in the Contacts field at the bottom of the Journal dialog box. Following the meeting, you can export the entry to a text file or send it to the person you spoke to or met with. You can manually create a new Journal entry using any of the following techniques:

- In the main Journal view, click the New button on the Standard toolbar or use the Ctrl+N keyboard shortcut.

- In any other main view, click the down arrow next to the New button on the Standard toolbar and select Journal Entry from the drop-down menu.

- In any main view, press Ctrl+Shift+J.

- In any Outlook composition dialog box that uses the new user interface, select New Journal Entry from the File menu displayed when you click the Office button in the upper-left corner of the window.

Adding information to an existing Journal entry

If you prefer to capture meeting notes in another application or have produced a Word document, Excel spreadsheet, or other document that relates to a meeting, call, or other interaction with a contact, you can open the Journal entry related to a meeting or call and insert that document directly into the Journal entry.

You can also use the rich editing tools Outlook 2007 provides to create supporting information directly in the Journal entry. You might add a table, Excel chart, SmartArt graphic, or Shapes-based drawing to capture the information exchanged in that interaction.

Just the facts

- The Journal provides powerful tracking capabilities to Outlook.

- To get more than the contact-specific information generated by the Activities control in a Contact dialog box, add the Contacts you interact with most frequently to the Journal.

- Navigate through the Journal timeline using the Date Navigator and zoom in or out using toolbar buttons.

- The Journal button is turned off by default in the Navigation Pane — if you plan to use the Journal, you should add it.

- Use the Timer control in Journal if you bill clients for your time or need to track how much time was spent in a phone call, meeting, or working on a task.

- Every contact or activity you add contributes to the Journal's file size, which can impact the performance and stability of Outlook — archive your Journal entries on a regular and frequent basis.

- Manually create a Journal entry to track a phone conversation, take meeting notes, or detail the steps required in a new project.

- Enhance Journal entries with notes, tables, graphics, and inserted files like most other Outlook items.

Outlook Power Beyond the Basics

PART III

GET THE SCOOP ON...
From e-mail to action ▪ Understanding Outlook's
data object model ▪ Transformations in Outlook ▪
Drag-and-drop tricks and tips

Magic Act Transformations

I**f you work in an e-mail-driven environment — and more and more of us do all the time — the majority of the new projects and activities you will engage in proba-bly arrive via e-mail. E-mail's virtually instant delivery and asynchronous nature makes it a primary carrier of informa-tion that requires an action from the recipient. Like all tech-nological "blessings," this has an upside and a downside.

The upside is that you can operate with greater speed and efficiency and at a lower cost than ever before. The incremental cost of every e-mail message is so small as to defy measurement, unlike the faxes and overnight pack-ages you previously relied on.

The downside is e-mail overload and Inboxes so stuffed with information that you seem to devote an ever-increas-ing percentage of your time simply trying to keep up with the flood of information that arrives on a minute-by-minute, all-day basis. Lacking an effective process for trans-lating the actions contained in these incoming messages into a more appropriate form, many people leave messages they have not yet decided how to deal with in their Inboxes.

This chapter describes how you can instantly convert e-mail messages into calendar appointments or tasks when they contain an action you must perform. Performing the magic transformations helps you get your Inbox emptied out and puts critical information in a more appropriate context where you are far less likely to overlook it.

Now, if you are one of those people who has a few hundred (or more!) e-mail messages currently stuffing your Inbox, you're probably thinking that this is easy to suggest but difficult to do. In this chapter, I show you one of Outlook's most powerful but least utilized capabilities — using drag-and-drop to instantly transform e-mail into appointments or tasks — that has the potential to change the way you process e-mail into actions from this point forward.

Outlook's data object model

Outlook allows you to create what I call data objects. These objects take the form of e-mail messages, calendar items, tasks, notes, and Journal entries. What makes Outlook unusual is the way it nicely separates the container from the content. The data object model allows powerful and easy transformations that help you move a piece of actionable information through a life cycle of sorts.

You receive an e-mail message that contains a requested (or required) action. To make the action visible and to allow you to assign it a start and due date and other attributes, you create a task. As the due date approaches, you may need to block out time on your calendar to complete the task, either individually or in a meeting with others, and you create an appointment or meeting. When moving information through this life cycle in Outlook, you are able to take advantage of the data object model to transform the content from one object type to another using a variety of techniques.

The new Color Categories and Follow-Up Flags in Outlook 2007, described in Chapter 1, enhance the data object model as these attributes now follow the information as you transform it from one form to another. Previous versions of Outlook did not allow category tags or follow-up information to be applied to all information objects. Labels, for example, were only available for calendar items. Outlook 2007 enhances the value of tagging information with these attributes early in the information life cycle by extending their applicability to most types of information objects.

Bright Idea

Take a look at your current Inbox and try to identify how many of the messages you have stored there contain actions you need or want to take. If you convert all of these e-mail messages into tasks, how much Inbox clutter might you be able to eliminate?

> **Inside Scoop**
>
> To make the most effective use of drag-and-drop techniques discussed in this chapter, I suggest you learn two critical keyboard shortcuts: Alt+F1 to show and hide the Navigation Pane and Alt+F2 to show and hide the To-Do Bar.

Transformations

While it is possible to copy and paste information from one object to another, transforming information helps reduce the amount of clutter you have to deal with in each of the main Outlook views. Once you have, for example, converted the actionable information in an incoming e-mail to a task, you can file the message away and get it out of your Inbox. Every time you perform a transformation like this, your Inbox gets closer to empty, and you can be less concerned about forgetting about an important action you needed to take.

E-mail to Task

When a new e-mail message arrives that contains an action you need to take, it's a great idea to create a task item for that action. Outlook 2007 provides three methods for transforming e-mail into tasks:

- As in previous versions, you can drag and drop an e-mail message from the Inbox (or other folder) Message List onto the Task icon or button in the Navigation Pane.

- Drag and drop an e-mail message from the Message List onto the Tasks list in the To-Do Bar that adds a Follow-up Flag to the message.

- Apply a Follow-Up Flag to an e-mail message from the Ribbon in the message dialog box that automatically generates an associated task, as pictured in Figure 12.1. Select Custom to create a task on your personal Tasks list. Select Flag for Recipients to create a task for yourself and send a task to each recipient

Figure 12.1. Apply a Follow-Up Flag to an e-mail message to generate an associated task.

which can be defined in the dialog box shown in Figure 12.2.

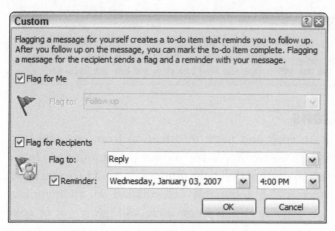

Figure 12.2. Choose Flag for Recipients to create a personal task and send a task to each recipient of the e-mail message.

E-mail to Appointment

You probably receive e-mail messages that contain requests from others to meet at a certain time and place or that ask you to make a suggestion. If you work with other Outlook users in your organization, these invitations may arrive in the form of a meeting request (as described in Chapter 8). However, more often than not, what shows up in your Inbox is a regular e-mail message asking if you have time to meet. You can use either of the following techniques to transform an e-mail message into a calendar item:

■ Drag and drop an e-mail message from the Inbox (or other folder) Message List onto the Calendar icon or button in the Navigation Pane.

■ Drag and drop an e-mail message from the Message List onto a date in the Date Navigator on the To-Do Bar.

Either of these actions creates and opens a new appointment dialog box containing the subject line and body of the message.

Task to Appointment

As an information object moves through the life cycle, it is often the case that a task needs to be converted into an appointment. Most frequently, this transformation is required when you either need to block out a specific amount of time to accomplish a specific activity or you set a meeting with someone as you complete the task itself. You can use either of the following techniques to transform a task into a calendar item:

- Drag and drop a task from either the main Tasks list or the list on the To-Do Bar onto the Calendar icon or button in the Navigation Pane.

- Drag and drop a task from the main Tasks list or the list on the To- Do Bar onto a date in the Date Navigator on the To-Do Bar.

Either of these actions creates and opens a new appointment dialog box containing the subject line and body of the task.

Appointment to Task

There may be occasions when you'll want to convert an appointment on your calendar to a task. I do this frequently when a meeting results in an action I need to take. The techniques you can use to perform this transformation are the inverse of those described in the Task to Appointment section above:

- Drag and drop an appointment from the Calendar onto the Task icon or button in the Navigation Pane.

- Drag and drop an appointment from the Calendar into the main Tasks list or the Task List on the To-Do Bar.

Any of these actions creates and opens a new appointment dialog box containing the subject line and body of the task.

Transformation techniques

Drag-and-drop is a powerful, fast way to perform these data object transformations. Outlook's UI contains a variety of targets for dragging and dropping data objects including:

- Navigation Pane buttons
- Navigation Pane icons
- To-Do Bar Date Navigator
- To-Do Bar Task List

In addition to these "precision" targets that are available regardless of the Outlook view you happen to be working in, you can also perform drag-and-drop operations using the Folder List view in the Navigation Pane, as shown in Figure 12.3.

When you drag and drop a data object onto one of the folders in the Navigation Pane, a new item appropriate to that folder is automatically generated and opened for you to edit. For example, an e-mail message dragged onto the Calendar folder in the Navigation Pane copies the e-mail message to a New Appointment form, populating the Subject field with the e-mail's subject line and copying the body of the message to the appointment's free text field.

Normal drag-and-drop transformations

When you click an object and drag it to any of the targets to perform a transformation using the left mouse button, Outlook's default behavior is to copy the information contained in the source to the target as described in the previous example. This

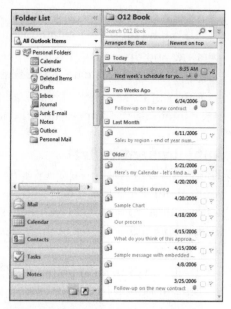

Figure 12.3. Drag an object to any folder in the Folder List displayed in the Navigation Pane to transform the object to another object type.

technique saves valuable time copying and pasting from one field in the source to the corresponding file in the target and is a welcome time-saver.

The net effect of this "normal" drag-and-drop is that the source object remains in its current location and the new target adds another data object to your Outlook information store. You can use this approach to extract the actionable information from an e-mail, transform it into a task or appointment, and then file the message to reduce the number of items in your Inbox.

Right-click drag-and-drop transformations

Outlook provides a number of options that make drag-and-drop transformations even more powerful when you use the right mouse button. In addition to the default behavior of copying the information from the source object to a new target, a right-click drag-and-drop allows you to:

▪ Copy the source object's text and attach the original object as an attachment in the new object you are creating.

▪ Move the source object to the new object you are creating that copies the text to the appropriate fields in the new object, attaches the source object to the new item, and removes it from the source folder.

■ Copy the source information and create a shortcut (or link) to the source object in the new object you are creating. This option is available when creating a new message or appointment but not when creating a new task.

These options appear on a context menu that pops open when you release the right mouse button on the destination target and are pictured in Figure 12.4.

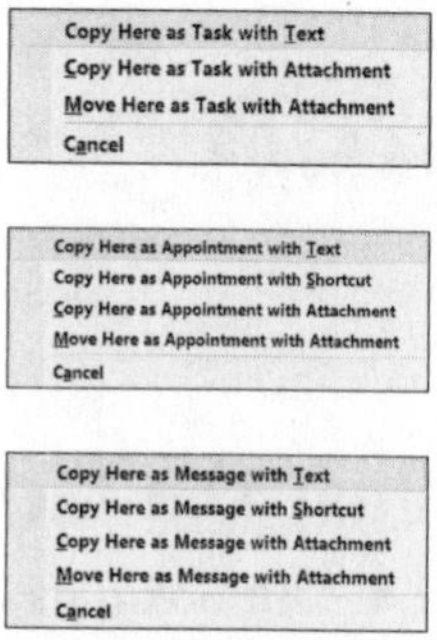

When you use the Move Here as (object) with an attachment, the new object contains the source object that is displayed in the free text field as shown in Figure 12.5, illustrating an e-mail message moved to a task object. You can add additional text or other information to the free text field of the new object, edit the subject line, and attach contacts, Color Category tags, and a Follow-Up Flag as appropriate.

Figure 12.4. The context menu displayed when dragging an object onto a Task target (top), an Appointment target (middle), and Message target (bottom).

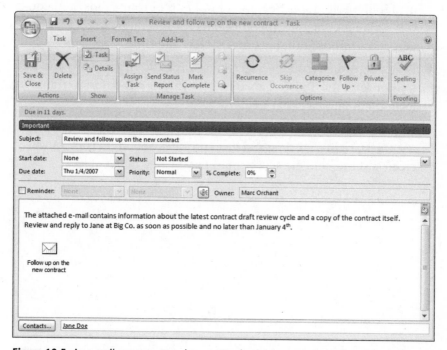

Figure 12.5. An e-mail message moved as an attachment to a new task appears in the free text field.

Watch Out!

It is all too easy to delete an attachment in the free text field of an Outlook item. Make sure you have clicked before or after the attached item to create an insertion point before you begin entering text or you may accidentally delete the attached object.

Just the facts

- Outlook data objects include e-mail messages, calendar items, tasks, notes, and Journal entries.

- Outlook's data object model separates container from content.

- Color Categories and Follow-Up Flags follow information as it moves through this cycle.

- To make drag-and-drop targets easily accessible, use the keyboard shortcuts for showing and hiding the Navigation Pane (Alt+F1) and To-Do Bar (Alt+F2).

- Convert e-mail messages requiring actions to tasks and file them in a mail folder to reduce the number of items in your Inbox, and convert e-mail messages to appointments (or meetings) when they contain event information on a specific day and time.

- Drag and drop e-mail messages onto Navigation Pane icons and buttons or onto the To-Do Bar's Date Navigator or Task List to transform them into calendar items or tasks.

- Left-click drag-and-drop copies the source object's data to the new target object; right-click drag-and-drop provides options to copy, move, or create a shortcut to the source object in the new target object.

GET THE SCOOP ON...
How Search Folders work ■ Outlook's default
Search Folders ■ Creating new predefined Search
Folders ■ Creating custom Search Folders ■
Modifying Search Folders

Find Anything with Search Folders

S earch Folders were first made available in Outlook 2003 and, along with the Reading Pane, were the most popular additions to that version of the application. Search Folders allow you to establish a set of criteria and display live results for all matching items every time you open them. This special type of folder can make finding virtually any message in Outlook fast and easy once you understand how it performs its magic.

How Outlook Search Folders work

The first thing to know about Outlook Search Folders is that they do not actually contain anything. Unlike the mail folders you are accustomed to using in Outlook to file and organize messages, a Search Folder presents a view of messages that match its criteria, regardless of where the actual message is actually stored in your Outlook PST file.

This has two important implications for working with the items displayed in a Search Folder and the folders themselves:

- If you delete an item displayed in a Search Folder, you delete the actual message.
- If you delete a Search Folder, you only delete the Search Folder and not the items that match its criteria.

243

Bright Idea

If you have been using Outlook for a while, there is probably a lot of old mail lying around in your PST file that you want to delete. Create a Search Folder that finds items older than a specific date and delete or archive unwanted e-mails that this Search Folder finds as they "show up."

In plain language, this means that Search Folders are a great tool for managing individual messages, but, as part of how they have been implemented, prevent accidental destruction of a large quantity of files. If you have ever accidentally pressed the Delete key when a folder in the Folder List was selected, you understand why this is a good thing.

In addition to finding matching items, Search Folders allow you to view a single message in multiple contexts. For example, if you receive an e-mail message that contains information related to two (or more) separate projects you are working on, you can see that single message in a Search Folder designed to collect all information about each project. It doesn't matter where the message is actually filed — Search Folders find and display it for you in as many Search Folders as it matches.

Before Search Folders were available, many Outlook users resorted to making copies of a message to store in each project folder the message related to. This approach added a lot of complexity to keeping information in sync and increased the size of PST files. Search Folders eliminate both of these concerns.

Outlook default Search Folders

When you installed Outlook 2007, three prebuilt Search Folders were added to your Personal Folders, as pictured in Figure 13.1. These default Search Folders — Categorized Mail, Large Mail, and Unread Mail — are good examples of how Search Folders can find all matching items that share a certain attribute.

Categorized Mail searches your Personal Folders for all e-mail messages you have attached one or more Color Category tags to. Large Mail finds all messages larger than 100K in size. Unread Mail, as you might expect, finds all unread messages.

In Figure 13.1, the Categorized Mail Search Folder in the Navigation Pane is selected. The Message List displays all of the messages in the Personal Folders PST file, and the Reading Pane shows the message selected in that list. If the Delete key was pressed, this message would be deleted just as if that action had been performed in the actual mail folder in which the message was filed.

Predefined Search Folders

Figure 13.1. Outlook 2007 includes three predefined Search Folders.

Of the three, I find the Large Mail Search Folder to be the most helpful. As mentioned earlier in this book and covered in greater depth in Chapter 25, anything you can do to trim the size of your Outlook PST files contributes to better performance and reliability. Large mail attachments are one the biggest reasons PST files grow at a sometimes alarming rate, often without you even being aware it is happening.

While the default setting for the Large Mail Search Folder is 100K, that number represents only the minimum threshold Outlook uses to populate the Search Folder. You can easily adjust the threshold used to characterize a message (including its attachments) as "large" if you like.

When you select the Large Mail Search Folder, Outlook performs a quick search and displays all files larger than 100K in size. I recommend you set the Message List filter for this Search Folder to group items, which organizes files into groups that you can collapse or expand in the Message List.

To set the Message List view to organize in groups, right-click on the Arranged by: Date bar just below the Instant Search field and select Show in Groups from the context menu, as shown in Figure 13.2. You can then use the small plus (+) or minus (-) sign in the

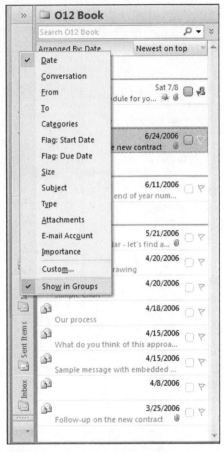

Figure 13.2. Select the Show in Groups command to organize items into groups in the Message List.

group header to expand or collapse that group. You can also collapse and expand the selected group or all groups from the View menu.

Bright Idea

Use the Large Mail Search Folder to find all of the big file attachments that may be lurking in your Outlook PST file. When you review these large messages, save a copy of the attachment to a folder on your hard disk and remove it from the e-mail message to reduce the size of your PST file.

Predefined Search Folders

The built-in Search Folders that Microsoft includes in your Outlook 2007 installation are a good start, but there are many ways to use Search Folders to give you powerful tools to look at your mail messages in more useful ways than is possible using standard folders. Outlook provides a number of predefined Search Folders to make creating additional Search Folders fast and easy. You can also create a completely custom Search Folder to meet a specific need.

To create a new Search Folder, choose Search Folder from the New drop-down menu on the toolbar in any main view, shown in Figure 13.3, use the keyboard shortcut Ctrl+Shift+P, or right-click Search Folders in the mail folder list.

Performing any of these actions opens the New Search Folder dialog box shown in Figure 13.4. The complete list of predefined Search Folders listed in the dialog box are:

Reading Mail

- Unread mail
- Mail flagged for follow-up

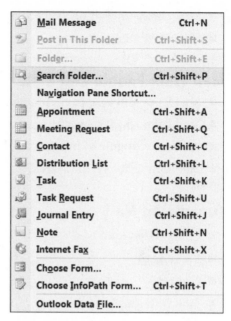

Figure 13.3. The New menu lists all of the data objects you can create in Outlook including Search Folder.

Figure 13.4. The New Search Folder dialog box.

- Mail either unread or flagged for follow-up
- Important mail

Mail from People and Lists

- Mail from and to specific people
- Mail from specific people
- Mail sent directly to me
- Mail sent to distribution lists

Organizing Mail

- Categorized mail
- Large mail
- Old mail
- Mail with attachments
- Mail with specific words

Custom

- Create a custom Search Folder

You can see the number of potential applications there are for Search Folders by reviewing this list. I use "Mail from specific people" to set up Search Folders for my most frequent and important correspondents — my boss, my wife, and my kids. "Categorized mail" folders lets me sort all mail messages with a specific category tag into a single consolidated view. And "Mail with attachments" is incredibly useful to find those space-hogging attached files hiding in my mail folders.

Setting up these predefined Search Folders is easy. For example, to create a folder that collects all mail from a specific person, open the New Search Folder dialog box from the New menu on the toolbar by pressing

---

Watch Out!

Search Folders are specific to individual PST files and cannot search across multiple files. If you use multiple PST files that contain information you'd like to access using Search Folders, you will need to create one for each PST file you want to search.

Ctrl+Shift+P or by right-clicking Search Folders in the mail folder list. In the dialog box, shown in Figure 13.5, select the Mail from specific people template from the list and either enter the person's name in the field at the bottom of the dialog box or click Choose to open a contact picker that allows you to find one or more people in your contacts list. Select the PST file you want to add the Search Folder to (applicable only if you use more than one PST file) and click OK. Your new Search Folder will be created and selected in the Folder List, displaying all matching items.

Figure 13.5. Creating a Search Folder for mail from a specific person.

Creating a custom Search Folder

Creating a custom Search Folder, while not quite as simple as using one of the predefined folders, is a relatively straightforward process and one that can produce very specific results. The Search Folder Criteria dialog box provides three tabs that allow you to select from and combine attributes of e-mail messages to zero in on the information you are looking for.

Follow these steps to create a custom Search Folder.

1. Open the New Search Folder dialog box from the New menu on the toolbar by pressing Ctrl+Shift+P or by right-clicking Search Folders in the mail folder list.

2. Scroll to the bottom of the list of predefined templates.

3. Select Custom ⇨ Create a custom Search Folder and click Choose. The Custom Search Folder dialog box shown in Figure 13.6 opens.

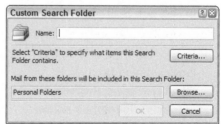

Figure 13.6. Custom Search Folder dialog box.

4. Enter a name for the new Search Folder.

5. Click Criteria to open the Search Folder Criteria dialog box shown in Figure 13.7 that displays the three criteria tabs mentioned earlier. Select the appropriate criteria from each of the tabs and click OK. The Messages tab, shown selected in Figure 13.7, contains criteria related specifically to sending and receiving messages. The More Choices tab, shown in Figure 13.8, contains criteria related to the state of all data objects, including category tags, attachments, priority, follow-up flags, and size. The Advanced tab, shown in Figure 13.9, provides access to every field of information in all Outlook objects and can be used to define very sophisticated filters. When you have selected the criteria you want to apply to the new Search Folder, click OK.

6. In the main Custom Search Folder dialog box, click Browse to open the Select Folder(s) dialog box shown

Figure 13.7. The Messages tab in the Search Folder Criteria dialog box relates to who sent and received messages.

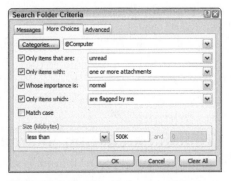

Figure 13.8. The More Choices tab relates to the state of messages.

Figure 13.9. The Advanced tab allows you to build sophisticated filters using every field of information in Outlook.

in Figure 13.10. By default, Outlook assumes you want to search all of your primary PST files (Personal Folders), including all subfolders.

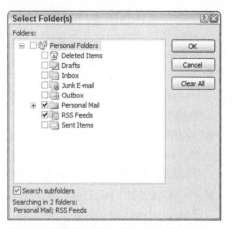

Modifying a Search Folder

You may find over time that you need to make adjustments to the criteria you have selected for a Search Folder. To do this, right-click the Search Folder you want to adjust and select the

Figure 13.10. The Select Folder(s) dialog box allows you to specify in which folders the Search Folder operates.

Customize this Search Folder command, as shown in Figure 13.11.

When you select a Search Folder you created from one of the predefined selections built into Outlook, you can modify the folder only within the parameters of the original definition. For example, if you had defined a Search Folder using the Mail from and to specific people option, the only adjustment possible is the person or people used as criteria for that search. This limitation does not apply to custom Search Folders, which can be freely modified in every way.

Figure 13.11. The Customize this Search Folder command can be accessed by right-clicking any Search Folder.

Just the facts

- Search Folders allow you to use predefined templates or custom settings to find mail messages in a specific folder or in an entire PST file.

- Search Folders do not actually contain any messages — they provide a view of all messages that match the criteria you have defined regardless of where they may be stored.

- Deleting a message from a Search Folder deletes the actual message, but deleting a Search Folder deletes only the folder, not its contents.

- Search Folders provide a handy tool for finding old mail messages or messages with large file attachments you can delete or archive to reduce the size of your primary PST file.

- Search Folders allow you to view messages in a variety of contexts — the same message might appear in a number of different Search Folders whose criteria it matches.

- Outlook 2007 provides an extensive selection of predefined Search Folders you can customize with a few mouse clicks.

- Custom Search Folders can be fine-tuned to find a very specific set of messages.

- You can modify a Search Folder once it has been created. Search Folders created using the predefined templates can be adjusted only within the confines of their original type of search. Custom Search Folders may be freely edited in any way you like.

GET THE SCOOP ON...
Modifying Outlook default view layouts ▪ Creating
custom views ▪ Special considerations for
custom views ▪ Customizing toolbars ▪
Outlook Today ▪ Custom Print Styles

Customizing Outlook Views

Chapter 14

As you saw in Part II, Outlook provides an extensive range of layouts for each of the main views in the application. Some of these layouts are graphical while others are list views that display information textually. Although the predefined views installed by default in Outlook are extensive, you may want to change the way information is organized and presented to better suit your preferences.

There are any number of reasons why you might want to adjust how Outlook displays and formats information. For example, I don't particularly care to see overdue tasks displayed in red, so I have adjusted my Tasks views to turn off the default coloring of overdue tasks defined in the Automatic Formatting rules. I also like to be able to see all tasks in every view of my Outlook environment that have a due date assigned and that have not been marked complete. So I have created a custom layout for the To-Do Bar that shows me that subset of my Tasks list.

The first part of this chapter discusses how the default layouts in Outlook's main views can be modified to better suit your work style. The second part of this chapter explores the many customization options you can use to modify the predefined layouts or create entirely new ones for Outlook's main views. The third part of this chapter discusses how to modify Outlook's toolbars by adding, removing, and rearranging icons that link to commands. The fourth and final portion of this chapter discusses Outlook Print Styles, which provide a variety of ways to view your information on paper.

Modifying Outlook's default view layouts

You can modify the predefined layouts in Outlook in a number of ways by choosing how the information in these layouts is sorted, filtered, and grouped. These changes can be made using a variety of techniques directly from Outlook's menus and toolbars.

As you switch from one main view to another in Outlook, the Navigation Pane can display a list of predefined layouts in every view except the Mail view, which displays the mail message folder list. In Mail view, you can select from the predefined layouts by choosing View ⇨ Current View and then selecting one of the layouts listed, as shown in Figure 14.1.

This same list of mail layouts can also be accessed by clicking the Advanced toolbar's Current View button, as shown in Figure 14.2. This control is available in all of Outlook's main views and is a quick way to switch between layouts, especially when the Navigation Pane is collapsed.

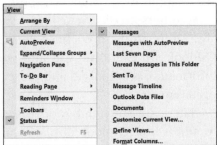

Figure 14.1. Use the View menu's Current View option to change the layout of the Mail view.

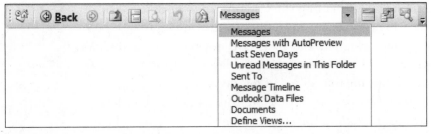

Figure 14.2. The Current View button on the Advanced toolbar provides quick access to all predefined layouts in any main view.

Inside Scoop

You can show or hide the predefined layouts and any custom views you define by choosing View ⇨ Navigation Pane from the menu bar and toggling the display on or off. You can also control the display of views by right-clicking the Navigation Pane when it is visible and minimized.

A third technique for switching between predefined layouts is to right-click the bar at the top of the list in any view where the column headers such as Category, Size, and Date are displayed. This opens the same menu accessed from the View menu and is shown in Figure 14.3. The predefined layouts are found on the Arrange By submenu.

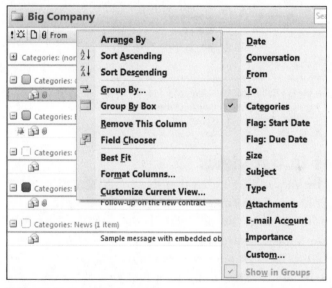

Figure 14.3. Access the Current View menu by right-clicking the column bar at the top of a list view.

The Calendar view has an additional option that controls the visibility of the Daily Task List in Day and Week views. When the Calendar view is active, a menu option labeled Daily Task List is added to the View menu, as shown in Figure 14.4. This submenu provides control over visibility and how tasks are sorted and displayed in the Calendar Day and Week views.

Watch Out!
Accessing the menu shown in Figure 14.3 is only possible when the Reading Pane is hidden. When the Reading Pane is displayed, right-clicking the bar at the top of the list pane shows only the predefined layout Arrange By menu, not the full Current View menu.

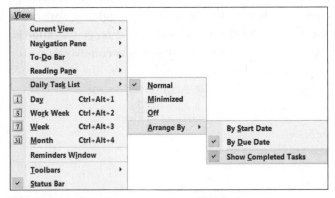

Figure 14.4. Use the View menu's Daily Task List view option to control the visibility and appearance of tasks in Day and Week view.

Sorting items in list views

At the top of every list view is the sort bar that shows the name of each column of information displayed. Common columns included in the predefined list view layouts include Subject, Start and Due Date, Categories, and Folder. You can add, remove, and rearrange columns in any list view using the Field Chooser dialog box shown in Figure 14.5. This dialog box can be opened by clicking the Field Chooser button on the Advanced toolbar, which, by default, is the next-to-last button on the toolbar. You can also access the Field Chooser dialog box by right-clicking the sort bar.

Figure 14.5. The Field Chooser dialog box.

When the Field Chooser dialog box is open, you can drag new fields onto the sort bar from the list in the dialog box, remove any existing columns by dragging them off the sort bar (the field displays a large "X" when dragged off the bar), or rearrange the order in which columns appear by dragging them to a new position on the sort bar.

Sort using column headers

You can sort items in list views by clicking the column header you want to sort by in the sort bar or by right-clicking the sort bar to display the Arrange By menu. Click the column header a second time to toggle the sort order between ascending or descending. This can also be done on the Arrange By menu that displays Sort Ascending and Sort Descending commands.

Sort using the Group By box

You can also perform sophisticated sorting of items in a list using the Group By box, pictured in Figure 14.6, which can be displayed by clicking the Group By button on the Advanced toolbar. This button appears, by default, immediately to the left of the Current View button. When the Group By box is displayed at the top of the list view, you can drag and drop any column header to the box to add it as a sorting criterion.

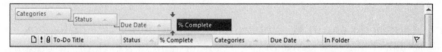

Figure 14.6. The Group By box allows you to drag and drop column headers to create sophisticated sort orders.

In Figure 14.6, the Group By box is sorting items in the Tasks view using the following criteria: Categories, Status, and Due Date. A fourth criterion, % Complete, is added. Note the arrows that indicate where in the sort order this criterion is added. As you add additional column headers to the Group By box, the display of items in the list resorts based on the new formula. You can drag and drop headers in the Group By box to dynamically resort the list items as you prefer. To remove a column header from the Group By box, drag it out of the Group By box and back to the sort bar.

Advanced customization

In addition to the toolbar, menu, and right-clicking techniques you can use to modify the predefined layouts in Outlook, the Customize View dialog box, shown in Figure 14.7, provides access to a complete set of controls that can be used to perform all of the changes I have just described, perform advanced layout customizations, or design a completely new layout. This dialog box can be a bit overwhelming when you first use it because it presents a set of buttons that each open an additional dialog box.

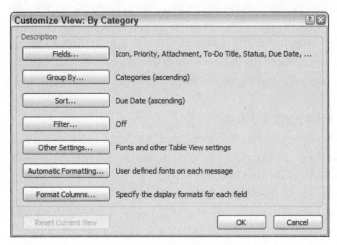

Figure 14.7. The Customize View dialog box provides access to a wide range of controls.

Despite the apparent complexity of the Customize View dialog box, it is actually quite easy to use once you understand how each of the options it provides affects your current or new layout. With a bit of practice and experimentation, you can define exactly how you want information to be displayed in any view in Outlook.

The Customize View dialog box can be opened from the View ⇨ Current View ⇨ Customize Current View menu option, or by right-clicking the sort bar in any list view and selecting the Customize Current View command. You can also modify an existing layout in the view you are currently working in by selecting the View ⇨ Current View ⇨ Define Views menu option, which opens the Custom View Organizer dialog box shown in Figure 14.8. Select the layout you want to adjust from the list and click Modify to open the Customize View dialog box. The Custom View Organizer dialog box shows all of the available layouts in the main view you are currently in. Figure 14.8 shows the list for the Tasks view.

Figure 14.8. The Custom View Organizer dialog box.

If you want to create a new layout, click New in the Custom View Organizer dialog box. The first step in creating a new layout is to make selections in the Create a New View dialog box shown in Figure 14.9. Enter a name for the new view and select from the list of layout templates presented. The Table layout is the most common choice when creating a new view. Then select one of the three options that affects who can use the new view you are creating. This applies only if you work in a Microsoft Exchange or Microsoft SharePoint Server environment.

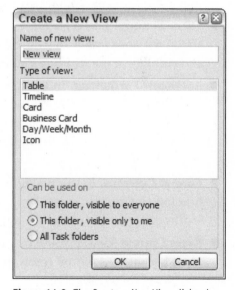

Figure 14.9. The Create a New View dialog box.

The Customize View dialog box

In the Customize View dialog box, you are presented with a set of buttons, each of which opens a second dialog box. A brief description of the items you can define or modify in each of these dialog boxes is shown to the right of the button.

- **Fields.** In this dialog box, you can select which fields appear in the view and in what order. This dialog box mirrors the actions you can perform with the Field Chooser dialog box shown in Figure 14.5.

- **Group By.** In this dialog box, you can select how items are grouped. This dialog box allows you to perform the same actions as the Group By box.

- **Sort.** In this dialog box, you can select the criteria used to determine how items are sorted. This dialog box allows you to define a sequence of sorting criteria not available working in the list view itself.

- **Filter.** Using filters, you can control what items are visible based on their characteristics. Filtering can only be done from this dialog box and provides an extraordinary level of control over what information is displayed in a view.

- **Other Settings.** This dialog box contains a variety of controls that affects the appearance of your view, including fonts, AutoPreview, and visibility of the Reading Pane.

- **Automatic Formatting.** In this dialog box, you can select which rules are used to automatically format items depending on their state. Outlook includes a number of predefined rules you can modify or turn on and off on a view-by-view basis. You can also create your own custom formatting rules.

- **Format Columns.** In this dialog box, you can set preferences for how information is displayed in each column, dictate how column widths are set, and control the alignment of text.

- **Reset Current View.** If you have made changes to one of the predefined layouts, this button resets that layout to its default settings.

Fields

The Show Fields dialog box, shown in Figure 14.10, provides access to every field Outlook can display. The appearance of this field varies depending on which main view you are working in. Some views, such as a list view in Tasks, can use more fields than a Day/Week/Month view in the Calendar. In general, the Show Fields dialog box defaults to a selection of fields labeled Frequently-used fields that lists the most common fields for the main view and layout you are customizing or creating. You can also select from lists of all fields organized by types, including Info/Status, Date/Time, All Mail fields, and other choices as shown in the drop-down menu in Figure 14.10.

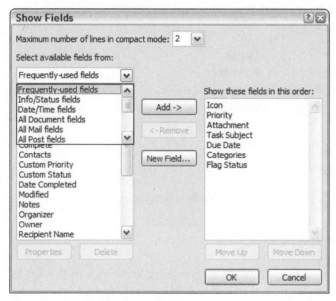

Figure 14.10. The Show Fields dialog box.

To add a field to the view, select it in the list on the left and click Add. To remove a field from the layout, select it in the list on the right and click Remove. Change the order in which fields are displayed by selecting the field in the list on the right and clicking the Move Up or Move Down button below the list to change its position. If you require a field that is not already defined in Outlook, click the New Field button in the center of the dialog box and provide a name, data type, and format options in the New Field dialog box.

Group By

The Group By dialog box, shown in Figure 14.11, allows you to select up to four fields to use in cascading order to arrange items in a list. When you apply multiple levels of grouping to items, each successive attribute is used to further separate and organize items, which match the attribute above. In the example shown in Figure 14.11, I have created a Group By setting that organizes the Tasks list first by Categories, then by Due Date, then by % Complete, and finally by Priority.

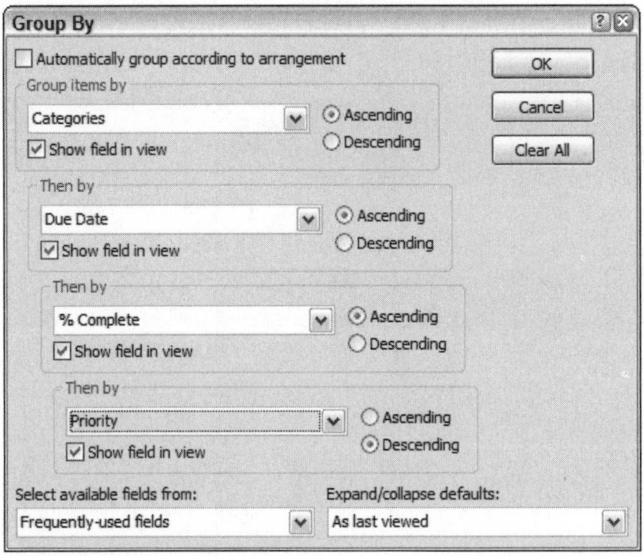

Figure 14.11. The Group By dialog box.

You can show or hide each of these grouping attributes in the list by selecting the Show field in view check box. When this option is selected, a separator bar appears in the list that contains a plus/minus sign that allows you to expand or collapse the view of all items matching the grouping attribute. Each subsequent level of grouping is indented from the left edge of the list pane, providing a visual representation of the grouping hierarchy you have defined for the view. Two radio buttons next to each grouping attribute allow you to select between ascending or descending sort orders.

At the top of this dialog box is a check box labeled Automatically group according to arrangement. Selecting this option overrides any settings in the dialog box and honors the arrangement you have created in the list view itself using right-click commands and field arrangements performed with the Field Chooser dialog box. You must deselect this check box to make changes in this dialog box.

At the bottom of this dialog box are two drop-down menus. The Select available fields from: menu allows you to choose from groupings of fields in similar fashion to the drop-down menu shown in the Show Fields dialog box in Figure 14.10. The groupings include the default choice of Frequently-used fields, Info/Status fields, Date/Time fields, and other sets of fields. The Expand/collapse defaults: menu controls the default for the expanded or collapsed view of items in the view. The default setting is As last viewed. The other options are All expanded and All collapsed.

Sort

The Sort dialog box, shown in Figure 14.12, has a number of elements in common with the Group By dialog box and is used to establish a hierarchy of sorting attributes for your custom view. Like the drop-down field selection menus in the Group By and Filter dialog boxes, the menus in the Sort dialog box are populated according to what you select in the Select available fields from: menu at the bottom of the dialog box. In the example image, I am creating a Sort order for a custom Tasks view and have selected Due Date followed by Priority and then Status to organize the Tasks list. Like the Group By dialog box, the Sort dialog box allows you to select either an ascending or descending order for each criteria and provides a Clear All button to reset the dialog box to apply no actions.

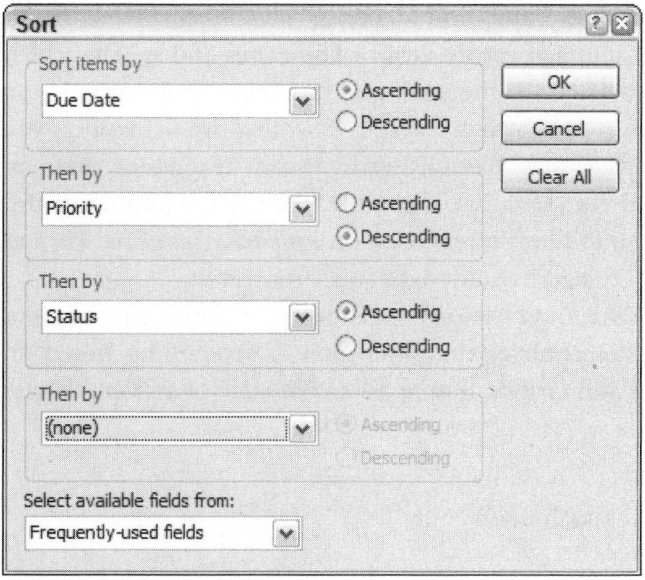

Figure 14.12. The Sort dialog box.

> **Watch Out!**
>
> When you define a custom view using both grouping and 'sorting settings, these operations are applied to the contents of the list you are viewing in that order. Because group and sort preferences can overlap or even conflict with each other, you can produce some "interesting" results. You might, for example, group by date descending and sort by date ascending and end up with an unsorted list as a result.

Filter

The Filter dialog box is the most powerful and complex of the dialog boxes available in Outlook for customizing a view. The Filter dialog box has four tabs that contain controls for filtering your list using virtually any item attribute. The first tab, shown in Figure 14.13, is specific to the main view you are working in. In this example, the tab is labeled Tasks. When creating a filter for a custom view in the Calendar, the tab would be labeled Appointments and Meetings.

Figure 14.13. The first tab in the Filter dialog box is labeled to reflect the main view you are customizing.

In this first tab, you can create keyword searches and specify which fields should be searched. In the example, this first tab also provides a field to filter based on the status of the task. The next two fields allow you to search for tasks that have been assigned to you (From) or that you have assigned to others (Sent To). The time fields at the bottom of this dialog box allow you to filter items based on time-based criteria, such as the date a task was created, modified, begun, or is due.

The next tab in the Filter dialog box, shown in Figure 14.14, is More Choices and provides controls that allow you to filter items based on assigned categories and criteria that apply to the state of an item. These options include:

- Read or unread
- With or without attachments
- Importance

- Flagged or unflagged
- Match case (of the keywords entered on the first tab)
- Size

The third tab in the Filter dialog box, shown in Figure 14.15, is Advanced. This tab allows you to construct complex filters by creating one or more condition statements, which can be combined to filter items with extraordinary precision. To build a condition statement, first select a field from the drop-down menu below the label that reads Define more criteria. Once you have selected a field, the Condition field displays a default value for the field you have just selected. Depending on the condition that the selected field defaults to, you may or may not need to assign a value in the final box. In the

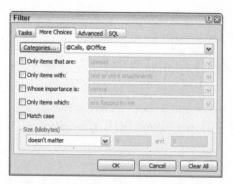

Figure 14.14. The More Choices tab in the Filter dialog box.

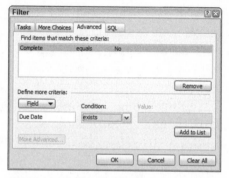

Figure 14.15. The Advanced tab in the Filter dialog box.

example, the field "Complete" has a default condition of "equals," and a default value of "No." Once the definition has been completed, click Add to List at the bottom of the dialog box, and that condition statement is added to the list box at the top of the dialog box.

To further refine the filter, you can add condition statements to the list. To remove a condition from the list, highlight the condition statement and click Remove. To reset the dialog box, click Clear All.

The final tab in the Filter dialog box is SQL. If you are familiar with structured query language and want to write your own filtering formula, you can enter it on this tab. By default, the SQL tab displays a structured query language statement that contains all of the criteria you have established using the controls in the Filter dialog box. At the bottom of this tab is a check box that reads Edit these criteria directly. If you choose to manually edit the SQL statement, the other tabs in the Filter dialog box are disabled.

Other Settings

The Other Settings dialog box, shown in Figure 14.16, provides a variety of controls for the display of your custom view. In this dialog box, you can choose the fonts used in columns and rows and how those fonts are displayed, whether or not gridlines should be used to separate items in the list, auto preview settings, whether the Reading Pane is displayed (and if so, where), and layout controls.

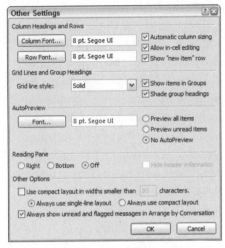

Figure 14.16. The Other Settings dialog box.

In the Column Headings and Rows section of the dialog box, there are three check box options. All three of these options are checked by default. Automatic column sizing tells Outlook to make its best guess about how wide each column in your custom layout should be. Allow in-cell editing makes it easy to correct or revise the text related to an individual item without having to open the item itself. Show "new item" row provides an easily accessed blank set of fields at the top of the list into which you can type to create a new item without opening a dialog box. When creating a new item using this new item row, you can navigate from field to field in the list layout using the tab or arrow keys. When you press Enter, the new item is added to your list. You can, of course, always open the item for further editing at any time.

Automatic Formatting

The Automatic Formatting dialog box, shown in Figure 14.17, includes six default formatting rules built into Outlook. You can make adjustments to any of these default formatting rules, create your own, turn rules on and off for a particular view, or delete a rule entirely.

To adjust one of the built-in rules, click on its name to highlight it. The Font button is active but the Condition button is not. You can modify the way Outlook formats items in the view that matches the criteria listed, but you cannot redefine the condition statement that defines these formatting rules.

To create a new automatic formatting rule, click Add and enter a descriptive name for the new rule. Click Font to show the Font

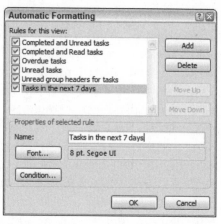

Figure 14.17. The Automatic Formatting dialog box.

dialog box pictured in Figure 14.18. In this dialog box, you can choose the font style and color item text that it is formatted with when meeting the criteria you establish for this rule. To set the actual criteria, click the Condition button and the Filter dialog box (described earlier in this chapter) is displayed. You can use the filtering capabilities to define precisely what conditions must be met for this formatting rule to be applied.

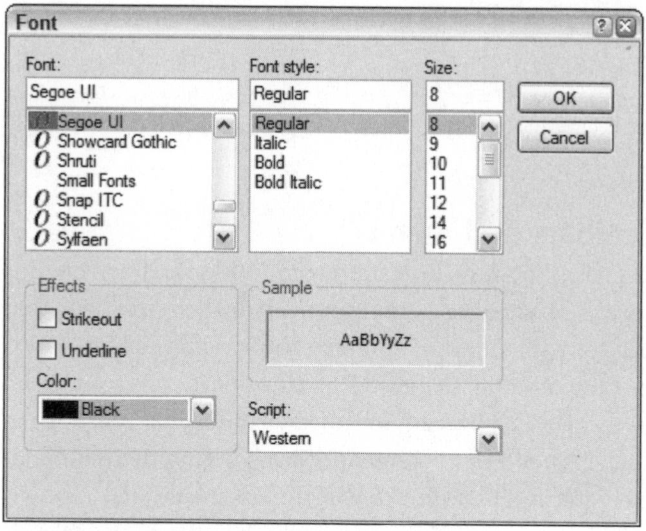

Figure 14.18. The Font dialog box.

Format Columns

The Format Columns dialog box shown in Figure 14.19 allows you to define how information is formatted and displayed in each column in a particular view. To redefine a column's format, click the column you want to modify in the list on the left, and the dialog box presents options that are available for that column and information type on the right. In this example, the Due Date column is highlighted, and options are provided to change the format of the date display, its label, the width of the column, and the alignment of text in the column.

As you can see, Outlook provides an extraordinary and rich set of tools that allows you to create an endless variety of customized views. Although the interface can be a bit intimidating, with some experimentation you can define views that meet your unique needs in no time at all.

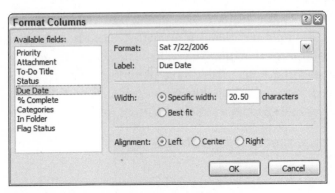

Figure 14.19. The Format Columns dialog box.

Customizing toolbars and menus

The process of modifying toolbars and menus in Outlook 2007 remains unchanged from previous versions. Outlook provides two toolbars that can be displayed in the main views: a Standard toolbar and an Advanced toolbar. Additional toolbars may be added by third-party programs that extend Outlook — a subject covered in Chapter 17. The position of these toolbars can be changed by clicking and dragging on the handle at the very left edge of each toolbar (the row of four vertical dots). To customize what is displayed on each of the toolbars, click the gray arrow at the right end of the toolbar to display a customization menu. Two choices are presented on this menu. The first displays the name of the toolbar with a submenu showing all of the standard buttons that can be shown or hidden on that toolbar, as shown in Figure 14.20.

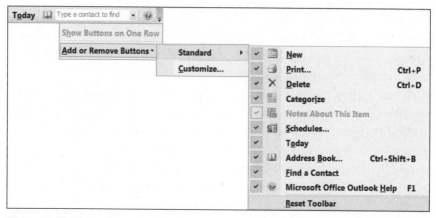

Figure 14.20. The toolbar customization menu.

Selecting the Customize command displays the Customize dialog box shown in Figure 14.21. Like the Filter dialog box, the Customize dialog box contains multiple tabs, each of which contains a set of customization options. The first tab, Toolbars, shows all of the toolbars that can be displayed in Outlook's main views. To make a toolbar visible, click the check box next to its name; to hide the toolbar, dese-

Figure 14.21. The Customize dialog box.

lect the check box next to its name. In this tab you can also create entirely new toolbars, or rename, delete, or reset an existing toolbar to its original configuration.

Inside Scoop

You can reset a toolbar to its default configuration at any time by selecting Reset Toolbar on the customization menu. All changes you have made to a toolbar are removed, including restoring any buttons you have hidden or removed and removing any new buttons you have added.

Creating a new toolbar

To create a new toolbar, click the New button on the Toolbars tab of the Customize dialog box. The New Toolbar dialog box, pictured in Figure 14.22, opens. Enter a name for the new toolbar and click OK.

Figure 14.22. The New Toolbar dialog box.

A new empty toolbar, shown in Figure 14.23, is displayed in the center of your screen next to the Customize dialog box. The next step in the process of creating a new toolbar is to populate it with commands. To do this, click the second tab, Commands, in the Customize dialog box. This tab, shown in Figure 14.24, displays a list of categories on the left side of the dialog box and a list of commands in

Figure 14.23. An empty toolbar, ready to have commands added.

each of those categories on the right. To add a command to a toolbar, click on a command in the list on the right and drag it to the new toolbar.

As you drag commands onto the new toolbar, you'll notice that some appear as icons and others may appear as text. You can control the state of each command you add to a toolbar by right-clicking its button or text label and adjusting its properties on the context menu. Figure 14.25 shows the sample Message Tools toolbar used in this example with a number of icon-based commands in place and a new command labeled Conversation" that is displayed by default as a text label.

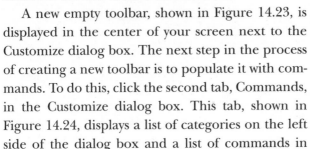

Figure 14.24. The Commands tab in the Customize dialog box.

Figure 14.25. The new button displayed in Text format.

Figure 14.27. Outlook includes a limited set of bitmap graphics you can use on custom toolbar buttons.

Figure 14.26. Right-click a button in Customize mode to display this context menu that provides controls to change the format and appearance of the button.

I prefer commands be displayed as buttons on my toolbars because they take up much less space and keep the toolbar as compact as possible. To change the display of the Conversation command, first right-click the text label of the command on the Message Tools toolbar, which displays the context menu shown in Figure 14.26. Select the Change Button Image menu option that displays a set of bitmap graphics you can select from, as shown in Figure 14.27. You can select one of these bitmap graphics to use as is or edit one of these button images using a simple set of tools accessed by selecting the Edit Button Image command, which opens the Button Editor dialog box shown in Figure 14.28. You

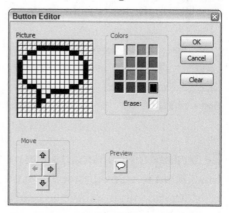

Figure 14.28. The Button Editor dialog box provides a simple set of pixel-editing tools to edit bitmap button images.

can also copy and paste a bitmap image from another toolbar into the button you are modifying.

After you have selected, and optionally edited, the button image, the final step in converting a default text label command to a graphic button is to right-click the toolbar and select the Default Style option as shown in Figure 14.29. Figure 14.30 shows the new Conversation button in its new graphic state inserted into the Message Tools toolbar.

Figure 14.29. Select the Default Style option to change a text button to a graphic button.

Any toolbar can be added to the toolbar dock at the top of the Outlook application window or dragged out of the dock and used as a floating window. To add the new Message Tools toolbar to the dock, drag it to the desired position in the dock and release the mouse button. Experiment with rearranging the toolbars, to see how they move out of the way as you drag a toolbar to a new position. Figure 14.31 shows the Message Tools toolbar added to the dock in the lower right.

Figure 14.30. The final result – a compact graphic button.

Figure 14.31. The new Message Tools toolbar added to the dock.

Rearranging commands on toolbars

In addition to all of the toolbar customizations discussed so far, Outlook provides you with the ability to rearrange commands on any of the default toolbars or menus in the application using the Rearrange Commands dialog box shown in Figure 14.32. This dialog box can be opened from the Commands tab of the Customize dialog box (see Figure 14.24).

Figure 14.32. The Rearrange Commands dialog box.

At the top of the dialog box are two radio buttons that allow you to select either a menu or a toolbar to customize. Use the drop-down menu next to either option to select the specific menu or toolbar you want to rearrange. In the example, the Standard toolbar is selected, and the Mark as Unread command is selected. Controls in the Rearrange Commands dialog box allow you to perform a variety of actions on the selected menu command using the buttons on the right side of the dialog box. Figure 14.32 shows the Modify Selection submenu.

Hack

Notice in the Rearrange Commands dialog box that an ampersand (&) precedes the letter "n" in the Mark as Unread menu command. This tells Outlook to assign Alt+N to this command as a keyboard shortcut. You can add, remove, or redefine these keyboard commands by changing where the ampersand appears.

General toolbar options

The third tab in the Customize dialog box, shown in Figure 14.33, is Options and provides controls that affect the behavior and appearance of all toolbars and menus in Outlook. These controls are organized in two sections: Personalized Menus and Toolbars, and Other.

Personalized Menus and Toolbars is a somewhat controversial feature introduced in prior versions of Microsoft Office that attempted to simplify the display of menus and toolbars by showing only a small selection of items until you clicked a button at the bottom of a menu or at the end of a toolbar to reveal all of the items available. By watching your behavior, Office would learn, over time, which commands and menu options you used most frequently and would personalize the display for you.

Figure 14.33. The Options tab in the Customize dialog box.

This turned out to be a rather unpopular feature and one that confused many Office users. The Office UI team listened to customer feedback and has changed the default setting for this feature to "off." If you are one of the minority of Office users who prefers the truncated, personalized menus, the feature is still available — you simply have to turn it on in this tab of the Customize dialog box. The other options in the dialog box are self-explanatory.

Outlook Today

Outlook Today is a page that can be customized to present information about your e-mail messages, tasks, and appointments on a single page. You can access the Outlook Today page by clicking the Personal Folders icon in the Folder List view or in the Mail view's folder list.

Like the other views in Outlook, the Outlook Today screen can be customized to present the information you prefer to see in a variety of layouts. On the Outlook Today screen is a link labeled Customize Outlook Today. Clicking this link opens the screen shown in Figure 14.34.

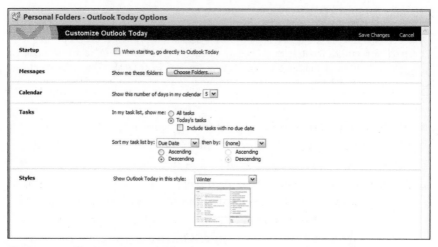

Figure 14.34. The Customize Outlook Today screen.

The Customize Outlook Today screen is divided into five sections:

■ **Startup.** Select the check box to make Outlook Today the default view when you first launch Outlook.

■ **Messages.** Click the Choose Folders button to select which e-mail folders are listed on the Outlook Today page. By default, your Personal Folders Inbox, Drafts, and Outbox folders are selected, but you can remove any of these folders or add any other folders you'd like. If you set up Outlook Rules to automatically route messages from specific senders or that contain specific keywords into new folders, it can be useful to summarize those destination folders on the Outlook Today screen. Outlook Rules are covered in Chapter 15.

■ **Calendar.** Use the drop-down menu to select how many days from today's date you want to have displayed on the Outlook Today screen. All appointments (both timed and all-day events) are listed.

■ **Tasks.** Use the radio buttons to select whether all tasks or just the current day's tasks are displayed on the Outlook Today screen. If you select the check box labeled Include tasks with no dates, the list can get extremely long, depending on the number of undated tasks you have on your lists. Below this set of controls is a second set of filters to control how tasks are sorted for display. You can set two criteria and decide whether to sort in ascending or descending order.

Hack

You can select any Outlook view as the default when you first launch the application from the Options dialog box accessed on the Tools menu. Select the Other tab and click Advanced Options. The first option in this dialog box allows you to choose which folder (main view) you want to see when Outlook is launched.

■ **Styles.** Outlook provides a selection of predefined styles for the Outlook Today page. There are a number of Web sites that offer customized designs for the Outlook Today page, which is, in essence, an HTML-generated Web page. Some of these page designs are little more than different visual treatments of the information described here. Others use VBScript (a scripting language used to create macros in Outlook and other Office applications) to produce more informative displays. Use your favorite search engine to conduct a search for "customize Outlook Today page" and you will find many examples.

Custom Print Styles

Depending on the view you are working in, Outlook provides one or more formats — called Print Styles — that allow you to control how the information you are viewing appears when printed. Like every other aspect of the application discussed in this chapter, Outlook Print Styles can be customized to meet your specific requirements.

When you invoke the Print command in Outlook, the Print dialog box, shown in Figure 14.35, is displayed. If you are like most Outlook users, you probably print e-mail messages more frequently than any other type of information in your Outlook Personal Folders and are probably accustomed to seeing two print styles listed: Table Style and Memo Style.

What you may not have noticed or investigated are the two buttons that appear to the right of the Print style list in this dialog box. And, if you have never or only rarely printed information from other views, you may not realize that Outlook Print Styles go beyond these two options. When you invoke the Print command from the Calendar view, you are provided with a much greater variety of Print Styles appropriate to printing calendar information. These styles are shown in Figure 14.36.

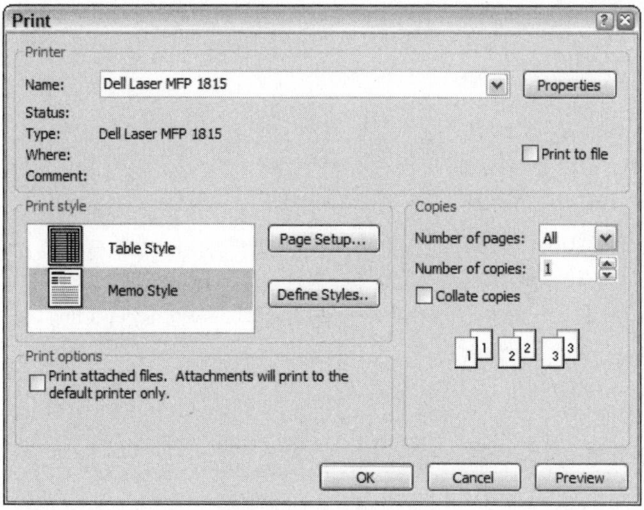

Figure 14.35. The Print dialog box in Mail view.

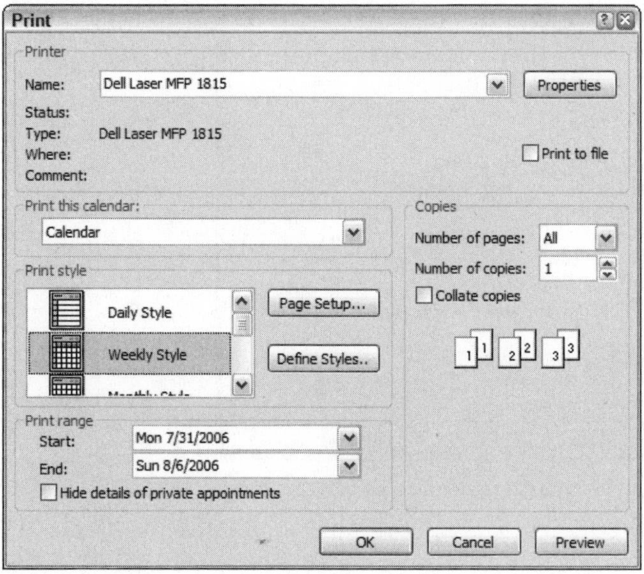

Figure 14.36. The Print dialog box in Calendar view.

To modify one of the existing styles or create a new one, click Define Styles. This opens the Define Print Styles dialog box shown in Figure 14.37. To modify one of the existing styles, select the style you want to customize in the Print style list and click Edit. To create a new Print Style, select the style you want to use as the basis for your new style and click Copy.

In either case, the Page Setup dialog box, shown in Figure 14.38, is displayed. This dialog box contains three tabs: Format, Paper, and Header/Footer. The Format tab changes based on the main Outlook view you are working in. The Paper and Header/Footer tabs are the same for all views. This example shows the Format tab for the Calendar view.

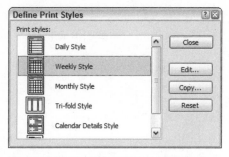

Figure 14.37. The Define Print Styles dialog box.

Figure 14.38. The Format tab in the Page Setup dialog box.

Note that you can preview how your information prints out by clicking Print Preview at the bottom of the dialog box. You can also issue a Print command directly from this dialog box.

To delete a custom Print Style, select it from the list in the Define Print Styles dialog box and click Delete. To reset Print Styles to their default state, select any of the default styles in the list and click Reset. You also can select a Print Style or access the Define Print Styles dialog box from the menu bar by selecting File ⇨ Page Setup.

Watch Out!
Clicking Reset resets all default styles to their original state. There is no way to reset only a single style to its default state other than to edit its properties in the Page Setup dialog box.

Just the facts

- Outlook provides an extensive set of tools and commands that allow you to customize many aspects of the application and how it presents controls and information.

- Show or hide the available view layouts in any main Outlook view by clicking the expand or collapse icon above the view list in the Navigation Pane when it is expanded or by right-clicking the Navigation Pane when it is collapsed.

- The Calendar view in Outlook 2007 adds a new view option — the Daily Task List that can be used in either Day or Week views of the Calendar. You can control the visibility of the Daily Tasks List from the View menu.

- You can select any view in Outlook or create a new custom view in the Custom View Organizer dialog box, which can be opened from the View menu.

- The Customize View dialog box provides one-click access to dialog boxes related to fields, grouping, sorting, filtering, and formatting.

- You can customize Outlook toolbars and menus to display the commands you use most frequently.

- Toolbars can be docked at the top of the application window or dragged out of the dock to display as floating toolbars.

- Toolbar commands can be easily rearranged by dragging and dropping when the Rearrange Commands dialog box is open.

- Outlook Today is an HTML-generated page that shows information about messages, appointments, and tasks on a single screen.

- Custom Print Styles allow you to control exactly how your mail messages, calendar, tasks lists, and other information appears when you print it.

GET THE SCOOP ON...
"Auto-magically" processing incoming e-mail messages ▪
Creating Outlook rules ▪ Modifying Outlook rules ▪
Third-party applications for automating and organizing
your e-mail

Automating Outlook E-Mail with Rules

Chapter 15

In the *Batman* comics and movies, Bruce Wayne has Alfred — a butler and companion who anticipates his master's needs and helps make his life simpler and less cluttered. Wouldn't you like to have an e-mail butler to review your incoming messages and automatically put them in the appropriate folder for you to review? This chapter introduces you to Outlook Rules, a powerful tool that allows you to set specific criteria for incoming messages, and define actions to be performed on messages that match those criteria.

Rules have been included in Outlook for some time but improve with every version as the defining criteria and actions that can be performed are enhanced by new features. The addition of color categories, improved flags, and other features in Outlook 2007 enhance what you can accomplish with rules.

Processing incoming messages "auto-magically"

One way to avoid the "Inbox trap" of messages stacking up more quickly than you can handle them is to create a set of folders for your most important and frequent correspondents, and others for information you are interested in but that is not as critical, such as newsletters and marketing

Bright Idea

The combination of Outlook Rules and Search Folders is very powerful. Use Rules to route incoming messages to the location you desire and Search Folders to provide a consolidated view of messages that match a certain set of criteria. As discussed in Chapter 13, Search Folders makes the actual location of a message much less critical.

promotions. Many people accomplish this sorting task by manually dragging new messages into these folders. With Outlook Rules, you can automate this process and save valuable time. Although the most common application for Rules is to process newly arrived messages, you can define a rule and apply it to existing messages in your Outlook environment as well.

Creating an Outlook rule

You can use two techniques to create a new rule in Outlook. If you need to quickly create a simple rule, the Create Rule dialog box provides a quick and easy set of options. If you need a more complex rule or want to do more than what Create Rule provides, Outlook's Rules Wizard provides an exhaustive list of options to create highly customized rules.

The Create Rule dialog box

To create a simple e-mail rule, right-click an e-mail in the message list and select the Create Rule command from the context menu. The Create Rule dialog box, pictured in Figure 15.1, opens.

Create Rule	? ⊠
When I get e-mail with all of the selected conditions	
☑ From Bob Smith (bob.smith@bigco.com)	⌄
☐ Subject contains Follow-up on the new contract	
Do the following	
☐ Display in the New Item Alert window	
☐ Play a selected sound: Windows XP Notify.w ▶ ▪ Browse...	
☑ Move the item to folder: Big Company Select Folder...	
OK Cancel Advanced Options...	

Figure 15.1. The Create Rule dialog box.

Outlook uses information from the message you selected to populate the first two information fields. In Figure 15.1, you see that the From and Subject fields in the top section of the dialog box have been filled in with Bob Smith's name and the subject line of the e-mail I selected. Click the check box for one or both of these criteria to establish the conditions that must be met to invoke the rule. If you select both the From and Subject criteria, a new message must meet both conditions for the rule to be applied.

In the lower section of the dialog box, under the heading Do the following, you can choose one or more actions that will be performed when a message meeting the criteria you have selected arrives. You can choose to:

- Display a New Item Alert
- Play a sound
- Move the message to a specific folder

When you click OK, Outlook presents a Success notification dialog box and asks if you want to apply the rule you have just created to messages in the current folder.

The Rules and Alerts dialog box

When you need to produce a more complex rule than what's possible with the Create Rules dialog box or you need rules to perform more complex operations on new messages, it's time to use Outlook's Rules Wizard. The Rules Wizard provides access to an exhaustive list of Outlook actions that can be performed on e-mail messages and an equally exhaustive list of criteria you can use to precisely pinpoint those messages that a rule should operate on.

You can access the Rules Wizard in one of three ways:

- Select Rules and Alerts from the Tools menu.
- Click the Rules and Alerts button on the Advanced toolbar.
- Click the Advanced Options button in the Create Rule dialog box.

When you invoke the Rules and Alerts command using either of the first two options above, the Rules and Alerts dialog box, pictured in Figure 15.2, is displayed. This dialog box is the starting point for creating, editing, and applying Outlook Rules. If you access the Rules Wizard from the Create Rule dialog box by clicking the Advanced Options button, the Rules and Alerts dialog box is bypassed and you enter directly into the first screen of the wizard.

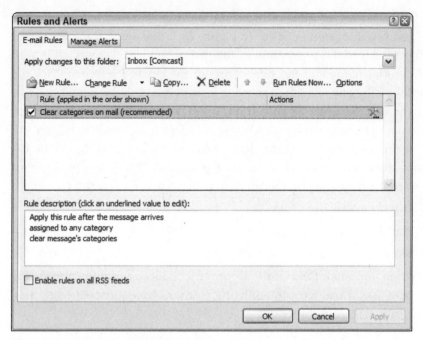

Figure 15.2. The Rules and Alerts dialog box.

At the top of the dialog box is a drop-down menu that lists which folders you want to apply the changes you make to.

The command bar just below this menu provides action buttons to:

- Create a new rule
- Change an existing rule
- Copy a rule to apply it to a new folder
- Delete a rule
- Change a rule's position in the stacking order using the up and down arrow icons (rules are run in sequential order and the sequencing can affect your results)
- Run rules manually using the Run Rules Now control
- Import or export rules (Options)

Below the list of rules is a description field that displays the criteria defined in the selected rule and the actions that will be performed on messages that match those criteria. At the bottom of the dialog box is a check box that allows you to enable rules for RSS feeds — a new preference in Outlook 2007.

Watch Out!
The option to apply rules to RSS feeds is an all-or-none setting. You cannot selectively apply rules to individual RSS feeds in Outlook 2007.

The Rules Wizard

When you click the New Rule action button on the command bar or modify an existing rule, the Rules Wizard is launched. The Rules Wizard dialog box, shown in Figure 15.3, provides a list of predesigned templates for rules under the headings Stay Organized, Stay Up to Date, and Start from a blank rule. The predesigned rules templates are a great way to get started with using Outlook Rules and address many of the common actions you may want to automate in Outlook. For maximum flexibility and the greatest degree over control of your rules, beginning with a blank rule is the best option.

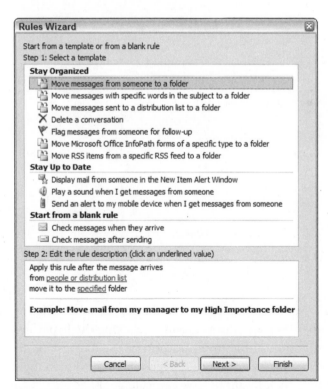

Figure 15.3. The Rules Wizard dialog box's opening screen.

After you have selected a template or decided to create an entirely new rule, the wizard displays a sequence of four screens that guide you through the process of building or modifying a rule. In the first of these screens, pictured in Figure 15.4, you select the conditions that must be met by a message for the rule to apply. A series of check box items are presented in a scrolling list in the top portion of the dialog box. As you select an item, it is added to a list displayed in the lower portion of the Wizard dialog box, where you edit the settings of each condition you have added.

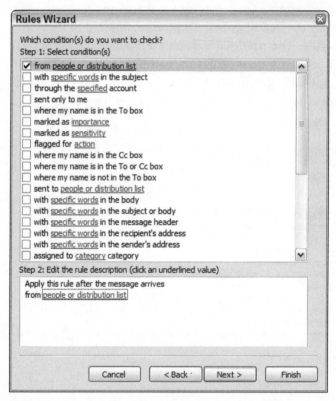

Figure 15.4. The first screen in the Rules Wizard — conditions.

After you have selected the conditions you want to use as criteria for the rule, edit the properties for each condition by clicking the hyperlink displayed for each condition in the lower portion of the dialog box. In Figure 15.4, you can see that I have selected from people or distribution list as the condition for which I want to have this rule apply.

In the second screen of the wizard, shown in Figure 15.5, you define the actions you want to have performed on the messages that match the conditions you selected in the previous screen. In this figure, I have selected the action labeled move it to the specified folder. In the lower portion of the dialog box, you can see that I have selected Jane Doe from The Big Company as the person whose e-mail I want this rule applied to.

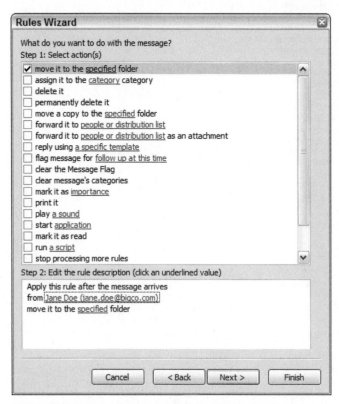

Figure 15.5. The second screen in the Rules Wizard — actions.

The third screen in the wizard, pictured in Figure 15.6, provides a list of exceptions that can be applied to the condition and action choices made in the previous two steps. In this illustration, I have chosen to exempt meeting invitations and updates from being routed to the Big Company folder (as you can see in the lower portion of the dialog box). If you work in an environment where you receive Outlook-generated meeting requests, you may want to do the same when you create rules that move messages out of the Inbox so you don't miss an invitation or schedule change pertaining to an important meeting.

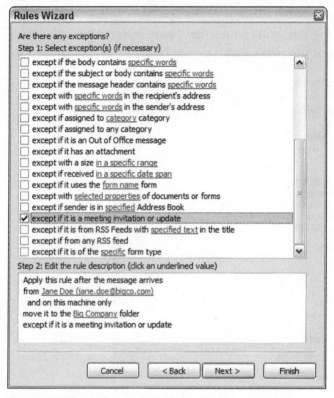

Figure 15.6. The third screen in the Rules Wizard — exceptions.

The fourth and final screen in the wizard, shown in Figure 15.7, lets you assign the rule a name and select options about how the rule will be applied. The lower portion of the dialog box provides an additional opportunity to make final changes to any of the attributes you have applied to the elements of the rule.

Hack

Create a Search Folder that finds all meeting requests and updates, and you'll always have a single view of all your pending invitations and updated meeting information. As an alternative, create a rule that puts all meeting requests and updates in a single folder and add that folder to the Favorite Folders list at the top of the Mail view's Navigation Pane.

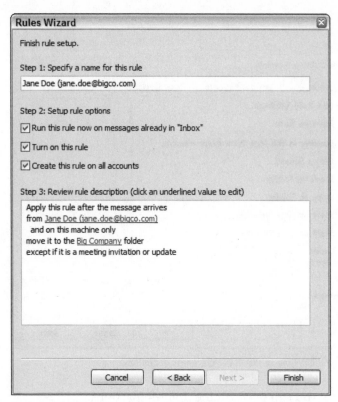

Figure 15.7. The final screen in the Rules Wizard — finish rule setup.

Changing an Outlook rule

You will inevitably find an occasion when you want to modify a rule you have built to automate message handling in Outlook. For example, if you have built a rule like the sample used in the preceding example that routes messages from a person to a specific folder, you may want to add an additional contact to that rule so that all messages from a particular company you are working with or collaborating with on a specific project are processed in the same way.

To change an Outlook rule, open the Rules and Alerts dialog box from the Tools menu or the Advanced toolbar and select the rule you want to modify. On the command bar, click the Change Rule button to display the menu shown in Figure 15.8.

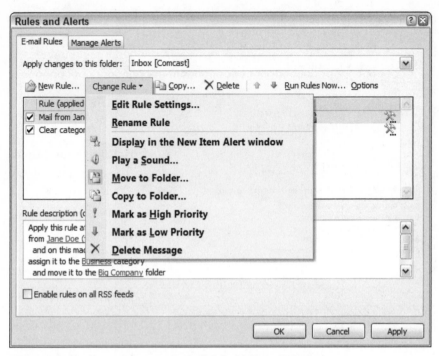

Figure 15.8. The Change Rule menu in the Rules and Alerts dialog box.

From this menu, you can perform the following actions:

■ **Edit Rule Settings.** This option opens the Rules Wizard and allows you to add, modify, or remove conditions, actions, or exceptions in the rule.

■ **Rename Rule.** This option lets you change the name displayed in the Rules and Alerts dialog box list.

■ **Display in the New Item Alert window.** This option tells Outlook to display an alert whenever a newly arrived message matches the criteria defined in the rule.

■ **Play a Sound.** This option allows you to associate a sound that will play whenever a newly arrived message matches the criteria defined in the rule.

■ **Move to Folder.** This option moves the selected rule from the currently designated folder to a different folder.

- **Copy to Folder.** This option copies the selected rule and applies it to another folder in your Outlook PST file and continues to apply it to the current folder.

- **Mark as High Priority.** Rules marked with High Priority are run first in the sequential order in which they are listed in the Rules and Alerts list. This menu option toggles the state of the selected rule between High Priority and Normal Priority.

- **Mark as Low Priority.** Rules marked with Low Priority are run last in the sequential order in which they are listed in the Rules and Alerts list. This menu option toggles the state of the selected rule between Low Priority and Normal Priority.

- **Delete Message.** This option selects the delete it action in the second screen of the wizard. When selected, this option instructs Outlook to delete the message after it has performed any other actions. Use this option carefully, and apply it only to spam or other unwanted messages you receive.

Running Outlook Rules manually

In fully automated mode, Outlook Rules monitor your incoming e-mail messages and are applied as matching items arrive. This automatic behavior is enabled if you select the option labeled Turn on this rule in the last screen of the Rules Wizard (see Figure 15.7) or if you check the box next to the rule in the Rules and Alerts dialog box list. You may build rules that you want to apply manually at specific times. This can be particularly useful if you create rules to locate and move messages to an archive folder or PST file or perform other maintenance tasks.

To run an Outlook rule manually, open the Rules and Alerts dialog box from the Tools menu or the Advanced toolbar and select the Run Rules Now action button from the command bar. The Run Rules Now dialog box, pictured in Figure 15.9, is displayed. Select the check box next to the rule you want to run, use the Browse button to select a folder in your PST file you want to process, optionally select the Include subfolders check box if the folder has subfolders you also want to process, and use the Apply rules to: drop-down menu to decide whether you want to apply the rule to all messages, unread messages only, or read messages only. When you have made all your selections, click the Run Now button to run the rule or rules you have selected.

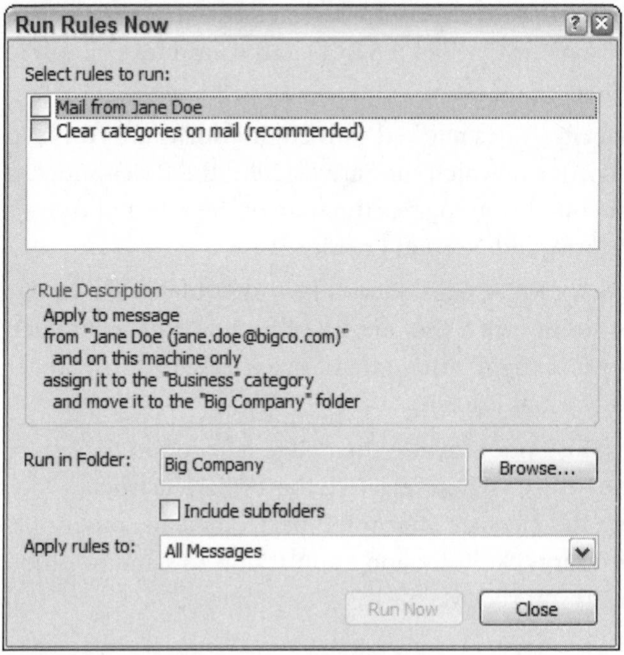

Run Rules Now
Select rules to run:
Mail from Jane Doe
Clear categories on mail (recommended)
Rule Description
Apply to message
from "Jane Doe (jane.doe@bigco.com)"
and on this machine only
assign it to the "Business" category
and move it to the "Big Company" folder
Run in Folder:
Big Company
Browse...
Include subfolders
Apply rules to:
All Messages
Run Now
Close

Figure 15.9. The Run Rules Now dialog box.

Import or Export Options

If you are migrating from a previous version of Outlook or want to add the rules you have built to an Outlook installation on another PC, use the Options button on the command bar in the Rules and Alerts dialog box to open the Options dialog box shown in Figure 15.10. You can import rules you have exported from another Outlook installation or export the rules in your current Outlook installation to a file you can use to migrate them to a different PC. If you have imported rules created in a previous version of Outlook (2003 or earlier) into your Outlook 2007 environment, the Upgrade Now button is activated.

Options
Import and export
Import or export your rules to and from previous versions of Outlook
Export Rules...
Import Rules...
Rules upgrade
We recommend that you upgrade your rules for better performance, unless you also use a previous version of Outlook.
Upgrade Now
OK
Cancel

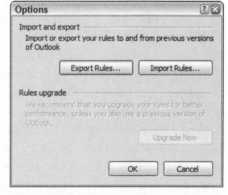

Figure 15.10. The Options dialog box allows you to import and export rules.

Inside Scoop

You should always run the Upgrade Now command on rules you import from another version of Outlook to make sure all the settings are updated to work properly in Outlook 2007. This is the best way to make sure your rules will work properly and avoid unpleasant surprises.

Outlook Alerts

The Rules and Alerts dialog box contains a second tab labeled Manage Alerts. If you work in an environment where you connect to a SharePoint Server from Outlook, you can create alerts to inform you when events take place on the server. These events might include the availability of new documents, events, or newly assigned tasks. You can create an alert by clicking the New Alert action button on the command bar and selecting the source from the dialog box shown in Figure 15.11. If you work in a SharePoint Server environment, your site administrator can help you set up these alerts and advise you on objects and events for which alerts can be created.

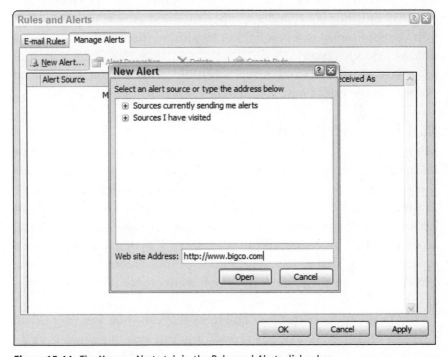

Figure 15.11. The Manage Alerts tab in the Rules and Alerts dialog box.

Third-party automation solutions

Outlook Rules are a powerful and easy-to-use feature to automate much of the routine filing of e-mail messages. The new Instant Search feature discussed in Chapter 16, and Search Folders, which are covered in Chapter 13, make finding information in Outlook easier than ever. For many users, these features and capabilities provide all the automation and organization they need.

A large and thriving aftermarket has grown up around Outlook over the years to further extend the application. Outlook has been designed by Microsoft to be an extensible communication and information management environment, and many enterprising developers have taken advantage of that design to create plug-in modules (generally referred to as add-ins), utilities, and full-blown applications that work inside Outlook by adding toolbars and other controls or alongside Outlook in a separate application window.

Chapter 17 provides an overview of a number of these applications that I have tested, reviewed, and used with Outlook over the years. These tools can enhance your Outlook experience and raise your productivity with the application to a new level. A handful of these add-ins and applications are specifically focused on automating how information is processed, organized, and made accessible. This section contains an overview of the ones I have found to be particularly useful.

NEO (Nelson* E-mail Organizer)

NEO (www.caelo.com) has been helping Outlook users get a handle on their information for many years. NEO is a stand-alone application that you use in conjunction with Outlook to provide a different interface to your e-mail. When a new message arrives in your Outlook POP3 or Exchange mail account (NEO does not support IMAP or HTTP e-mail accounts), NEO is notified and adds a reference to that new message to a separate catalog that it maintains outside of your Outlook environment. NEO also indexes the content of the e-mail to enable powerful searches of your messages.

NEO's strength are its filters and views that can show you your e-mail messages organized in a variety of ways. You can look at messages organized by sender, subject, category, and other criteria and filter on any of those views. Much of this capability can be created in Outlook by building customized views (see Chapter 14), Search Folders (see Chapter 13), and rules, but if you're not inclined to invest the time required to build out these capabilities and prefer to use a prebuilt tool, NEO may be worth taking for a test drive. NEO is available in two versions — a free version and a commercial Pro version with more features and capabilities.

ClearContext

The ClearContext Inbox Management System (IMS) is an add-in utility that provides a set of toolbars and custom Inbox views and enhancements to address the needs of people who receive lots of e-mail and tend to leave many messages in their Inboxes. ClearContext groups related e-mail messages together into threaded conversations and prioritizes the Inbox Message List view to show you the highest-priority information first using a sophisticated set of preferences and observed behavior.

ClearContext figures out who is most important by watching the frequency and quantity of e-mail you exchange with each person and treats your most frequent correspondents as most important. ClearContext toolbars in both the main view and in the new Ribbon UI in message windows, as well a right-click context menu, provide action buttons to file, delegate, defer, and prioritize messages and create tasks or calendar items from messages with a single click. Find them at www.clearcontext.com.

Omea Pro and ViaPoint

Two other Outlook organizers that work in similar fashion to NEO but offer their own unique twists on organizing your information are Omea Pro (www.jetbrains.com/omea/) and ViaPoint (www.viapoint.com). Both programs index and organize all your Outlook data, not just e-mail, and allow you to create virtual folders, which are similar to Outlook Search Folders but which organize a greater number of information sources. Omea Pro has excellent support for RSS subscriptions and Newsgroups. ViaPoint provides a similar set of features and capabilities and adds integration with Google Desktop Search or Windows Desktop Search. Both extend beyond Outlook information and can include Office documents, Web bookmarks, and other files on your local PC and network shares in its organize and search environments.

Just the facts

- Outlook Rules can replace the drudgery of manually dragging e-mail messages to folders, assigning categories and flags, and other repetitive and time-consuming processes by automating them.

- Create a simple rule based on an e-mail message in your Inbox (or other folder) by right-clicking the message and choosing the Create Rule command.

- The Rules and Alerts dialog box provides a variety of predesigned rules templates to perform common filing and tagging tasks that you can customize for your specific needs.

- Rules can be run on an automatic or manual basis.

- The Rules Wizard presents a sequence of screens that provide extensive lists of conditions, actions, and exceptions that you can select from to construct your rules.

- Use the Change Rules menu in the Rules and Alerts dialog box to modify or reprioritize your rules.

- Alerts can notify you of changes on a SharePoint Server.

- A number of third-party tools are available that enhance Outlook's built-in automation tools or provide a new UI for working with your Outlook information.

GET THE SCOOP ON...

Instant Search in Outlook 2007 ▪ Simple searches ▪ Advanced searches using the Query Builder ▪ Windows Desktop Search ▪ Third-party search tools ▪ System-level search in Windows Vista

Find Anything in Outlook... Fast

The impact that search has had on the way we work with information has been profound. The advent of Web-based search engines from Microsoft, Google, Yahoo!, and a host of others has changed how we research topics of interest. Travel search engines like Expedia and Travelocity have completely disrupted that industry. Web-based purchasing engines like Amazon.com and Buy.com have made buying online a commonplace alternative to getting in the car and driving around in search of stuff. And eBay has given us a worldwide garage sale.

It was inevitable that this search-based behavior would trickle down to the desktop. Although Windows and Office have offered search tools for years, they have been slow, inefficient, and downright frustrating for most people who try to use them. As hard drive capacities have increased and price-per-megabyte (nowadays price-per-gigabyte) has plummeted, we're storing more information than ever before. And that creates significant challenges when you need to find a particular document or e-mail.

The most popular offerings in desktop search come from the same companies that dominate Web search. Microsoft and Google built their own tools. Yahoo! acquired its desktop search technology from a third-party company: X1. And Copernic, a company long associated with search tools for the desktop and local network, has managed to grab a loyal following large enough that it was acquired in 2005 by Mama.com, a big player in the domain registration sector. All these tools are, as you might expect, free.

This chapter begins with an exploration of the new Instant Search feature in Outlook 2007 powered by the Windows Desktop Search engine in Windows XP and the system-level search in Windows Vista. Compared to the complicated and frustrating search tool in previous versions, Instant Search is a breakthrough in terms of ease of use and quality of results. Later in the chapter, I provide an overview of the desktop search tools offered by Microsoft, Google, Copernic, and Yahoo! The chapter closes with a look at how search is integrated into Windows Vista and the implications for search in Outlook 2007.

Outlook 2007 Instant Search

Outlook 2007 sports an all-new, integrated search feature that is built into every main view of the application and prominently displayed for easy access. In the main Mail view, the Instant Search box is located directly above the message list as shown in Figure 16.1. In all other views, the Instant Search box is located above the display area in the upper left.

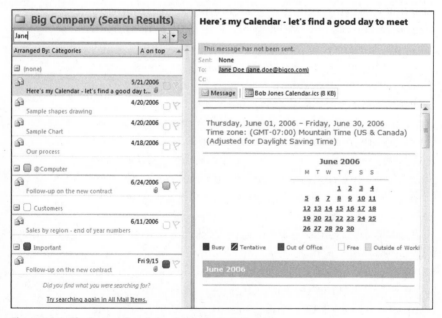

Figure 16.1. The Instant Search box in the main Mail view.

This feature is called Instant Search because, as you begin typing text in the text area of the search box, Outlook begins displaying results immediately. This is sometimes referred to as "word wheeling," and the more you type, the more the results are narrowed down.

Simple searches

In its default state, Instant Search conducts simple text searches, looking for any match to the text you enter in the search box's text field. The search box turns orange when you click in its text field to indicate that search is active. The words (Search Results) in parentheses are appended to the name of the folder you are currently viewing and now searching. When you complete your search or click the cancel button (the "X" next to the text entry field), the search box reverts to its normal state, matching the rest of the UI, and the parenthetical disappears.

When you access the Instant Search field in Mail view, you are, by default, searching only the message folder you are currently working in. If no matching items are found in the current folder, Outlook displays a text link in the results below the search box that offers to extend your search to all mail folders. You can also extend your search across all message fold-

ers by clicking the triangle icon at the end of the search box to show the Search Options menu shown in Figure 16.2. Select the Search All Mail Items command. After selecting the command, the display at the top of the message list reads "Search Results (All Mail Items)." This mode also can be activated using the keyboard shortcut Ctrl+Alt+A.

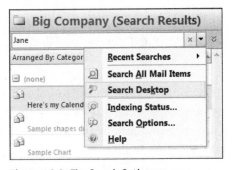

Figure 16.2. The Search Options menu.

Watch Out!

After you have selected the Search All Mail Items option, you must reset the Instant Search box if you want to return to single-folder search mode. This can be done by clicking the cancel icon or by selecting any folder in the Navigation Pane.

Advanced Search using the Query Builder

Instant Search is not limited to simple text searches. You can construct multi-value searches by defining additional criteria that must be matched.

To expand the search box to display the Query Builder, used to define an advanced search, click the double-arrow icon at the right of the search box to provide additional field definitions, as shown in Figure 16.3.

Outlook presents four additional fields you can use to refine your search parameters. In Mail view, Outlook initially displays the From, Body, Subject, and To fields. You can change any of these pre-selected fields to another by clicking the triangle icon following the field name as pictured in Figure 16.4. Note that at the bottom of this menu is the Remove command, which, as the name implies, deletes the selected criterion from the query. To add additional fields to your advanced search, use the Add Criteria command at the bottom of the Query Builder box.

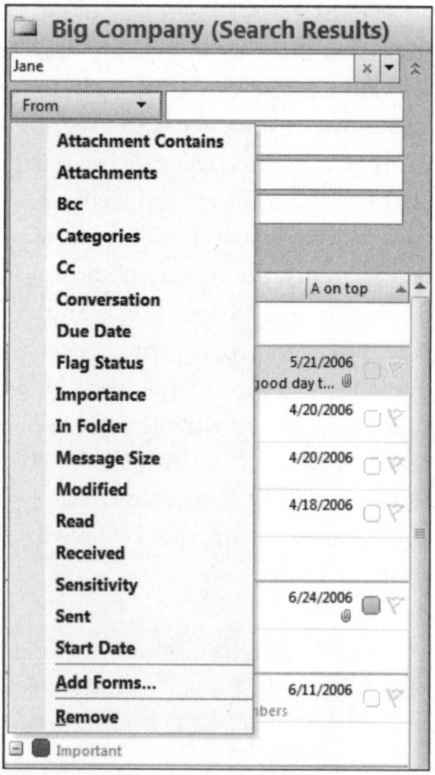

The Query Builder is presented in a different format in Outlook's other views. Unlike the Mail view, the other main views in Outlook do not use a message list pane by default, and the right side of the view is a single pane used to display information. The Query Builder is displayed in a wide

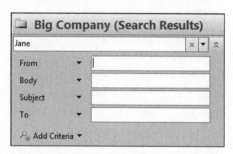

Figure 16.3. The Query Builder is used to construct advanced searches.

Figure 16.4. The field menu allows you to select which field to use in your search.

format above the information area as shown in Figure 16.5, which shows an advanced search in the Calendar view. This illustration also shows the Reading Pane turned on to display the content of the selected search result.

If you prefer this layout, it's a simple matter to reconfigure the Mail view to follow this format by changing the Reading Pane position to Bottom. This setting extends the Message Pane across the right side of the main view and repositions the Instant Search box to the upper right corner as in the other main views.

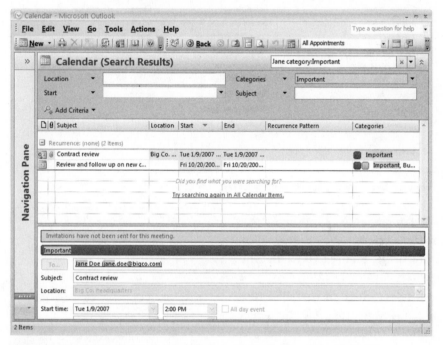

Figure 16.5. The Query Builder in Calendar view with the Reading Pane displayed.

Search Options

The Instant Search feature in Outlook 2007 on PCs running Windows XP is powered by Windows Desktop Search (WDS), which is described in detail later in this chapter. Many of the options for WDS can be set from the system tray, but some options specific to Outlook can be set from the Instant Search menu, shown in Figure 16.6, which is located on the Tools menu.

On the Instant Search menu, note that keyboard shortcuts are available for a number of search actions. The two shortcuts I find most useful are Ctrl+E, which moves the focus to the Instant Search box in any of the main views, and Ctrl+Alt+A, which expands a mail search to extend across all mail message folders. The Search Desktop command transfers your current query to the WDS interface described later in this chapter. Indexing Status reports the number of items indexed in your Outlook PST file and the current number of new items that have yet to be indexed.

Tools			
Send/Receive	▶		
Instant Search	▶	⌕ Instant Search	Ctrl+E
Address Book... Ctrl+Shift+B		⌄ Expand the Query Builder	Ctrl+Alt+W
Organize		⌕ Search All Mail Items	Ctrl+Alt+A
Rules and Alerts...		⌕ Search Desktop	Ctrl+Alt+K
Mailbox Cleanup...		⌕ Indexing Status...	
Empty "Deleted Items" Folder		⌕ Search Options...	
Forms	▶	Advanced Find...	Ctrl+Shift+F
Macro	▶	Related Messages...	
Account Settings...		Messages from Sender...	
Trust Center...			
Customize...			
Options...			

Figure 16.6. The Instant Search menu.

The Search Options command opens the dialog box shown in Figure 16.7. In the Search Options dialog box, you can select which of your PST files are indexed for search, select options that affect what is searched and how results are displayed, and set the default behavior for Instant Search to look only in the folder you are currently viewing (the default setting in Outlook) or to always search all folders.

The Advanced Find command invokes the old Outlook Find interface from prior versions shown in Figure 16.8. While

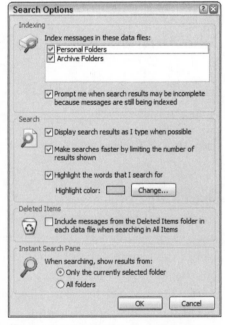

Figure 16.7. The Search Options dialog box.

very powerful, it demonstrates why Instant Search is such an improvement. The three-tab interface is rather complicated and quite cumbersome to use compared to the new search interface in Outlook 2007. Still, the ability to construct very refined queries may come in handy from time to time, and if Instant Search fails to meet your needs, this is a powerful alternative for occasional use.

Figure 16.8. The Advanced Find dialog box.

The final two commands on the Instant Search menu are actually preconfigured queries that use the Advanced Find tool. Related Messages executes a search using a query defined with the Conversation criterion applied to the message you have selected. Messages from Sender executes an Advanced Find Search using the sender's name (in the From field) as the query term. You can achieve similar results using the appropriate field criterion in the new Instant Search interface, but these menu commands make it a one-click operation based on the currently selected message.

Windows Desktop Search

Windows Desktop Search (WDS) is a free Windows XP tool offered by Microsoft to enable system-wide search of your files. Introduced prior to the release of the 2007 Office system to provide desktop search for any Windows system, you must enable Instant Search in Outlook 2007 on a Windows XP system. Windows Vista, the successor to XP, has a system-level search engine that eliminates this requirement.

WDS not only enables Instant Search in Outlook, it also provides similar search features to Office OneNote 2007 and adds a search bar to the Windows Task Bar. As you type in this search bar, WDS begins searching for all matches to your search term in the files on your PC it has indexed and shows results in a pop-up sheet as you type, as pictured in Figure 16.9.

If the file or Outlook object you are searching for is displayed in the results, select it to open the desired item. If you want to use a more advanced interface for searching your file system and Outlook information, click the Search Desktop button at the bottom of the pop-up sheet to open

Figure 16.9. Windows Desktop Search displays results as you type.

the WDS window pictured in Figure 16.10. A series of filters is presented immediately below the search box at the top of the window to restrict your search to a specific file type. The drop-down menu shown in this illustration provides a complete list of filters. The Communications filter searches in your e-mail messages, calendar items, Instant Messaging chat transcripts, and tasks.

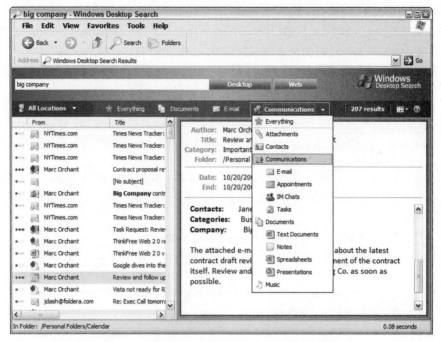

Figure 16.10. The Windows Desktop Search interface showing the filters menu.

The combination of these two tools — Instant Search inside Outlook and Windows Desktop Search — delivers the right tool for just about any search you may need to conduct. And it's important to note that only in WDS can you search against your entire Outlook PST file at once. Instant Search works on a view-by-view basis so you cannot use it to find all e-mails, appointments, tasks, contacts, and notes related to a particular project. WDS handles that type of search quite well and adds the ability to also include any related Office documents and other files.

> **Watch Out!**
>
> The Windows Desktop Search indexer can index your Outlook PST file only when Outlook is running. If you receive new e-mail messages or create new appointments, contacts, or tasks in Outlook and exit the application before the indexer has "caught up," you may not see these new items show up in searches immediately.

Windows Desktop Search uses a system-level engine to create an index that is used for both Instant Search and WDS queries. This indexing engine runs in the background and indexes any new files and Outlook items whenever your PC is idle. You can check the status of indexing, pause the indexer if you are performing a particularly CPU-intensive task such as burning a CD or DVD, or force the indexer to update immediately from a context menu accessible from the WDS icon in the system tray. This menu, pictured in Figure 16.11, also provides instant access to the WDS interface and Help files. The Search Now command is particularly helpful if you have chosen not to display the Deskbar in the Windows Task Bar.

Figure 16.11. The Windows Desktop Search context menu.

To define what is indexed on your PC and perform maintenance on your index file, select the Windows Desktop Search options command from the context menu to display the Indexing Options dialog box shown in Figure 16.12. This dialog box displays the Outlook PST files and file folders on your PC that are currently being indexed and presents two buttons to modify what is indexed and to access advanced options.

To add additional folders to the index or exclude folders you do not want the indexer to include in search results, click the Modify button to open the Indexed Locations dialog box shown in Figure 16.13. Select the

Figure 16.12. The Indexing Options dialog box.

Inside Scoop

Rebuilding your WDS index compacts the size of the file, which can get quite large over time. Assuming that you are performing regular backups of your PC, you should allow the index to rebuild just before performing a backup. A complete index rebuild can take some time, so schedule accordingly.

check box next to an Outlook PST file or file folder you want to include or deselect a check box to exclude a PST file or folder. When you first select a folder, all subfolders inside that folder also are selected. Use the plus sign next to a parent folder to display its subfolders for inclusion or exclusion.

The Advanced Options dialog box, shown in Figure 16.14, is accessed by clicking the Advanced button in the Indexing Options dialog box. In this dialog box, you can rebuild or reset your index file and change the location of the index file. Options also are available that control how encrypted files are handled and to address words with diacritical characters found in a number of languages. It's a good idea to rebuild your index file if you've recently deleted a significant number of files from your system, as is the case when you perform a backup and delete files to make room on your hard drive. This reduces the potential for "false positive results" that take place when WDS lists a file in its search results only to complain that it can't be found when you try to open it.

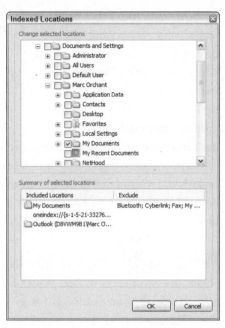

Figure 16.13. The Indexed Locations dialog box.

Figure 16.14. The Advanced Options dialog box.

When the indexer is active, the magnifying glass icon in the system tray animates (pulses white and blue). To view the current indexing activity and set a "snooze" period longer than the default 15 minutes that you can select from

Figure 16.15. The Windows Desktop Search Indexing Status dialog box.

the context menu, select the Indexing status command from the context menu to display the dialog box shown in Figure 16.15. This dialog box reports the number of items indexed on your PC, shows the number of new items that have yet to be scanned, and provides snooze controls and an Index now command to force the indexer to run immediately.

Third-party search tools: Do you need them?

Given the requirement that Windows Desktop Search be installed to provide the Instant Search features in Outlook, does it make sense to even consider using a third-party desktop search tool after you've upgraded to Office 2007? The answer, in the best tradition of consultants everywhere, is "it depends." A number of excellent alternatives to WDS are available, and you can certainly opt to use another tool. There are consequences to making this decision, but none of them is particularly troublesome as long as you know how things will work.

The most obvious and immediate consequence of electing to use a third-party desktop search tool in addition to WDS is that you will have two indexing engines competing for system resources and you will be maintaining two index files, which can consume a sizable chunk of hard disk space. It is possible to use Outlook 2007 without WDS installed, but Instant Search will not be available. If WDS is not installed on your PC, an option to tell Outlook to stop nagging you about the need to install the search engine can be found in the Options dialog box.

Should you decide that a different approach to desktop and Outlook search is right for you, two of the most popular options are offered by Google and Copernic.

Google Desktop Search

Google Desktop Search brings the familiar Google Web search experience down to the desktop and uses your browser as its primary interface for searching and viewing found results. Integration with Outlook comes in the form of a toolbar added to the main views as shown in Figure 16.16. When you execute a search using this toolbar, results are displayed in a pop-up window also shown in this figure.

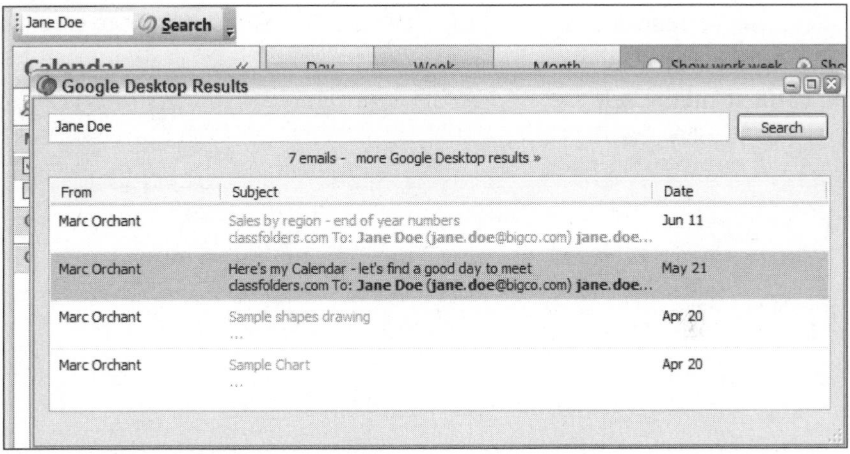

Figure 16.16. Google Desktop Search in Outlook.

Unlike Outlook Instant Search, Google Desktop Search displays all matching items in a single results window. To expand your search to include all files on your PC as well as Outlook items, click the more Google Desktop results link at the top of the pop-up window to open a browser window that displays all matches in a browser window, as pictured in Figure 16.17. In the browser interface, you can sort the results by date or relevance and filter the results using the links at the top of the page. Although Google Desktop Search does not provide previews like Windows Desktop Search and Copernic Desktop Search do, an icon representing common file types does appear to the left of each result, giving you a visual indication of what kind of file each result was found in.

Like all of these search tools, Google Desktop Search provides a Deskbar that can be added to the Windows Task Bar to execute a search even when Outlook is not running or visible. Google Desktop Search also adds the option to display a Sidebar that can be docked to the edge or a screen that can be used to execute searches and run a wide assortment of small programs called gadgets. These gadgets can display news, RSS information, weather, system performance information, and a variety of other kinds of information and entertainment.

>
> **Watch Out!**
> Like WDS, the Google Desktop Search indexer can index your Outlook PST file
> only when Outlook is running. If you receive new e-mail messages or create
> new appointments, contacts, or tasks in Outlook and exit the application
> before the indexer has "caught up," you may not see these new items show up in searches
> immediately.

Figure 16.17. Google Desktop Search in a browser window.

Copernic Desktop Search

Copernic has been making tools to search your PC and local area network for years, long before the current proliferation of desktop search
tools began. When Copernic released its free desktop search tool, it
quickly received praise from the tech media and bloggers for its speed
(both indexing and searching), well-designed user interface, and preview support for a wide variety of file types. In September 2006, Copernic
released a new version of the utility that improved performance and
added the ability to save searches for reuse. Unlike the Recent Searches
feature in Outlook Instant Search, which lists the most recent searches
you have conducted, these saved searches are permanent.

Figure 16.18 shows the Copernic Desktop Search window with a preview of a selected Outlook e-mail message. Note that the preview provides immediate access to the message's file attachments and commands to open, reply to, forward, and print the message as well as a command to search for related messages. A similar set of commands is presented for any file or Outlook item found. Along the top of the screen, Copernic displays all the file types that it is configured to index and find. Clicking a file type serves to filter the search results. The number of items of each file type found is displayed below its icon.

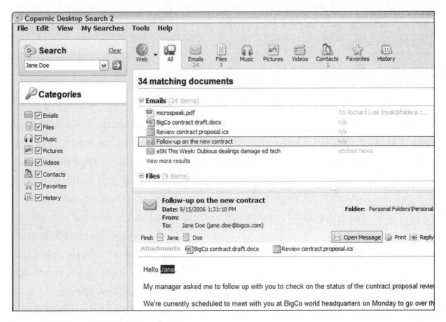

Figure 16.18. Copernic Desktop Search.

Copernic also provides a Deskbar in the Windows Task Bar from which searches can be initiated. Like WDS and Google's Deskbars, results begin appearing as you type and are refined as more information is entered. The Copernic Deskbar display is sorted by file type, making it easy to select the most likely match directly from its pop-up results window.

Yahoo! Desktop Search

In addition to these third-party options, Yahoo! offers a free desktop search tool based on the commercial X1 search product. It was incompatible with Outlook 2007 at the time of this writing, but will undoubtedly be updated and available by the time you read this. The X1 interface in Yahoo! Desktop Search is rather different from the tools described in this chapter, and it is the only desktop search tool of the four described here that does not offer a deskbar, relying instead on keyboard shortcuts to invoke a search. Yahoo! Desktop Search provides integration with Yahoo! Instant Messenger and can optionally install a Yahoo! Search toolbar in your browser to mirror the system-wide capabilities offered by the other tools.

Windows Vista system-level search

By the time you have this book in your hands, Windows Vista will have shipped and will be the default operating system installed on all new PCs. Vista has a search indexing engine built directly into the operating system, and this engine provides search services to Office applications as well as desktop search. It remains to be seen how this inclusion of search directly into the operating system will impact the third-party market.

On a PC running Vista, Instant Search in Outlook works identically to how it operates on a Windows XP system with Windows Desktop Search installed. The biggest difference in how search works on a Vista system is on the desktop. To begin a search on a Vista system, you open the Start menu and type into the search box at the bottom of the menu. As you begin entering text, the Start menu begins word wheeling and displays results right on the Start menu itself, temporarily replacing the application icons normally displayed in the left pane.

Clicking the Show all Results link above the search box opens the Vista search interface, which is, in essence, a variation on the standard Windows Explorer window. The controls for filtering search results are very similar to those in Windows Desktop Search on Windows XP systems.

The tight integration with system-level search and indexing and the easy access to Instant Search inside Outlook suggests that Outlook users running Windows Vista will be hard-pressed to justify adding another search tool on top of what the operating system already provides. It will be interesting to see how third-party providers react to this competitive challenge. While it is possible to turn off the system-level indexer in Vista and subsequently bypass the Instant Search tool in Outlook in favor of an alternative solution, the value proposition will have to be fairly high to convince most users that it will be worth the hassle.

I suspect some Microsoft competitors will cry foul and claim that Microsoft is not competing on a level playing field. From my perspective, it appears they are addressing a profoundly broken process in the best way possible by building fast and accurate search features directly into both the operating system and applications. If you are using a system running Windows Vista, I suggest you use the built-in tools and see for yourself how well they perform. If you are able to find what you're looking for, you will certainly benefit from not having yet another potential source of conflict introduced into your PC environment by a third-party application.

If you're still running Windows XP on your PC, you have more of a choice. Windows Desktop Search is an additional installation you can decide whether or not to perform. If a third-party tool looks more appealing, you can turn off Instant Search in Outlook 2007 and use a different search tool quite easily.

Just the facts

- Desktop search tools have become commonplace and are offered by a number of companies including Microsoft, Google, Yahoo!, and Copernic.

- Outlook 2007 introduces a new built-in search tool called Instant Search, which uses the same index file as Windows Desktop Search on Windows XP systems.

- The Instant Search box can be expanded to reveal the Query Builder, in which you can add, remove, and change the fields used to structure your search.

- The Advanced Find dialog box, which is carried over from Outlook 2003, can be opened from the Instant Search menu accessed from the Tools menu to perform complex, fine-tuned searches.

- Windows Desktop Search is a free utility from Microsoft used to power Instant Search in Outlook 2007.

- Google Desktop Search provides similar features to Windows Desktop Search and adds a unique Sidebar that can be configured to display news and entertainment, run a slide show of pictures on your PC, and monitor the state of your system.

- Copernic Desktop Search is another alternative that provides a similar set of features to Windows Desktop Search in a very easy-to-use interface.

- Windows Vista has an index and search engine built directly into the operating system that Outlook 2007 uses to power Instant Search.

GET THE SCOOP ON...
Add-in alchemy ▪ Favorite add-ins for Outlook ▪ Basic
filing tools ▪ Finding add-ins ▪ External applications to
enhance Outlook ▪ Outlook Express ▪ Windows Live Mail
Desktop ▪ Instant messaging ▪ Other Microsoft Office
applications ▪ Third-party applications

Using Other Programs to Extend Outlook

A few years ago, I got into a blog conversation with a couple of Microsoft developers on the topic of "Outlook is a platform." In that discussion, we all agreed that one of the great strengths of this application is the way it has been designed to accept add-in programs and integrate with other applications to enhance and extend its core capabilities. A vast aftermarket exists for these utilities and companion programs, and more are released all the time.

This chapter explores how Outlook 2007 can be made even more useful and adapt better to the way you work through the use of additional software. In the first part of this chapter, I discuss what I call "add-in alchemy," the art and science of keeping Outlook running well with these extensions. The second part of this chapter describes some of my favorite add-ins for Outlook — ones that have stood the test of time for me and that I consider essential for using Outlook optimally in my work. The third part of this chapter discusses external programs that can enhance how you access and use the information in your Outlook environment and extend the program's capabilities. By the way, neither of these lists is intended to be exhaustive — there are literally hundreds of add-ins and dozens of applications that integrate with Outlook.

Outlook "add-in alchemy"

Add-ins are a great way to enhance your Outlook experience, but they can produce some nasty side effects if you get too enthusiastic about how many you're using or combine the wrong ones. The sheer number of add-ins and the variety of functions and features they offer is simply too great to provide specific advice on which ones you can use safely and in what combinations.

If you get overly excited about the potential to redesign Outlook through add-ins, you can easily make Outlook unstable. Trust me, I've been there more often than I care to admit. But in doing so, I've learned some valuable lessons in personal restraint and in managing add-ins as well as how to troubleshoot and repair Outlook when add-in alchemy goes wrong.

Too many add-ins can cause big trouble

I would love to give you a simple formula like "use no more than n add-ins, and everything will work well," but it's not as simple as basic arithmetic. These enhancements hook into Outlook in a variety of ways to perform a wide range of operations that can greatly enhance your use of Outlook. They also can create utter havoc in performance and stability. And, like baking soda and vinegar (or, more popularly, Mentos and soda), two elements that are benign on their own can produce explosive results when combined.

For that reason, these are my rules of add-in alchemy:

■ **Be conservative.** Ask yourself whether you really need the capability an add-in provides and how frequently you will use it. If the answer is "not very often" or "well, it would be cool to be able to do that, but...," you are probably better off resisting temptation and leaving well enough alone.

■ **Add one at a time.** I recommend that you add one add-in to your Outlook environment at a time and spend some time — at least a few hours and preferably a day or more of steady use — to learn how your most recent addition affects the performance and stability of Outlook. This makes it much easier to identify the culprit when Outlook begins running slowly or crashes start to occur.

- **Use System Restore before installing a new add-in.** System Restore is a utility built into Windows XP and Vista that takes a snapshot of the System Registry, called a Restore Point, that you can use to "roll back" the state of your system to a previous state. It's beyond the scope of this book to get into the nuances of this feature, but you can get additional information by opening Help and Support from the Windows Start menu and searching for "System Restore." For our purposes, I illustrate the simple process of creating and restoring from a System Restore point.

To create a Restore Point, open the System Restore utility from the Control Panel's Performance and Maintenance category. Look in the See Also list in the Explorer bar on the left edge of the window, and click the System Restore link. You see the screen pictured in Figure 17.1, which provides two options:

1. Restore my computer to an earlier time

2. Create a restore point

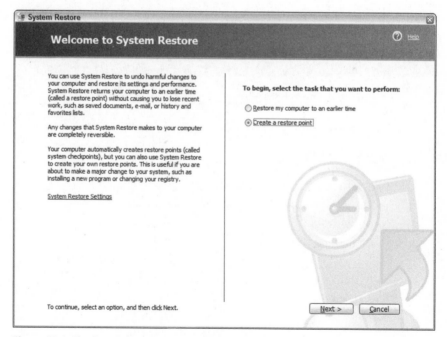

Figure 17.1. The System Restore opening dialog box.

Inside Scoop

Windows XP's System Restore function is continually creating snapshots of your system state. In theory, a restore point should be created prior to every software installation. Not all installer programs follow Microsoft's specifications. When dealing with Outlook add-ins, I recommend that you manually create a restore point before you begin any software installation.

In this first screen, click the Create a restore point radio button and the Next button. The screen shown in Figure 17.2 appears, which provides a field to give the restore point a name. As the warning text on the page indicates, the name of a restore point cannot be edited once created, so give the restore point a meaningful name — I suggest a format like the one in the illustration that references the installation of an Outlook add-in with the specific name of the software you are about to add.

After you have entered a name, click the Create button to save a system restore point. After the restore point has been created, a success screen appears; close it, and proceed with your installation of the add-in software.

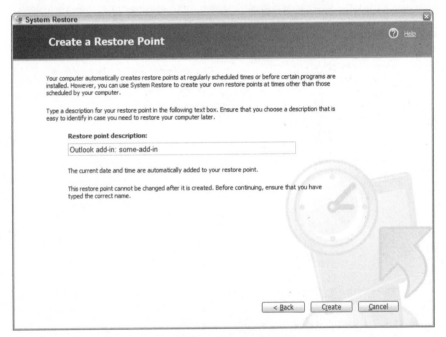

Figure 17.2. The second screen in the System Restore process.

Should you encounter instabilities or problems with a particular add-in, first run the uninstaller that should have been included with the software to remove it from your system. After the uninstaller has removed the software, run Outlook and verify that no visible traces of the add-in remain. If, even after uninstalling the software, you either see visible traces of the add-in or stability and performance do not return to normal, you can roll back your system registry using the restore point you created in the preceding steps.

To restore your system registry to its state prior to installing a problematic add-in installation, open the System Restore utility, select the Restore my computer to an earlier time option, and click Next. The screen shown in Figure 17.3 appears, from which you can select the restore point you created. Click the calendar grid to select the date on which you created the restore point, and then select the restore point from the list box on the right. Click the Next button, and System Restore rolls back the system registry state to its previous state.

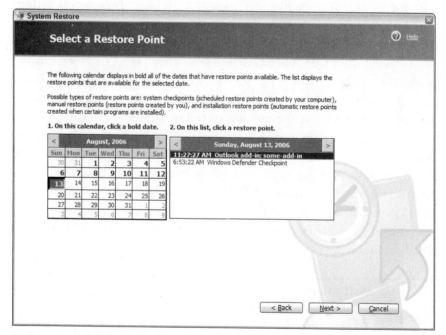

Figure 17.3. The System Restore dialog box for restoring your system registry.

Enabling and disabling add-ins

Another consideration regarding add-ins is the additional system memory and resource demands they may add to the already hefty chunk of both that Outlook consumes. As a general rule, the more features or capabilities an add-in provides in Outlook, the more memory and resources it requires. Most PCs these days are equipped with 512 megabytes of memory, and it is increasingly common to find even consumer systems configured with 1 gigabyte. As adoption of Windows Vista escalates, I fully expect these two numbers to double to a "standard" of 1 gigabyte and an increasingly common 2-gigabyte configuration for power users, gamers, and people who tend to have a number of applications open at the same time.

As an alternative to uninstalling add-ins, you can turn add-ins on and off in Outlook 2007 using the COM Add-Ins dialog box. I like to use a few specialized add-ins when I'm doing a certain sort of work, but I really don't need them most of the time. I also test lots of Outlook add-in software for writing projects like this book and my blog. Turning off add-ins allows me to create as level a playing field as possible for new titles I am reviewing.

To access the COM Add-Ins dialog box, select Trust Center from the Tools menu. The Trust Center dialog box, pictured in Figure 17.4, is a central location for managing all the controls that Outlook 2007 provides to help you protect the information stored in Outlook and your identity and privacy when you connect to the network. Chapter 27 discusses Outlook security, and the Trust Center is described in depth as part of that discussion. For the topic at hand — managing Outlook add-ins — the Add-ins screen pictured in Figure 17.4 is where we will focus. The Trust Center dialog box view lists all the add-ins that have been installed, the path to where they reside on your hard disk, and whether they are active or disabled.

Watch Out!

You must almost always quit and restart Outlook to completely disable an add-in. Outlook loads as much of its program code, including add-ins, as possible into memory, and the only way to be certain that an add-in is no longer running is to exit the application entirely.

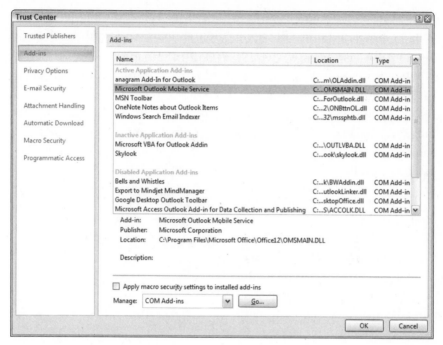

Figure 17.4. The Trust Center dialog box.

To manage the add-ins installed in Outlook, make sure COM Add-ins appears in the selection box at the bottom of the Trust Center dialog box and click Go. The COM Add-Ins dialog box, shown in Figure 17.5, opens. A list of all installed add-ins is displayed. Checked add-ins are active, and unchecked items are disabled. To disable an add-in that you suspect is making Outlook unstable, deselect its check box, click OK, exit Outlook, and then launch the application again to make sure the add-in has been unloaded from your system's memory.

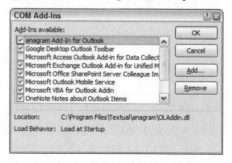

Figure 17.5. The COM Add-Ins dialog box.

Where did my add-in go?

Occasionally, an add-in creates a severe crash, and Outlook unexpectedly quits. When you restart the application, Outlook may present a dialog box stating that an add-in was the source for the crash and asks if you want to disable it before the application launches. Allow Outlook to do this, and after the program has restarted properly, perform the following actions:

1. Exit Outlook.

2. Run SCANPST.exe on your Outlook PST files to repair any damage that may have resulted from the crash. This utility is discussed in Chapters 3 and 26.

3. Restart Outlook.

If you want to re-enable the offending add-in after performing these repairs, open the Trust Center dialog box, select Disabled Items from the drop-down menu at the bottom of the dialog box, and click Go. The Disabled Items dialog box, shown in Figure 17.6, lists any add-ins Outlook has automatically disabled at startup. To

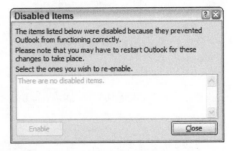

Figure 17.6. The Disabled Items dialog box.

re-enable an add-in, select it from the list and click Enable. You need to exit and restart Outlook once more to reload the add-in.

If everything works as expected, you have most likely encountered a one-time glitch. If the behavior repeats itself, you should uninstall the offending add-in package and check with the developer of that tool to see if others have reported similar issues and if an updated version or patch is available.

Favorite add-ins for Outlook

The extensible nature of Outlook's design has created a robust and thriving add-in ecosystem. A Web search using Windows Live Search finds 127,821 results for the phrase "Outlook add-ins." The range of options can be utterly bewildering, and offerings range from freeware to commercial tools to entire suites of related add-ins.

Over the years that I have been using Outlook, I have found a handful of these add-in tools that I recommend all the time to friends and coworkers. These recommendations are based on my own first-hand experience using the tools as well as feedback from the people who have tried them and found them both useful and stable. Some of the new features in Outlook 2007 have made a number of my standard add-in recommendations unnecessary because the functionality I used to get from the add-ins is now baked right into the application. But some remain useful, even in places where Outlook offers basic functionality.

RSS add-ins

RSS (Really Simple Syndication) is an increasingly popular way to subscribe to an information feed on a Web site or blog and have new content delivered using a tool commonly referred to as an aggregator. Web-based aggregators, stand-alone aggregator applications for your PC, and add-ins for Outlook allow you to aggregate and view RSS subscriptions inside the application.

Built-in RSS tools in Outlook 2007

With the advent of Outlook 2007, Internet Explorer 7, and Windows Vista, RSS has become a system-level source of information. You can subscribe to an RSS feed in either Outlook 2007 or in Internet Explorer 7 and have that feed registered in a system-level master file that Vista manages. The file format for these subscription lists is an emerging industry standard called OPML (Outline Processor Markup Language). Although OPML has other applications besides managing and exchanging RSS subscription lists, that is the task it is used by these application and operating environments to accomplish.

Although the primary discussion in this chapter concerns add-ins, any conversation about RSS add-ins must be had in the context of the built-in capabilities provided by Outlook 2007 — the first version of the application to natively support this subscription format. Although third-party alternatives like ones I describe later in this chapter offer additional features and functionality above what Outlook 2007 provides, you may decide the built-in tools will suffice for your needs.

The Import and Export Wizard screen, shown in Figure 17.7, lists two options for importing a subscription list if you already have been using an aggregator application and have exported an OPML file from that environment or have been subscribing to RSS feeds using Internet Explorer 7. If you have been using a non-Microsoft application to subscribe to and read RSS, choose the OPML import option and locate the file on your PC. If you have been using Internet Explorer 7 to subscribe to and read RSS, choose the System Feeds list option.

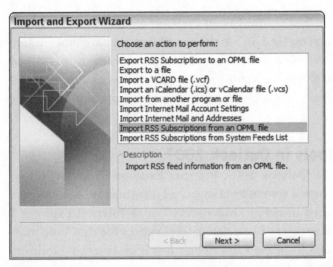

Figure 17.7. The Import and Export Wizard dialog box showing RSS import options.

A second option is to add RSS subscriptions one at a time directly into Outlook as you encounter blogs or Web sites you want to subscribe to. Copy the RSS feed link address from the blog or site in your Web browser, and then, in Outlook, open the Account Settings dialog box from the Tools menu and click the RSS Feeds tab, as pictured in Figure 17.8.

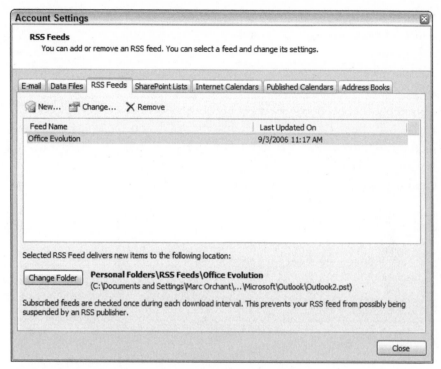

Figure 17.8. The RSS Feeds tab in the Account Settings dialog box.

Click the New button on the command bar above the list area in the dialog box. As you add feeds to Outlook, they are displayed in this list. The New RSS Feed dialog box, shown in Figure 17.9, is displayed. Paste the link you copied in your browser into the dialog box, and click Add.

Outlook checks the link and displays the RSS Feed Options

Figure 17.9. The New RSS Feed dialog box.

dialog box, shown in Figure 17.10. In this dialog box, you can set a number of preferences that affect how the feed is displayed in Outlook, where its content is stored on your PC, and how frequently it checks for updates. The last option in this dialog box, Update Limit, determines from the publisher's site how frequently the source should be queried for new content. You can override this setting by deselecting the check box. If you do, Outlook checks the feed whenever a scheduled or manual Send/Receive command is issued.

Figure 17.10. The RSS Feed Options dialog box.

You can adjust these feed properties at any time by accessing the RSS Feeds tab in the Account Settings dialog box. Select the feed whose properties you want to adjust in the list, and click the Change button on the command bar to access the RSS Feed Options dialog box for that subscription.

After you have successfully subscribed to an RSS feed in Outlook, it is listed under the RSS feeds icon in the Folder List in the Mail view, as shown in Figure 17.11. RSS posts are displayed in essentially the same fashion as e-mail messages in the Message List Pane and are shown in the

Watch Out!

Constantly querying (or "pinging") a blog or site for updates is considered bad etiquette. Every time you check a feed, you are consuming cycles on your PC and adding to the bandwidth load on the server you are checking. In general, you should allow the publisher to specify the frequency and honor that setting.

Reading Pane when selected. Some feeds, like the one for my Office Evolution blog at ZDNet, do not send the entire content but are set up to provide only a summary of the post. To read the full post, you can right-click the orange status message at the top of the post and choose either to have the full content downloaded for viewing in Outlook or to open the blog or Web site in your external browser.

Figure 17.11. An RSS feed in Outlook 2007 with options for reading a full post displayed.

NewsGator Inbox for Microsoft Outlook

www.newsgator.com

NewsGator Inbox has long been a favorite tool for people who want to aggregate, organize, and read RSS feeds inside Outlook. NewsGator Inbox is part of a family of products that also includes FeedDemon, a stand-alone application for working with RSS; NewsGator Online, a browser-based way to read your subscriptions; and NewsGator Mobile, a specially designed view of your RSS feeds meant for reading using the browser on your mobile phone or PDA.

NewsGator provides synchronization across all these platforms, which means that after you have read a particular article or post in one place, it

Hack

If you listen to podcasts — Internet programs produced by amateur and professional commentators — you know that you can subscribe to your favorite programs using their RSS feeds. Both NewsGator and Attensa can be configured to automatically download the MP3 files of the podcasts you subscribe to, as can Outlook's built-in RSS feature.

is marked as read in all other environments. The ability to check on RSS updates in all these environments and always have only new information presented is a great time-saver and has made NewsGator a perennial favorite for Outlook users.

NewsGator provides a custom summary page that you can access by selecting the folder you designate as the location for all RSS subscriptions in your Outlook Folder List. This summary page provides a "river of news" view — a listing of the latest information across all your subscriptions in chronological order from newest to oldest.

Attensa for Outlook

www.attensa.com/products/outlook/

Attensa is a relative newcomer, but offers a very interesting and potentially useful capability called AttentionStream. Like NewsGator, Attensa provides synchronized access to your RSS subscriptions in Outlook, on the Web, and on your handheld mobile device. With AttentionStream, Attensa learns over time which RSS feeds you pay the most attention to and provides a special view where content from those most important feeds is filtered to the top of the RSS list in Outlook.

Attensa also provides a static, hierarchical folder view like the one Outlook and NewsGator provide and a "river of news" view similar to the one provided by NewsGator Inbox. Another nice feature in the Attensa offering is the option to add a toolbar to Internet Explorer or Mozilla Firefox that makes adding subscriptions to Attensa a one-click operation in either browser.

Filing Tools

As with RSS, Outlook 2007 provides basic filing tools. On the Edit menu are the Copy to Folder and Move to Folder commands, which, as their names imply, allow you to file selected e-mail messages or RSS articles into folders in your PST file. Move Items, pictured in Figure 17.12, also can be invoked with the keyboard shortcut Ctrl+Shift+V or by clicking a button on the Standard toolbar. Note in the illustration that you can create a new folder on the fly when moving items using this command.

These basic filing commands, along with the drag-and-drop tech-niques described earlier in the

Figure 17.12. The Move Items dialog box.

book for transforming e-mail messages into calendar items and tasks, may be all you need to perform your filing and organizational actions. However, a number of third-party utilities can enhance these basic capabilities. The following have proved to be very useful.

SpeedFiler

SpeedFiler (www.claritude.com) by Claritude Software is a small yet very powerful add-in that enhances the filing and organizing process in Outlook in four ways:

- Quickly file received messages
- File outgoing messages as you send them
- Find and jump to folders with ease
- Find-as-you-type folder search

SpeedFiler adds a new toolbar to Outlook, pictured in Figure 17.13. From this toolbar, you can perform the actions listed above and set pref-erences for how sent mail is automatically filed. SpeedFiler uses the same Ctrl+Shift+V keyboard shortcut as Outlook's built-in Move to Folder command to invoke the similar but more powerful dialog box shown in Figure 17.14. The SpeedFiler version of this Move Items dialog box allows you to type the first few letters of the folder name in which you want to file your message and automatically presents a pick list of match-ing folders in any PST files you currently have open. SpeedFiler also builds a list of recently accessed folders that you can select from the drop-down menu in the dialog box.

Figure 17.13. SpeedFiler adds this toolbar to Outlook.

Figure 17.14. SpeedFiler's enhanced Move Items dialog box.

Onfolio

Onfolio (`http://toolbar.live.com`) is included in the Windows Live Toolbar enhancement for Internet Explorer. Formerly a third-party application, Onfolio was acquired by Microsoft in March 2006. Onfolio is a rich tool that allows you to collect information from your Outlook e-mail, Web pages, files on your PC, and RSS subscriptions and organize these items for retrieval, review, and sharing at any time.

Inside Outlook, Onfolio adds a small toolbar, pictured in Figure 17.15, that contains two buttons. The first, represented by the application's icon, opens the Onfolio Deskbar, shown in Figure 17.16, a resizable window that

Figure 17.15. The Onfolio toolbar.

Figure 17.16. The Onfolio Deskbar.

can float on top of all other open windows or be docked to the left or right side of your display. The second button, labeled Capture, provides the option to add either e-mail messages or selected message text to an Onfolio collection. The advantage Onfolio offers is that it makes the information you capture from Outlook, as well as other sources, accessible and sharable even when Outlook is not running.

Onfolio also includes an RSS aggregator. You can add feeds individually or import an OPML file to create your subscription list. Onfolio can capture RSS articles you aggregate in Outlook or through its own Feeds tab into any of the collections you create. Onfolio displays a preview of each post in the Deskbar and uses your browser to display the actual blog post or Web page when you select a post in the Deskbar, as pictured in Figure 17.17.

Watch Out!

Onfolio collections can become very large if you add a substantial number of documents. Although Onfolio attempts to manage file bloat, an option in the Preferences dialog box allows you to manually compress the size of your Collection files. I recommend doing this as part of your regular Outlook maintenance if you decide to use this tool.

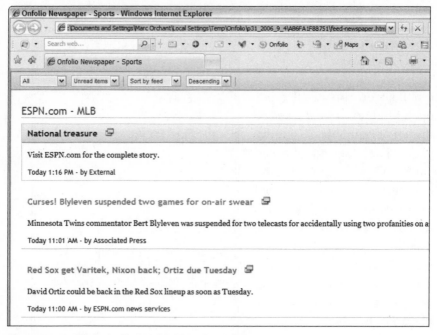

Figure 17.17. RSS feeds displayed in IE7 using Onfolio.

GTD add-in for Outlook (NetCentrics)

Getting Things Done (GTD) is a personal productivity system developed by David Allen. Many Outlook users have worked to adapt Outlook to the practices and principles taught in Allen's books and seminars. For years, Allen has offered a guide to setting up Outlook to support a GTD workflow, but some of the ideas in his system require abilities Outlook simply does not provide. Find more information at http://gtdsupport.netcentrics.com.

In response to continued demand from GTD practitioners who use Outlook, Allen teamed up with NetCentrics to produce the GTD add-in for Outlook. Like SpeedFiler, the GTD add-in provides one-click filing. And, like the ClearContext Inbox Management System (described in Chapter 15), the add-in provides additional tools to generate tasks and appointments from e-mail messages. The add-in also provides tools to Defer and Delegate messages (two of the four Ds in Allen's decision-making — the other two are Do and Delete).

The big deal about the add-in is that it overcomes Outlook's uni-dimensional category tagging by allowing a second project tag to be applied to e-mail messages, tasks, and appointments. If you're familiar with GTD, you know why this is important. The add-in will be updated for Outlook 2007, but development on the update had not begun as of this writing.

Bells and Whistles for Outlook

www.emailaddressmanager.com/outlook-bells.html

I can't say enough about this add-in suite for Outlook. Bells and Whistles for Outlook packs a number of useful tools into a single add-in managed from the Options dialog box shown in Figure 17.18.

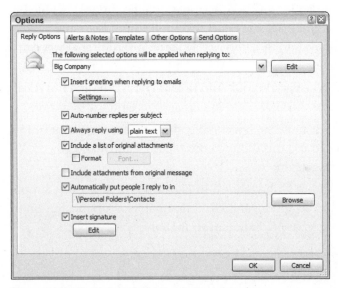

Figure 17.18. The Bells and Whistles Options dialog box.

For the price of most single add-ins ($29.95), Bells and Whistles for Outlook provides a suite of tools that provide the following capabilities:

- Automatically add smart reply greetings and e-mail signatures
- Track message exchanges by adding customizable tracking IDs and reply counters
- Create quick e-mail text templates, or use one of the more than 30 predefined templates
- Send personalized e-mails using the BCC field for mail merge

- Automatically compress file attachments on your outgoing e-mails
- Automatically select the e-mail account through which certain e-mails are sent
- Smartly manage your address book by automatically adding to your Contacts the addresses of people you reply to
- Give reminders to add attachments or message subjects
- Add e-mail notes to Inbox e-mails
- Manage third-party Outlook add-ins

That last feature — the ability to manage third-party add-ins — is a particular favorite of mine for three reasons:

1. You can manage add-ins without having to open Outlook, enable or disable specific add-ins, and restart the application. Bells and Whistles' Outlook Add-in Utility is a separate program that you can run at any time.

2. The Bells and Whistles Outlook Add-in Utility lists a number of third-party add-ins that the COM Add-in Manager in Outlook does not.

3. Should an add-in cause such instability that you are unable to run Outlook, you can use this utility to disable the culprit and get Outlook running again.

The Outlook Add-in Utility, shown in Figure 17.19, has a very simple interface. Select a listed add-in, and click the Enable or Disable button to change its state. Click Save & Exit, and your changes are applied.

Figure 17.19. The Bells and Whistles Outlook Add-in Utility.

Sources for Outlook add-ins

You can find add-ins for Outlook in many places. The natural place to start is your favorite search engine, although as I pointed out at the beginning of this chapter, the sheer number of results can be a bit overwhelming. Popular download sites like C|Net's Download.com and Tucows provide a better experience but still require a substantial amount of searching and filtering to find just what you are looking for.

Over time, I have come to rely on two sites as my primary hunting ground when I need a new add-in to add a specific feature to Outlook. The first is Sperry Software whose home page is shown in Figure 17.20 (www.sperrysoftware.com), which has collected more than 30 high-quality add-ins that add a wide variety of capabilities to Outlook. Sperry Software add-ins range in price from around $10 for a single add-in to $80 for a bundle of related tools. One of my favorite add-ins from this company is the Hide Fax Numbers Add-In ($19.95). If you have ever clicked the To: button when composing an e-mail and been frustrated by the fact that Outlook treats both e-mail and fax numbers as valid addresses, you will see the value in this add-in. It prefixes fax numbers in your Contact list with the word "fax," which has the effect of preventing Outlook from recognizing the number as an address.

The second source I rely on is Slipstick Systems (www.slipstick.com), whose home page is shown in Figure 17.21. This site has collected links to more than 500 add-ins for Outlook and Exchange. Slipstick was started by Sue Mosher, a veteran Microsoft MVP (Most Valuable Professional), and is now operated by Diane Poremsky, another long-time Outlook MVP. Diane's company, CDOLive, runs a number of excellent Outlook sites, many of which are listed in Appendix C. One of the things I really appreciate about Slipstick is that the site offers an RSS feed that provides information on new and updated add-ins on the site.

Inside Scoop

Many Outlook add-ins provide a trial period during which you can evaluate the software to decide whether it provides sufficient value to warrant a purchase. I strongly recommend that you take full advantage of these evaluation periods, which range from 14 to 30 days, before plunking down your hard-earned cash on something that may not meet your needs.

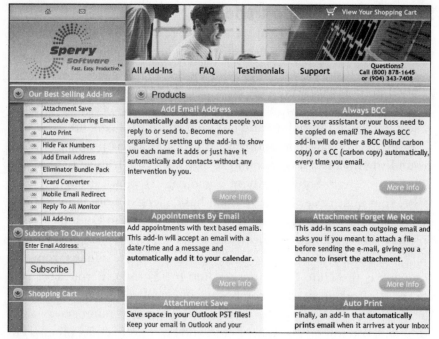

Figure 17.20. The Sperry Software site.

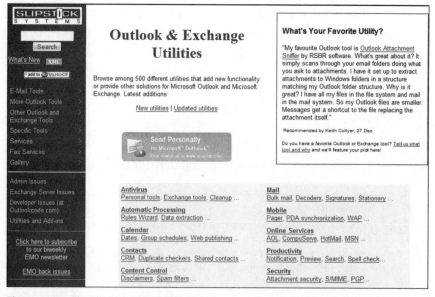

Figure 17.21. The Slipstick Systems site.

External programs that enhance Outlook

Outlook's extensible architecture not only makes add-ins possible, it also provides a wealth of opportunities for other applications to integrate their features and capabilities into your Outlook environment. Microsoft provides integration with a number of its own applications to enhance Outlook's core capabilities, and a number of third-party companies have done the same.

As was the case with add-ins, providing an exhaustive catalog of applications that can work with Outlook is beyond the scope of this book. However, a few applications provide important capabilities that Outlook lacks, and I have some recommendations to make as well.

Outlook Express — Outlook's newsgroup reader

Outlook Express is the e-mail and newsgroup reading application included with Windows and bundled with Internet Explorer 6. Most people, especially those who do not use Microsoft Outlook, are confused by the similar names of these two applications, thinking that Outlook Express is a "light" version of Outlook. Much has been made over the years of Microsoft's questionable decision to name these applications in such a confusing fashion.

The fact is the two applications have only two things in common. First, both applications are e-mail clients. Of course, Outlook (the Office variety) offers a wide range of additional information management and collaboration capabilities. Second, Outlook has long used Outlook Express as a helper application to provide newsgroup reading.

Newsgroups — public or private discussion forums where conversations about a wide variety of topics take place — have been around for as long as there has been a public Internet. Microsoft hosts hundreds of public newsgroups where users, Microsoft employees, and partners like resellers and MVPs engage in conversations about the company's products. Microsoft also uses newsgroups to conduct private conversations with beta test groups and other communities.

Over time, more and more people access newsgroups using a Web browser, but a stand-alone application is still a popular choice because it allows you to read and reply to conversations even when you are not connected to the network. The de facto choice for reading newsgroups for Outlook users has always been Outlook Express.

Follow these steps to access Outlook newsgroups using Outlook Express. In this example, you will add a subscription to Microsoft's public Outlook newsgroup.

1. Launch Outlook Express. If asked whether you want to make Outlook Express your default e-mail program, click No.

2. On the Tools menu in Outlook Express, click Accounts.

3. In the Internet Accounts dialog box, click the Add button, and then click News, as shown in Figure 17.22.

4. The Internet Connection Wizard opens. Type your name in the Display name field, and click Next. Type your e-mail address in the e-mail address field, and click Next.

5. Type **msnews.microsoft.com** in the News (NNTP) Server field.

6. Click Next, click Finish, and then click Close to exit the wizard.

7. A dialog box pops up asking, "Would you like to download newsgroups from the news server you added?" Click Yes.

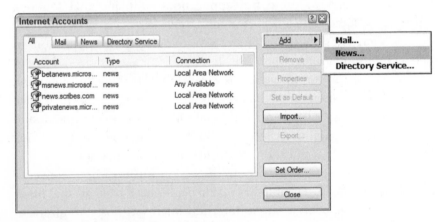

Figure 17.22. The Internet Accounts dialog box.

8. In the Newsgroup Subscriptions dialog box, type **outlook** to display all Outlook newsgroups, as pictured in Figure 17.23. Select the microsoft.public.outlook newsgroup (and any others you're interested in), and click Subscribe.

9. Select the newsgroup in the Folders list in the left pane of the Outlook Express window, and a list of posts appears in the top pane on the right side of the application window. Select a post that looks interesting, and its text is displayed in the Reading Pane, as shown in Figure 17.24.

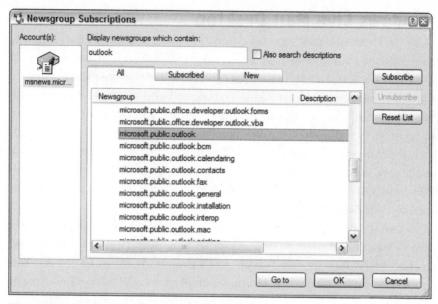

Figure 17.23. The Newsgroup Subscriptions dialog box.

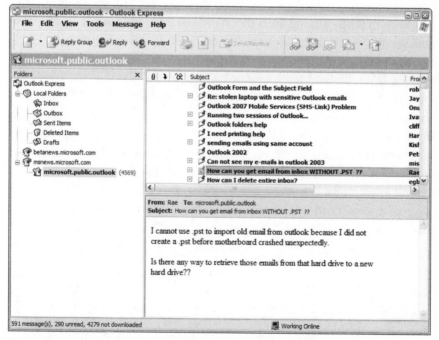

Figure 17.24. Outlook Express displaying the public Outlook newsgroup.

Windows Live Mail Desktop

Outlook Express is getting a bit dated. The program hasn't had a significant update in a number of years, and with the imminent release of Windows Vista and a whole new user interface for the operating system, a number of applications are being redesigned and renamed to align with the Live brand. As part of this overhaul, Outlook Express is being retired in favor of the all-new Windows Live Mail Desktop (not to be confused with the Web-based Windows Live Mail that is replacing Hotmail). A program very much like Windows Live Mail Desktop will be included with Windows Vista. Windows Live Mail Desktop is available as a free download for Windows XP systems.

So what's new in Windows Live Mail Desktop? A few things. In addition to e-mail and newsgroups, Windows Live Mail Desktop can be used to read RSS subscriptions (which you can already do in Outlook). You can send content from your Hotmail e-mail to your Windows Live Spaces blog. But for most Outlook users, think of this mostly as a user interface upgrade for Outlook Express. It has a few nice touches, like the search bar at the very top of the window and an icon and link showing whether you are currently signed into the Windows Live Messenger application and service. Everything looks more modern, as shown in Figure 17.25, but the essential functionality as an adjunct to Outlook for newsgroup reading is unchanged from Outlook Express.

If you install Windows Live Mail Desktop on a Windows XP system, it copies all the newsgroup subscription (and e-mail account) information from your existing Outlook Express setup. If you have newsgroup subscriptions set up already, Windows Live Mail Desktop displays the alert dialog box shown in Figure 17.26, asking if you want to make it the default application for newsgroup reading. If you're not sure you want to say goodbye to Outlook Express, click No. As long as the check box in this dialog box is selected, Windows Live Mail Desktop asks you the same question every time you launch it. Even if you uncheck the box in this

Watch Out!

You must be running Windows XP with Service Pack 2 (SP2) installed and complete a Windows Genuine Advantage (WGA) validation check to download and install Windows Live Mail Desktop and an increasing amount of other free stuff from Microsoft. WGA is one way Microsoft is trying to discourage people from using pirated copies of Windows.

dialog box, you can make Windows Live Mail Desktop your default news-group reader at a later time in its Options dialog box.

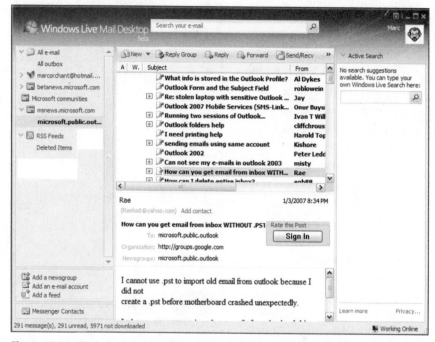

Figure 17.25. Windows Live Mail Desktop updates the look of Outlook Express.

Instant messaging and Outlook

Microsoft has built integration hooks into Outlook 2007 for use with several of their instant messaging (IM) services, includ-ing Microsoft Windows Live Messenger and Microsoft Office Communicator. These services

Figure 17.26. The default newsgroup reader alert dialog box.

allow you to communicate using text chat or a Voice over IP (VoIP) audio and video connection with people in your Contacts list in real time. A number of different IM products are available from Microsoft, and the names can get a bit confusing (it's the Outlook/Outlook Express thing all over again):

- **Microsoft Windows Live Messenger**, pictured in Figure 17.27, is the new thing in the Windows Live family of services and shares a similar interface with Windows Live Mail Desktop, Windows Media Player 11, and other Live-branded applications from Microsoft. You can chat online via text or voice, or have a video conversation with others using the service. Live Messenger includes a Remote Assistance screen-sharing feature that lets you connect to a friend or support technician who can view your computer desktop over the Internet and take control of your cursor to show you how to deal with a problem you may be having. Microsoft and Yahoo! have agreed to allow users on their respective networks to connect, so you can also communicate with people using that instant messaging service. Windows Live Messenger is a free download from Microsoft.

Figure 17.27. Windows Live Messenger.

- **Microsoft MSN Messenger** is the IM tool included with the MSN software suite. If you subscribe to MSN, this is most likely the IM application you have been using.

- **Microsoft Windows Messenger** is included with Microsoft Windows XP. It is essentially identical in features and functionality to MSN Messenger with a different interface.

In Outlook, a contact's online status can be displayed when you rest the cursor on the person's e-mail address in a message. When you are viewing a new meeting request, the online status is displayed when you rest the pointer on the attendee's name. Online status is visible for any person whose IM e-mail address you have added to your instant messaging application's Contact list.

In Outlook, you can add a person's instant messaging address to the IM address text box for that contact, as shown in Figure 17.28. When this person sends you e-mail from the e-mail address saved in his Contact record, his instant messaging address is used to check and display his online status.

Figure 17.28. Add an IM address to your Contact records to enable online status display.

To enable online status, open the Options dialog box from the Tools menu and click the Other tab. Under Person Names, shown in Figure 17.29, check the Display online status next to a person name check box.

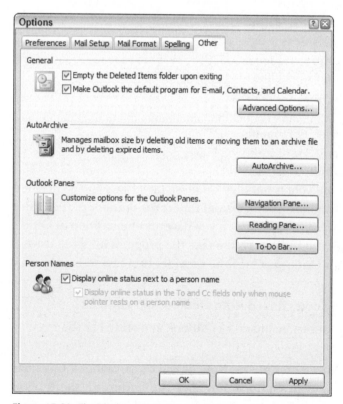

Figure 17.29. The Display online status option.

Other Microsoft Office applications

Outlook is generally installed as the default e-mail handler for the operating system and, as such, can be used by any application installed on your PC that has an e-mail feature builtin to compose and send messages. All 2007 Microsoft Office system applications have this feature on either the Office button menu in Ribbon-driven applications (Word, Excel, and PowerPoint) or from the File menu. The Send command in Office Word 2007 is shown in Figure 17.30. This command allows you to send the current document as a file attachment in an e-mail message.

The Office 2007 system application that is most tightly integrated with Outlook is Office OneNote 2007. OneNote is a digital information capture and reference application that works like a notebook, allowing you to organize meeting notes, information captured from other documents and Web pages, and even audio and video recordings using sections and pages. OneNote is bundled on most Tablet PCs and is included in the Home and Student, Ultimate, and Enterprise editions of the Office suite. It can be purchased separately if you have another edition of Office. A 60-day trial is offered to allow you to take the program for a test drive.

Figure 17.30. The Send e-mail command on the Office button menu in Word 2007.

When used with Outlook, OneNote provides two ways to use the programs together:

- Create meeting notes linked to an Outlook appointment
- Create tasks that can be linked to Outlook and added to the Tasks list

To create meeting notes in OneNote linked to an Outlook Calendar event, open the event in Outlook and click the button on the Ribbon highlighted in Figure 17.31 that shows the OneNote application icon and is labeled Meeting Notes. This icon is added to Outlook automatically when you install OneNote.

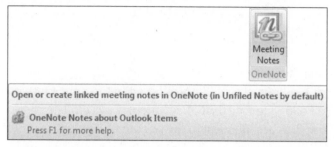

Figure 17.31. The Meeting Notes icon on the Appointment dialog box's Ribbon and its Super Tooltip.

A new page is added to the Unfiled Notes section of your OneNote notebook, and an appointment information grid is automatically generated, as pictured in Figure 17.32. At the bottom of the information grid is a spot to begin capturing notes from the meeting. The link between the meeting notes page and the Outlook event is maintained when you file the notes in a different section of your OneNote notebook.

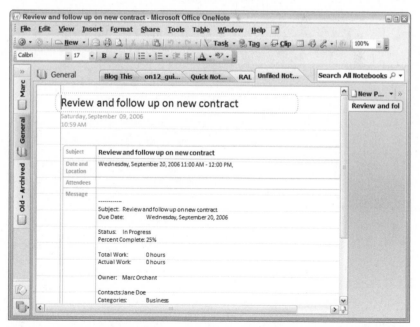

Figure 17.32. A new meeting note in OneNote linked to an Outlook appointment.

Inside Scoop

You can add tasks that synchronize with Outlook on any page in your OneNote notebooks — they are not limited to Meeting Notes pages. To see all the tasks you have created in your OneNote notebooks, you can generate a Note Flags Summary in OneNote at any time.

As you add meeting notes, if you come with up with an action that needs to be taken, you can generate a task that will be added to your Outlook Tasks list by adding a Follow Up Flag from the Outlook Tasks toolbar, shown in Figure 17.33. These flags are identical to the ones in Outlook.

Figure 17.33. The Outlook Tasks toolbar in OneNote.

Clicking the last button on the toolbar opens the associated Task item in Outlook when you select the text of a flagged item in OneNote. As you can see in Figure 17.34, the Outlook item has a OneNote item embedded in the Notes area of the Task item. Double-click this item to open the associated page in your OneNote notebook.

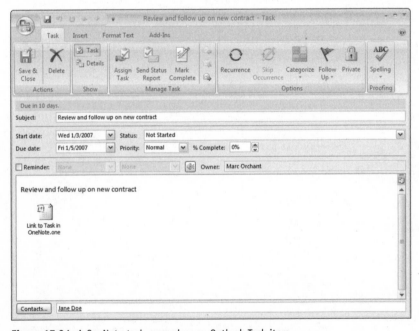

Figure 17.34. A OneNote task opened as an Outlook Task item.

You also can create notes linked to Calendar events or Contacts using the OneNote icon that is added to Standard toolbar in those Outlook main views. As discussed in Chapter 10, Outlook's built-in Notes tool is very basic and not terribly useful for capturing more than a small amount of information. This integration with OneNote is a welcome addition to Outlook 2007 and provides a very rich environment for capturing a variety of information with great synchronization to your Outlook objects and lists.

Third-party applications

The variety of applications, utilities, and add-ins created by third-party developers to enhance and extend the Office suite is rich with options. An entire book could be devoted to this topic alone and would require several chapters just to cover the application software that contributes new functionality to Outlook. In this section, I'd like to introduce you to two utilities and one application that I have found indispensable to my work and that make Outlook a far more useful tool. I've often written that the utilities described here actually make my PC smarter.

ActiveWords

www.activewords.com

This utility does so many things that it's difficult to fit it into a specific category. In essence, ActiveWords is a macro recorder — that is, it allows you to create a simple shortcut (a few letters or a single word) to perform an action on your PC. That action may be something as simple as launching an application or opening a Web page in your browser, or as sophisticated as launching an application, creating a new document, and inserting boilerplate text you've saved for frequent reuse. The possibilities are virtually endless.

A number of macro recorders and keyboard shortcut generators are available. Here are three things that set ActiveWords above and apart from all of them for me:

■ The ActiveWords Outlook Agent, shown in Figure 17.35, is a plug-in "application" that includes dozens of preconfigured commands to invoke actions in Outlook using a simple phrase. For example, the Outlook Agent turns every record in your Contact list into an ActiveWord. I can open the ActiveWords ActionPad, shown in Figure 17.36, and type "Jane Doe" to open her Contact record at any time, no matter what I happen to be doing or what application is on my screen. I can also type a contact name in any application and press the ActiveWords trigger key (F8 by default) to have ActiveWords look at the text I have just typed and match it to any ActiveWord I have defined.

- A very easy-to-learn yet incredibly powerful scripting language makes it easy to construct complex sequences without having to be a programming genius (which I definitely am not!).

- The ActiveWords InkPad allows Tablet PC users to write ActiveWords on a small floating palette to invoke actions.

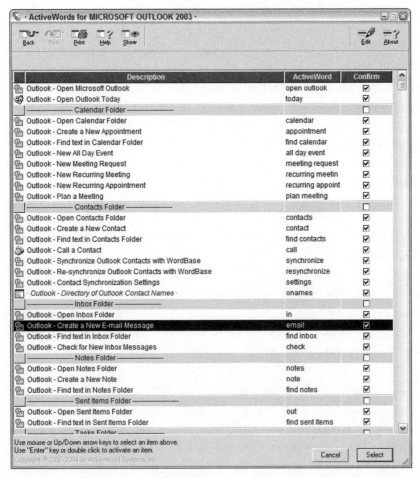

Figure 17.35. The ActiveWords Outlook Agent.

Figure 17.36. The ActiveWords ActionPad.

Building your own ActiveWords is a straightforward process. To create an ActiveWord that will send an e-mail message to Jane Doe requires three simple steps. First, choose Add new ActiveWords from the menu on the ActiveWords toolbar to open The ActiveWords Add Wizard, shown in Figure 17.37.

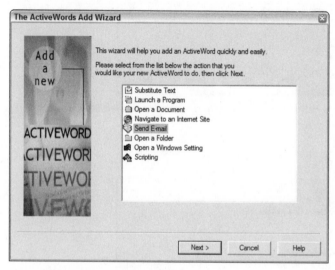

Figure 17.37. The ActiveWords Add Wizard.

Select Send E-mail from the list of actions, and click Next. The next screen has two fields. Add the e-mail address of the person you want to send messages to in the first field, and give the ActiveWord a descriptive name in the second field, as illustrated in Figure 17.38.

In the final wizard screen, shown in Figure 17.39, enter the actual text you want to associate with this ActiveWord. For this example, I've chosen "jdmail." I can type "jdmail" into the ActionPad or anywhere I'm working, followed by the ActiveWords trigger key (F8 by default), and a new Outlook e-mail addressed to Jane opens. If Outlook is not running, the application is launched and the new e-mail message is created and addressed, ready for me to enter text.

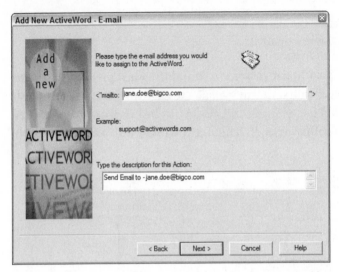

Figure 17.38. Enter an e-mail address and name for the action in this second screen.

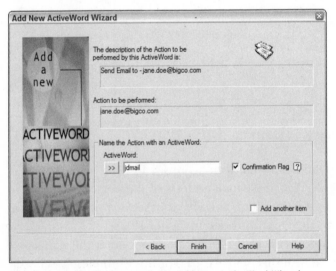

Figure 17.39. The final screen in the Add New ActiveWord Wizard — define the new ActiveWord.

Another way I use ActiveWords is to automate the creation of standard e-mail responses I send on a regular basis. Using the text substitution feature, I create an e-mail response to a frequently asked question I receive, such as a pitch to review a new software product on my blog. I receive an average of 10 requests like this every week, and I just don't have enough time to look at all the products being offered. So I've composed a brief "no thank you" e-mail response that I can generate by typing the ActiveWord "nothx." This ActiveWord issues the Reply command, inserts my boilerplate response, and issues a Send command. I figure I save at least 15 minutes each week using this one ActiveWord. Multiply that savings by the dozens of ActiveWords I have constructed, and the time-savings becomes very significant.

A 60-day evaluation of ActiveWords is available to provide plenty of time for you to see if the utility is right for you. When you request the 60-day trial license, you'll receive a helpful set of tutorial e-mails to guide you through some of the application's features, and you can try the Outlook Agent and the other add-in applications the company offers free to all users.

Anagram

http://getanagram.com

Occasionally, you find a piece of software that fundamentally changes the way you work. For me, that application is Anagram. This small utility sits invisibly in the system tray waiting to perform its magic at the press of a key. What Anagram does is intelligently parse whatever text is selected — on a Web page, in an e-mail message, or in a document — and determine whether it should create a new Contact, Calendar event, Task, or Note in Outlook.

It puts each piece of text into the correct field automatically and cuts the time required to create a new data object in Outlook from minutes to a few seconds. Its accuracy is uncanny, and on the rare occasion that the text I've selected is somewhat ambiguous, I can ask Anagram to rescan the text as the object type I intended with a click of the appropriate button in its dialog box, which is shown in Figure 17.40.

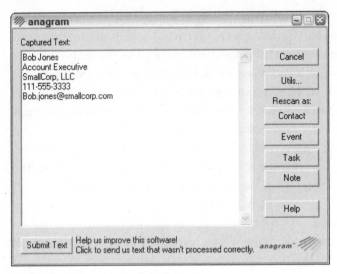

Figure 17.40. The anagram dialog box.

Anagram provides an extensive set of preferences to control how text is captured, parsed, and rendered. Figure 17.41 shows the Addresses tab in the Preferences dialog box.

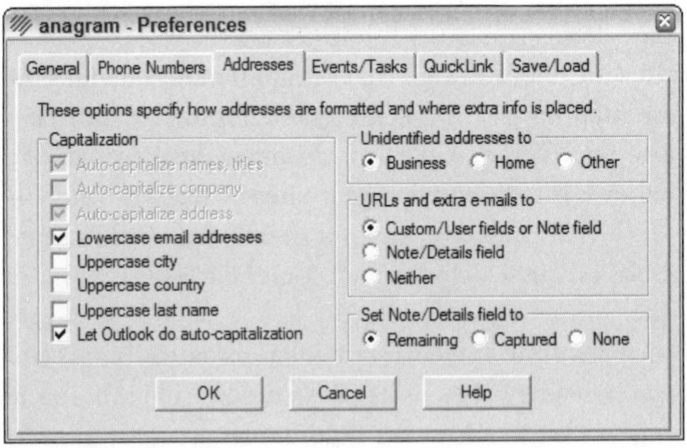

Figure 17.41. anagram's Preferences dialog box.

Anagram offers a 45-day evaluation period to test-drive the utility; it also offers a generous licensing scheme that allows you to add licenses for additional PCs at a nominal price. Like ActiveWords, Anagram saves time every single time I use it, and the aggregate savings these two utilities provide translates into an hour or more every week that I can spend getting real work done rather than performing repetitive tasks.

Mindjet MindManager Pro

www.mindjet.com

MindManager is an application for creating mind maps on your PC. Mind mapping is a technique popularized by Tony Buzan, a deep thinker from the UK who has spent his career documenting how the human brain works and how creativity happens. Mind maps can be used in a variety of ways — to brainstorm, outline a document, plan a project, or collect and organize research. I use MindManager Pro to do all these things.

Mindjet, the company that developed MindManager, has gone to extraordinary lengths to provide integration with the Microsoft Office suite. You can export maps to Word, PowerPoint, or Project and can import spreadsheet data from Excel. MindManager Pro's integration with Outlook is, not surprisingly, one of my favorite features in the application. You can create Outlook data objects as elements of your mind map that synchronize with your Outlook PST file.

As Figure 17.42 shows, MindManager Pro includes map parts to create new contacts, appointments, and tasks. Once created and synched to Outlook, these objects can be updated or modified in either environment and updated in the other with a single mouse click. MindManager Pro installs toolbar buttons in Outlook (and the other Office applications it integrates with) and provides toolbar buttons for synching with Outlook and other Office applications in its own interface.

Using a mind map to manage meetings and projects is a powerful and very engaging change from other methods of sharing and capturing information. Mindjet offers a 21-day evaluation period to try out MindManager Pro and see how it works for you.

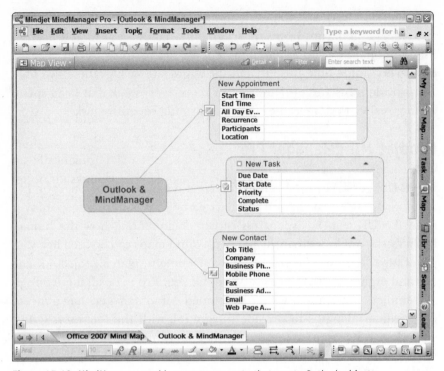

Figure 17.42. MindManager provides smart map parts that create Outlook objects.

Just the facts

- Add-ins can provide Outlook with new features and functionality, but exercise caution and restraint to avoid making Outlook unstable.

- Third-party RSS tools like NewsGator Inbox and Attensa provide more options than the built-in feature in Outlook at additional cost.

- Outlook 2007 has basic filing tools such as SpeedFiler, Onfolio, Bells and Whistles, and GTD to assist you in organizing your e-mail messages.

- Many applications have Outlook integration built in and can extend and enhance how you use the program.

- Outlook Express and Windows Live Mail Desktop provide newsgroup reading features that Outlook itself does not offer.

- Microsoft offers a number of instant messaging applications that can integrate with Outlook for real-time text, voice, or video chat.

- Office OneNote 2007 offers bi-directional integration with Outlook for creating meeting notes and tasks that can be accessed from both applications.

- ActiveWords can automate many Outlook operations and perform complex sequences of actions from a single command.

- Anagram intelligently parses selections of text and automatically creates properly formatted contacts, calendar events, tasks, or notes depending on the text you have selected with the press of a hot key.

- Mindjet MindManager Pro allows you to create mind maps with embedded Outlook objects that synchronize with your PST files.

GET THE SCOOP ON...
The Research Pane ■ Using the Research Pane ■
Quick tips ■ Configuring Research Pane options ■
Adding new research services

Using Outlook as a Research Tool

Chapter 18

Microsoft first introduced the Research Pane in Office 2003, and it was a welcome, if overlooked, addition to the suite. Prior to that release, something as simple as looking up the meaning of a word or consulting a thesaurus for an alternative choice meant launching a browser or other application. Looking up information about a company or referencing an online encyclopedia posed similar context switching costs. The Research Pane changed all that by providing access to these and other sources of information inside Outlook and other Office applications.

In Office 2007, many of the Task Panes have been eliminated and their functions replaced by clusters of commands on the Ribbon. The Research Pane is one of the few that justly survived this purge, and it returns essentially unchanged in the latest version of Office. This chapter introduces the Research Pane, explains its use, and discusses how it can be configured to present the reference sources most useful for your work.

An Overview of the Research Pane

The Research Pane can be displayed as a floating window, as pictured in Figure 18.1, or it can be docked to the right edge of the e-mail or task window you are working in. In either display mode, the pane includes a field where you can enter a word or phrase, a drop-down menu listing all of the available research services you can use, a large results field, and a link at the bottom that provides access to options. In actual use, the field at the top is automatically populated with the word or phrase you have selected in the text of the object you are working with.

The Research Pane utilizes information sources on the Web, your PC, or depending on the environment in which you use Outlook, your intranet. A number of services are available in the Microsoft Windows Marketplace, and later in this chapter we look at how additional services can be added to your list of references. Office 2007 includes a number of pre-installed services that you can reference in the standard installation of Outlook. These sources include:

Figure 18.1. The Research Pane in floating window mode.

Reference books

- Microsoft Encarta English Dictionary
- A thesaurus
- Translation dictionaries

Research sites

- Microsoft Encarta Online Encyclopedia
- MSN Search
- Factiva iWorks (premium)
- Highbeam Research (premium)

Business and financial sites

- MSN Money Stock Quotes
- Thomas Gale Company Profiles (premium)

Inside Scoop

Premium services require a per-item purchase or a subscription. The premium services Microsoft includes in standard Office installations provide a brief abstract in the results field and a link to the premium service site where you can access the full article.

As this chapter was being written, Microsoft was still making the transition from the MSN Search brand to the new Windows Live Search brand. Results in the Research Pane appear under the MSN Search banner but display in a Windows Live Search page in your browser when you click the link at the bottom of each result.

Using the Research Pane

The Research Pane is available only in certain contexts when working in Outlook. You can access the Research Pane in the following views:

- Main Mail view with the Reading Pane displayed
- Mail message window
- Appointment or Meeting Request window
- Contact record window
- Journal entry window

You can access the Research Pane in two ways when working in these contexts. To look up the meaning of a word and open the Research Pane, press the ALT key and click the word you are interested in. In Figure 18.2, the word "contract" has been looked up in an e-mail message window and the Research Pane, in docked mode, shows the results of that search.

The second technique, which can be used to look up the meaning of a single word, uses the Thesaurus to find a synonym, conduct research on a phrase, or perform a translation of selected text, is illustrated in Figure 18.3. Select the word or phrase and right-click the selection to display the context menu. On the menu, choose the Look Up, Translate, or Synonyms command and the Research Pane opens, as shown in Figure 18.4.

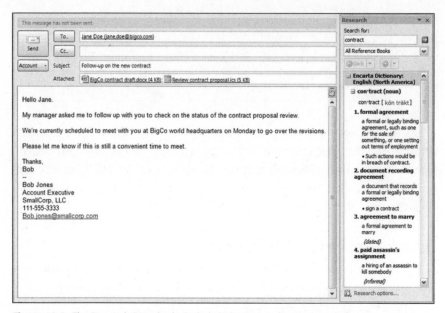

Figure 18.2. The Research Pane in docked mode in an e-mail message window.

Figure 18.3. The Look Up command on the right-click context menu.

Hack

You can make your research much more efficient by selecting the reference book or research service you want to use from the drop-down menu to reduce visual clutter. With the Research Pane visible, select the resource you want to use; enter the word or phrase you want to look up, translate, or research; and press Enter to get just the results you are looking for.

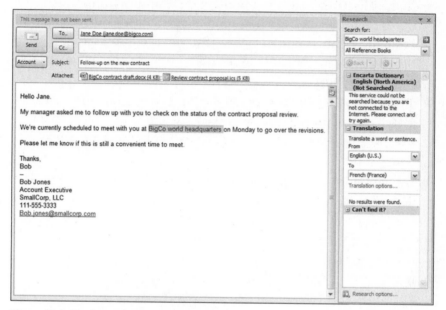

Figure 18.4. The Research Pane displaying results of a phrase search.

By default, Outlook displays results from its reference books but not the research or business sites it can access. To search those resources, either you can select a different service from the drop-down menu directly below the search text field, or you can expand the section labeled "Can't Find It?" at the end of the results listings and click one of the links presented under the heading Other places to search.

You can expand and collapse sections in the Research Pane listings using the plus and minus icons next to each section heading. These controls work in identical fashion to the ones in Outlook's list views.

Research Pane Quick Tips

These tips tell you how to get the best results from the Research Pane and provide some additional options for putting those results to work:

- The Research Pane has Back and Forward buttons like the ones found in a Web browser. During an Outlook session (that is, until you exit the application), you can access any of the results you have generated using these buttons. Clicking the button itself moves you back or forward one result at a time. Clicking the arrow next to the button displays a menu listing all the available results in that direction.

- In the Thesaurus, when you position the cursor over one of the words in the results list, a box appears with a drop-down menu icon. From the menu, shown in Figure 18.5, you can insert the word at the current insertion point in the object you are working in or copy it to the Clipboard.

- To find additional synonyms if the initial results from a Thesaurus search do not provide what you need, use the Look Up command from the drop-down menu described earlier to use that word as the search term.

- You can Move, Size, or Close the Research Pane using commands accessible from the small triangle icon on the pane's title bar.

Figure 18.5. Access useful commands in Thesaurus results from this menu.

Configuring the Research Pane

To control which services are available in the Research Pane and set other preferences, click the Research options link at the bottom of the pane to display the dialog box shown in Figure 18.6. The Research Options dialog box lists all the services available to Outlook and the other Office applications you have installed on your system. These services are grouped into the same four categories displayed in the pane itself: Reference Books, Research Sites, Business and Financial Sites, and Other Services.

To add a service to the Research Pane, select its check box. To disable a service, deselect its check box. Each service has a Properties sheet that you can view by selecting a service in the list and clicking the Properties button pictured in Figure 18.6. The Service Properties dialog box, shown in Figure 18.7, provides information about the service publisher, a brief description, copyright information, and the address from which the service is hosted. Some services provide configuration options from this Properties dialog box.

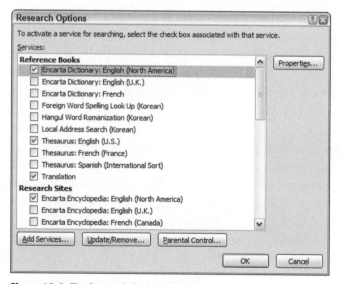

Figure 18.6. The Research Options dialog box.

Figure 18.7. The Service Properties dialog box.

Clicking the Update/Remove button in the Research Options dialog box opens the dialog box shown in Figure 18.8. In this window, you can update services currently available in the Research Pane or remove unneeded services.

If you use Office on a shared PC and some of the users are children, you may want to enable the Parental Control feature. This option enables blocking of inappropriate content in the Research Pane from those services that provide a filtering option. Not all services do. The Parental Control dialog box, shown in Figure 18.9, provides two check box options to allow you to enable these controls. The first enables filtering from those services that have Parental Control available. The second restricts the use of services that do not provide these filters. You can (and should) specify a password to lock the Parental Control feature if it applies to your PC environment.

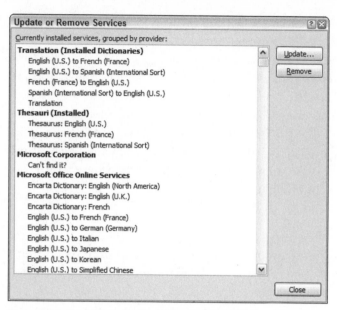

Figure 18.8. The Update or Remove Services dialog box.

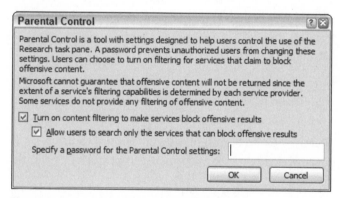

Figure 18.9. The Parental Control dialog box.

Adding new research services

You can add commercial research services to your Office installation and subscribe to services your company may have set up on your intranet. The best place to find commercial service offerings is the Office Marketplace

Web site. Office Marketplace is accessible from the Office Online Web portal. You can access this resource by selecting Microsoft Office Online from the Help menu. After the Office Online page is open, select the Downloads tab and enter "research services" in the search box. You can access this page directly from the Research Pane by clicking the Get Services on Office Marketplace link at the bottom of the pane.

If you are interested in technical information about how to build research services yourself, visit MSDN, the Microsoft Developer Network Web site, and navigate to the Office Developer Center, where a variety of articles, templates, and tools are available.

Just the facts

- The Research Pane can provide a number of handy reference and research options that formerly required opening a Web browser or using an external application.

- Research services installed with Office 2007 include reference books, research sites, and business and financial sites.

- The Research Pane is accessible only in certain views in Outlook — the main Mail view and Message, Appointment, Task, Contact, and Journal item windows.

- To open the Research Pane, press the ALT key and click a word in the text you are viewing, or select one or more words and choose Look Up from the right-click context menu.

- Thesaurus results provide an action menu you can use to insert or copy a result into the object you are editing or to perform a secondary lookup.

- Parental Controls are available to filter inappropriate material if your Office installation is on a PC used by children.

- Additional commercial services can be found in the Office Marketplace at the Microsoft Office Online Web portal.

- Information about developing your own research services can be found on the MSDN Web site.

Using Outlook with Business Contact Manager

Microsoft first introduced the Business Contact Manager in Office 2003 to provide a lightweight Customer Relationship Management (CRM) system for sales professionals and small business owners. Business Contact Manager is an add-in application for Outlook that provides a set of tools for defining accounts and contacts, managing sales opportunities and marketing campaigns. Outlook 2007 with Business Contact Manager also can be used with Microsoft Small Business Accounting to manage inventory, create invoices, and track payables and receivables. Outlook 2007 with Business Contact Manager is included in the Office 2007 Small Business, Office 2007 Professional, and Office 2007 Ultimate editions of the suite.

This chapter includes an overview of Business Contact Manager but is in no way intended to be a complete guide to its use. After reading this chapter, if you decide that the capabilities Business Contact Manager provides are applicable to your work, you can learn more about the product on the Microsoft Office Online Web site (http://office. microsoft.com) and access a product guide, tutorials, and other resources to assist you in using the add-in.

Chapter 19

What is Business Contact Manager?

Sales professionals and small business owners face a unique challenge when it comes to tracking their interactions with their contacts. Keeping on top of opportunities, managing correspondence, and tracking the results of marketing campaigns can be a complex and challenging operation. In its standard form, Outlook provides some, but not all, of the tools needed to manage this information.

Larger organizations rely on CRM software to consolidate and organize contact, sales, and marketing information, but such software tends to be too complex and expensive for individuals or small businesses to use. Microsoft offers a product called Dynamics CRM for larger organizations that allows sales teams to share customer information. Outlook 2007 with Business Contact Manager provides the most essential tools offered in CRM systems and integrates them directly into the familiar Outlook interface for individual use.

Business Contact Manager adds tools and views to Outlook 2007 that provide consolidated views of the information related to accounts, individual contacts, opportunities, and marketing campaigns. This information is maintained in a database file separate from your Outlook PST files using SQL Server Express, a runtime version of Microsoft SQL Server that is installed with Business Contact Manager.

Business Contact Manager uses other Office applications, including Word, Excel, PowerPoint, and Publisher, to produce the reports, documents, and marketing tools. It is designed to generate and link to accounts, contacts, and campaigns. In Word, for example, the Office menu displays a new Business Contact Manager submenu, as shown in Figure 19.1.

Business Contact Manager provides the following capabilities.

Figure 19.1. Business Contact Manager integration in Word 2007.

> **Watch Out!**
>
> SQL Server Express launches at startup, consumes a significant amount of memory and system resources, and runs in the background even when Outlook is not running. On a system with 512 MB of RAM, the performance hit will be noticeable, especially if you tend to keep a number of applications running at one time.

Customer information

- Access all information related to a contact — including e-mail messages, phone calls, appointments, tasks, notes, and documents.

- Share customer information with coworkers using password-protected network access.

- View customer financial history at a glance when Business Contact Manager is used with Microsoft Office Small Business Accounting.

- Simplify billing when Business Contact Manager is used with Office Small Business Accounting. You can track billable time on your Outlook calendar and then convert it into invoices.

Sales activities

- Collect and manage contact information, lead sources, documents, appointments, tasks, and all communications history.

- Track and monitor sales opportunities by type, progress, products and services offered, projected sales amount, and likelihood of closing. Leads can be assigned to employees or co-workers.

- Track prospects and customers from initial contact through closing and after the sale.

- Convert sales opportunities into quotes, orders, and invoices when Business Contact Manager is used with Office Small Business Accounting.

- Forecast sales and prioritize tasks in Business Contact Manager's main views to provide a customizable overview of your company's sales pipeline.

- Provide a variety of customer, prospect, and opportunity reports to help you sort and filter information. You can export information to Office Excel 2007 for more in-depth analysis.

Marketing activities

- Use wizards to guide you through the process of developing marketing campaigns and planning and completing campaign activities.

- Create targeted mailing lists by filtering prospect and customer data — and then use Business Contact Manager's e-mail merge feature to generate personalized mailings. Lists can be exported to Office Publisher 2007 or Office Word 2007 to produce personalized documents.

- Track every marketing campaign you send to your contacts automatically in their communications history.

- Measure the success of your campaigns using the Marketing Campaign tracking feature, so you can increase the effectiveness of future initiatives.

Project information

- Collect and organize all your project information, including activities, e-mail messages, meetings, notes, and attachments, using the Business Projects feature.

- Assign tasks to others and transfer task information to their Outlook environments using the Project Tasks feature.

Installing Business Contact Manager

When you install Business Contact Manager, the installer checks the version of the .NET Framework on your PC and applies any required patches before beginning the installation of the SQL Server Express engine and the Business Contact Manager application. After the initial installation is complete, a setup wizard guides you through the process of making initial decisions about how Business Contact Manager will work in your Outlook 2007 environment.

In the first step of the wizard, shown in Figure 19.2, I recommend you select the Express option unless you have previously worked with Business Contact Manager and already have a database file set up specifically to meet your needs.

Welcome

Microsoft Office Outlook 2007 with Business Contact Manager (Beta) can help you:

- Market your products and services directly to customers and leads.
- Customize forms and lists to best fit your business needs.
- Better manage your business projects with detailed scheduling capabilities.
- Integrate seamlessly with your accounting application for improved cost management.
- Take your business contact information with you on your laptop for quick access.
- Better add, track, and convert key opportunities to maximize sales.

Click one of the following options:

⊙ **Express**
Create a new or use an existing local Business Contact Manager database.

○ **Advanced**
Create or select a Business Contact Manager database on this computer, or select an existing database on a different (remote) computer.

Figure 19.2. The first screen in the setup wizard.

The second screen in the wizard, shown in Figure 19.3, registers your Business Contact Manager installation. Two options are provided. If you are willing to provide your contact information, Microsoft provides you with credits that you can use to create mailing lists using their List Builder service and subscribes you to an e-mail newsletter that provides tips and ideas for using Business Contact Manager. A second, anonymous option registers you without requiring you to provide any personal information or opt in to any further marketing communications.

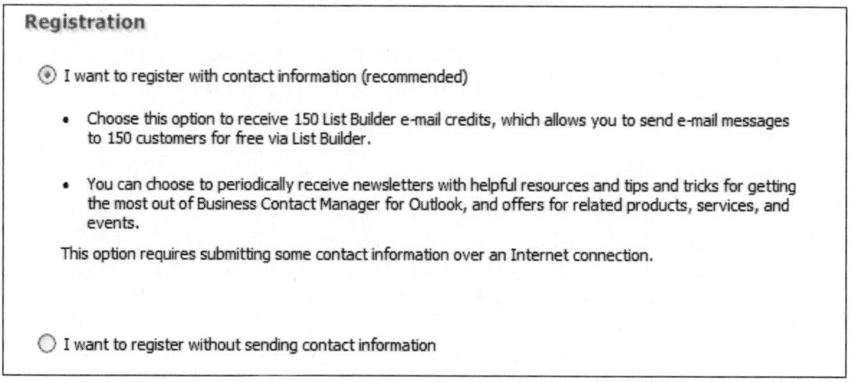

Registration

⊙ I want to register with contact information (recommended)

- Choose this option to receive 150 List Builder e-mail credits, which allows you to send e-mail messages to 150 customers for free via List Builder.

- You can choose to periodically receive newsletters with helpful resources and tips and tricks for getting the most out of Business Contact Manager for Outlook, and offers for related products, services, and events.

This option requires submitting some contact information over an Internet connection.

○ I want to register without sending contact information

Figure 19.3. The second screen in the setup wizard.

If you elect to provide the requested personal information, the third wizard screen, shown in Figure 19.4, is displayed. Enter your e-mail address (required) and any other information you care to share, select the e-mail information you're willing to receive, and click Next. This completes the setup of Business Contact Manager. The remaining screens in the wizard provide an introduction to the additions Business Contact Manager makes to the Outlook UI and provide links to helpful information online.

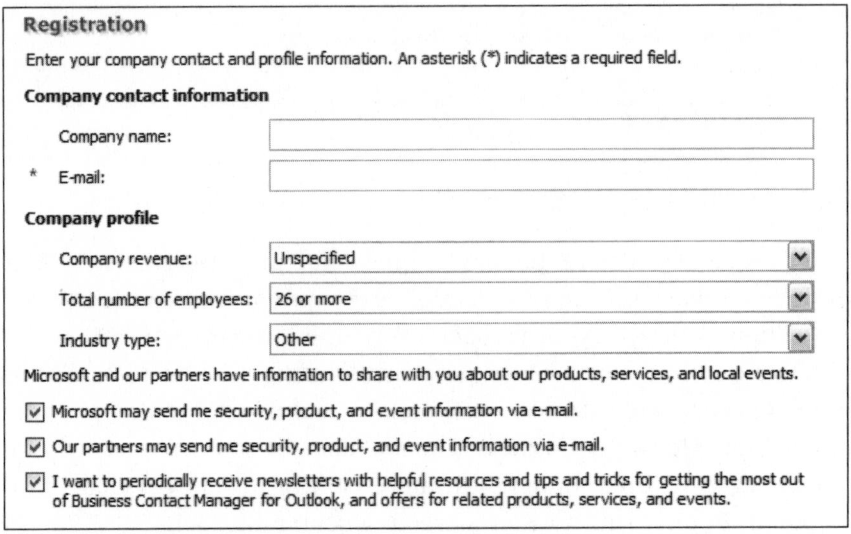

Registration

Enter your company contact and profile information. An asterisk (*) indicates a required field.

Company contact information

Company name: [   ]

*   E-mail: [   ]

Company profile

Company revenue: [Unspecified   ▼]

Total number of employees: [26 or more   ▼]

Industry type: [Other   ▼]

Microsoft and our partners have information to share with you about our products, services, and local events.

☑ Microsoft may send me security, product, and event information via e-mail.

☑ Our partners may send me security, product, and event information via e-mail.

☑ I want to periodically receive newsletters with helpful resources and tips and tricks for getting the most out of Business Contact Manager for Outlook, and offers for related products, services, and events.

Figure 19.4. The third screen in the setup wizard.

The next wizard screen, shown in Figure 19.5, illustrates the Business Contact Manager menu, toolbar, and folder contents.

Inside Scoop

The List Builder credits may come in handy when you need to build a new prospecting list and the e-mails Microsoft sends to Business Contact Manager users are generally pretty helpful. You can opt out and unsubscribe at any time, so I suggest getting the credits and taking a look at a couple of issues to decide if there's value for you.

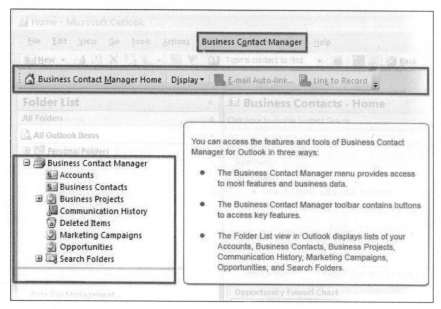

Figure 19.5. The first introduction screen in the setup wizard.

The second screen in the setup wizard's introduction, shown in Figure 19.6, explains three of the key components in Business Contact Manager:

- Accounts and Business Contacts help you keep track of the companies and individuals you do business with. These contact records are distinct from those in your Outlook Contact list and are stored in Business Contact Manager's SQL database.

- Business Projects let you organize and manage business activities and relate them to Accounts and Business Contacts.

- Marketing Campaigns help you select and target your best customers and leads with promotions, discounts, and other marketing communications.

The final screen of the startup wizard, shown in Figure 19.7, contains some very useful links to resources that address a number of helpful topics. Much of this information is also contained in the Business Contact Manager Help file, but I strongly recommend that you click each of these links and review the information before you proceed. You may want to print the material out for handy reference as you begin working with Business Contact Manager.

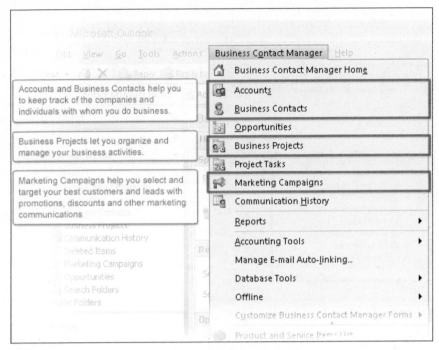

Figure 19.6. The second introduction screen in the setup wizard.

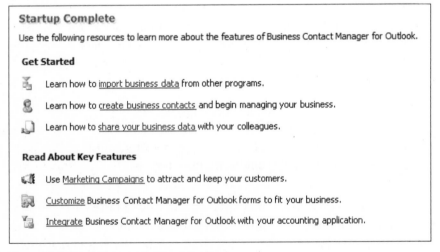

Figure 19.7. The final screen in the setup wizard.

After setup is complete, you will find one or two e-mail messages in your Inbox welcoming you to Business Contact Manager and, if you provided registration information, a confirmation of your registration with a code to enable your List Builder credits. The welcome e-mail, shown in Figure 19.8, describes some of the new and improved features in Outlook 2007 with Business Contact Manager and is similar to the welcome e-mail you saw in your Inbox when you first installed Outlook.

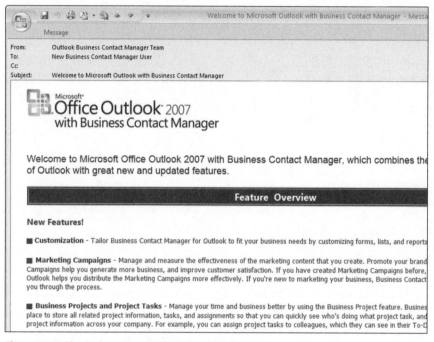

Figure 19.8. The Business Contact Manager welcome e-mail.

Using Business Contact Manager

Business Contact Manager makes substantial changes to Outlook. As shown in Figure 19.9, a new menu, toolbar, and folder are added to the main Outlook screen. Controls are also added to e-mail, appointment, and task item windows to assist you in linking existing information to the business accounts and contacts you create.

View tabs

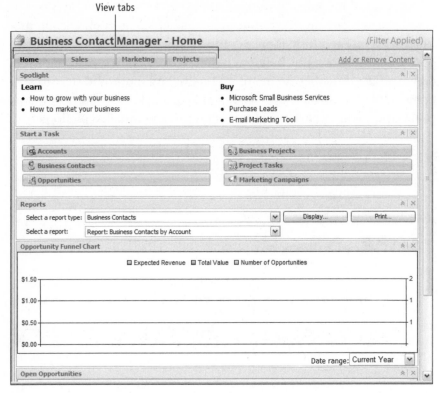

Figure 19.9. The main Business Contact Manager view.

The Home screen is the dashboard for all Business Contact Manager activities and provides a set of buttons for creating new Business Contact Manager items, a section for selecting reports and generating them, and a summary graph of your sales opportunities from all accounts. Along the top of the main view area are a series of tabs labeled Sales, Marketing, and Projects, which display specific sets of tools and actions related to each of those activity areas.

Along with these additions to the user interface, the New menu in Outlook main views is changed after Business Contact Manager is installed. As you can see in Figure 19.10, a new section is added to the menu that lists all the data objects you can create in Outlook with Business Contact Manager. You will notice a Business Note object listed in this new menu section. These notes are linked to an account and are far more useful than the very basic sticky notes Outlook provides. The Phone Log option is virtually identical to the Business Note form with the addition of a timer so you can track how long you spend on a call — especially helpful if you bill for your time.

The Business Manager Home screen is highly customizable and can be configured to display the information you find most useful. To make changes to what is shown on the home page, click the link labeled Add or Remove Content in the upper-right corner of the Home screen view to display the dialog box shown in Figure 19.11. This Add or Remove Content dialog box presents a series of check boxes that you can select or deselect to customize the Home screen.

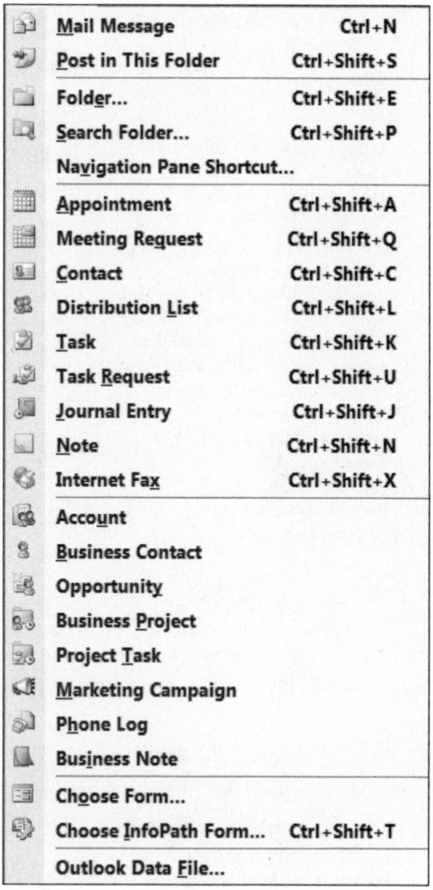

	Mail Message	Ctrl+N
	Post in This Folder	Ctrl+Shift+S
	Folder...	Ctrl+Shift+E
	Search Folder...	Ctrl+Shift+P
	Navigation Pane Shortcut...	
	Appointment	Ctrl+Shift+A
	Meeting Request	Ctrl+Shift+Q
	Contact	Ctrl+Shift+C
	Distribution List	Ctrl+Shift+L
	Task	Ctrl+Shift+K
	Task Request	Ctrl+Shift+U
	Journal Entry	Ctrl+Shift+J
	Note	Ctrl+Shift+N
	Internet Fax	Ctrl+Shift+X
	Account	
	Business Contact	
	Opportunity	
	Business Project	
	Project Task	
	Marketing Campaign	
	Phone Log	
	Business Note	
	Choose Form...	
	Choose InfoPath Form...	Ctrl+Shift+T
	Outlook Data File...	

Figure 19.10. The New menu with Business Contact Manager commands added.

Navigating in Business Contact Manager view

Business Contact Manager provides a number of ways to navigate through its views. You can use the buttons and links presented on the Home screen when you are working in the Business Contact Manager folder to access the Marketing, Sales, and Projects tabs in that view. In any view, you have the ability to jump to the Home screen or the major work areas in Business Contact Manager from the toolbar shown in Figure 19.12.

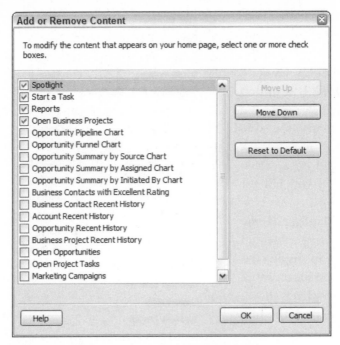

Figure 19.11. The Add or Remove Content dialog box.

Figure 19.12. The Business Contact Manager toolbar.

The toolbar contains three buttons and a navigation menu:

■ **Business Contact Manager Home,** as its name implies, takes you to the Home screen.

- **Display** presents a drop-down menu as shown in Figure 19.12 with links to the Accounts, Business Contacts, Opportunities, Business Projects, Project Tasks, Marketing Campaigns, and Communication History views in the Business Contact Manager.

- **E-mail Auto-link** establishes a link between the sender of a selected e-mail message and a Business Contact Manager Account.

- **Link to Record** establishes a link between a selected e-mail message, calendar item, or task and a Business Contact Manager Project.

The Business Contact Manager menu, shown in Figure 19.13, duplicates the listings on the toolbar's Display menu and provides additional commands to access reports, the Configuration and Options dialog boxes for Business Contact Manager, and an interface that allows you to import data about your products and services from a database or Excel file. It is outside the scope of this chapter to investigate all the reports, configuration options, and tools Business Contact Manager provides, but you can find excellent reference information about these tools and options in the Business Contact Manager help file and on the Office Online Web site.

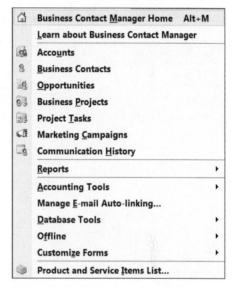

Figure 19.13. The Business Contact Manager menu.

Business Contact Manager inserts itself into the Ribbon in e-mail, task, and appointment dialog boxes as well. The mail message Ribbon, shown in Figure 19.14, has a new group labeled Business Contact Manager that includes buttons labeled Link to Record and E-mail Auto-link that perform identical functions to those on the Business Contact Manager toolbar. In appointment and task windows, the Link to Record control is displayed in similar fashion.

Figure 19.14. New Ribbon controls added by Business Contact Manager.

When you click Link to Record, either on the Business Contact Manager toolbar or in one of the content forms, the dialog box shown in Figure 19.15 is displayed. In this dialog box, you enter the name of the Business Contact to whom you want to link the data object you have selected or are viewing, identify the Folder in which you want to search, and press Enter to perform a search. Select the contact from the results list to link that e-mail, event, or task to that contact. Using the Linked Records field in the lower portion of the dialog box, click the Link To button to connect the object to one or more of the Business Accounts that the Business Contact is associated with.

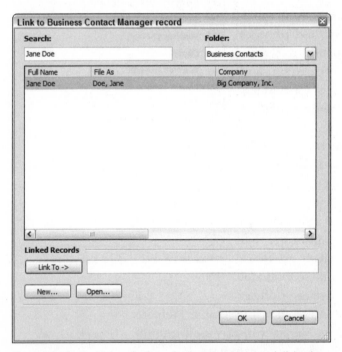

Figure 19.15. The Link to Business Contact Manager record dialog box.

 Inside Scoop

The power of a relational database at work is the ability to create these connections between contacts, accounts, and individual data objects. This provides a rich set of relationships that Business Contact Manager uses to update the main view screens and generate reports.

The E-mail Auto-link command opens the Manage E-mail Auto-linking dialog box shown in Figure 19.16. Using the Search for: field, you can assemble a list of Business Accounts and Business Contacts you want to link together. Select those who have a relationship with each other, and click OK to establish a relationship between those entities. This linkage allows Business Contact Manager to tag an e-mail sent to or received from any entity in the relationship and show it in the History screen and in reports related to that Account or Contact.

The Search and Link control in the lower portion of this dialog box can be used to search through your existing e-mail records for communications you have stored in your PST file that were generated prior to installing Business Contact Manager, that are located in an archival PST file, or that are located on a remote server that you have been provided access to.

Figure 19.16. The Manage E-mail Auto-linking dialog box.

Working with Business Accounts and Business Contacts

Business Accounts and Business Contacts are two of the essential building blocks in Business Contact Manager and are distinct from the contact records or groups you may have in your standard Outlook Contacts folder. These records are stored in the SQL database that Business Contact Manager employs and have a number of additional elements not present in the standard contact record form described in Chapter 7.

The Business Account form, shown in Figure 19.17, looks similar to a standard Outlook Contact form at first glance, but as you can see in the illustration, a number of fields are present in the Classification section that relate to account status and assignment, a Source information section identifies how the account was developed, and the bottom of the form provides a list that displays the individual Business Contacts that are linked to the account.

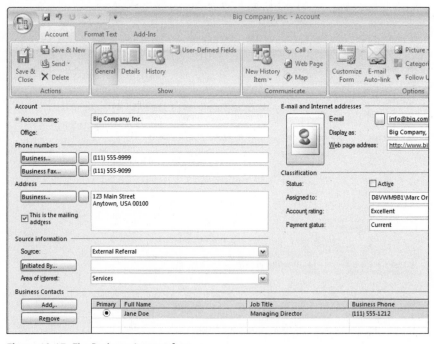

Figure 19.17. The Business Account form.

The Ribbon is dramatically different in this form, too. The Actions group is identical to the one found in the standard Outlook Contact record, but everything else is quite different. The Business Account Ribbon displays a Show group with controls to display the General screen (shown), as well as Details and History screens. The Communicate group provides a New History Item, which features a drop-down menu from which you can log any of Business Contact Manager's data objects such as a Business Note, Phone Log, or Opportunity. The Options group adds Customize Form and E-mail Auto-link controls to the options available on the Ribbon in the standard Outlook Contacts form.

Business Contacts, like the example shown in Figure 19.18, are similarly enhanced. The same Source information and Classification fields presented in the Business Accounts form are included, as is a Linked account button that allows you to associate a Business Contact with a Business Account. The Ribbon in this form is identical to the one described previously.

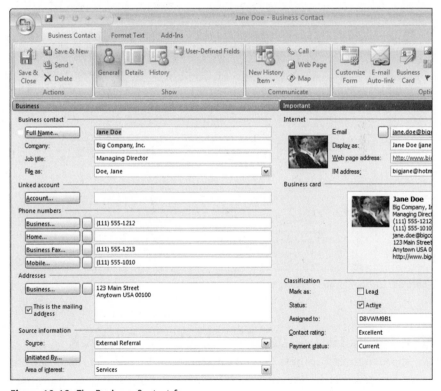

Figure 19.18. The Business Contact form.

The Business Project dialog box, shown in Figure 19.19, is another form that utilizes many of the same fields and controls as the Business Accounts and Business Contacts forms. A Business Project can be created for every significant engagement with a prospect or customer that you want to track discreetly, and the Project form, as shown, presents a detailed history of the correspondence, events, and activities that have transpired or been scheduled. This form provides a complete record of the events and actions that have gone into the pursuit of an opportunity or campaign.

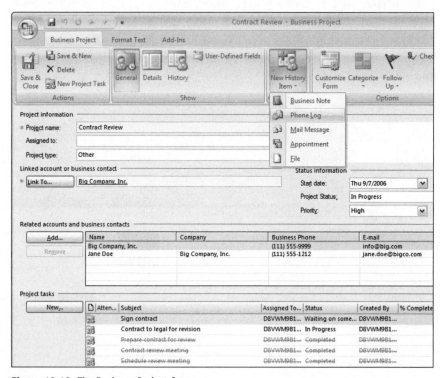

Figure 19.19. The Business Project form.

Managing two sets of contacts in Outlook

Any discussion of Business Contact Manager must address the complexity and potential challenges you face in managing two sets of contact records in a single Outlook environment. If you want to maintain a standard Outlook Contact record for an individual and a Business Contact Manager record as well — as might be the case for a friend with whom you also have a business relationship — it is critical that you understand that each record is stored in a different environment and no connection between the two records exists. If such a contact were to change his or her mailing address or mobile phone number, you would need to update each of the contact records for that person manually.

A final piece of advice regarding Business Contact Manager: Be sure to use the database maintenance commands in the Manage Database dialog box, shown in Figure 19.20, to regularly back up and check for errors in your Business Contact Manager database file. Business Contact Manager automatically creates a reminder task when you install the add-in to remind you to perform the first backup shortly after installation. I recommend that you create a recurring event in your calendar with a reminder alarm to perform this database maintenance on a regular basis.

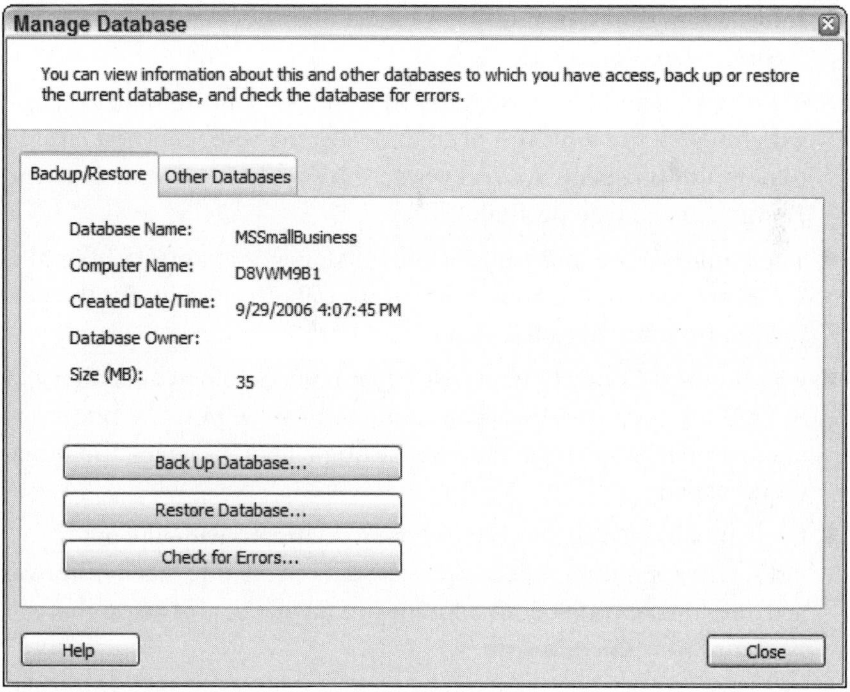

Figure 19.20. The Manage Database dialog box.

Watch Out!

You can make a standard Outlook Contact into a Business Contact Manager Contact by dragging the record from the Outlook Contact list to the Business Contact Manager list or folder item. This deletes the contact record from the Outlook Contact list, and it is a one-way street — you cannot drag a Business Contact Manager Record to the Outlook Contact list.

Just the facts

- Business Contact Manager consolidates information about accounts, contacts, opportunities, and marketing campaigns in a new set of views added to Outlook.

- In contrast to the PST file used to store standard Outlook data, Business Contact Manager uses a runtime SQL Server Express database to store its data, which provides rich tracking and reporting features.

- Information stored in Business Contact Manager can be shared securely with other Outlook users.

- The tracking and history features in Business Contact Manager provide you with the tools you need to determine who your best customers and prospects are and where you should focus your time and energy to maximize profitability.

- The Home screen in Business Contact Manager is your dashboard for all activities in the application and can be accessed from the new menu or toolbar installed with the add-in.

- The Business Contact Manager toolbar is accessible in all main views in Outlook and provides access to different views in the application and commands to create links to existing e-mail messages and other Outlook data.

- Creating links among accounts, contacts, and individual e-mails, tasks, and appointments provides the data needed to track historical activities, make projections about future projects, and assess the health of your sale pipeline.

- Managing two sets of contacts in Outlook can be tricky, so you must understand the differences between standard Outlook Contacts and Business Contact Manager's Business Contacts.

PART IV

Connect with Outlook

GET THE SCOOP ON...
Services provided by Exchange Server 2007 ▪
Outlook Web Access ▪ Connecting to Exchange
Server from Outlook 2007 ▪ Cached Exchange
Mode ▪ Remote access to Exchange Server

Outlook and Exchange Server

Chapter 20

Exchange Server is a product designed to meet the needs of larger organizations — a complex server technology that, while relatively easy to use from the Outlook client side, is a great deal of work to set up and administer. As organizations of all sizes have become more mobile and teams more distributed, the services offered by Exchange have become more desirable to all kinds of organizations. Because of the complexity and expense involved in setting up and running your own Exchange Server, a thriving marketplace of service providers has grown over the years who provide the option of using a hosted Exchange environment on a subscription basis for smaller companies or even individuals.

When Exchange Server was first released, it focused primarily on being a server for e-mail messages. Today, combined with other Microsoft server products like Live Communication Server, Exchange has become the central switchboard for all kinds of communications and information including e-mail, calendar, contacts lists and task items, faxes, and voice mail messages.

Microsoft Exchange Server 2007 provides access to all these types of messages in one central location — your Outlook Inbox. Actually, thanks to Exchange Server's

Outlook Web Access (OWA), you can even access your information when away from your PC, anywhere you can connect to the Web. And, as discussed in Chapter 24, the information on an Exchange Server also can be accessed using a Windows Mobile-powered device via Mobile Outlook.

Exchange Server is a big topic and well outside the scope of a book about Outlook 2007. This chapter focuses on the services that Exchange Server provides to Outlook 2007 and how they differ from using Outlook in stand-alone or Internet mail mode. If, after sampling some of what Exchange Server has to offer, you're interested in learning more about these features and services, Microsoft's Office Online site (`http://office.microsoft.com`) has an entire section devoted to Exchange, including links to a wide range of additional information such as product guides, training courses, and white papers that explore the applications for this server. A search in your favorite search engine for "hosted Exchange" also can provide a wealth of options to explore.

Exchange Server services

Depending on how Exchange Server is configured, it can provide a range of services including some or all of the following:

- **E-Mail.** In an Exchange environment, all your e-mail resides on the server and you access it in Outlook on your PC, via Outlook Web Access (OWA) in a web browser, or using Mobile Outlook on a Windows Mobile device.

- **Public Folders.** Exchange can provide shared folders that can be used to store and share Office documents and other files with other people who have access to the server.

- **Free/Busy Service.** This service allows you to see the availability of others on your team when using Outlook to schedule meetings.

- **Unified Messaging.** This service uses your organization's telephony network and combines all types of messaging into a single system that can receive, store, and deliver e-mail, voice mail, and fax messages to your Inbox. Unified Messaging is new in Exchange Server 2007.

Inside Scoop

Outlook Web Access Premium requires Internet Explorer 6.0 or newer. Outlook Web Access Premium is not supported on other browsers. Outlook Web Access Light is supported on recent versions of Netscape Navigator, Opera, Mac OS X Safari, and Mozilla Firefox.

Outlook Web Access

Outlook Web Access is one of the greatest benefits provided by Exchange for Mobile Outlook users. OWA makes your Exchange mailbox available in any Web browser. Exchange 2007 provides two versions of Outlook Web Access: Premium and Light. OWA Premium provides access to all your Exchange 2007 mailbox data. OWA Light provides access to e-mail, calendar, and contacts only. It does not support tasks or notes.

Outlook Web Access in Exchange Server 2007 has been enhanced in a number of ways from the service provided by Exchange Server 2003. Here are some of the new or enhanced features:

- **Flexible Message Views.** New view controls allow you select how the message list is displayed, choose the position of the Reading Pane, and configure multiple grouping and sorting options just as you can in Outlook itself.

- **Scheduling Assistant.** This helps you schedule meetings with coworkers. The Scheduling Assistant provides suggested times and uses color to code potential dates as Good, Fair, or Poor, depending on the availability of the people you are inviting.

- **File Access.** OWA lets you access documents and document libraries on Windows SharePoint and file servers on your network.

Exchange and Outlook 2007

If you are in the office using Outlook 2007 and are connected to your local network, you can view e-mail messages, calendar data, contacts, tasks, and notes. If you receive a voice mail message, you can play that message through your computer speakers. If you receive a fax message, Unified Messaging automatically routes it to your mailbox as an attachment to an e-mail. Simply open the attached file to view or print your fax.

Exchange Server 2007 makes it easier to connect when you are working from home or on the road. In the past, a virtual private network (VPN) connection was required to "tunnel" through the company firewall to reach the Exchange Server. The new version eliminates this requirement and, if configured by your Exchange administrator, provides a way to connect over the Internet using an encrypted connection without the need for a VPN client application.

Setting up an Exchange Account in Outlook 2007

The procedure for setting up an Exchange Server account in Outlook 2007 is essentially the same as for a POP3 or IMAP connection. Outlook 2007's automatic account setup requires only a few pieces of information to connect to the server and establish your account. Because Exchange Server is administered by the IT person or department in your organization, you should always ask how to set up your connection to the Exchange Server before attempting to do it on your own.

You can use the Add New E-mail Account Wizard to quickly get your account set up. You'll need the following information from your administrator:

- The name of your Exchange Server on the network.

- The name of the mailbox your administrator has set up for you. This is usually your user name on the network, but again it's always best to check in advance.

- If you plan to access the Exchange Server from Outlook when outside the company network, you also should get the URL required in the Microsoft Exchange Proxy Server Setting dialog box.

With this information in hand, you are ready to set up your Exchange Server account. Unlike POP3, IMAP, or HTTP accounts, you cannot create an Exchange Server account while Outlook is running, so the first step is to make sure you have exited Outlook. At the desktop, access the Control Panel from the Start menu and select the User Accounts icon shown in Figure 20.1.

On the User Accounts screen, shown in Figure 20.2, click the Mail icon to open the Mail Setup dialog box. If your Control Panel is in Classic mode, you can double-click the Mail icon directly.

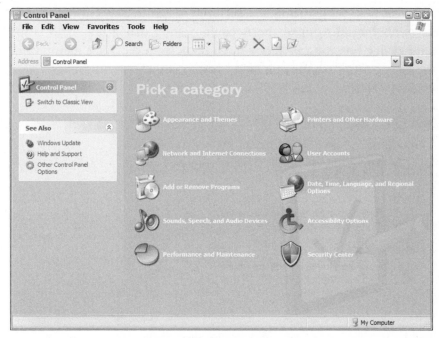

Figure 20.1. The User Accounts icon in the Control Panel.

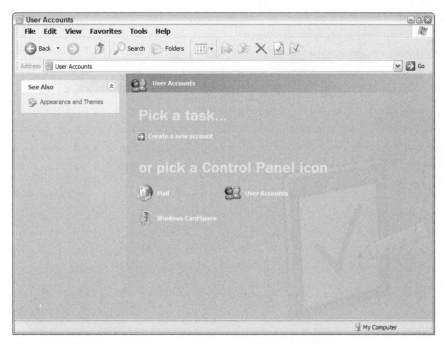

Figure 20.2. The Mail icon on the User Account screen in the Control Panels.

In the Mail Setup dialog box, pictured in Figure 20.3, click the E-mail Accounts button to open the Account Setting dialog box. This is the same dialog box you can access in Outlook from the Tools menu. Click the New control on the command bar to launch the Add New E-mail Account Wizard.

Figure 20.3. The Mail Setup dialog box.

In the first screen of the wizard, shown in Figure 20.4, make sure the first radio button, labeled Microsoft Exchange, POP3, IMAP, or HTTP, is selected and click Next.

In the second screen of the wizard, select the Microsoft Exchange option and click Next. The third screen of the Wizard, shown in Figure 20.5, provides two fields. Enter the name of the Exchange Server in the first field and the name of your mailbox in the second, and click Next. That should be all the information required to set up your account on the server.

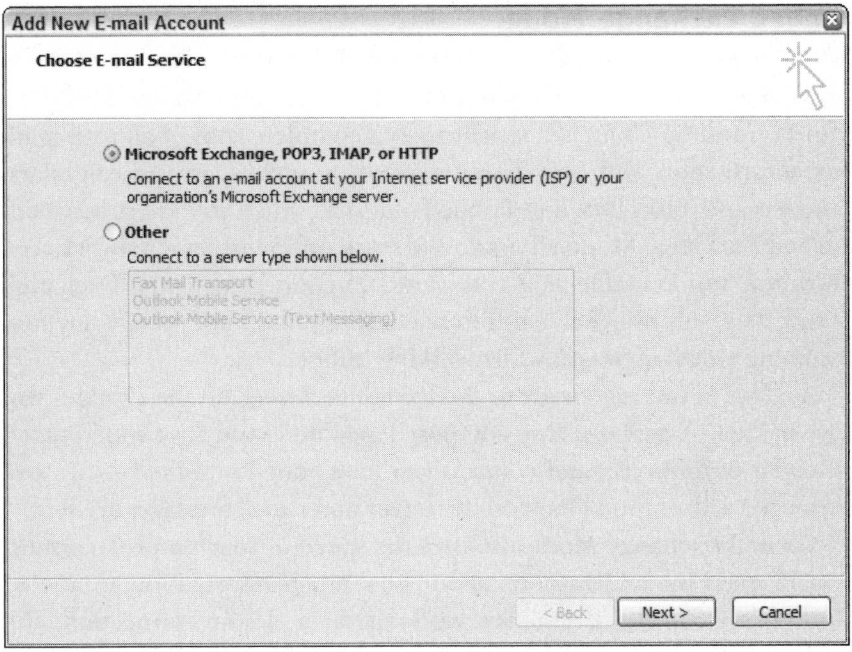

Add New E-mail Account

Choose E-mail Service

⦿ **Microsoft Exchange, POP3, IMAP, or HTTP**
Connect to an e-mail account at your Internet service provider (ISP) or your organization's Microsoft Exchange server.

○ **Other**
Connect to a server type shown below.

Fax Mail Transport
Outlook Mobile Service
Outlook Mobile Service (Text Messaging)

[< Back] [Next >] [Cancel]

Figure 20.4. The first screen in the Add New E-mail Account Wizard.

Add New E-mail Account

Microsoft Exchange Settings
You can enter the required information to connect to Microsoft Exchange.

Type the name of your Microsoft Exchange server. For information, see your system administrator.

Microsoft Exchange server: |

☑ Use Cached Exchange Mode

Type the name of the mailbox set up for you by your administrator. The mailbox name is usually your user name.

User Name: [   ] [Check Name]

[More Settings ...]

[< Back] [Next >] [Cancel]

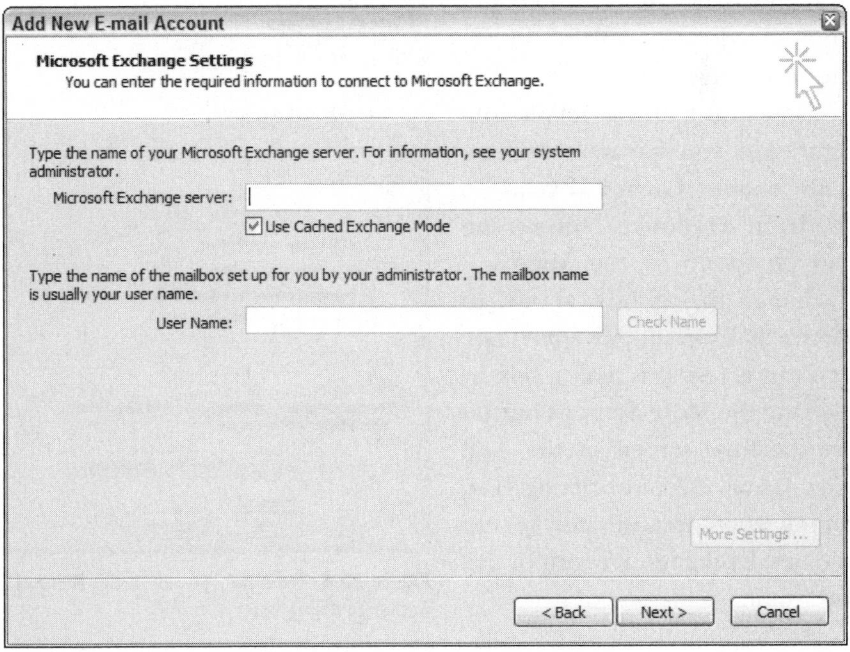

Figure 20.5. The final screen in the Add New E-mail Account Wizard.

Cached Exchange Mode

Ask your Exchange Server administrator if Cached Exchange Mode is available. If it is, the data file Outlook uses to store information locally on your PC (and OST file) can synchronize a complete copy of all your mailbox information and any shared resources, such as group calendars, Contacts and Tasks lists, and Public Folders to which you are subscribed. Cached Exchange Mode allows you to work offline when a network connection is not available as if you were still connected to the Exchange Server. The only noticeable difference is that you do not receive any new incoming e-mail messages while working offline.

As soon as you reconnect to the Exchange Server, all the changes you have made — e-mail you have composed, new items you have added to the Calendar or Tasks list, and contacts you have added or edited — are synchronized with your mailbox on the server and e-mail messages are sent.

Cached Exchange Mode also uses the speed of your network connection to make smart decisions about how much information to add to Outlook's OST file. If you are working on a slower connection, the Exchange Server may send Outlook only the headers of new e-mail messages at first and then fetch the rest of the message as you open them. With a faster connection, Outlook downloads the entire message immediately.

Depending on the server configuration, you may need to manually enable Cached Exchange Mode in Outlook. This setting can be found in the Microsoft Exchange dialog box, shown in Figure 20.6, on the Advanced tab. You can access this dialog box by clicking the More Settings button on the final screen of the Add New E-mail Account dialog box, either when you initially set up the new Exchange account or at a later time.

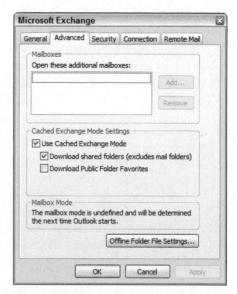

Figure 20.6. The Advanced tab in the Microsoft Exchange dialog box.

Exchange proxy settings

If your administrator has set up remote access to the Exchange Server over the Internet, you may need to manually set up the Exchange proxy settings that allow Outlook to use an HTTP connection to access the server when you are outside the company firewall. In the Microsoft Exchange dialog box, select the Connection tab and click the Exchange Proxy Settings button shown in Figure 20.7.

In the Microsoft Exchange Proxy Settings dialog box, shown in Figure 20.8, enter the URL supplied by your server administrator and select the appropriate connec-

Figure 20.7. The Connection tab in the Microsoft Exchange dialog box.

tion options as appropriate for your server's configuration. Using this secure connection, Outlook can access the Exchange Server from any location.

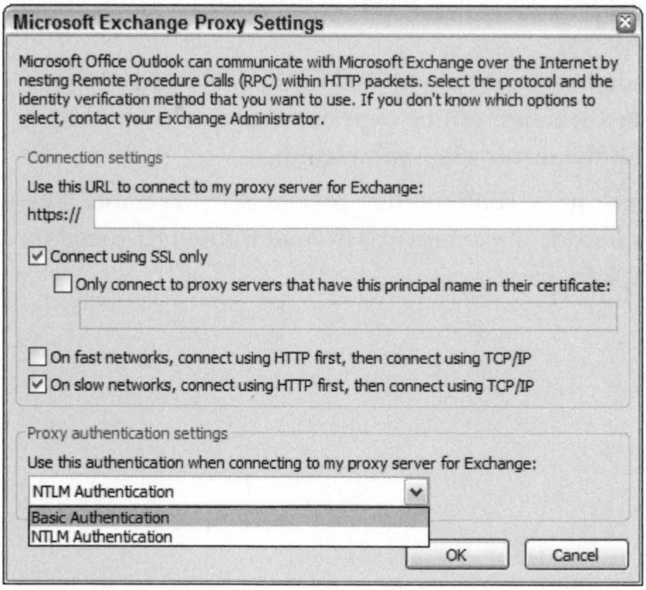

Figure 20.8. The Microsoft Exchange Proxy Settings dialog box.

Watch Out!

At the risk of sounding like a broken record, always ask your Exchange Server administrator about how to make changes to your account before you attempt to do it on your own. You can make a serious mess of things if you select the wrong options.

Just the facts

- Exchange Server is much more than just an e-mail server and can provide a unified Inbox for all the communications you receive.

- Exchange can act as the central switchboard for e-mail, shared calendars, public Contacts and Tasks lists, faxes, and voice mail messages.

- Outlook Web Access allows you to connect to the Exchange Server from any Web browser and work in an Outlook-like environment on any Internet-connected PC or Mac.

- Exchange Server can be configured to provide Public Folders where Office documents and other files can be stored and shared.

- Outlook Web Access provides two options depending on the browser you connect with: Premium and Light.

- Setting up an Exchange account in Outlook 2007 is similar to setting up a POP3, IMAP, or HTTP account, provided that you have the right information.

- If your server administrator has enabled Cached Exchange Mode, use it to provide a seamless offline experience and automatically synchronize with the server when you reconnect.

- Exchange Server can be configured to provide secure remote access when you work outside the company's firewall without the need for additional VPN software.

Outlook and SharePoint

ike Exchange Server, SharePoint is a product — actually a family of products — designed to meet the needs of larger organizations, not individuals or small organizations where everyone works in the same location. As we've become more mobile and the people with whom we collaborate more distributed geographically, the benefits offered by a SharePoint site start making more sense for organizations of smaller size or even ad-hoc teams working at a distance. SharePoint is like Exchange in another way. It is a complex server technology that, while relatively easy to use, is a substantial project to set up and administer. A third way that SharePoint and Exchange are similar is that a large number of service providers are happy to host your company on their SharePoint servers for an affordable monthly subscription fee.

In this chapter, we look at the tools and capabilities a SharePoint site can make available to your team and how Outlook 2007 connects to SharePoint. The improvements in the connection between Outlook 2007 and SharePoint Server 2007 are substantial, and it is much more practical to consider using Outlook as a front-end tool for collaboration via SharePoint than with previous versions of the two products.

This chapter provides an overview of the potential for collaboration and information-sharing possible with Microsoft SharePoint Server 2007. The Office Online Web site (http://office.microsoft.com) has a link to a wide range of additional information including product guides, training courses, and white papers that explore the application for this server. If you need to collaborate with others and want to be able to access important information related to that collaboration in Outlook 2007, SharePoint Server might meet your needs.

Overview of SharePoint 2007 for Outlook users

SharePoint Server 2007 allows you to create resources that can be accessed in a Web browser by members of a project team and then connected to Outlook. This allows team members to access the SharePoint resources on their local PCs, as well as in a browser where SharePoint sites have traditionally been used. Working in Outlook has a number of advantages over using the browser — especially when network connections are slow or unavailable.

The improved connectivity in the 2007 versions of both products allows you to work directly on SharePoint resources in your local Outlook environment. For people who do not always have access to a network connection, these resources, once connected, can continue to be used offline. Any offline changes made are synchronized when you are next online and Outlook reconnects to the SharePoint server.

Five types of SharePoint resources can be connected to and used in Outlook 2007:

- **Calendar.** As with an Exchange calendar, a SharePoint 2007 calendar can be viewed side by side with your local Outlook 2007 calendar, or the two calendars can be overlaid to view all items at once.

- **Tasks list.** After a SharePoint Tasks list for a project is connected to Outlook, team members can see all project-related tasks in the main Tasks view and can view tasks assigned only to them in the To-Do Bar.

- **Document Library.** Team members can preview, search, and open project documents from a connected library. Site members can edit documents locally while connected or even when offline. If your team uses Office OneNote 2007, meeting notes synchronized with calendar events can be shared in the library and used as a collaborative note-taking space synchronized to everyone's local notebook.

- **Discussion Board.** Discussion Boards are a great way to discuss specific topics related to a project. Unlike e-mail discussions, which tend to get disorganized, out of sequence, and very messy with quoted text and mangled subject lines, Discussion Boards keep all the messages related to a conversation in a single place and in the right order.

- **Contacts List.** SharePoint Contacts Lists help team members stay in touch with each other and with people outside the team who have a role in the project. Because they are synchronized with the server, when anyone on the team adds or edits contacts, everyone gets the new information immediately (or when they next connect).

Connecting SharePoint resources to Outlook

After you accept an invitation to a SharePoint site and sign in, you can connect any of the resources described in the preceding section to your local copy of Outlook. In Figure 21.1, a SharePoint calendar is being viewed. Selecting the Actions menu displays a number of options, including the ability to connect this calendar to Outlook.

Figure 21.1. A SharePoint calendar is connected to Outlook from the Actions menu.

Inside Scoop

Note that the Actions menu on a SharePoint site also allows you to subscribe to an RSS feed for the resource you are viewing. If you subscribe to and display the RSS feed in Outlook, you receive a new post whenever a change is made to the resource.

After you have selected the Connect to Outlook option, SharePoint confirms that you have the appropriate account privileges to make the connection and displays a dialog box, similar to the one shown in Figure 21.2, asking you to confirm that you want to make the connection.

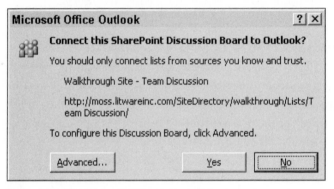

Figure 21.2. The Microsoft Office Outlook dialog box asks you to confirm your connection to a SharePoint server.

SharePoint sites use a sidebar similar to the Navigation Pane in Outlook to provide access to the resources the site administrator has set up for each project. In Figure 21.3, the project Tasks list is shown. Along the left side of the screen is a sidebar labeled View All Site Content that provides access to the site's resources. Because browsers make it notoriously difficult to create a right-click context menu, SharePoint uses a drop-down menu on each item to provide specific commands related to that resource or information object. In this figure, you see that a task item can be viewed, edited, or deleted, its permissions can be changed, or an alert can be set to notify you if the item is modified.

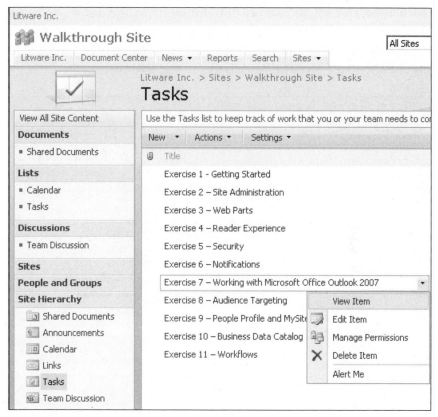

Figure 21.3. The Tasks list in a SharePoint site.

As mentioned earlier in this chapter, tasks are one of the resources you can connect to your local Outlook environment. When you establish a connection between a SharePoint Tasks list and Outlook and you view the connected list, all of the project's tasks are displayed in the Tasks main view in Outlook, but only those tasks assigned to you appear in the To-Do Bar. You can sort and filter tasks in the main view in Outlook by the Assigned To value to group tasks by owner.

The process of creating a new item in SharePoint is simple, and after a resource has been connected to Outlook, the new event, task, document, or discussion is synchronized with Outlook immediately if you are connected to the Internet or, if you are working offline, the next time you are online and launch Outlook. Figure 21.4 shows the Calendar: New Item screen on the SharePoint site. You can use text formatting, attach files, and set recurrence for the event in this form. Note the Workspace check box at the bottom of the dialog box, which creates a new point of collection for the people and information objects related to this event, called a Meeting Workspace, on the SharePoint site.

Litware Inc. > Sites > Walkthrough Site > Calendar > New Item
Calendar: New Item

	OK	Cancel

📎 Attach File	🔤 Spelling...	* indicates a required field

Title *	Contract Review
Location	Conference room - Building 200
Start Time *	10/31/2006 4 PM ▼ 00 ▼
End Time *	10/31/2006 6 PM ▼ 00 ▼
Description	A A⁻ **B** *I* U̲ ≡ ≡ ≡ ⦂☰ ⦂☰ ☰⦂ ☰⦂ A ⬙ ▸¶ ¶◂
	Review the contract before our signing meeting
All Day Event	☐ Make this an all-day activity that doesn't start or end at a specific hour.
Recurrence	☐ Make this a repeating event.
Workspace	☑ Use a Meeting Workspace to organize attendees, agendas, documents, minutes, and other details for this event.

	OK	Cancel

Figure 21.4. The Calendar: New Item screen on the SharePoint site.

When Outlook synchronizes with the SharePoint server, the calendar item is added to the SharePoint Calendar displayed next to, or as an overlay on, your local Calendar. The event window, shown in Figure 21.5, has a few notable changes from the normal Appointment dialog box displayed for a local event in your Calendar.

Watch Out!
Meeting Workspaces are very convenient but are not one of the resources that can be connected to Outlook 2007. In order to see the information gathered into the Workspace, you must access the SharePoint site directly in your Web browser.

In the Actions group on the Appointment tab, two new controls are displayed. Open in Browser takes you to the calendar item on the SharePoint site. Copy to My Calendar places a copy of the event on your local Outlook Calendar so that it is visible even when you elect not to display the SharePoint site Calendar. Placing the event on your Calendar also allows the event to be displayed on an Exchange Server, if you work in that environment, and also allows the event to be synchronized to a Windows Mobile device, Palm OS Treo Smartphone, or Blackberry.

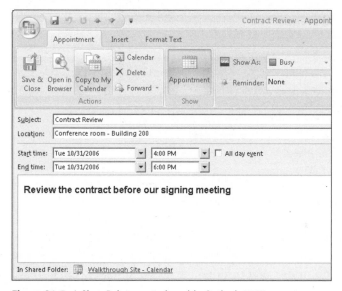

Figure 21.5. A SharePoint event viewed in Outlook 2007.

Also note the link added to the bottom of the Appointment window. This link describes the SharePoint site in which the shared object is located — especially helpful when you are connecting to more than one SharePoint project at a time — and contains a link that opens the original appointment in your browser.

Outlook, OneNote, and SharePoint

Chapter 17 discusses the integration between Outlook 2007 and Office OneNote 2007 to create linked meeting notes that can be accessed from the Appointment dialog box in Outlook. The same technique can be applied to a SharePoint site and calendar events connected to Outlook from the server.

Setting up a shared notebook in OneNote that can be added to a library on the SharePoint server is a simple, three-step process. In OneNote, choose File ⇨ New ⇨ Notebook to open the New Notebook Wizard. In the first screen of the wizard, shown in Figure 21.6, select one of the Shared Notebook templates and click Next.

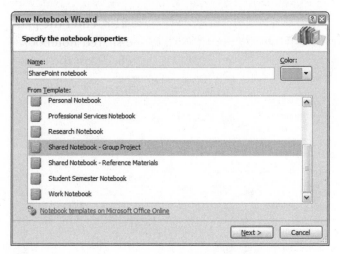

Figure 21.6. The first screen in the New Notebook Wizard.

In the second screen of the wizard, shown in Figure 21.7, select the third radio button labeled Multiple people will share the notebook and the first radio button under that option labeled On a server. Click Next.

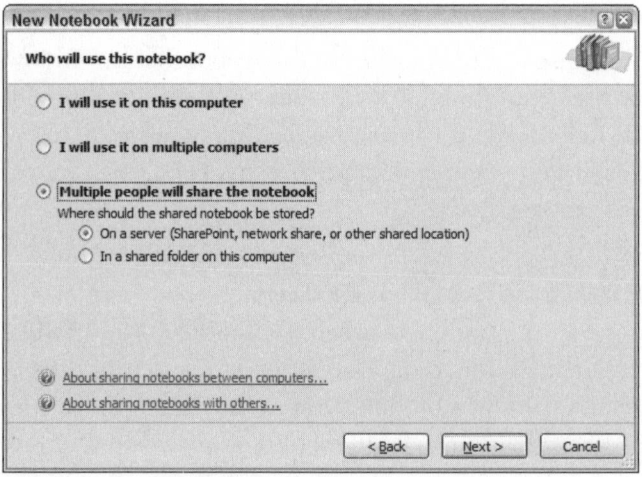

Figure 21.7. The second screen in the New Notebook Wizard.

Inside Scoop

You do not have to use the Shared Notebook templates in OneNote if you have defined your own template or prefer to use a different layout. The Shared Notebook templates have helpful sections and page definitions already included that make them ideal for group use.

In the final screen of the wizard, shown in Figure 21.8, enter the path to the SharePoint site library you want to use as the shared notebook's location and click Create. OneNote creates the notebook on the server and a synchronized copy on your PC. If you select the check box in the dialog box, OneNote creates an e-mail invitation in Outlook ready for you to send to other team members with whom you want to share the notebook. When the recipient clicks the link included in the e-mail invitation, his local copy of OneNote has a synchronized copy of the shared notebook on the server added. Any changes made by a team member to the shared notebook are synchronized with all connected copies on team members' PCs as they are made.

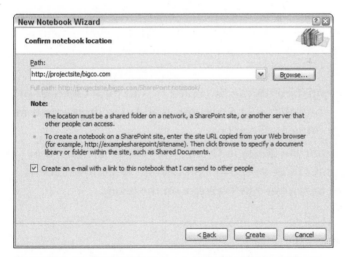

Figure 21.8. The third and final screen in the New Notebook Wizard.

Bright Idea

While the setup and maintenance of a SharePoint Server is not a trivial undertaking, either from a financial or resource perspective, many hosted service providers can provide access to the benefits of a SharePoint Server for a monthly subscription fee. A search for "hosted SharePoint" in your favorite search engine provides you with a number of choices to investigate.

Just the facts

- SharePoint Server 2007 and Outlook 2007 make it easier than ever to access shared resources from the server directly in Outlook.

- Changes or additions made to connected resources are synchronized between the SharePoint Server and Outlook in real-time when you are connected and when you reconnect to the network and launch Outlook if you have been working offline.

- SharePoint provides five resources that can be connected to Outlook: Calendar, Tasks list, Document Library, Discussion Board, and Contacts List.

- SharePoint 2007 also allows you to subscribe to an RSS feed for resources that sends a new post to Outlook, Internet Explorer, or another RSS aggregator every time a resource is updated or changed.

- SharePoint Tasks lists can be viewed in the main Tasks view in Outlook but only those tasks assigned to you are displayed in the To-Do Bar.

- A new item created on the SharePoint site is immediately synchronized to your local Outlook environment if you are connected to the Internet.

- SharePoint calendar events can be copied to your local Calendar or opened in your browser using new controls added to these events in Outlook's Appointment dialog box.

- Meeting notes that you create in OneNote 2007 that are linked to an Outlook event can be stored in a SharePoint Document Library, where they can be accessed by everyone on the team.

GET THE SCOOP ON...
Web-based access to your e-mail and contacts ■
Using Hotmail Plus with Outlook ■ Importing
Outlook contacts into Hotmail Plus ■ Differences
between Hotmail Plus and MSN Premium

Outlook and Webmail

A migration is underway to use the Internet as a place where we can store and access personal information no matter where we are or what PC or connected device we are using. Microsoft, Google, Yahoo!, and others have online offerings that provide e-mail, instant messaging, file sharing, and other services that require nothing more than a browser on your device. There's been lots of talk about Web 2.0 in the past few years as a significant evolutionary period in this seemingly inevitable migration.

As an Outlook user, how does this migration affect you? As explained in Chapter 20, Microsoft offers Outlook users in an Exchange environment access to their e-mail, contacts list, and other information through a Web service called Outlook Web Access. But if you don't work in an Exchange Server environment and don't want to pay the cost of a hosted Exchange account, do you have other options?

In 2005, Microsoft introduced a product called Microsoft Office Outlook Live (MooL) to provide a "personal Exchange Server" on a subscription basis. MooL combined a copy of Outlook for your PC with a Hotmail account that synchronized all the information in your local e-mail PST file with a Web-based application. I thought MooL was a great idea, and I recommended it to many people I advised who expressed a need to get at their information from a number of different devices and locations. Unfortunately,

Chapter 22

409

MooL was discontinued in Fall 2006 just prior to the release of Outlook 2007 and the new Office Live services described in Chapter 23.

With the elimination of MooL, those seeking an easy and inexpensive way to access e-mail and contacts from more than one device in more than one location using a combination of the Web and a local copy of Outlook still have options. This chapter begins with a general discussion of how Webmail and Outlook can work together. As an example of this integration, I show you how to use a Hotmail Plus account to create an online version of the e-mail and contacts components of your Outlook environment and discuss what you can do to keep everything in sync. To wrap things up, I discuss the differences in cost and capability between Hotmail Plus and another Microsoft offering — MSN Premium with Outlook Connector.

Connecting Outlook to Webmail

Outlook 2007 supports Webmail services from Microsoft and other providers that use standard POP3, IMAP, or HTTP protocols. If you have an e-mail account with popular Webmail services like Google's Gmail, Yahoo! Mail, or AOL, you can configure an e-mail account in Outlook that will download new e-mail from those accounts into the familiar Outlook environment on your PC.

Depending on the protocol used by your Webmail provider, what you gain by doing this is, at minimum, capture e-mail from these Web-based services into a local PST file, and, at best, create a synchronized copy of your online mail in your local Outlook environment. The protocol offered is the key to how you can work with messages delivered to your Webmail address:

- POP3 service connections simply download e-mail to your PC. You can tell Outlook to leave a copy of mail on the server (highly recommended) so that when you access mail in the browser, all your messages are still available. You also can tell Outlook to delete a message on the server when you delete it locally.

- IMAP service connections provide true synchronization with the server. An IMAP account in Outlook is really a view of the mail residing on the server. The advantage is that you are always in sync, whether you access your e-mail account in Outlook or in the browser. The disadvantage to IMAP is that, unless you allow full synchronization, it's hard to work with IMAP mail when discon-nected from the network. Full synchronization is great if you have an always-on broadband connection, but it can seriously impact per-formance on a dial-up connection depending on the size of your IMAP account because the entire folder structure is updated every time you connect to the server. Of the major providers, only AOL offers IMAP access at this time.

■ HTTP service connections provide a view of mail on the Web server providing account access and are fully synchronized with what you see in Outlook each time a Send/Receive operation is carried out. Hotmail and MSN Webmail services both use HTTP to connect with Outlook and are preconfigured in the Add New E-mail Account dialog box shown in Figure 22.1. A Hotmail Plus or an MSN Premium account, which carries a monthly or annual sub-scription fee, is required to make the connection in Outlook. If you use an alternate Webmail provider that offers HTTP access, you need to manually enter the server information in the Add New E-mail Account dialog box.

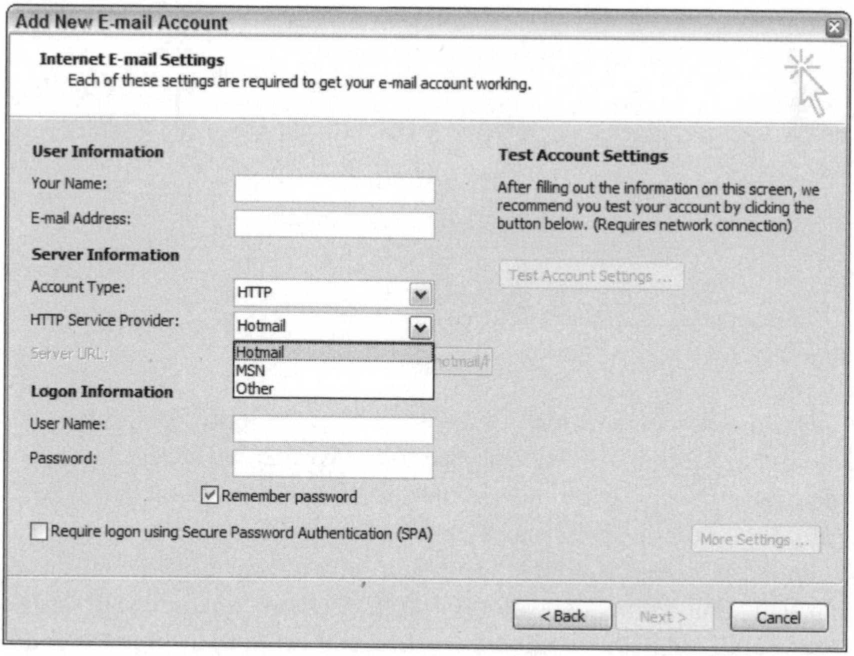

Figure 22.1. The Add New E-mail Account dialog box with HTTP account options shown.

Watch Out!

Use extreme caution when selecting the option to delete messages on the server when you delete them locally in a POP3 account. When this option is selected, you cannot recover a message after it has been deleted. It's gone for good.

Managing e-mail messages

When you first create a new account in Outlook to work with your Webmail account, what happens is largely controlled by the mail server. In the case of Google's Gmail, for example, you can make a selection to receive only new e-mail, or you can opt to download older mail to your local Outlook environment. Gmail's options are shown in Figure 22.2. Depending on the preference you have set, you receive new mail as it arrives at your Gmail address or all e-mail received since the date shown is downloaded to Outlook on the next Send/Receive operation.

Settings

General   Accounts   Labels   Filters   **Forwarding and POP**   Chat   Web Clips

Forwarding:	⊙ Disable forwarding
	○ Forward a copy of incoming mail to
	[email address] and [keep Gmail's copy in the Inbox ▾]
	Tip: You can also forward only some of your mail by creating a filter!
POP Download: Learn more	**1. Status:** POP is enabled for all mail that has arrived since Mar 6
	○ Enable POP for **all mail** (even mail that's already been downloaded)
	⊙ Enable POP only for **mail that arrives from now on**
	○ **Disable POP**
	2. When messages are accessed with POP [keep Gmail's copy in the Inbox ▾]
	3. Configure your email client (e.g. Outlook, Eudora, Netscape Mail) Configuration instructions
	[Cancel] [Save Changes]

Figure 22.2. Gmail POP3 preferences.

Other services provide varying levels of support for adding an account in Outlook. AOL, for example, provides no direct help, but Microsoft offers an extensive article on Office Online (search for AOL mail) that describes the steps required to add an AOL account to Outlook. AOL uses the IMAP protocol, so you do get full synchronization with the online state of your AOL account, as discussed earlier. Yahoo! Mail offers only Outlook synchronization in their Premium Mail subscription, which costs, at this writing, around $20 per year.

Inside Scoop

Gmail uses POP3 to provide an Outlook connection so messages from this Webmail account will arrive in your primary Inbox by default. You can use an Outlook Rule (see Chapter 15) to reroute incoming e-mail from your Gmail account to another folder if you prefer.

Managing contacts lists

All these Web-based mail services provide an address book and support import of your Outlook Contacts list. With the non-Microsoft services, this is accomplished by exporting a Comma Separated Values (CSV) text file from Outlook, which you then import into the Webmail account. This process is similar to the Import process described in Chapter 3. To create a CSV file, follow these steps:

1. Select File ⇨ Import and Export to display the Import and Export Wizard shown in Figure 22.3. Select the Export to a file option, and click Next.

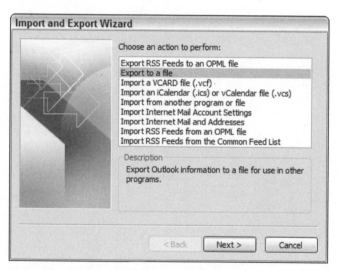

Figure 22.3. The Import and Export Wizard – Step 1.

2. In the next Wizard screen, shown in Figure 22.4, select the Comma Separated Values (Windows) option and click Next.

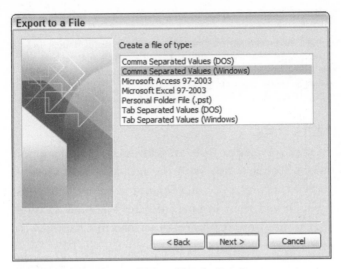

Figure 22.4. The Import and Export Wizard – Step 2.

3. In the next Wizard screen, shown in Figure 22.5, select the Contacts folder from the Outlook folder list and click Next.

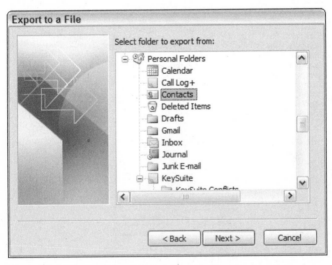

Figure 22.5. The Import and Export Wizard – Step 3.

4. In the next Wizard screen, enter a name for the export file and use the Browse button to select where the export file will be saved. Click Next.

> **Inside Scoop**
>
> This export and import process duplicates the current state of your Outlook Contacts list in your Webmail address book. As you add new contacts in one environment or the other, the two lists will no longer be identical. If you always create new contacts in Outlook and regularly perform this export and import process, you can manually keep both lists in sync.

5. In the final Wizard screen, accept the defaults, which show the Contacts folder from your primary PST file as the source, and click Finish. The button labeled Map Custom Fields allows you to change the order in which individual fields in the Contact record are exported, but this is unnecessary for preparing a file for Webmail service import.

After the export operation is complete, open your Webmail account in a Web browser and use the import feature in that service to add your Outlook Contacts list to the Webmail address book. If you have existing contacts in your Webmail address book, you may need to manually remove duplicate entries.

Also, be aware that many Webmail address books do not provide the same fields as Outlook, so some of your contact information may not transfer. All the major services support commonly used name, address, phone, and e-mail fields.

Hotmail Plus

If you do not yet have a Webmail account established, you may want to consider using Microsoft's Hotmail Plus to set up a synchronized e-mail and contact environment with Outlook. A subscription to a Hotmail Plus account costs $19.95 per year. At the time this book was written, Microsoft was in the process of migrating the Hotmail brand to the new Windows Live Mail identity, and by the time you read this, a Hotmail Plus account may very well be called a Windows Live Mail Plus account.

Windows Live Mail, the Webmail service, should not be confused with Windows Live Mail Desktop, described in Chapter 17. That PC-based e-mail and newsgroup application is a replacement for Outlook Express on Windows XP systems and will be the default e-mail application on Windows Vista systems. The two Live Mail environments can work together in much the same way I'm describing, although Hotmail integration with Windows Live Mail Desktop lacks the Calendar, Tasks, Notes, and Journal features offered by Outlook.

Hotmail uses an HTTP connection and synchronizes in near real-time with Outlook as mail operations like sending, receiving, and filing are performed. I say "near" real-time, because Outlook and Hotmail update their respective views of your Hotmail environment as part of a Send/Receive operation initiated from Outlook or when you switch to a different e-mail account folder in Outlook and then back to your Hotmail Plus account folder.

A Hotmail Plus message in Outlook, shown in Figure 22.6, and the same message in Windows Live Mail (the new version of the venerable Hotmail Web interface), shown in Figure 22.7, are displayed identically. Working in either environment from a mail reading perspective is essentially the same. Both environments display a folder list, a message list, and a reading pane.

If you prefer, you can (at least for now) continue to use the old Hotmail interface on the Web. You also can elect to use a "lite" version of the new Windows Live Mail interface if your network connection doesn't deliver a satisfactory experience with the full version of the interface. These and other options can be configured on the Windows Live Mail Options page shown in Figure 22.8.

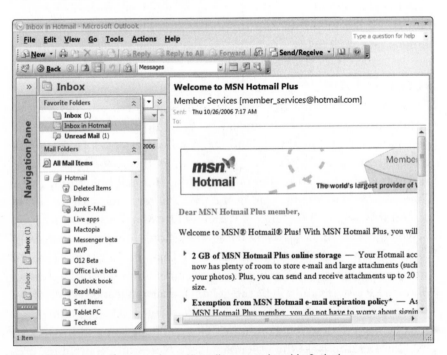

Figure 22.6. An e-mail message in my Hotmail account viewed in Outlook.

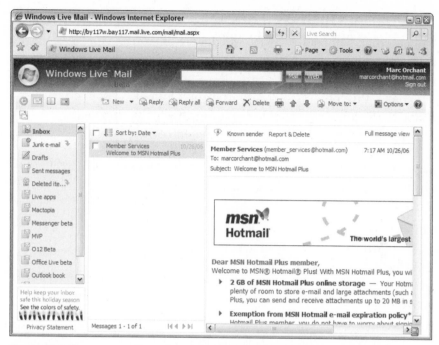

Figure 22.7. The same e-mail message viewed in Windows Live Mail in a Web browser.

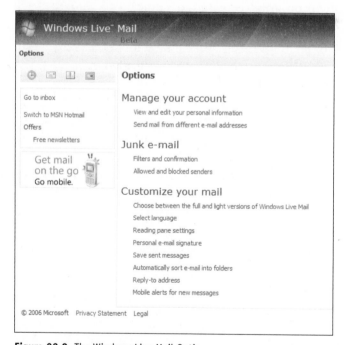

Figure 22.8. The Windows Live Mail Options page.

Importing Outlook contacts into Hotmail Plus

Unlike other Webmail services, which rely on you manually exporting your Contacts list from Outlook to a CSV file, Hotmail Plus provides a utility that automates this process. To import your Outlook contacts to your Hotmail Plus account, begin by clicking the Options link in the upper-right corner of the Windows Live Mail screen to display the Options panel shown in Figure 22.9. Select the Import contacts command and an Application dialog box displays, asking if you want to run the application or save it to disk. Select Run.

Figure 22.9. The Windows Live Mail Options menu.

The Windows Live Contact Importer utility launches and displays a status screen as it searches your PC for Outlook contacts and Outlook Express or Windows Live Mail Desktop address books. This status screen, shown in Figure 22.10, isn't particularly informative — the progress bar uses a pulsing green activity animation but doesn't really provide any true measure of progress achieved or time remaining.

When the search has completed, Windows Live Contact Importer displays the contact lists and address books it has found. Note that if you have the Outlook Business Contact Manager add-in installed, its unique Business Contacts and Business Accounts lists appears in the list of found items shown in Figure 22.11.

Select the contacts lists you want to import into your Hotmail Plus account, and click Next. The Windows Live Contact Importer displays a list of all the found contacts and allows you to select those contacts you want to import. After you have made this selection and clicked Next, the utility prompts you to supply your Windows Live ID (formerly called your Passport ID; this is usually your Hotmail Plus e-mail address and password) as pictured in Figure 22.12.

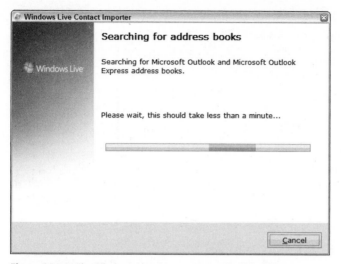

Figure 22.10. The Windows Live Contact Importer dialog box Searching for address books screen.

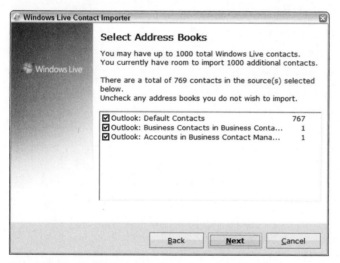

Figure 22.11. The Windows Live Contact Importer dialog box Select Address Books screen.

When the import operation is complete, you can view the imported information using the Contacts list or Search box. Figure 22.13 shows a contact record in Windows Live Mail.

Figure 22.12. Enter your Windows Live ID information to complete the import.

Figure 22.13. Windows Live Mail showing the imported contacts.

Hotmail Plus versus MSN Premium

Microsoft also offers a comprehensive subscription service through its MSN division called MSN Premium. This service costs $9.95 a month or $99.00 annually and provides a number of enhancements for creating HTML-formatted e-mail using a library of templates, antivirus and anti-spyware protection, and a variety of other benefits. The most important distinction related to the subject of this discussion — integration with Outlook 2007 — is that MSN Premium includes the use of a tool called the Outlook Connector. This tool provides real-time synchronization with all your Outlook information and the online MSN Premium environment.

If you spend a significant amount of time working away from your primary PC, this alternative may provide enough value to offset the additional cost of the subscription because it provides fully synchronized access to your Contacts, Calendar, and Tasks lists. Unlike Hotmail Plus addresses, which end in @hotmail.com, MSN Premium e-mail addresses end in @msn.com.

A number of Internet Service Providers and telecommunication companies like Qwest here in the Rocky Mountain region include MSN Premium with their DSL Internet connectivity. The ISP or telecommunication company provides the connection to the Internet and Microsoft provides the software and services. If you are a DSL subscriber, you should inquire with your ISP or telecommunications company to see if MSN Premium is included in your service.

Just the facts

- Web access to your Outlook e-mail and Contacts is available using a variety of Webmail providers like Google, Yahoo!, AOL, and Microsoft.
- Outlook 2007 supports all the major e-mail protocols used by Webmail providers, including POP3, IMAP, and HTTP.
- POP3 should be configured to leave a copy of e-mail on the server so all your messages are available in Outlook and via the browser.
- IMAP connections provide true e-mail synchronization because all messages are stored on the server; only AOL currently offers IMAP access to Webmail from Outlook.

- HTTP connections provide near real-time synchronization between the Webmail server and Outlook. This is the connection type used by Microsoft Hotmail and MSN Premium.

- Use Outlook's Import and Export Wizard to create a CSV file containing your Outlook Contacts information for import into Webmail accounts from companies other than Microsoft.

- Hotmail Plus uses the Windows Live Contact Importer utility to access and import your Outlook, Outlook Express, and/or Windows Live Mail Desktop addresses into your Hotmail/Windows Live Mail account.

- MSN Premium is a more expensive and more fully featured alternative to Hotmail Plus that provides the Outlook Connector, which delivers full synchronization between Outlook and your online MSN account.

GET THE SCOOP ON...
What Office Live offers ▪ Using Office Live Basics,
Essentials, or Premium with Outlook ▪ Office
Live for personal use

Microsoft Office Live

Chapter 22 discussed migration to the Web as a place where an increasing amount of your information and application functionality will be found in the future. Microsoft is well aware of this trend, and the company's Chief Technical Officer and industry luminary Ray Ozzie issued a manifesto of sorts in October 2005, titled "The Internet Services Disruption." Intended as a rallying cry to the 70,000 employees of the company, Ozzie painted a picture that, as you read this, has already begun to take shape.

Barely six months later, the company announced Office Live. Microsoft has a curious tendency of coming up with confusing product names. There's the classic case of Outlook, the application this book is about, and Outlook Express, an e-mail client that has nothing at all in common with Outlook except that they both provide e-mail services. And most recently, we have Windows Live Mail, the replacement for Hotmail, and Windows Live Mail Desktop, the replacement for Outlook Express.

Office Live created confusion because the immediate expectation was that Microsoft was planning to release an online, Web-based version of its ubiquitous suite of productivity applications. And Office Live is something decidedly different.

This chapter provides a look at Office Live and describes the three versions of the service: Basics, Essentials, and Premium. All three versions provide useful online services that can extend what you do with the information and documents you produce in the applications in the Office suite, including Outlook.

What is Microsoft Office Live?

Microsoft Office Live is a set of three online services that help organizations easily and inexpensively establish a presence on the Internet.

Office Live Basics

Office Live Basics is a free service, provides Web-based e-mail, Web site hosting, and a domain name (yourname.com). Live Basics includes 25 e-mail addresses (you@yourname.com), a Web domain hosted by Microsoft (www.yourname.com), an easy-to-use, template-driven Site Designer tool to create your Web site, basic reporting tools, and technical support via e-mail. The Site Designer tool walks you step by step through the process of creating a basic Web site, beginning with the selection of a design template as shown in Figure 23.1.

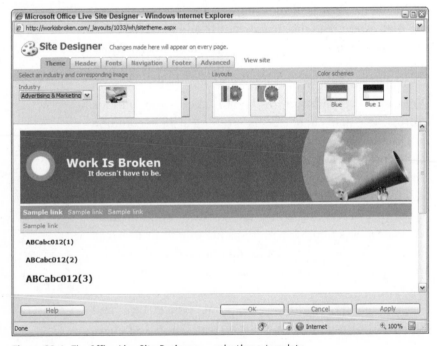

Figure 23.1. The Office Live Site Designer — selecting a template.

Inside Scoop

Office Live is *not* an online version of the Office suite of productivity applications. In October 2006, there were reports that Microsoft was considering developing a set of online applications based on the Microsoft Works suite that is bundled on many PCs. Works, while not as powerful as Office, provides many of the same capabilities.

You can easily add pages to your site using Site Designer. The application's interface, shown in Figure 23.2, is well organized and uses point-and-click buttons and navigation icons to assist you in creating and managing pages on your site, building an image library to illustrate your pages, and uploading documents you can make available to site visitors to download.

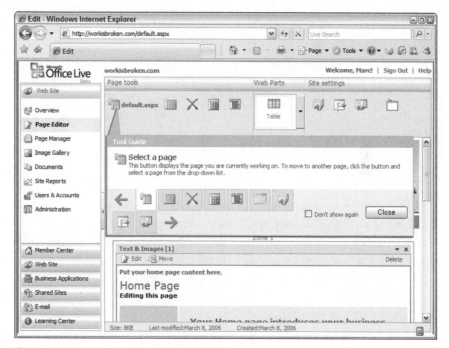

Figure 23.2. The Page Editor view in Site Designer.

Office Live Basics includes a basic set of Web reports that help you track site traffic, page popularity, browser preferences of your site's visitors, and other statistics. These reports can be viewed in an online interface, as shown in Figure 23.3, or downloaded as CSV (Comma Separated

Values) files that you can import into an application like Excel to perform analysis and charting for reports you can distribute to others in your organization.

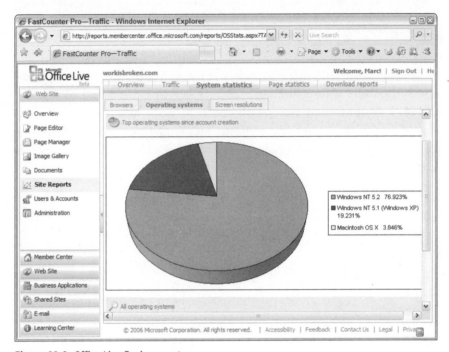

Figure 23.3. Office Live Basics reports.

Office Live Basics provides 25 Webmail accounts, each of which is provided with 2GB of storage space. These Webmail accounts are accessed using Windows Live Mail or a Windows mobile-powered cell phone. Each account in Windows Live Mail includes a Contacts list and a calendar with a Tasks list. Contacts can be imported from your Outlook Contacts list using the same Windows Live Importer utility described in Chapter 22. There is no import feature available for calendar information from Outlook, although you can share your Windows Live Mail calendar with others.

Also included with Office Live Basics is access to the Office Live adManager, which provides a source of revenue-generating ads that you can display on your Office Live Web site, and access to Office Accounting Express 2007, a free version of Microsoft's small business accounting package.

Office Live Basics provides a Learning Center that offers helpful articles like the one pictured in Figure 23.4. The article shown talks about e-mail management and how to integrate Office Live with Outlook. Unfortunately, Office Live Basics e-mail cannot be accessed from Outlook. You will need to upgrade to the subscription-based Office Live Essentials or Premium editions, which employ the same Outlook Connector described in Chapter 22. This software, installed on your PC, provides a real-time synchronization between your Office Live account and Outlook.

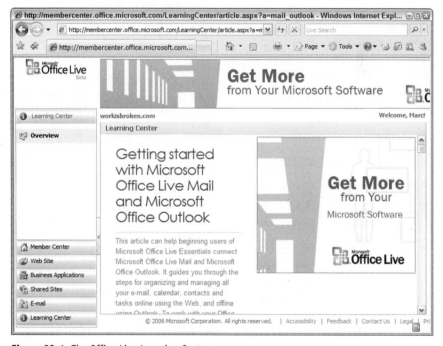

Figure 23.4. The Office Live Learning Center.

Watch Out!
If you have an Office Live Basics account, be prepared for many invitations and solicitations to upgrade to an Office Live Essentials or Premium account. Also be prepared to have ads displayed everywhere in your Office Live environment. Putting up with ads is the price you pay for getting a free account.

Office Live Essentials and Premium

Office Live Essentials and Premium accounts are where things get really interesting if your organization needs a combination of the e-mail and Web presence components in Basics and a set of business applications and tools to share information among employees and with partners and customers. These subscription accounts also provide the critical ability to use the Outlook Connector to access and synchronize all your Web-based information from Outlook on your PC.

Essentials pricing begins at $19.95 and includes the following:

- 1GB of Web site storage (compared to 500MB in Basics)

- Custom Web site uploading to the Office Live server

- 500MB of shared Workspace storage (not available in Basics)

- Advanced Web traffic reports

- 50 e-mail accounts (compared with 25 in Basics), each with 2GB of storage space

- A 20MB e-mail attachment limit (compared to 10MB in Basics)

- 10 Business applications/Workspace users

- 500MB of Business applications/Workspace storage

- Office Live Business Contact Manager — a Web-based version of the Outlook add-in described in Chapter 19

- Online, e-mail, and 24-hour toll-free phone support (Basics provides online and e-mail support only)

Premium pricing begins at $39.95 and adds the following to the Essentials offering:

- 2GB of Web site storage

- 20 Business applications/Workspace users

- 1GB of Business applications/Workspace storage

- Application modules for project management, sales, document management, company administration, and time management

You can, at additional cost, add more users, Web storage, Business applications/Workspace storage, domain names, bandwidth, and e-mail accounts as needed to the core Essentials or Premium packages.

Using Office Live Essentials with Outlook

The inclusion of the Outlook Connector in Office Live Essentials and Premium makes those editions the most interesting to an organization that uses Outlook 2007 looking for a way to connect all its users without getting into the expense and administration issues raised by self-hosting Exchange and SharePoint. The business applications and Workspaces provided by Office Live Essentials and especially Premium deliver similar value to a SharePoint environment. The e-mail, calendar, and Tasks list sharing in both editions provides similar benefit to an Exchange server.

If your organization is distributed across multiple locations, allows telecommuting, or needs to provide on-the-road connectivity to road warrior salespeople and account managers, Essentials or Premium is an offering with a great deal of potential value. If you already have hosted e-mail and a Web site for your company, you can easily transfer your MX records (e-mail) and domain name to Office Live Essentials or Premium and use Microsoft as your host for these services.

The Outlook Connector allows you to set up a new account profile in your local copy of Outlook that connects to the Office Live server. Account setup is similar to connecting to any other e-mail server providing an HTTP connection like Hotmail and MSN Premium. Office Live Essentials provides server-side antivirus and spam-filtering services as well as offering daily backups of all your information. All in all, it's quite a nice package if your organization includes enough people to justify the expense. When you consider that hosted Exchange accounts average $10 per user per month, it's hard to find much fault with the pricing for Office Live Essentials or Premium.

Office Live for personal use

Office Live Basics is a nice way to get a free domain name, basic Web site, and five e-mail accounts. Although you can't connect directly to Office Live e-mail in Outlook, there may be value in having Webmail accounts for you and the other members of your household, club, or small organization.

Bright Idea

Office Live Basics is a great way to grab a domain name at no cost. If you have been thinking of developing a Web site and already know the domain name you'd like to use as your address, secure it now in a free Basics account. You can move the domain to another host 60 days after creating your Basics account. You will be responsible for domain registration fees if you move to another host.

As of this writing, Microsoft has announced that all Office Live accounts will be connected to eBay to create the ability to set up an online shop. Along with the eBay connection comes the ability to conduct online transactions via PayPal, which is now owned by eBay. If you have been interested in participating in online commerce, that may be another reason to explore the potential benefits that an Office Live subscription can provide. After all, the price of an Office Live Basics account is hard to argue with.

Just the facts

- Microsoft Office Live is not an online version of Microsoft Office.
- Microsoft Office Live is available in three editions: Basics, Essentials, and Premium.
- Office Live Basics is a free service that provides 25 e-mail addresses, a domain name, and a basic Web site.
- Office Live Essentials and Premium are subscription services that add shared Workspaces, business applications, and the ability to connect to your Office Live information from Outlook using the Outlook Connector.
- You can easily transfer your existing e-mail and domain name to Office Live.
- For personal use, Office Live Basics offers great value, but you can't access your Webmail from Outlook.
- All Office Live accounts provide the ability to use eBay and PayPal to conduct online commerce.

GET THE SCOOP ON...
Taking Outlook with you ▪ Outlook and Windows
Mobile ▪ Outlook and Palm OS PDAs ▪
Outlook-on-a-stick ▪ Outlook and UMPCs

Outlook and Mobile Devices

When I was a kid, I looked forward to two TV shows and was always diligent about finishing homework and chores to make sure I did not miss *Batman* or *Star Trek*. *Batman* had such amazing gadgets — I'm sure that this early impression has a lot to do with the passion I have for cool toys today. But Star Trek left an even more indelible mark because of two devices familiar to anyone who's ever watched the show — the communicator and the tricorder. What passed for science fiction nearly 40 years ago, in many ways, is the reality of today.

Today, increasing numbers of people carry a small device that fits in their pocket and provides instantaneous communication with people all over the planet, access to just about any information desired in a matter of seconds, and the ability to carry vast amounts of personal information on tiny cards not much bigger than a thumbnail. That surely sounds like the communicator and tricorder to me. We just call them by different names, like Smartphone or Treo.

If you've been around for some or all of the past 40 years and have watched the rate at which technology has accelerated, you can appreciate that the small, portable devices have more computing power and memory than the behemoths we kept in climate-controlled computing centers or the incredibly large, noisy, and lumbering desktop computers we once used. And the next generation of information workers are growing up in a world where everything is connected and information is located on the network where it can be accessed from a variety of devices.

This chapter looks at the three most popular mobile devices that provide you with the ability to carry some or all of your Outlook information with you wherever you may be. I look at Windows Mobile devices that provide a mobile version of Outlook and Outlook companion applications for the Palm OS-based Treo models. The corporate standard for e-mail is the Blackberry, and while this device is a great e-mail tool and allows you to review Office documents when connected to a Blackberry server, it's less capable as a mobile Outlook device and not well suited for personal use. Each of these mobile platforms has become a vital tool for conducting business, accessing calendar and task information, working with documents, and sending and receiving e-mail. Oh yes...they also are cellular phones and, in some configurations, modems that allow you to get connected to the Internet when no wireless service is available.

Take Outlook with you

Despite the increased availability of Internet connectivity via wireless or WiFi connections in cafes, libraries, hotels, and airports, there are times when it's simply not convenient to pull out your notebook computer to check your calendar, look up a phone number, or refer to an e-mail message about an upcoming meeting or event. At the end of 2005, there were 207.9 million cell phones in the U.S., a 14 percent increase over the previous year. That trend appears likely to continue and illustrates the ever-increasing need or desire for mobile connectivity in our lives.

The power and capabilities of these small devices is increasing at a similar rate. The features available on a relatively inexpensive device like the recently introduced $200 Motorola Q Smartphone cost two to three times that amount less than a year ago. The number of these so-called "converged devices" that combine conventional telephony with personal information management and Internet access is on the rise.

For Outlook users, this is very good news. Because it's the most popular e-mail and personal information management application on the planet, Outlook has near-universal support for synchronization of your data on these mobile devices. On devices running Microsoft's Windows Mobile operating system, the support is delivered through a mobile-friendly version of Outlook itself. The Folder List view in Outlook Mobile, shown in Figure 24.1, is consistent with the display on your PC and pops open in much the same way that the folder list does when the Navigation Pane is minimized in Outlook 2007.

On Palm OS Treo Smartphones, you have the option to use the built-in calendar, contacts, tasks, and e-mail applications, or you can choose from a number of third-party alternatives that provide a more Outlook-like experience and better fidelity to the information on your PC. Whichever mobile platform you elect to use, you can stay completely in sync with your Outlook data while on the go.

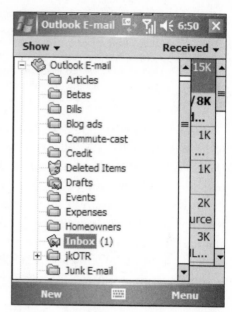

Figure 24.1. The folder list in Outlook Mobile on a Windows Mobile device.

Outlook and Windows Mobile devices

No big surprise — the most Outlook-like experience on a mobile device is delivered by Microsoft itself. The mobile version of Windows has gone through almost as many permutations as the Windows OS we use on our PCs and, like its "big brother," has matured and improved significantly over the years. The mobile experience offered by devices powered by Windows Mobile 5, the latest version, is very good indeed, offering mobile versions of Word, PowerPoint, and Excel in addition to Mobile Outlook.

The way you work on a Windows Mobile device has a lot to do with the actual device you choose. An increasing number of Smartphones have a full QWERTY keyboard that, although tiny in size compared to the keyboard on your notebook or desktop PC, is very functional and good for composing short e-mails, text messages, and Instant Messaging chat posts and for performing light editing. A number of devices still provide only a standard ten-key dial pad, and entering text on these keys requires a bit of practice. Ten-key devices use a technique called predictive input to guess what word you're typing as you add each letter. It sounds hard, but it's actually a very fast method of entering text after you get the hang of it.

Bright Idea

If you want a good teacher to help you master the ten-key pad method, look no further than the nearest teenager or college student in your life. Most young people today use text messaging on their conventional cell phones as a primary means of communicating with their friends and are amazingly fast at text entry.

Most Windows Mobile devices support Bluetooth, a wireless protocol for connecting devices like headsets, keyboards, and mice. If your Windows Mobile device has Bluetooth built in and you plan to do a lot of text entry, you may want to consider getting a wireless keyboard for more extensive work. A variety of foldable keyboards are available that you can toss in your briefcase, purse, laptop bag, or coat pocket that open up to a standard-sized keyboard but take up a small amount of space when folded. This setup — a Windows Mobile device and foldable keyboard — is actually a great way to work on airplanes, in cafes, and in other locations where space is at a premium.

Sending and receiving e-mail

Working with e-mail in Mobile Outlook couldn't be simpler. Composing messages is performed in a simple form shown in Figure 24.2. Select the account you want to send from if you have more than one configured, add the contact(s) you want to send the message to, enter your message text, and click Send. Mobile Outlook uses the Contacts list in the same way Outlook 2007 does and performs auto-complete on names as you begin entering text. When the right contact name is shown, tap on it with the stylus or press the select button on the device and it is added to the recipient field. Note the keyboard icon in Figure 24.2. Windows Mobile provides an onscreen keyboard that you can tap on with the device's

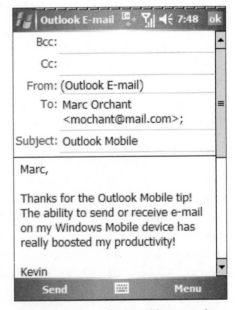

Figure 24.2. The mail composition screen in Mobile Outlook.

stylus. This is slower than entering text on a QWERTY or ten-key keypad, but it works well enough for small amounts of text.

Reading e-mail in Mobile Outlook is a one-handed affair because you can use the D-pad, the four-way directional navigation button on Windows Mobile devices, to scroll up and down in the message text. On some Windows Mobile devices, you can rotate the display to read mail in a landscape orientation, which makes the line lengths a bit longer and easier to read.

Working with contacts

Mobile Outlook displays all the information related to a contact just as you entered it in Outlook 2007, including the person's picture if you've included it. An advantage to using contact photos in Windows Mobile is that the person's picture is displayed as part of the Caller ID screen on your device when you receive a call from that person. Figures 24.3 and 24.4 show the contact record display. The first figure shows the first screen of information, and the second shows the rest of the contact methods you can use on a Windows Mobile device as you scroll down the page.

Figure 24.3. A first screen in a contact record in Mobile Outlook.

Hack

If your Windows Mobile device has a camera, you can snap a picture of a contact and add it to that person's contact record on the mobile device. When you sync with Outlook, the picture is stored on your PC and appears in the contact record on your PC.

Note that you can use any of the communication methods supported by the device if you have entered the contact's phone number(s), e-mail address, IM screen name, and Web site URL. When you click any of the action buttons shown in these figures, the appropriate application is launched. E-mail is, of course, handled by Mobile Outlook. Phone calls and SMS text messaging are handled by the device's phone and text messaging application interfaces. IM chats are conducted using Windows Messenger Mobile. Web browsing is accomplished using the mobile version of Internet Explorer included in Windows Mobile.

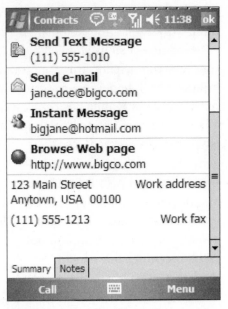

Figure 24.4. The rest of the contact record in Mobile Outlook.

Managing your calendar, tasks, and notes

Mobile Outlook includes Calendar, Tasks, and Notes views that synchronize with their counterparts in your Outlook 2007 environment on the PC. The calendar, shown in Day view in Figure 24.5, displays events in much the same way as in Outlook on your PC. Tapping or selecting an appointment block opens a details screen where you can view any notes attached to the appointment, linked contacts, and other related information. The Tasks and Notes

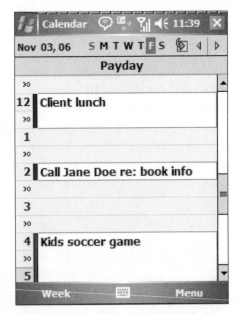

Figure 24.5. The Mobile Outlook Calendar in Day view.

views in Mobile Outlook are very similar, presenting a streamlined view of the information from your Outlook 2007 environment designed to be easy to read and manipulate on the small screen.

Setting up e-mail for Mobile Outlook

Setting up Mobile Outlook to connect to your e-mail account(s) is every bit as easy as in Outlook 2007. The mobile edition uses the same smart technology to automate the process of figuring out the server addresses and other information required for you. To set up an account, enter your name in the first screen in the account wizard as shown in Figure 24.6 and click Next.

The second screen in the wizard, pictured in Figure 24.7, appears and displays the progress of the auto-detection process. If your e-mail account is typical, Mobile Outlook sets up everything for you and you're ready to send and receive e-mail. If the wizard is unable to figure things out, you're provided with a series of screens that walk you through the process of manually providing the information required about your incoming and outgoing servers.

Figure 24.6. The initial screen in the account wizard in Mobile Outlook.

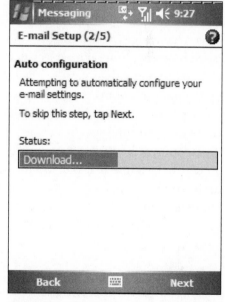

Figure 24.7. The second screen in the account wizard in Mobile Outlook.

After your account setup is completed, you can set preferences for how frequently your Windows Mobile device should check for e-mail and how the connection should be made — either using the Internet or your cellular provider's network, as appropriate for your account. This configuration screen, shown in Figure 24.8, reminds you that connection charges may apply against the minutes or bandwidth provided by your account. If you are on a plan that provides a set number of minutes or data download quota, you may want to consider a long interval between checks or sticking with a manually initiated check you perform yourself.

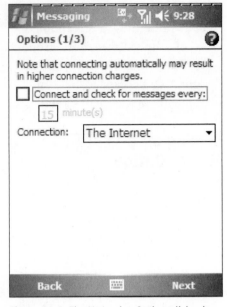

Figure 24.8. The Messaging Options dialog box.

If you work in an Exchange environment or use a hosted Exchange account (see Chapter 20 for information about Exchange Server and hosted Exchange), you configure your account setup in ActiveSync, the PC-based utility application used to synchronize content between your PC and your Windows Mobile device. ActiveSync can perform a synchronization operation whenever you connect your mobile device to your PC by placing it in a docking cradle or using a USB cable. Depending on how your PC is configured, you also may be able to synchronize using Bluetooth. Although Bluetooth sync is much more convenient because there are no wires to contend with, be aware that Bluetooth connections are much slower than USB cable connections, and if you have lots of new data in either Mobile Outlook or Outlook 2007 on your PC, the sync can take quite a while.

Watch Out!

ActiveSync is a cranky piece of software and can create serious headaches when problems do crop up. You can find advice on properly configuring ActiveSync for your Windows Mobile device in the documentation that came with your device or online. It's worth investing a bit of time to make sure you have everything set up properly.

Outlook and Palm OS PDAs

Many people are unaware of the fact that Palm, prior to being a hardware purveyor of Personal Digital Assistants (PDA), was a software company that developed a product called Graffiti for the short-lived Apple Newton. The original Newton's handwriting recognition was widely and justifiably criticized (and the subject of a pretty famous Doonesbury cartoon) and Graffiti was a big hit among the early adopters. When Palm first introduced the Palm Pilot a couple of years later, Graffiti was the ink-recognition system that helped catapult the device to the top position in the market.

Palm has had its ups and downs since then, but the company's Treo line of converged phone-PDA devices has been a runaway success. At the time of this writing, there are five different Treo models available. Two, the 700w and 700wx, run Windows Mobile 5 and provide the Mobile Outlook solution described earlier in this chapter. The other three, the 650, 680, and 700p, run the Palm OS. A sixth, the 750, is about to be released that will run the Windows Mobile OS.

In the past, Palm PDAs required a third-party set of conduits — software tools that allow data to be synchronized between a PDA and a PC — to work with Outlook. With the introduction of the Treo 650 a couple of years ago, Palm began including Outlook connectivity in the box. The Palm OS includes a basic but capable set of information management tools that sync with Outlook's calendar, contacts, tasks, and notes. With the advent of the Treo line, an e-mail client was added to the mix.

Although there is nothing wrong with the Palm applications, they are very basic and have limitations on record size and number of categories that can be defined, and their formats lack many of the fields present in Outlook. So although the ability has existed for some time to synchronize some of your Outlook data with a Palm device, compromises had to be made.

The Palm platform has long enjoyed a thriving community of third-party developers, and a number of companies recognized the opportunity to provide a more satisfying experience for Outlook users. Three have stood out as great alternatives for Outlook users who want to keep their Treo and their PC in perfect sync. All three of these programs have similar core capabilities that map to Outlook, but each has taken a slightly different approach to how it presents those capabilities. I've used all of them and can recommend any of them to an Outlook user who also carries a Treo, depending on which best matches the user's needs.

Chapura KeySuite

KeySuite is the Outlook companion program I use on my Treo 700p. Chapura, the developers of KeySuite, has a long history of support for Palm to Outlook synchronization with its PocketMirror synchronization conduits, which have been a staple for Outlook users with Palm devices for years. KeySuite maps every field in Outlook to a matching field on the Treo (or other Palm OS device) and provides the same set of main views as Outlook on the PC (as do all of these programs):

Figure 24.9. The KeyToday screen.

- KeyToday (shown in Figure 24.9) maps to Outlook Today — a summary screen of the day's events, tasks, and any new e-mail messages.

- KeyDates maps to the Outlook calendar and provides daily, weekly, monthly, and annual calendar views, with or without task integration in daily and weekly views. Daily view with tasks is shown in Figure 24.10.

- KeyContacts maps to Outlook's contact list and also functions as the address book for the Treo's phone.

- KeyTasks maps to the Outlook Tasks list.

- KeyNotes maps to Outlook's Notes.

Figure 24.10. The KeyDates daily calendar with task integration.

KeySuite does not include an e-mail client for the Treo. It does integrate with VersaMail, which is bundled on all Palm OS Treos, and with SnapperMail, a popular alternative mail application for the Treo.

One consideration you must take into account when deciding to adopt KeySuite is that the suite uses its own data files, not the data files used by the built-in Palm applications. If you have been using a Palm device for a while and have populated the Address, Calendar, and Tasks applications, you will consume additional memory on your Treo. If you do decide to switch to KeySuite, you'll want to delete the records in your built-in Palm data files to save space, especially if you have a lot of information in these applications and are using a Treo 650, which has half the memory of newer devices.

DataViz BeyondContacts

DataViz develops Documents to Go, the Office companion bundled on most Treos. The company has been in the Palm business for a long time and also has a long history of providing excellent translation tools that allow files to be used on both Macs and Windows PCs (which is less of an issue today but used to be a very big deal). Like KeySuite, BeyondContacts uses its own data files to provide complete fidelity to Outlook's data structures.

BeyondContacts includes the same five applications as KeySuite and adds Inbox to Go, a completely integrated e-mail client. If you also have Documents to Go installed (all new Treos include this Office companion suite), you can open the following attachments in e-mail messages with a single tap of the stylus: MS Word, WordPerfect, WordPro, RTF, PDF, MS Excel, Quattro Pro, Lotus 1-2-3, MS PowerPoint, JPEG, GIF, and BMP. Figure 24.11 shows BeyondContact's Today screen.

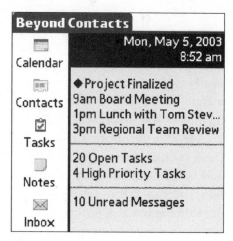

Figure 24.11. The Today screen in BeyondContacts.

Iambic Agendus

Agendus has an interesting history. The application, like Palm's Graffiti gesture script, has its roots in the Apple Newton. Originally called Action Names, the software was ported from the Newton to the Palm platform when the first Palm Pilot appeared on the market. Agendus takes a different approach than the other two programs described in this chapter because it uses the built-in Palm data files and makes a trade-off between full Outlook field matching and a host of useful features the other two suites do not provide. In essence, syncing with Agendus is the same as syncing with the built-in Palm application. In fact, Agendus actually uses the conduits Palm supplies and adds one of its own called Agendus Extras.

Agendus uses a lot of icons, as illustrated in Figure 24.12, which shows the Agendus Today screen. The suite also provides a number of application modules and features that go beyond Outlook compatibility, such as a Task matrix system that allows you to define priorities in a more useful fashion than simple high or low priority, a set of Over-the-Air (OTA) applications that fetch weather, travel, and other information in real time, and a powerful built-in Internet search tool.

Figure 24.12. The Agendus Today screen.

Agendus also does a neat trick with contacts. Although all three of these companion programs do a good job of linking contacts to events and tasks, Agendus takes contact linking a step further. In this application, you can define relationships between contacts and display all connected contacts as a group, as shown in Figure 24.13. In this figure, you can see two hierarchical levels of contacts linked to the primary contact being viewed.

The final distinction that Agendus provides is that it can synchronize with either Outlook or Palm Desktop, making it a great tool for people who have Outlook on a PC at work and Palm Desktop on a PC at home. Iambic also produces Agendus for Windows, which provides a view of your Outlook or Palm Desktop data in a different interface that features some of the same enhancements as Agendus for the Palm. The company also sells a full-featured e-mail application that integrates with the Agendus suite.

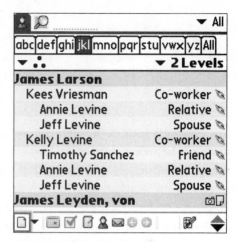

Figure 24.13. The Agendus contact screen showing contact links.

Outlook in your pocket

Another approach to taking Outlook with you is to carry all your data on a USB flash drive or hard drive for use on any PC you happen to have access to. The attraction to this approach is that you avoid synchronization issues because your one true set of data is always with you and up to date. The only real downside to this approach is that you have to be even more diligent about creating a backup than when storing data files on a notebook or desktop PC because it's much easier to misplace a small USB drive than it is a computer.

There are some very complex ways to achieve this kind of Outlook portability that I won't go into precisely because they are complex and require a level of technical knowledge and "joy of geek" that most people aren't interested in achieving. Fortunately, an excellent alternative is inexpensive (under $30), flexible, and quite easy to use. It's called Migo.

Migo organizes and stores a backup of the data and e-mail from your computer onto just about any portable storage device, such as a USB flash drive, a memory card, or even an MP3 music player like an iPod. As long as the storage device can be mounted as a drive in Windows, Migo can use it to make Outlook portable.

Watch Out!
Outlook 2003 and 2007 use a new PST file format. You cannot use your Outlook 2007 PST files on a borrowed computer running any version older than 2003. If you use an application not installed on the borrowed PC that uses a proprietary file format, you cannot work on that file.

To access your data when you are on the go, plug your Migo-enabled device into a PC running Microsoft Windows 2000 or later, and the Migo engine temporarily transforms that PC into your own. All the data from your PC, including your Outlook data, your browser favorites (Internet Explorer or Firefox), and your desktop complete with files and folders, appears. After the Migo environment is running, you can work on documents, manage your calendar and tasks, and receive and answer e-mail just as you would on your own PC. Migo lets you use the borrowed computer's software, hardware, and network connections, including Internet access. The only condition is that the borrowed PC must have Office 2007 and any other application software you use installed.

When you're finished using a borrowed computer, Migo keeps all the work you've done on your USB device, including your Internet history and cookies. No trace of your activity is left behind on the borrowed computer. When you get back to your home or office PC, Migo synchronizes the data it carries with the files on your own computer, so you're always working on the latest versions of your data. Your e-mail folders also are updated, so there's less need to leave copies of your messages on your mail server. If you use more than one computer, Migo can even create a portable version of each that you can carry on your USB device, allowing you to choose which one you want to run on the borrowed PC.

The new Ultra Mobile PC

In 2006, a number of Microsoft OEM partners began producing a new kind of PC called the Ultra Mobile PC (UMPC). The small devices, about the size of portable DVD player, run the Windows XP Tablet PC operating system and allow you to use both a stylus and your finger to tap on the screen to open folders and applications, click buttons, and enter text.

These devices, like the TabletKiosk i7200 shown in Figure 24.14, generally have a 7" display and a variety of connectivity options including

WiFi and Bluetooth, allowing you to access a network connection and use wireless peripherals like a keyboard, mouse, or headset. Because UMPCs are full Windows XP computers, you can install and run Office 2007 on them just as you would any PC.

Figure 24.14. The TabletKiosk i7200 Ultra Mobile PC. (Image courtesy of TabletKiosk)

When you are working at your desk, you can plug the UMPC in to your local network, and use a full-size monitor, keyboard, mouse, and printer. Many UMPCs either include or make available as an option a docking cradle that lets you keep all these peripherals plugged in and ready to use as soon as you place the device in the cradle. Although they are not as powerful as conventional notebook computers, UMPCs are very portable and allow you to carry your PC with you with much less hassle than a full-sized notebook PC. If a Windows Mobile device or Treo is just too small and a notebook a little too big to allow you to use Outlook when you are on the go, a UMPC may be a great balance between portability and power. UMPCs are currently being offered by companies like Samsung, Asus, and TabletKiosk. As the new platform matures, I expect to see other manufacturers introduce their own UMPC models.

Just the facts

- The emergence of converged devices that incorporate a cellular phone and a portable computer provides new mobility options for people who want to access their Outlook information and e-mail on the go.

- Because Outlook is the most popular e-mail and information management application in the world, virtually every device supports it.

- The two most popular choices to take Outlook with you are devices running Windows Mobile 5 or the Palm OS-powered line of Treo Smartphones.

- Windows Mobile devices provide the most faithful Outlook experience because they run Mobile Outlook — a companion version of the application on your PC.

- Mobile Outlook synchronizes with your PC using a utility called ActiveSync, which keeps all your Outlook data on both the mobile device and your PC up-to-date no matter where you last made changes to it.

- Mobile Outlook provides the same automated e-mail account setup as Outlook 2007, and setting up most accounts requires little more than your e-mail address.

- Palm OS Treos can synchronize with Outlook using software conduits that map Outlook information to the built-in Palm applications or third-party Outlook companion programs.

- A number of applications can act as a mobile companion to Outlook on the Palm OS, including Chapura KeySuite, DataViz BeyondContacts, and Iambic Agendus.

- Migo software creates a snapshot of your desktop or notebook PC, including your Outlook data, that you can carry with you on a USB storage device and plug into any borrowed PC.

- Ultra Mobile PCs are small, portable Windows XP Tablet PC-based devices that provide a great balance between portability and usability.

Keep Outlook Working

PART V

GET THE SCOOP ON...
Backing up your data files ▪ Archiving strategies ▪
Putting your data files on a diet ▪ Staying calm when
things go wrong ▪ Slimming down your data files by
managing attachments ▪ Storing file attachments

Care and Feeding of Outlook Data Files

Chapter 25

O ver the past 25 years, I've taught many computer classes, and I invariably share my three rules of personal computing with my students. They're trite and overused, and they probably ended up being ignored on more than a few occasions, but no one — not ever — has come back to me and complained that following these rules did anything other than get them out of a serious jam.

These are my three rules of personal computing:

1. Save early and often.

2. Back up your work frequently.

3. When things go wrong on your system, don't panic (assuming you are practicing the first two rules).

You've probably heard the first two rules many times. So let me ask you, when was the last time you backed up your data? That's what I thought.

Expanding on rules one and two, let me suggest the following thoughts. The keyboard shortcut for saving your work in every program worth using is Ctrl+S. If you remember only one keyboard shortcut, this should be the one. If you can handle two, also memorize Ctrl+Z, which is the equally universal Undo command. Having memorized the command, use it. A lot. Whenever you stop to stare off into the middle distance, save your work. When you get up from your PC, save your work. When you pause to take a sip of the refreshing beverage you have close to your PC, save your work. Whether you work from the keyboard or prefer to use the mouse to click the Save button in the application you're working in, you get the idea.

As for rule number two, the question I'm most frequently asked after dispensing this advice is, "How often is frequently?" Of course, I have developed what I think is the perfect response: "How much work are you willing to lose?"

I probably sound like a wise guy saying that. But I'm completely serious. If you think about it, Murphy's Law (and remember, he was an optimist) states that things inevitably go wrong and at the worst possible time. So the likelihood that your hard drive will crash or your power supply will suddenly go "poof" or some other unanticipated tragedy will occur is directly proportional to how badly you need to access your data at any given time. Backing up frequently means just that. If you are the kind of person who uses the PC occasionally except for activities like e-mail and Web surfing, back up accordingly. If, on the other hand, your entire life's work is on your PC and it's absolutely essential that you never lose even a single day's work, then you should be backing up every day.

This chapter begins with my three rules for Outlook happiness. They're not quite the same as my three rules for personal computing, but they are intended to accomplish the same thing — to keep you safe, secure, and stress-free. The chapter concludes with some tips and tricks to maintain your Outlook data files in tip-top condition to provide the best performance possible on your PC.

Rule number one: Back up data files regularly

Reinstalling Outlook is not much fun, but it's not a terribly difficult task to accomplish. Rebuilding your Outlook environment, by contrast, is a task that falls somewhere between traumatic and impossible, depending on what kind of mail server you connect to. So rule number one is to back up your Outlook files on a regular basis.

Assuming, as we have throughout this book, that you are using Outlook in stand-alone mode and not connected to an Exchange Server, you can accomplish this critical task in two ways. You can manually back up your Outlook PST files, or you can use an external application to automate the process. In either case, you first need to decide where to store your backup files. Your options include using removable media like a CD, DVD, or USB flash drive, an external hard drive, or a server located on your local area network or the Internet. Each of these approaches has advantages and disadvantages depending on your budget, network setup, and Internet connection.

Removable media

The biggest advantage to removable media is cost. Optical storage media — CDs or DVDs — is very inexpensive and can be purchased just about anywhere. I can buy competitively priced, recordable CD and DVD media at my local supermarket and have recently seen blank discs being sold in airport book shops (admittedly at somewhat less competitive prices). Assuming your PC has an optical drive capable of burning CDs and/or DVDs, you can choose between two kinds of media in one or both formats. CD-R and DVD-R are one-time discs that you make a backup on and then file it away. CD-RW and DVD-RW discs can be written to many times.

The RW (read/write) discs tend to be a bit more expensive, but they provide much more flexibility, especially for use in a regular backup schedule. I have a set of backup CD-RW discs for each day of the week and use them every Monday, every Tuesday, and so on. This means that, at any given time, I have a full week of backups available. That may be a little over the top for your needs, but I prefer to be excessive when it comes to my data, and the daily backup takes just a few minutes and is part of my end-of-the-workday routine.

Recently, USB flash drives — sometimes called thumb, pen, or jump drives — have dropped in price so precipitously that they have become very affordable options for this kind of backup activity. For example, I saw an advertisement from one of the big-box electronic stores recently offering a three-pack of 1GB (gigabyte) drives for under $100. If you were to use these drives on a three-times-a-week backup rotation, you'd have a very nice setup for a relatively nominal investment.

Watch Out!

Recordable optical discs need to be stored and handled with a modest amount of care and common sense. They should never be exposed to direct sunlight for any significant period of time, and they can be scratched more easily than commercial music CDs or movie DVDs. Store them in jewel cases or a disc binder.

All of these removable mediums have the same advantage: portability. You can store your backups in a separate location from your PC, and you can easily take a backup disc or USB drive with you when you're traveling with a notebook PC. I keep my backup discs in a fireproof media safe in my office.

External hard drives

External hard drives have likewise become very inexpensive and are an excellent option for backing up all your files or even creating an image of your entire PC. Most modern PCs are equipped with USB 2.0 connections, and the performance of an external hard drive connected through one of these ports is much better than writing to an optical disc. Keep in mind, though, that these hard drives, like the one inside your desktop or notebook PC, are mechanical devices that will wear out someday. The odds of both your internal and external hard drives failing at precisely the same time are slim, but natural disasters like flooding, fire, and electrical surges have the potential to take out your entire system.

In addition to their backup usefulness, these drives can be used to store working files and applications and your photo and music library if you use a digital camera or portable MP3 player. If your PC's internal hard drive is getting full — and in this day and age of digital camera and downloadable music and video that's not uncommon — an external drive may be a great addition to your system to give you room to work and to handle backup chores.

Server storage

If your Internet Service Provider or your employer provides access to file storage on its server, you may want to consider network backup as an option. These servers are generally backed up on a daily basis and reside in very secure data environments. The biggest drawback to network storage, especially over a broadband connection, is that they take much longer to accomplish. If you tend to be highly mobile, this can be an excellent option in spite of this performance issue because you can access your backup files from any location with a net connection.

Manual backup

No matter which approach you select for *where* you back up your files, you have an additional decision to make about how these backups are accomplished. The simplest route to take is to manually back up your

Outlook data by opening the folder where the files are stored and then dragging and dropping them to the desired backup location on an optical, USB, or external hard drive. If you elect to back up your files to a server, the process varies based on the provider and server you are connected to, and instructions for the specific actions you need to take should have been provided to you.

Assuming that you are backing up to local media or a server on your local network, the first step is to locate and open the folder that contains your Outlook PST files. These files are, by default, stored in your Windows profile folder along a path similar to this: C:\Documents and Settings\yourname\Local Settings\Application Data\Microsoft\Outlook.

It's quite a bother to click your way through all these folders to get to your files. Fortunately, there is a much faster way to access this folder inside Outlook and from the Control Panel. If Outlook is running, select Account Settings from the Tools menu to display the dialog box shown in Figure 25.1, and click the second tab labeled Data Files. On the control bar above the list of files, select the last command to open the folder where your files are stored.

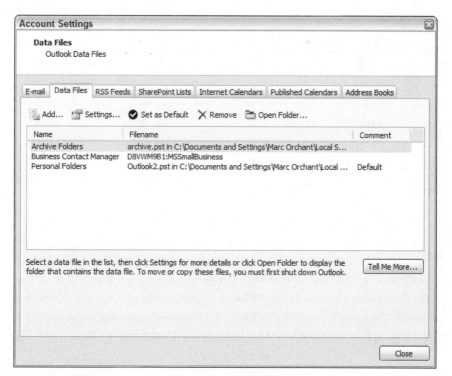

Figure 25.1. The Data Files tab in the Account Settings dialog box.

Watch Out!

It's important that you exit Outlook before you begin the backup process to make sure the files have been properly closed and are ready to be copied. If Outlook is not running and you want to perform a backup, open the folder manually or use the Control Panel Mail applet as described in this chapter.

If Outlook is not running, you can access the Account Settings dialog box from the Control Panel. Open the Control Panel from the Windows Start menu, and open the Mail applet. If your Control Panel is set to Category View, click User Accounts to access the Mail applet and open it by clicking its icon. If your Control Panel is set to Classic View, locate the Mail applet and open it by double-clicking it. The dialog box pictured in Figure 25.2 is displayed, and you can open the Account Settings dialog box by clicking the Data Files button.

Figure 25.2. The Mail Setup dialog box.

When you select the Open Folder control in the Account Settings dialog box, a Windows desktop folder similar to the one shown in Figure 25.3 opens. It contains your data files and a number of other settings files that Outlook uses to configure and store settings for your account. If you have previously run the SCANPST.exe repair utility on your data files and allowed the utility to create a backup before attempting repairs, those files also are in this folder. They are easily identified by their .bak file extensions and can be quite large in size because they are essentially backup copies of your PST files. I recommend you do not back up these files as they contain errors that were subsequently repaired by the utility.

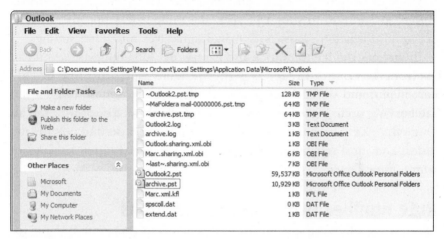

Figure 25.3. A Windows desktop folder containing PST and other Outlook data files.

To create the backup, select the PST file or files and drag them to your backup media. If you are backing up to an optical disc and are using the Windows CD Burning Wizard, a window to drag the files into is opened when you insert the blank disc. If you are using a third-party application to record CDs or DVDs, drag and drop the files to that application's window. If you are backing up to a USB drive or external hard drive, drag the files to that drive's icon in the My Computer window or open the drive from My Computer and drag the files to a folder you have created on that drive.

Automated backup applications

Many external hard drives come bundled with backup utility software, and a variety of third-party general-purpose utilities are available commercially and as shareware (try before you buy). It is outside the scope of this book to wander too far in that direction, but, as I described in Chapter 3, there is an excellent backup tool specifically designed to assist you in performing a complete backup of your Outlook files and settings that I have used and recommended for years.

The use of OutSource-XP 2 is documented in Chapter 3. For the regular routine backup I am discussing here, the steps are identical to those described for preparing your previous Outlook installation for an upgrade to Outlook 2007. The advantage that OutSource-XP 2 provides is that, in addition to your PST files, the utility backs up other critical account information, passwords, e-mail signatures, and other settings.

If you pay the fee to unlock and license the full application, you can compress these backup files as well. The utility works just fine in unlicensed or demo mode, and the compression feature is most useful if you are backing up to a smaller-capacity USB flash drive. Restoring from an OutSource-XP 2 backup requires only a couple of clicks and is easily the fastest and most reliable way I've found to perform routine backups of your Outlook data.

Rule number two: Archive old items

Outlook has offered the ability to archive items to a separate PST file for a long time. By moving older items you don't need immediate access to from your primary PST file into an archive file, you can keep your primary file smaller, which enhances Outlook's performance and stability. I like to call this technique "near-line" backup as opposed to the offline backup strategies described in rule number one.

The advantage to near-line backups is that the information remains accessible when you are working in Outlook — the archive PST file is located in the folder list in the Navigation Pane, is indexed for Instant Search, and can be used in exactly the same fashion as your primary PST file. The disadvantage to near-line storage from a data security perspective is that the archive files are stored in the same place as your primary files and are equally susceptible to data corruption, hardware failures, and other evils. A combination of near-line and offline strategies is the ideal approach to maintaining optimum performance and guarding against catastrophe.

In typical Outlook fashion, you can perform archive tasks in a number of ways — some automatic and some manual. The controls used to set up automatic archiving are scattered throughout the application and can initially be confusing as you encounter them, but the placement of these controls and the way they all work together makes sense after you become familiar with how archiving works.

Manual archiving

The most direct way to archive a folder in your primary PST file is to select the folder you want to move items out of in the folder list in the Navigation Pane and then select the Archive command from the File menu. The Archive dialog box, shown in Figure 25.4, is displayed, allowing you to choose the date you want to use to determine what is archived. Any items prior to the date you select are moved to an identically named folder in the archive PST

Figure 25.4. The Archive dialog box.

file. By default, this file is named archive.pst, and it resides in the same folder as your primary PST file. You can create your archive file wherever you like, either on your primary hard drive, an external hard drive, or a network share on a server on your local network.

At the top of the dialog box are two radio buttons that allow you to use the default AutoArchive settings, which are discussed in the next section, or manually set the cut-off date for the folder you have selected. You also can force Outlook to archive items that have been marked to ignore auto-archiving using the check box below the folder list. The Archive file: field allows you to select the destination file if you have more than one archive file available or if your archive file has been set up in a location other than the default.

Another manual archiving technique is to move an entire e-mail message folder to your archive file. I use this technique all the time when I have completed a project and am ready to move all the correspondence associated with that project out of my primary PST file. To manually archive an entire folder, select it in the folder list in the Navigation Pane

Inside Scoop

Any folder can be archived — not just e-mail folders. You can select the Archive command in the File menu when working in any other view in Outlook to archive the contents of that view. For example, you may want to archive your calendar or Tasks list every few months.

and drag and drop it into the desired location in your archive.pst folder. If that file is collapsed, hold the cursor over the top-level folder icon and it expands to show the folder hierarchy.

If you have previously used the Archive command on the File menu to archive some of the contents of the folder you want to move, you need to use a different technique to avoid replacing the existing folder in the archive.pst file with the folder in your primary PST file. In this case, select all the messages in the source folder in your primary PST file in the message list pane and drag and drop them to the corresponding folder in your archive.pst file. After the messages have been moved, you can safely delete the now-empty folder in your primary PST file.

AutoArchive

Automatic archiving is a great way to regularly reduce the size of your primary PST file, especially if you tend to forget to perform routine maintenance tasks. By default, Outlook asks if you want to AutoArchive folders in your Outlook environment every 30 days. You can change the default auto-archiving setup from the Other tab in the Options dialog box accessed from the Tools menu shown in Figure 25.5.

When you click the AutoArchive button, the dialog box pictured in Figure 25.6 is displayed. Although the number of choices presented may seem intimidating, it's actually a very clearly designed and labeled dialog box. The first two check boxes define how frequently AutoArchive runs (every 30 days is the default) and whether you want to be prompted before AutoArchive runs. I recommend that you leave this second check box selected so you always know when Outlook is performing this task.

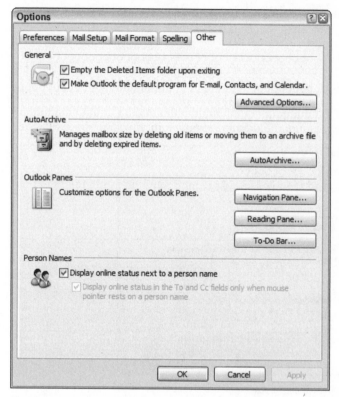

Figure 25.5. Access AutoArchive settings from the Other tab in the Options dialog box.

The next three options, under the heading During AutoArchive:, control what actually takes place when an AutoArchive run is conducted. Delete expired items refers to dated items like meeting requests whose dates have passed. Archive or delete old items refers to all other data objects — you determine which of the two actions is performed in the next section of the dialog box. Show archive folder in folder list controls whether your archive.pst file is visible in the folder list. I recommend keeping this check box selected to make the manual archiving technique that I described previously for archiving an entire folder as easy as possible and to keep your archived items accessible when you need them.

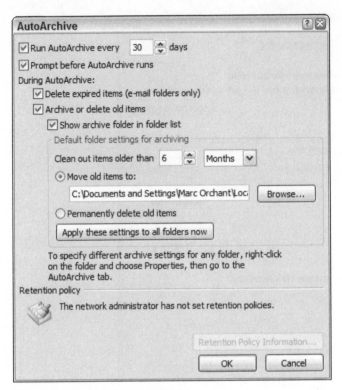

Figure 25.6. The AutoArchive dialog box.

In the center section of the dialog box, you can choose between moving old items to a designated archive file and permanently deleting them. Outlook defaults to archive.pst, but you can browse to a different file and/or location if you prefer. The button at the bottom of this section allows you to apply the default AutoArchive settings to all folders in your Outlook PST files. Be aware that if you do this, you replace any folder-specific AutoArchive settings you may have previously defined.

Hack

Regardless of the choice you make in the AutoArchive dialog box regarding visibility of the archive file, you can always open an archive file by choosing Outlook Data File from the Open command on the File menu. You can always close a file other than your primary PST file by selecting it in the folder list and choosing Close from the file menu.

The dialog box contains an unusually helpful reminder message immediately below this section. It reads: "To specify different archive settings for any folder, right-click on the folder and choose Properties, then go to the AutoArchive tab."

As an example, the Inbox Properties dialog box is shown in Figure 25.7 with the AutoArchive tab selected. You can establish a different AutoArchive setting for each folder as dictated by the nature of the information in that folder. When you invoke the AutoArchive command or the next scheduled run falls due, the specific settings you establish for each folder are honored.

The final option regarding retention policy settings is enabled only if you work on a business network and your administrator has set such a policy. Network policies, if they exist, override any changes you make locally.

Figure 25.7. The Inbox Properties dialog box.

Mail Cleanup

The Mail Cleanup dialog box, shown in Figure 25.8, contains a number of tools to assist you in maintaining your Outlook PST files. With respect to AutoArchive, this is the dialog box from which you can initiate an archiving run between regularly scheduled intervals. To begin an AutoArchive process, click the AutoArchive button in this dialog box. Mail Cleanup provides a number of other tools that I explore in the discussion of Outlook rule number three.

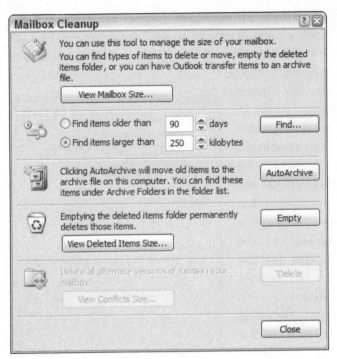

Figure 25.8. The Mail Cleanup dialog box.

Rule number three: Compact your Outlook files

If you can do one thing to improve the performance of Outlook, it's keeping the size of your PST file as small as possible. While the theoretical limit of a single Outlook data file is 2GB, it takes a powerful PC and a very knowledgeable Outlook user to keep things working well with such a large file. Most people never approach this limit, and if you follow my advice in rule number two about archiving manually and automatically, you will probably never have to worry about this limitation.

Even with smaller PST files, there is a decided benefit to keeping file size under control and there are a few simple things you can do to accomplish this. The next sections in this chapter discuss strategies you can use with regard to attachments and sent and deleted mail to put your PST file on a diet. Before exploring those ideas and techniques, an explanation is in order about how Outlook PST files can be optimized.

Just as your hard disk can become fragmented over time, breaking files into pieces scattered about your drive, so too does your Outlook PST file become inefficient as you delete and archive items. To reduce the inefficiencies in your PST files, Outlook provides a Compact command that reorganizes the structure of your file and reduces the amount of disk space it consumes.

To access this command, right-click the Personal Folders icon in the folder list in the Navigation Pane or the top-level icon for any other PST file you want to compact and choose Properties from the context menu. The Properties dialog box shown in Figure 25.9 is displayed.

Click the Advanced button in the lower-right corner to display the dialog box shown in Figure 25.10. Click the Compact Now button, and Outlook reorganizes and optimizes the PST file. This can take anywhere from a few seconds to a minute or more, depending on how scrambled your PST file is.

Figure 25.9. The Outlook Today — [Personal Folders] Properties dialog box.

I recommend that you run this optimization command before you perform your regular backup procedure. There is little sense in backing up a file that's bigger than it needs to be, and in the event that you do need to restore from a backup, you have the added benefit of having an already compacted file ready to resume your work.

What to do when things go wrong

As I said earlier in the chapter, Murphy was an optimist. Things do go wrong from time to time, no matter how many precautions you take to keep your PC running in optimal fashion. If you've adopted my three Outlook rules and something does happen to make your Outlook installation unstable, or even worse, unusable, remember this first:

Don't panic.

Figure 25.10 The Compact Now button in the Personal Folders dialog box.

Confident that you have a backup should it be required, you can use the Inbox Repair Utility included with Outlook to attempt a repair on your PST file. Using SCANPST.exe is covered in detail in Chapter 3. Follow the steps outlined in that chapter to run the utility and, if errors are detected, create a backup file and allow the utility to repair your PST file. As I suggest in Chapter 3, run the repair utility until it reports that no errors have been found. It can, on occasion, require more than one pass to completely repair a damaged PST file.

If SCANPST.exe doesn't resolve your problem and the issue did not occur following the installation of a new add-in (see Chapter 8 for a discussion on troubleshooting add-in problems), you can attempt to determine if something is amiss in your Outlook application installation using the Office Diagnostics command on the Help menu. When you launch this tool, you are presented with the opening screen shown in Figure 25.11.

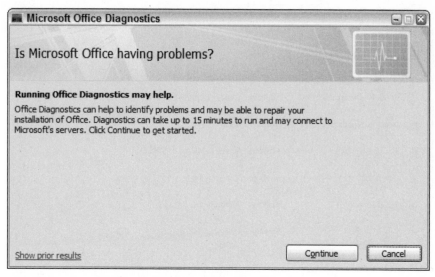

Figure 25.11. The initial Microsoft Office Diagnostics screen.

Take note of the information displayed on this opening screen. The tests that this utility performs can take some time, depending on the configuration and status of your PC, so allow up to 15 minutes for the diagnostics to run and make sure that you are connected to the Internet. After the tests have been run, the Office Diagnostics tool provides the option to connect to Office Online to access information and possible fixes for any problems it does find. Click Continue to advance to the next screen shown in Figure 25.12, which lists the diagnostic tests that are run.

Click Run Diagnostics to run the tests. You cannot pick and choose which tests to run in this utility. It's an all-or-none proposition, and while I generally prefer software that provides choices, when you are trying to diagnose a significant problem, it's really best that you be as thorough as possible.

After the test run is completed, the results screen shown in Figure 25.13 is displayed. If any errors were found, specific information about what steps to take to resolve the problem are displayed. If none of the tests reveal any issues, click Continue to connect to the Office Online Web site, pictured in Figure 25.14, for additional suggestions and resources.

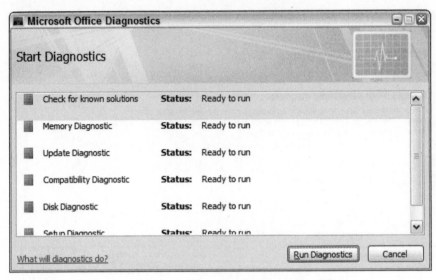

Figure 25.12. The second screen in the Microsoft Office Diagnostics utility.

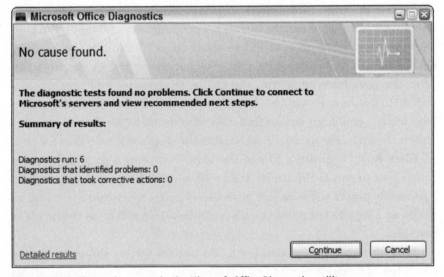

Figure 25.13. The results screen in the Microsoft Office Diagnostics utility.

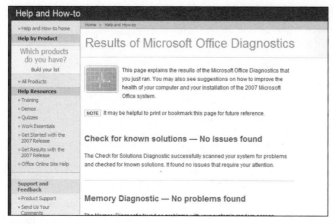

Figure 25.14. The Office Online diagnostics page.

Restoring from your backup files

Depending on whether you've chosen to perform manual backups or to use a backup utility like OutSource-XP 2, the process of restoring from a backup is simple. If you are using a manual backup strategy, open the folder containing your Outlook data files as described earlier in this chapter, drag the current PST files to the Recycle Bin, and then drag and drop your backup files to the data files folder.

If you have chosen to use OutSource-XP 2 to perform your backups, launch the utility and click the Restore tab to display the options pictured in Figure 25.15. Locate the backup set you want to restore from using the Browse For A Backup button. When the backup set is loaded, select the PST files and settings you want to restore and click the button labeled Restore All Selected Files And Registry Settings Now! to perform the restoration.

> **Watch Out!**
> Outlook must not be running when you perform a restoration from backup files. Windows will not allow you to move an open PST file to the Recycle Bin. Make sure that you have exited from Outlook before performing a restore operation, regardless of whether you create your backups manually or with a utility program.

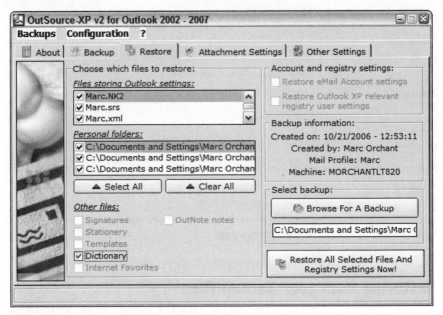

Figure 25.15. OutSource-XP 2's Restore tab.

Additional ideas

To help keep your Outlook PST files in optimal operating condition, you should know about a few archiving and file management ideas that I have been using for a number of years that allow me to keep my PST files to a manageable size. Depending on the volume of mail and file attachments you receive, your results may be more or less dramatic than mine, but I have been able to reduce the size of my primary PST files by up to 60 percent by using the techniques described in this section.

Regularly archive the Sent Items folder

I have my Sent Items folder set to AutoArchive every two weeks. Because I use two PST files in my setup, I have set the Sent Items folder in each to archive on this schedule. I have AutoArchive set to move all e-mail that is at least 30 days old. The Windows Desktop Search indexing engine is very good at keeping up to date on the location of these relocated sent messages, and finding them with Instant Search is every bit as easy as when they resided in my primary PST files. With data stored on both your primary and arcl..ve PST files, using the Search All Mail Items option in Instant Search works best. The search results are grouped to indicate which of the files the matching information is located in.

If you prefer to manually archive your Sent Items, create a Sent Items folder in your archive.pst file, select the messages in your primary PST file's Sent Items folder that you want to move, and drag and drop them onto the archive folder. Remember to use the Compact Now command after an archiving operation to reduce the size of your primary PST file as much as possible, especially if a large number of files were relocated.

Empty the Deleted Items folder regularly

Outlook does not, by default, permanently delete items when you use the Delete control on the Ribbon or press the Delete key when working in the main views. It simply moves those items you have marked for deletion to the Deleted Items folder. I actually know some people who use their Deleted Items folder as another file folder! Needless to say, I don't recommend that practice because I am a big believer in the old saying, "out of sight, out of mind." I think it's far better to move files you may need one day and are reluctant to delete to an archive instead.

You can manually empty the Deleted Items folder by right-clicking it in the folder list in the Navigation Pane and selecting the Empty Deleted Items Folder command from the context menu. If you tend to experience remorse after deleting files on your PC, sticking to this manual approach may be the safest strategy; you can easily retrieve any item from this folder before emptying it. If you do choose to take a manual approach, my advice is to make reviewing the contents of this folder a regular part of your Outlook maintenance schedule so you can empty it before you perform backup or compacting actions.

Outlook can be set to automatically empty the Deleted Items folder when you exit the application. To set this option, open the Options dialog box from the Tools menu and click the Other tab. Select the option to Empty the Deleted Items folder upon exiting in the General section at the top of the dialog box, shown in Figure 25.16.

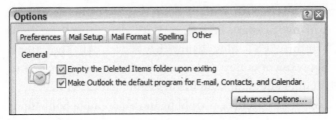

Figure 25.16. The Empty the Deleted Items folder option.

You can find the size of your Deleted Items folder in the Mailbox Cleanup dialog box, shown in Figure 25.8, or by right-clicking the folder in the list in the Navigation Pane and choosing the Properties command. In the Properties dialog box, click the Folder Size button.

Managing file attachments

The single largest contributors to Outlook file size are the file attachments we send and receive. If you're like many e-mail users I've worked with, you may never have given a moment's thought to the fact that every file attachment you send lands in your Sent Items folder and stays there (unless you practice good archiving discipline). If you've had the same e-mail account for years and have never looked at the size of your Sent Items folder, you may be in for a real shock.

In typical Office fashion, you can use numerous ways to find the size of your mail folders to identify opportunities to slim down your PST file. One way to look at the size of your PST file and each folder inside it is to use the Mailbox Cleanup tool described earlier in this chapter. If you refer to Figure 25.8, you see a button labeled View Mailbox Size at the top of the dialog box. Clicking this button displays the Folder Size dialog box shown in Figure 25.17, which displays the total size of your primary PST file and the size of each folder contained within it. As you can see from the figure, Calendar, Contacts, Journal, and other data are actually stored in folders in the PST file.

Hack

Get into the habit of reviewing your Sent Items folder and removing attachments from the messages you have sent regularly. Because you sent the file, it already exists somewhere on your hard drive. You really don't need another copy hogging space in your PST file.

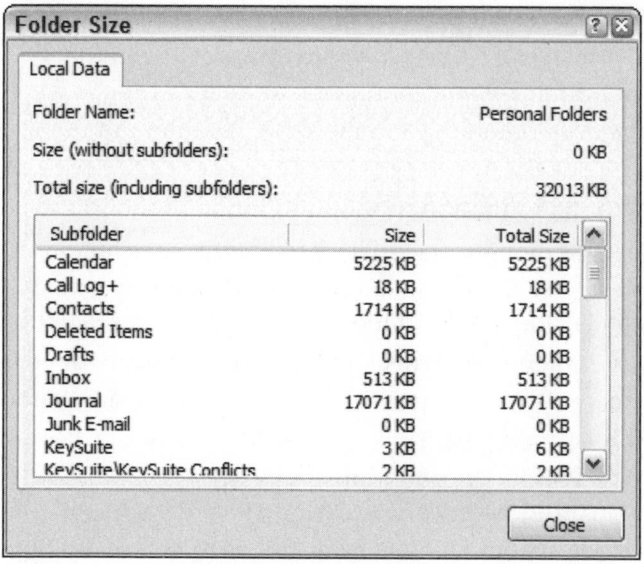

Figure 25.17. The Folder Size dialog box.

You can access this same dialog box by right-clicking the Personal Folders icon in the folder list in the Navigation Pane, selecting Properties, and then clicking the Folder Size button in the Properties dialog box. I prefer using the Mailbox Cleanup dialog box when performing maintenance work on my Outlook environment because it contains a number of useful tools in a single location.

Having determined which folder or folders contain a large amount of data, you can click the Find button in the Mailbox Cleanup dialog box to search for files above a certain size (or older than a certain date) to archive or delete. This allows you to establish your own threshold for what constitutes a "big" file attachment and makes it easy to quickly locate those files consuming significant amounts of disk space.

After you have identified the space-consuming files, you can right-click the file attachment to save it to your file system and then right-click a second time to remove the attachment from the mail message. Save the message after you've removed the attachment, or simply close the message. Outlook asks you if you want to save the change.

It's also possible to use a Search Folder, discussed in Chapter 13, to find large files. Outlook comes with a prebuilt Large Files Search Folder that you can customize to meet your exact criteria. The advantage to using the Search Folder is that it provides one-click access to a list of the largest files in your primary PST file at any time. If you use multiple PST files, remember that Search Folders are specific to each PST file and you need to define a new Search Folder for each of the PST files you use.

Where to store attachments

There are two schools of thought regarding keeping file attachments in e-mail. Some people prefer the redundancy of having a file in e-mail as well as in the standard file system. Others who receive hundreds of megabytes of file attachments every week and perform regular backups see it as a waste of space. While it is ultimately a personal decision based on what works best for you, my advice is to get into the habit of storing files in your file system and not in your Outlook environment.

Third-party add-ins and utilities are designed to detach and file attachments in your file system automatically and assist you in keeping track of where the attachment associated with an e-mail message has been stored. These tools generally add a text link in the body of the e-mail message that points to the physical location of the file on your PC. Some of them recreate the folder structure that you have created in Outlook in a folder on your desktop, so the location of the attachment in the file system follows an identical path to the location of the message in your Outlook folder hierarchy.

While this functionality is a welcome aid to automating this process, it's not terribly difficult to set it up yourself. Create a folder in your My Documents folders labeled Outlook Attachments and create a folder structure there that mirrors your Outlook folder setup. When you add a new folder to Outlook, add one to your file folder setup in My Documents. I find using Windows Explorer to work in this file system hierarchy is more productive because the file tree is identical to the folder list in Outlook and allows easy expansion of nested folders.

Carrying this organizational strategy to its logical conclusion, you can do the same thing with your physical filing system for any information you print out, clip from magazines or newspapers, or receive from co-workers in paper form. It requires a bit of work to maintain this system, but I guarantee you'll spend much less time looking for material in any of these locations if you adopt a single filing system strategy for all your storage locations.

Why Outlook blocks certain file types

Security is a big concern, and one of the principal ways that viruses and other so-called "badware" gets onto PCs is e-mail. Spammers send unsolicited e-mail containing tracking and sniffing programs designed to reveal personal information about you without your knowledge. Hackers trying to gain access to your system often attach small applications to e-mail messages that masquerade as images or are labeled to appear to be software updates.

Outlook has had its security paranoia increased with every major release in an effort to protect you from this badware. As a result, certain known file types are permanently blocked and cannot be received by e-mail in Outlook. These file types include executable files (.exe), Compiled Help files (.chm), and other types of files that can contain program code. It's a long list. Type "blocked attachments" into the box labeled Type a question for help in the upper-right corner of any Outlook main view for more information about what types of files are blocked and advice on how to avoid sending or receiving such files.

Just the facts

- Regular backups of your Outlook data file are your best insurance against losing valuable, and often irreplaceable, information when files get corrupted or hardware failures occur.

- You can back up your Outlook data to a variety of media including recordable optical discs (CD or DVD), USB flash drives, external hard drives (USB or FireWire), or network servers.

- Archiving old information moves it out of your primary PST file to a secondary file and helps keep your primary file smaller and faster.

- Any folder in Outlook including the Calendar, Contacts, or Tasks folder can be archived using the Archive command, not just e-mail.

- Archived PST files can be opened, displayed in the folder list in the Navigation Pane, and used in Outlook like any other PST file.

■ The Mail Cleanup dialog box accessed from the Tools menu provides a number of useful tools to assist in keeping your Outlook data
files in tip-top condition.

■ If things start working badly (or stop working entirely), first try using
SCANPST.exe, the Inbox Repair Tool, to fix any data file corruption.

■ If problems persist, run the Office Diagnostics Utility located on the
Help menu to perform a number of tests on your Office installation,
operating system, and hardware.

■ Empty the Deleted Items folder regularly or consider setting a
preference to have Outlook do it for you whenever you exit the
application.

■ Search for large e-mail messages containing big file attachments
using the search tool in the Mail Cleanup dialog box or the Large
Mail Search Folder installed with Outlook.

GET THE SCOOP ON...
Microsoft Update ▪ New and improved Office Online ▪
Where did Office Update go? ▪ All sorts of free stuff

Keeping Outlook Up to Date

Unless you have just begun using Microsoft Windows and Office, you know the importance of updating the operating system and Office suite. Microsoft has put a lot of work into making updates more predictable and manageable, especially in the last few years following the release of Windows XP Service Pack 2. That significant update to the operating system was the first to seriously promote the use of Automatic Updates, a setup where Microsoft would post important security and stability updates to its servers and your PC could automatically download and install them.

This system was implemented because too many people simply never bothered to check for updates, and a tremendous number of systems were left unpatched and vulnerable to widely publicized exploits that would allow badware to find its way onto those systems. These security and stability updates affect both the operating system and the Office suite, and it's important to keep your system up to date for your own protection as well as to prevent the inadvertent spread of badware to the other PCs on your network and to those with whom you exchange files.

Of course, there's more to keeping your system and applications updated than just keeping the bad guys at bay. The Microsoft Office suite tends to hang around for a few years between major version releases, and regular updates enhance and extend the functionality of the applications

475

Chapter 26

in the suite in that intervening time. It's safe to assume that with a release as sweeping in nature as Office 2007, a number of updates will be made available as time passes.

This chapter begins with a look at the update mechanisms available to Office 2007 users — Microsoft Update, Windows Update, and Office Update. The chapter concludes with a look at the resources available on the Office Online Web site, including clip art and templates you can download and Internet calendars and newsletters you can subscribe to.

Microsoft Update

If you've been using Windows and Office for more than a year or two, you've probably become accustomed to updating your Windows operating system using the Windows Update site and keeping Office up to date using Office Update. In mid-2005, Microsoft began testing a unified update service called Microsoft Update. The unified service has been officially released and is the most comprehensive way to make sure your operating system and Microsoft applications like Windows Media Player, Windows Defender, and the new Live applications are kept up to date with the latest security and stability patches and driver updates. Office updates that affect application security are now released via Microsoft Update as well.

Windows Update is still the default update service for Windows XP systems. You can switch to Microsoft Update by clicking the prominently displayed link on the Windows Update Web page if you prefer to use the new, more comprehensive service. Frankly, I can't think of any reason not to switch to Microsoft Update and have all the PCs I administer set to use the new service.

Until this year, these update services could be accessed only using Internet Explorer. Users of the Firefox and Opera browsers can now access the updates as well when configured with an ActiveX extension or plug-in. Netscape 8.0, the most recent version of that browser, provides users access to both the IE and Mozilla rendering engines and automatically uses the IE renderer when accessing the Windows Update or Microsoft Update sites.

In order to access either update site, you must have Windows Genuine Advantage (WGA) installed. WGA is an ActiveX control that checks to make sure the copy of Windows installed on your PC is legitimate.

Microsoft Update is accessible only from PCs running Windows XP with Service Pack 1 or 2 installed or PCs running Windows Server 2003.

When running Windows Vista, Microsoft Update is no longer Web-based. In the newest version of Windows, the service is accessed and run from a Control Panel applet installed locally on the PC. This change potentially makes the update process much more secure because there are concerns about using a Web browser as the agent for making significant changes to the operating system.

Keeping your system up to date with Microsoft Update

Windows Update or Microsoft Update can be accessed from the Tools Menu in Internet Explorer or Outlook. When you select whichever update service your PC is configured to access from the Outlook Tools menu, it is opened in Internet Explorer. If you prefer using a different browser, you need to make sure it has been properly configured with the ActiveX extension or plug-in required to access the site. You also can launch Windows Update from the All Programs menu accessed from the Windows Start menu. The initial screen you encounter when you begin the update process is shown in Figure 26.1. The illustrations in this chapter show Microsoft Update, but the differences between the two services from a user interface perspective are minimal, and you'll see much the same layout and controls if you're still using Windows Update.

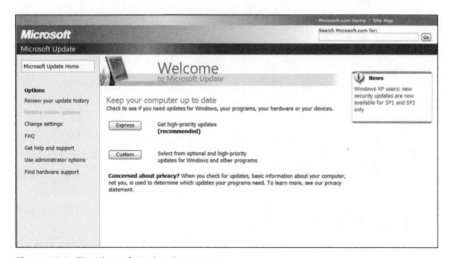

Figure 26.1. The Microsoft Update home page.

On the Microsoft Update home page, you are presented with two buttons labeled Express and Custom. The Express button scans your Windows installation only to determine if you need what Microsoft calls high-priority updates, which address critical security and stability issues only. This is the same set of updates delivered to your PC if you have Automatic Updates enabled on your system. The Custom button performs a more comprehensive scan of your system hardware and software to determine if any driver or application updates are also available, resulting in a slightly longer scanning process.

You can review the updates that have been applied to your system by clicking the link labeled Review your update history in the sidebar on the left side of the Microsoft Update page. This history page, pictured in Figure 26.2, lists all the updates that have been successfully applied to your system as well those that have been cancelled or failed. In the case of failed updates, you can click the red icon (a circle with an "X") to retry installation of that patch.

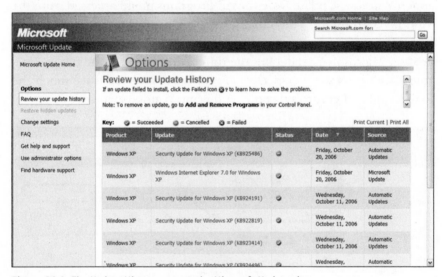

Figure 26.2. The Update History page at the Microsoft Update site.

Keeping Office up to date

Security-related updates to Office applications are generally delivered via Microsoft Update. There are other updates that will certainly be made available for Office 2007 as the suite is enhanced and improved over the next few years. Some of these releases may take the form of monolithic Service Pack releases while others will be specific to Outlook or another application in the Office system.

In previous versions of Microsoft Office, you could access the Office Update service from the Help menu in Outlook. Although there is still a Check for Updates command on the Help menu in Outlook 2007, it now takes you to Microsoft Update. To access the Office Update service available on the Office Online Web site, select the Microsoft Office Online command on the Help menu. Office Online, as mentioned throughout this book, is a great resource for training, tips and tricks, newsletters and RSS feeds, and other Office-related resources. When the Office Online home page opens, you see a prominently displayed button labeled Check for Updates. Click this control to access the Office Update service to see if any updates are available for your Office installation.

When you click the Check for Updates button, the Office Online engine scans your system to create a snapshot of your system. This is compared to the list of available updates, and if updates to one or more of the Office applications you have installed on your PC are available, they are displayed on a results page like the one shown in Figure 26.3. Office Update displays both Required Updates and Optional Tools that are available.

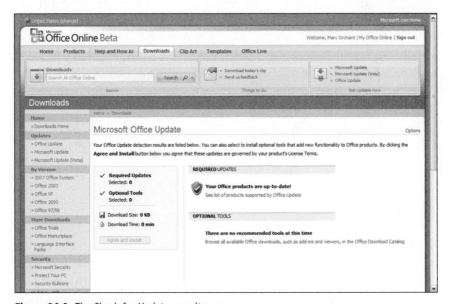

Figure 26.3. The Check for Updates results page.

Inside Scoop

The illustrations in this book were created while the latest Office Online site was still in beta, just as the Office suite itself was. The appearance of the site may be different when you visit it, because Microsoft is constantly updating its online look.

Other updates and resources

The Office Online site offers a number of free resources that you can use to extend and enhance your out-of-the-box Office 2007 experience. You can find a continually updated clip art library, templates, and Internet calendars to subscribe to and add to your personal calendar.

In addition to these downloads, the Office Online site allows you to search both the Office site and Windows Marketplace for additional services and add-ins for Outlook, which include ratings supplied by other users to help you choose wisely. A number of training resources are available as well, and you can subscribe at the site to one of the best newsletters Microsoft publishes.

Clip art

Microsoft's online clip art library has matured nicely over the years and is continually updated with graphic images, photographs, and multimedia files that you can incorporate into your e-mail messages, meeting invitations, and other Office documents. You can search for just the right graphic embellishment directly on the Web site, as shown in Figure 26.4, or while working in any of Outlook's composition forms by invoking the Insert Picture command that opens the Clip Art Pane, as shown in Figure 26.5. Note that when working in Outlook, you can use the pop-up menu next to each online image, denoted by the small globe icon next to the graphic in the clip art palette, to make the image available offline by adding it to your local clip art collection.

Templates

The Templates tab on the Office Online site appears, at first glance, to offer little for Outlook, because the majority of the templates listed on the main page are oriented toward the productivity applications in Office 2007. If you search for e-mail templates, you are presented with a number of choices that can be used to generate very attractive e-mail messages. A small sample of what is available on the site is shown in Figure 26.6.

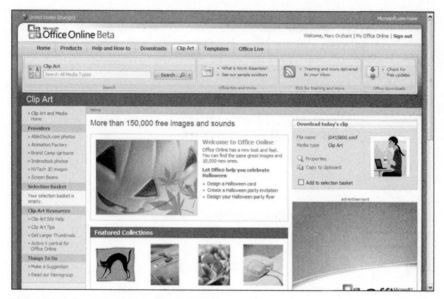

Figure 26.4. The Office Online clip art library.

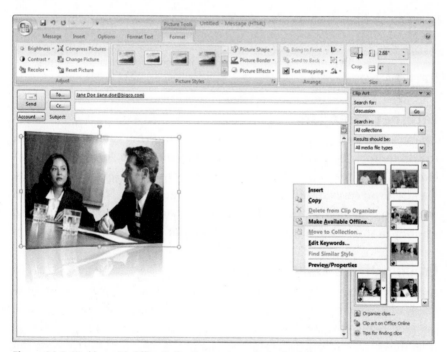

Figure 26.5. Working with Office Online images in an Outlook window.

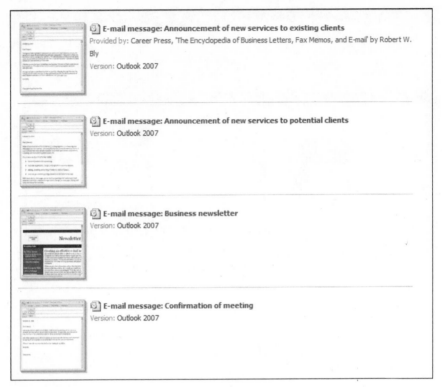

Figure 26.6. A sample of the e-mail templates available from the Office Online site.

Internet calendars

Chapter 8 provides a thorough discussion of Internet calendars and how to add them in both side-by-side and overlay modes to your personal calendar in Outlook. The Office Online site provides a selection of calendars that you can subscribe to, as shown in Figure 26.7. Note that you can find these calendars on the Products tab, not on the Downloads tab where you might initially expect to find them.

Crabby Office Lady newsletter

As you might expect from a company as big as Microsoft, they publish hundreds of newsletters on a variety of topics that you can subscribe to. I have sampled many of these newsletters over the years, and the one I think provides the greatest information and entertainment value for Office users is the Crabby Office Lady newsletter. This newsletter has informed and amused since 2002, and a fully searchable archive of the articles from this newsletter is available on the Help and How-to section of the Office Online site.

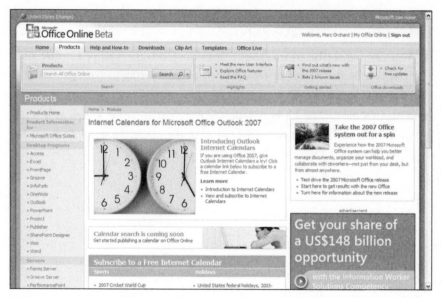

Figure 26.7. Internet calendars are accessed from the Products tab on the Office Online site.

You can subscribe to the Crabby Office Lady newsletter by e-mail, or you can add an RSS feed to your subscriptions, which delivers every new article directly to Outlook and Internet Explorer. She discusses Outlook tips and techniques on a regular basis.

Just the facts

- Microsoft provides critical system and Office suite updates via two services — Windows Update and Microsoft Update.

- Microsoft Update is the more comprehensive of the two services and provides updates for hardware drivers and applications in addition to Windows security and stability patches.

- Only PCs running Windows XP with Service Pack 1 or 2 installed, Windows Server 2003, or Windows Vista can access Microsoft Update.

- Microsoft Office Online provides access to Office application updates and a variety of add-ons, training resources, and other tools to extend and enhance your Office experience.

- Office Update checks all the Office system applications installed on your system and lists any updates available for any of them.

- Office Online provides access to an extensive clip art library in your browser or while working in Outlook's composition forms.

- You can subscribe to Internet calendars from the Office Online site that can be displayed side-by-side or as an overlay to your personal calendar in Outlook.

- The Crabby Office Lady newsletter is a great source of tips and techniques for using Outlook and the rest of the Office suite and can be subscribed to as an e-mail newsletter or RSS feed.

GET THE SCOOP ON...
Junk E-mail filters ▪ External content filtering ▪
Protecting yourself from phishing and fraud ▪
Attachment blocking ▪ Digital certificates and e-mail ▪
Macros and security ▪ Virus and badware protection

Outlook Security

Chapter 27

You've probably heard the old saying that an ounce of prevention is worth a pound of cure. This bit of folk wisdom certainly applies to keeping your Outlook environment secure. Because of the way Microsoft has wired Outlook into the Windows operating system to take advantage of services provided by the OS like HTML rendering, RSS subscription management, and integration with the file system, Outlook is often criticized when it comes to security and labeled a "bad" or inherently unsecure product.

Nothing could be further from the truth. While these hooks into the operating system do provide avenues for badware to penetrate your Outlook environment that other applications providing e-mail services may not expose, Outlook 2007 is the most secure version of the application yet. With some basic security settings and the addition of software that any Windows-based PC should be running, you'll have little to fear from viruses and other malicious code.

No one who uses e-mail on a regular basis for work or personal life needs to be told what an issue spam or junk e-mail has become. In a July 2006 article, the BBC reported that a study conducted by e-mail security firm Return Path showed that 99 percent of the machines they monitored (over 20 million e-mail addresses) had been compromised by spammers or viruses and were generating junk e-mail traffic. In the same report, IronPort, a company that monitors approximately 25 percent of all e-mail sent over the Internet, stated that 80 percent of all e-mail traffic was junk.

This raises two issues you need to be concerned with. The first is how to keep your PC safe from infection and compromise by these spammers and virus writers. The second is, even if your machine is secure and well-protected from infection by badware, how do you ward off the flood of junk e-mail that bombards everyone with an e-mail address?

Security is a multi-faceted issue, and this chapter touches on a number of different things you should be doing to keep your PC, your e-mail, and your personal information secure. This chapter begins with a look at the junk e-mail filtering built into Outlook 2007. It continues with a look at the all-new Trust Center, which provides Office-wide controls for security and privacy. The Trust Center controls how Outlook uses digital certificates to encrypt e-mail, sign messages, and request receipts, and how the program filters external content, suspicious links, and file attachments that may contain potentially dangerous code and macros. The chapter concludes with a brief discussion about antivirus and anti-spyware tools and why they are so important for e-mail security.

Outlook's Junk E-mail filters

The Junk E-mail Options dialog box, shown in Figure 27.1, is essentially unchanged from the one introduced in Outlook 2003. Junk E-mail settings are accessed from the Options dialog box on the Tools menu. This dialog box presents five tabs that provide complete control over the level of filtering applied to incoming mail, management of lists of known safe and unwanted senders, and filters to block mail from specific countries and messages using specific character sets. From time to time, Microsoft releases updated Junk E-mail filter settings files via Microsoft Update and Office Update to keep your baseline settings up to date.

The Options tab is the default view in the Junk E-mail Options dialog box and provides controls that allow you to set how aggressively Outlook filters incoming e-mail messages and what should be done with messages flagged as junk. In the top portion of the dialog box, you can choose from four levels of filtering:

■ **No Automatic Filtering.** Mail from blocked senders is still moved to the Junk E-mail folder.

- **Low.** Move the most obvious junk e-mail to the Junk E-mail folder.

- **High.** Most junk e-mail is caught, but some regular mails may be caught as well. Check your Junk E-mail folder often.

- **Safe Lists Only.** Only mail from people or domains on your Safe Senders List or Safe Recipients List is delivered to your Inbox.

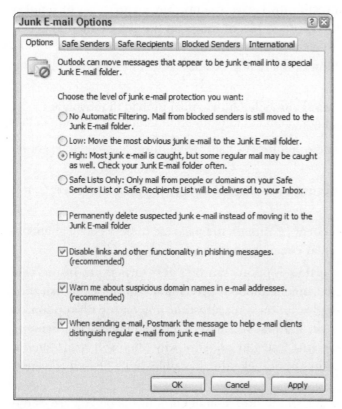

Figure 27.1. The Options tab in the Junk E-mail Options dialog box.

I recommend that you try the High setting and make a point of checking what ends up in the Junk E-mail folder on a daily basis to retrieve any legitimate e-mail that has been incorrectly tagged as junk. In my experience, the current filter set is quite good, and you can always "teach" Outlook that a specific sender is safe, as described a bit later in this chapter.

If you find that too much of the e-mail you receive is being tagged as junk and it comes from too many senders to make teaching Outlook what kind of mail you consider to be desirable a practical matter, you can switch the setting to Low and see if that produces more acceptable results. I cannot think of a good reason to suggest that anyone turn filtering off. Even if you prefer to use a different tool to filter your inbound e-mail, Outlook's Junk E-mail filter is a good second layer of defense. I also recommend that you not turn on the Safe Lists Only mode unless you absolutely only want to receive e-mail from a known set of senders and are prepared to perform lots of triage on the Junk E-mail folder to keep Outlook up to date on who you want to receive e-mail from.

The lower portion of the dialog box allows you to turn the following options on or off:

- Permanently delete suspected junk e-mail instead of moving it to the Junk E-mail folder

- Disable links and other functionality in phishing messages. (recommended)

- Warn me about suspicious domain names in e-mail addresses. (recommended)

- When sending e-mail, Postmark the message to help e-mail clients distinguish regular e-mail from junk e-mail

The last three of these options can be safely turned on. In the best case, they'll provide some additional protection, and in the worst, they do no harm. I strongly caution you against turning on the first option, at least until you are certain that you have built a complete Safe Senders List and Safe Recipients List. I'm not sure why Microsoft made such a draconian, no-recourse option like this so visible, but at least it is turned off by default.

The next three tabs in the Junk E-mail Options dialog box are essentially identical in appearance and are used to manage your Safe Senders, Safe Recipients, and Blocked Senders lists. You build these lists as you process legitimate incoming e-mail that Outlook incorrectly tags as junk

---

Watch Out!

If you check the option to permanently delete mail identified as junk, there is no way to recover those messages. They are permanently deleted, and you will not even know that delivery was attempted. This can cause problems when someone you're expecting mail from sends a message that is deleted because it looks like junk to Outlook.

and sends to the Junk E-mail folder or, conversely, junk e-mail that Outlook fails to catch that appears in your Inbox.

In either case, right-click an incorrectly filtered message and choose Junk E-mail from the context menu to display the submenu pictured in Figure 27.2. For junk e-mail mes-

sages that Outlook misses, choose Add Sender to Blocked Senders List. All future e-mail from that address will be tagged as junk and sent to the Junk E-mail folder upon arrival. In the case of legiti-

Figure 27.2. The Junk E-mail menu.

mate e-mail that is incorrectly identified as junk, you have a few options.

In the Junk E-mail folder, select a message that Outlook has incorrectly identified as junk e-mail and take one of the following actions:

- Click the Not Junk button on the toolbar. This opens a dialog box where you can move the message to the Inbox, add the sender to the Safe Senders List and, optionally, add any or all of the recipients of the message to the Safe Recipients List if the message was sent to others besides you.

- Right-click the message, select Junk E-mail, and on the submenu choose Add Sender to Safe Senders List if you want to receive all future e-mail messages from that person in your Inbox.

- Right-click the message, select Junk E-mail, and on the submenu choose Add Sender's Domain to Safe Senders List if you want to receive all future e-mail messages from that domain in your Inbox. Any e-mail address from that domain is now considered safe no matter who at that domain sends it. Use caution when selecting this option. If the domain is a company or organization you trust, it's probably safe to add it to the list. I recommend not adding common domains, especially those that offer free e-mail addresses (such as @yahoo.com or @hotmail.com) to the Safe Senders List.

- Right-click the message, select Junk E-mail, and on the submenu choose Add Recipient to Safe Recipients List if you want to receive all future e-mail messages sent to that recipient in your Inbox. It's common practice for many people when they send a message to a large group of recipients to put all the individual names in the BCC: field to hide their addresses from the other recipients in the list and to put their own e-mail in the To: field. This has long been a common trick used by spammers, and Outlook sometimes guesses that a legitimate message sent in this fashion is junk.

■ Right-click the message, select Junk E-mail, and on the submenu choose Mark as Not Junk. This is the same as clicking the Not Junk toolbar button.

The final option on the context menu, Junk E-mail Options, opens the dialog box shown in Figure 27.1 directly.

In the Junk E-mail Options dialog box, the next three tabs display the addresses you have added to the Safe Senders, Safe Recipients, and Blocked Senders lists. Figure 27.3 shows the Safe Senders tab. All three tabs present a list field showing those addresses you have added to the respective list and provide Add, Edit, and Remove buttons to manage your lists. You can save any of these lists to a text file by clicking the Export to File button and add a batch of names from a list you have previously saved by clicking the Import from File button.

Figure 27.3. An example of the List tabs in the Junk E-mail Options dialog box.

The Safe Senders tab differs from the other two tabs in presenting two additional options at the bottom of the dialog box. The first option, marked Also trust e-mail from my Contacts, tells Outlook to trust e-mail sent by anyone in your Contacts list and is turned on by default. The second option instructs Outlook to automatically add to the Safe Senders List any address you send an e-mail message to.

The final tab in the Junk E-mail Options dialog box, shown in Figure 27.4, controls which top-level domains and what character-set encodings you want to block. Top-level domains are country-specific. Encodings are language-specific. If you consistently receive junk e-mail from a particular country or in a particular language, you can block any future e-mail using these controls.

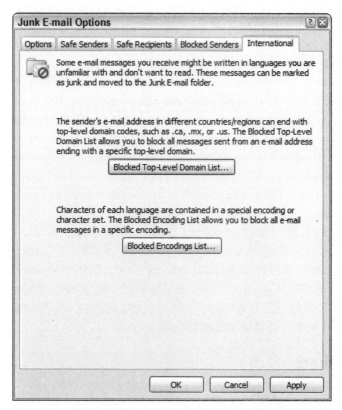

Figure 27.4. The International tab in the Junk E-mail Options dialog box.

Inside Scoop

In the past, there have been barrages of junk e-mail from certain countries. In 2005, spammers favored Korea as a country from which they would send their unsolicited messages. When enough people blocked Korea's top-level domain, the spammers moved on. According to a BBC article from July 2006, the number-one country from which spam originates is the United States.

Filtering content in Outlook

Microsoft is in the unique position of providing the operating system and application software used by the vast majority of people in the world. That has produced enormous successes for the company but has also made Windows and Office the target of people on the dark side of the net world. The company is continually challenged by new attacks and has responded with a continual stream of improvements to how their software is built and an increasing number of built-in and optional tools to provide a layered defense against badware attacks.

Because Outlook is the most widely used e-mail client in the world, and due to the way it has been integrated with the underlying Windows operating system, security is a big concern. Outlook 2003 introduced the Junk E-mail filters you've just explored, and in Outlook 2007, the latest bid by Microsoft to provide a secure application environment is the Trust Center, accessed from the Tools menu. The Trust Center combines many of the existing security settings Outlook has provided, adds some new features, and presents it all in an easily accessed and well-designed set of screens that make it easier than ever to lock down your PC and e-mail.

In Chapter 17, you looked at the Add-ins screen in the Trust Center. With respect to security and junk e-mail, the rest of the Trust Center is your next area of exploration. You navigate through the Trust Center using the buttons located on the sidebar on the left side of the dialog box. The selected screen's tab is highlighted in orange.

Trusted publishers

The Trusted Publishers screen lists those publishers whose code, which can take the form of ActiveX controls, macros, or add-ins, you have explicitly recognized as coming from a trusted source. Trusted publishers must meet all the following criteria:

- The code is signed by the developer with a digital signature.

■ The digital signature is valid (checked against a certificate authority's database and found to be legitimate, current, and not expired or revoked).

■ The certificate associated with the digital signature was issued by a reputable certificate authority (CA) — a commercial organization that issues digital certificates, keeps track of who is assigned to a certificate, signs certificates to verify their validity, and tracks which certificates are revoked or expired.

If you try to run published code that does not meet these criteria, the Trust Center disables the code by default, and the Message Bar appears to notify you of a potentially unsafe publisher. This is similar to the warnings generated in Internet Explorer when a Web site you are viewing attempts to run an ActiveX control without your explicit permission.

Privacy options

The Privacy Options sheet in the Trust Center, shown in Figure 27.5, allows you to control what kind of application-level communications you want to allow with Microsoft and its service partners. These options are universal for all Office applications you have installed on your PC.

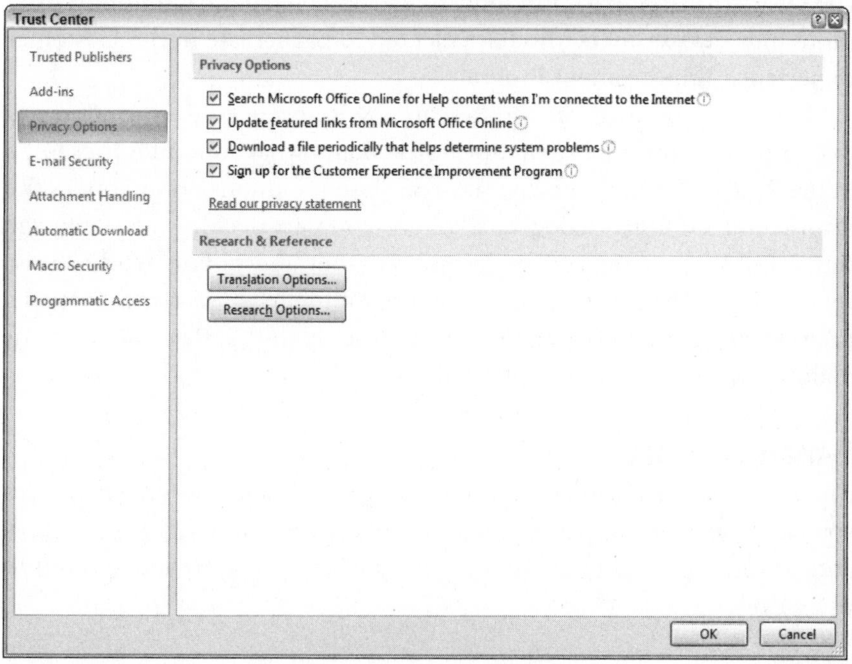

Figure 27.5. The Privacy Options screen in the Trust Center.

The first option controls whether the Help file installed locally on your PC is augmented with the latest content available from Office Online when you're connected to the Internet. I recommend that you turn this option on if you have a broadband connection (DSL, cable, or company LAN) because the online help for all Office applications is substantially enhanced with the online content.

The second option does not apply to Outlook, but in other Office programs (Access, Excel, PowerPoint, Word, and Visio), this option adds featured templates, tutorials, and other content to the New dialog box under the Featured heading.

The third option adds a small software agent application that runs in the background on your system that collects error information and asks, on occasion, for your permission to share that information with Microsoft. The information it collects is anonymous and cannot be traced back to you.

The last check box option collects usage information as you work with the Office applications on your PC and sends that information to the Office team to help them track what features are being used, how frequently they are used, and other behavioral data. Like the previous option, all information is anonymous. The sweeping changes in Office 2007 were, in large part, influenced by data collected from hundreds of thousands of customers who have elected to participate in this Customer Experience Improvement Program.

The two options under the Research & Reference heading allow you to control how translations are performed and what content is presented in the Research Pane. Clicking the Translation Options button opens the Translation Options dialog box, where you can decide what language translations you want to enable and whether the online World Lingo service should be accessed when you are online to assist in those translations. Clicking the Research Options button opens the Research Options dialog box discussed in Chapter 18.

E-mail security

The E-mail Security screen, shown in Figure 27.6, addresses the measures you can take to secure your e-mail with encryption and digital signatures and provides controls that affect how e-mail is displayed and allowed to use scripts.

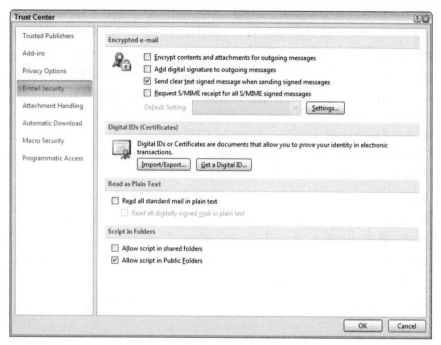

Figure 27.6. The E-mail Security screen in the Trust Center.

The first section in the E-mail Security screen deals with encrypted e-mail. Most e-mail is sent as clear text, meaning that the potential exists for someone to intercept a message you send and read it. If you're sending an e-mail that does not contain personal information or proprietary or confidential company information, it's arguable whether you need to encrypt your e-mail messages. But the capability is there if you prefer that all your communications be kept completely private.

You can encrypt messages on an individual basis as you compose each message or use the setting in the Trust Center to make it the default for all messages. To encrypt an individual message, click the small arrow icon on the More Options group on the Options tab of the Ribbon in the message window. This opens the Message Options dialog box. In that dialog box, click the Security Settings button to open the Security Properties dialog box and check the box labeled Encrypt message contents and attachments. These dialog boxes are shown in Figure 27.7.

There's more to encrypting e-mail than simply checking a box in Outlook. In order for your recipient to decrypt the message (and any attachments), he needs a copy of your private key, which is generated as part of acquiring a digital certificate. Acquiring a digital certificate to encrypt and to sign documents is addressed below. You can send your private key in a digital certificate to a recipient in several ways:

- Send a digitally signed message (this option is available in the same Security Properties dialog box). The recipient adds your e-mail name to his Contacts list and, by doing so, also adds your certificate.

- Send an e-mail message with your CER file attached, or send the CER file on a disk. The recipient can import the CER file into your contact card.

- Create a contact card with your CER file, and send the contact card.

- Publish your certificate to an LDAP directory or another directory that is available to the other person.

- Post the certificate on a shared network volume that is available to the other person.

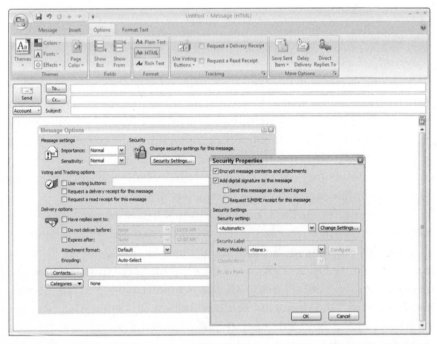

Figure 27.7. A message window, Message Options dialog box, and Security Properties dialog box.

The Outlook Help file has a lengthy article with additional information about encryption you can refer to. The important thing to understand is that without your certificate, the message you send will be unreadable, so it's a very good idea to make sure this is all working before sending critical correspondence that has been encrypted. You don't want to miss an important deadline because you were troubleshooting encryption!

The second section in the E-mail Security screen focuses on the digital certificates described in the preceding discussion on encryption. If you are interested in digitally signing your e-mail messages and Office documents and being able to send encrypted e-mail messages, you need a digital certificate. Assuming that you, like most people, do not have one, Microsoft has set up an Office Marketplace page that lists Certificate vendors who will be happy to sell you your own certificate — the average cost is under $20.00. To review the vendors and options currently available, click the button labeled Get a Digital ID and the E-mail Security dialog box shown in Figure 27.8 is displayed.

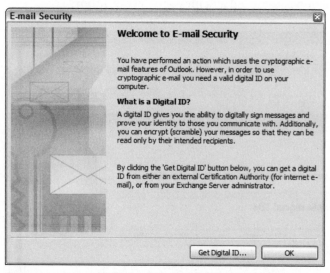

Figure 27.8. Get a digital ID (certificate) via this dialog box.

After reading the text in this dialog box, click Get Digital ID, which opens the Office Marketplace page, shown in Figure 27.9, that lists vendors of digital certificates in your browser. As the dialog box suggests, if you work in an Exchange Server environment, your network administrator may have configured the server to act as a CA. In that case, you can get a certificate from your company's server.

Watch Out!

Depending on the volume of e-mail you send, you may want to give careful thought about whether you really want to receive a receipt acknowledgement for every piece of mail you send. I find it's far more practical to request a receipt only for important correspondence.

This page and the extensive article in the Outlook Help file provide lots of useful information about how a digital ID or certificate can be used to digitally sign documents, enable data encryption, and request an S/MIME (Secure Multipurpose Internet Mail Extensions) receipt when an e-mail you send is received. Like encryption, this receipt function can be enabled on a per-message or application-wide basis. An S/MIME receipt is used to request confirmation that a message was received unaltered. It also includes information about who opened the message and when it was opened. This verification information is returned as a message in your Inbox.

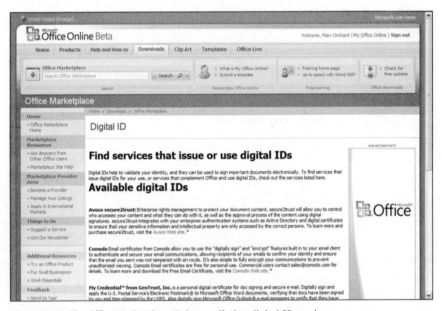

Figure 27.9. The Office Marketplace Web page listing digital ID vendors.

Attachment handling

File attachments to e-mail messages are a potential security risk, and the next screen in the Trust Center, shown in Figure 27.10, provides controls to prevent the exposure of your personal information in Office files you send and to affect how attached files are previewed in the Outlook Reading Pane. Given the fact that e-mail has become one of the most common ways to share files, understanding how to configure these controls can potentially save you from a lot of trouble.

Most Office applications provide a preview feature that allows a document to be shared, reviewed, and changed by multiple authors. The changes each person makes are tagged with his or her identity so that each subsequent reviewer can see what changes have been suggested and comments added by each person. This is an excellent way to collect feedback from the people you are collaborating with on a document, but it does expose your name and e-mail address to anyone who subsequently receives a copy of the document.

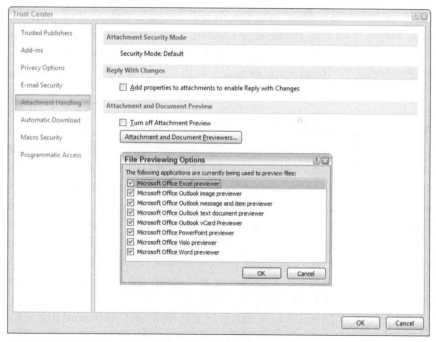

Figure 27.10. The Attachment Handling screen in the Trust Center.

If you do not use the Track Changes or other review features in Office, you can have Outlook automatically strip this personal information from any Office documents you send by deselecting the check box labeled Add properties to attachments to enable Reply with Changes. If you do use this feature in Office applications, leave the check box selected.

The second option in the Attachment Handling screen controls whether file attachments are previewed in the Reading Pane and, if so, which file formats you want to have displayed. To disable all attachment previews, select the check box labeled Turn off Attachment Preview. If you prefer to selectively control which files can be previewed in the Reading Pane, leave the check box selected and click the Attachment and Document Previewers button to open the File Previewing Options dialog box, shown inset in Figure 27.10.

A number of exploits or attacks have been created by virus and bad-ware creators that can compromise your system simply by previewing an infected file. The most common file formats for this sort of exploit have traditionally been Word files containing malicious macro code or scripts and image files in the Windows Metafile format. Assuming that you are running up-to-date antivirus and anti-spyware software on your system, these utilities catch most infected e-mail messages before they arrive in your Inbox. The File Previewing Options are a second layer of defense that you can use to fortify your PC. If there are file types you do not generally receive or don't care to preview in Outlook, by all means turn those preview options off.

Automatic download

The next screen in the Trust Center, shown in Figure 27.11, controls the automatic download of images in the e-mail messages you receive. As I mentioned in the previous section that discussed file attachments, infected images are a known exploit vector used by bad guys trying to compromise your system. Slightly less sinister but a legitimate privacy concern are images that contain a cookie or other tracking code that silently tells the server that hosts the image that you have opened or pre-viewed a message. This is a common technique used by both legitimate e-mail senders and spammers.

Mailers want to know how many of the messages they send are actually seen by the recipients on their list. This is often referred to as the "open rate" for a message. In and of itself, this information is innocuous, but it can be used to target additional advertising and spam or junk e-mail to you by attempting to learn what you find interesting.

The options in this screen are clearly explained and self-explanatory. I recommend that you leave all the check boxes selected to provide the best balance between security and functionality. The two possible exceptions are the controls related to RSS items and SharePoint discussion boards. If you do not subscribe to RSS feeds in Outlook and do not connect to any SharePoint sites, you're safe in deselecting those two options without affecting the usefulness of Automatic Download.

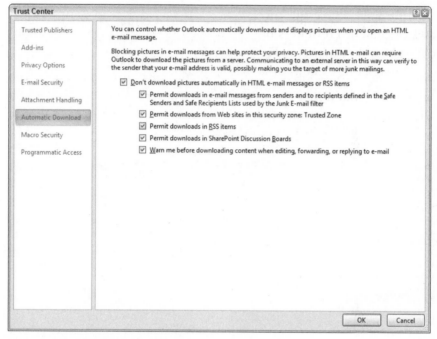

Figure 27.11. The Automatic Download screen in the Trust Center.

Macro security

Macros are executable code created using Visual Basic for Applications (VBA) that extends the capabilities of Office applications. There is a thriving community of VBA developers that create some amazing extensions to Office applications using these tools, but as is the case with most tools, the person wielding them dictates whether they are used for good or evil.

Because macros are relatively easy to construct from previously written chunks of code, this has become a favored technique for novice badware authors who are often referred to by information security folks as "script kiddies." Fortunately, Outlook and the other Office 2007 applications have robust controls that can eliminate the potential for unauthorized macro code to be executed on your PC.

Watch Out!
Under no circumstances do I recommend that you disable security checks on macros. In fact, I can't think of any good reason why Microsoft provided such easy access to this potentially disastrous option.

The Macro Security screen in the Trust Center, shown in Figure 27.12, provides this control. Depending on your level of paranoia — and when it comes to security, paranoia is a good thing to have a healthy amount of — you should select one of the first three options in this screen. I've found that the second option works fine for me because it allows macros signed with a digital certificate by a Trusted Publisher to execute and disables all other macros.

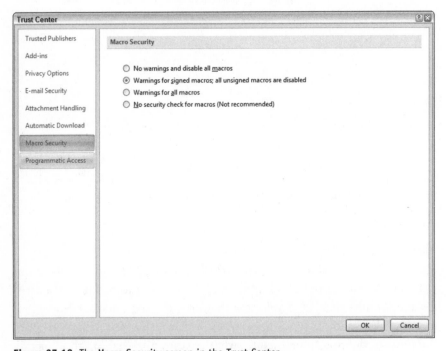

Figure 27.12. The Macro Security screen in the Trust Center.

Programmatic access

The final screen in the Trust Center, shown in Figure 27.13, provides options to control how Outlook alerts you when an external program attempts to access Outlook's Contacts list, the Windows Address Book, and Outlook's e-mail services. As with the Macro Security screen described in the previous section, there are only two legitimate choices and one you should never select. Actually, in this screen, there is only one option I can recommend with confidence, and that is the option labeled Always warn me about suspicious activity.

The only reason I can think of for selecting the first option that Microsoft has labeled as recommended is if you have an application on your system that you know is legitimately trying to access Outlook that generates a warning message every time it runs. This most commonly occurs with third-party applications that attempt to use Outlook's e-mail services or ones that synchronize Outlook data with another device like a remote PC or a PDA.

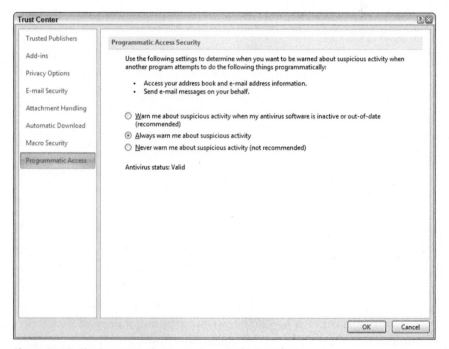

Figure 27.13. The Programmatic Access screen in the Trust Center.

Personally, I'd rather get the warning and manually permit the access, but that's just me. If you find that the warnings appear too frequently and are an annoyance, go with the first option and make sure your antivirus status, which is displayed in this screen, is valid. Under no circumstances can I think of a good reason to completely disable these warnings. Don't do it.

Antivirus and anti-spyware utilities

To wrap up this discussion about Outlook security, let me briefly touch on the subject of antivirus and anti-spyware software. This is a big topic — one that entire books are devoted to — that I can't possibly do justice to in this book. There are so many options available to secure your PC, applications, and information that it's equally impossible for me to make any specific recommendations about which tools you ought to use.

What I can do, with complete confidence, is offer the following thoughts about antivirus and anti-spyware software:

- ANY antivirus software is better than no antivirus software. Most knowledgeable PC users have their preference for a particular tool but YMMV (your mileage may vary) with a particular brand depending on how your system is configured in terms of compatibility and performance.

- Cost is not a reason to justify not running these utilities. Excellent tools are available at no charge for private, non-commercial use. If you're a business person, consider it another form of insurance for your business and buy a license for every PC you own.

- Set up your antivirus and anti-spyware software so that they automatically update themselves as new definition or signature files are released. This works best if you have a broadband, always-on connection, but even if you're still using a dial-up connection, always keep your utilities up to date.

- Run a firewall on your PC. Software firewalls control what kinds of information can be sent from and received by your PC. Windows XP includes a basic firewall. It works, and you should use it. If you want stronger, more configurable protection, any number of alternatives that range from no cost to around $50 per PC are available. In this day and age, there is no excuse for not running a firewall. It will not slow down your PC.

Thanks. I feel better having gotten that off my chest. I feel confident in making those statements for a couple of reasons — ones I think are very good. First, I worked for five years in the information security industry and have seen firsthand the consequences of failing to secure your PC. It's not a pretty picture.

Second, as the father and network administrator for a home with two net-surfing kids, I can tell you in all honesty that I have never had a PC in our home compromised by a virus or other badware. Not once. And I have not gone to any extraordinary lengths to secure my kids' laptops. I have installed antivirus and anti-spyware utilities on both of their PCs and have set them up to automatically update whenever a new signature or definition file is published. I've turned on the Windows firewall. That's been good enough.

On a closing note, I should point out that Windows Vista will include a utility called Windows Defender, shown in Figure 27.14, which protects against spyware. Windows Defender is available at no charge from Microsoft today for Windows XP systems, and if you are not running any anti-spyware software, you should put this book down, go to Microsoft's Web site, and download and install Windows Defender now. Like the Windows XP firewall, it's a good tool. If you are already using other tools, never mind. But if you've not yet erected any kind of barrier against spyware on your system, this is a smart way to add another layer of defense to your PC.

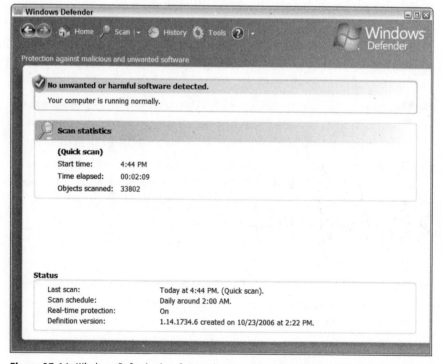

Figure 27.14. Windows Defender is a free anti-spyware tool from Microsoft for Windows XP and is built into Windows Vista.

Just the facts

- Outlook uses services from the Windows operating system and provides services to other applications that create security risks you should address.

- Outlook's Junk E-mail filters provide extensive controls that let you add people you want to hear from to a Safe Senders List and block spammers by listing them on a Blocked Senders List.

- Outlook allows you to block all traffic from country-specific top-level domains and messages encoded in certain character sets.

- Trust Center settings apply to all Office applications installed on your PC.

- The E-mail Security screen in the Trust Center specifically addresses Outlook and provides the ability to use digital IDs to encrypt and sign outgoing e-mail messages and to request receipt confirmation when your messages are received and opened.

- The Attachment Handling screen in the Trust Center provides control over how file attachments are previewed in Outlook's Reading Pane and whether personal information is included in the Office documents you send to others.

- The Automatic Download screen in the Trust Center addresses the downloading of images in HTML e-mail you receive, allowing you to make smart decisions about what images you want to view or block.

- The Macro Security screen in the Trust Center prevents malicious macro code from executing on your PC when included in an e-mail or file attachment.

- The Programmatic Access screen in the Trust Center gives you the ability to choose how Outlook alerts you when another program tries to access its information or services.

- Configure your antivirus and anti-spyware utilities to automatically download and install the latest signature or definition files as they are published.

Appendixes

PART VI

Outlook Keyboard Commands

Outlook contains hundreds of keyboard shortcuts that perform commands with the press of one or more modifier keys (Shift, Ctrl, or Alt) and a letter or number. The following list describes many of the keyboard commands available in Outlook.

When working in the content forms featuring the Ribbon UI, pressing the Alt key displays the letters used to switch between tabs on the Ribbon in each form.

Table AA-1: Basic Navigation

Action	Keyboard Command
Switch to Mail view	Ctrl+1
Switch to Calendar view	Ctrl+2
Switch to Contacts view	Ctrl+3
Switch to Tasks view	Ctrl+4
Switch to Notes view	Ctrl+5
Switch to Folder List (Navigation Pane)	Ctrl+6
Switch to Shortcuts	Ctrl+7
Switch to next message (in an open message window)	Ctrl+period

continued

Table AA-1 *continued*

Action	Keyboard Command
Switch to previous messages (in an open message window)	Ctrl+comma
Switch focus to the Navigation Pane, main view area, the Reading Pane, and the To-Do Bar	F6 or Ctrl+Shift+Tab
Switch focus to the Outlook window, the smaller panes in the Navigation Pane, the Reading Pane, and section in the To-Do Bar	Tab
Go to Folder (dialog box)	Ctrl+Y
Activate the Instant Search box	F3 or Ctrl+E
Next Message in Reading Pane	Alt+down arrow or Ctrl+period or Alt+Page Down
Previous Message in Reading Pane	Alt+up arrow or Ctrl+comma or Alt+Page Up
Page down through Message text	spacebar
Page up through Message text	Shift+spacebar
Expand or collapse a Folder group in the Navigation Pane	Shift+plus sign or Shift+minus sign
Collapse to expand a selected group in the e-mail Message List	left arrow or right arrow
Back to previous view in main window	Alt+B or Alt+left arrow or Alt+Backspace
Forward to next view in main window	Alt+right arrow

Table AA-2: Search

Action	Keyboard Command
Activate Search box	F3 or Ctrl+E
Clear Search results	Esc
Expand Search to All Items (Mail, Calendar, or Contacts views)	Ctrl+Alt+A

Action	Keyboard Command
Advanced Find	Ctrl+Shift+F
New Search Folder	Ctrl+Shift+P
Search for text in an open message or other item window	F4
Find next occurrence in a text search in an open message or other item window	Shift+F4
Find and Replace text	Ctrl+H
Expand Search to include desktop items	Ctrl+Alt+K

Table AA-3: Create New Items

Action	Keyboard Command
New appointment	Ctrl+Shift+A
New contact	Ctrl+Shift+C
New distribution list	Ctrl+Shift+L
New folder	Ctrl+Shift+E
New journal entry	Ctrl+Shift+J
New meeting request	Ctrl+Shift+Q
New e-mail message	Ctrl+Shift+M
New note	Ctrl+Shift+N
New Office document	Ctrl+Shift+H
New Search Folder	Ctrl+Shift+P
New task	Ctrl+Shift+K
New task request	Ctrl+Shift+U

Table AA-4: File Operations

Action	Keyboard Command
Save	Ctrl+S or Shift+F12
Save and close	Alt+S
Save as	F12
Undo	Ctrl+Z or Alt+Backspace
Delete an item	Ctrl+D
Print	Ctrl+P
Copy an item	Ctrl+Shift+Y
Move an item	Ctrl+Shift+V
Check names	Ctrl+K
Check spelling	F7
Flag for follow-up	Ctrl+Shift+G
Forward	Ctrl+F
Send	Alt+S
Turn on editing in a field (except icon view)	F2
Left align text	Ctrl+L
Center text	Ctrl+E
Right align text	Ctrl+R

Table AA-5: E-mail Operations

Action	Keyboard Command
Switch to Inbox	Ctrl+Shift+I
Switch to Outbox	Ctrl+Shift+O
Choose account from which to send a message	Ctrl+Tab (with focus on the To: field, then Tab to the Accounts button)
Send	Alt+S
Reply to message	Ctrl+R

Action	Keyboard Command
Reply all to a message	Ctrl+Shift+R
Forward a message	Ctrl+F
Mark a message as not junk	Ctrl+Alt+J
Display blocked external content in a message	Ctrl+Shift+I
Check for new messages	Ctrl+M or F9
Go to previous message	up arrow
Go to next message	down arrow
Create a new message (in Mail view)	Ctrl+N
Open a received message	Ctrl+O
Open the Address Book	Ctrl+Shift+B
Convert HTML or RTF message to plain text	Ctrl+Shift+O
Add a Quick Flag to an unopened message	Insert
Display the Flag for Follow Up dialog box	Ctrl+Shift+G
Mark as read	Ctrl+Q
Mark as unread	Ctrl+U
Display the message options menu (download pictures, change automatic download settings, or add a sender to the Safe Senders list)	Ctrl+Shift+W
Find or Replace	F4
Find next	Shift+F4
Send	Ctrl+Enter
Print	Ctrl+P
Forward	Ctrl+F
Forward as attachment	Ctrl+Alt+F
Show properties	Alt+Enter
Mark for Download	Ctrl+Alt+M
Display Send/Receive progress	Ctrl+B (when Send/Receive is in progress)

Table AA-6: Calendar Operations

Action	Keyboard Command
New appointment (in Calendar view)	Ctrl+N
New appointment (in any Outlook view)	Ctrl+Shift+A
New meeting request	Ctrl+Shift+Q
Forward a meeting or appointment	Ctrl+F
Reply to a meeting request with a message	Ctrl+R
Reply All to a meeting request with a message	Ctrl+Shift+R
Show 10 days in the calendar	Alt+0
Show 1-9 days in the calendar	Alt+1-9
Go to a date	Ctrl+G
Switch to month view	Alt+= or Ctrl+Alt+4
Go to the next day	Ctrl+right arrow
Go to the next week	Alt+down arrow
Go to the next month	Alt+Page Down
Go to the previous day	Ctrl+left arrow
Go to the previous week	Alt+up arrow
Go to the previous month	Alt+Page Up
Go to the start of the week	Alt+Home
Go to the end of the week	Alt+End
Switch to Full Week view	Alt+minus sign or Ctrl+Alt+3
Switch to Work Week view	Ctrl+Alt+2
Go to previous appointment	Ctrl+comma or Ctrl+Shift+comma
Go to next appointment	Ctrl+period or Ctrl+Shift+period
Set up recurrence for an appointment or task	Ctrl+G

Table AA-7: Contacts Operations

Action	Keyboard Command
Dial a new call	Ctrl+Shift+D
Find a contact or other item	F3 or Ctrl+E
Enter a name in the Search Address Books box	F11
In Table or List view of contacts, go to first contact that starts with a specific letter	Shift+*letter*
Select all contacts	Ctrl+A
Create a new message addressed to selected contact	Ctrl+F
Create a journal entry for the selected contact	Ctrl+J
Create a new contact (when in Contacts)	Ctrl+N
Create a new contact (from any Outlook view)	Ctrl+Shift+C
Open a contact form for the selected contact	Ctrl+O or Ctrl+Shift+Enter
Create a new distribution list	Ctrl+Shift+L
Print	Ctrl+P
Update a list of distribution list members	F5
Go to a different folder	Ctrl+Y
Open the Address Book	Ctrl+Shift+B
Use Advanced Find	Ctrl+Shift+F
In an open contact, open the next contact listed	Ctrl+Shift+period
Close a contact	Esc
Open a Web page for the selected contact (if one is included)	Ctrl+Shift+X
Open the Check Address dialog box	Alt+D
In a contact form, under Internet, display the E-mail 1 information	Alt+Shift+1
In a contact form, under Internet, display the E-mail 2 information	Alt+Shift+2
In a contact form, under Internet, display the E-mail 3 information	Alt+Shift+3

Table AA-8: Tasks Operations

Action	Keyboard Command
Show or hide the To-Do Bar	Alt+F2
Accept a task request	Alt+C
Decline a task request	Alt+D
Find a task or other item	Ctrl+E
Open the Go to Folder dialog box	Ctrl+Y
Create a new task (when in Tasks)	Ctrl+N
Create a new task (from any Outlook view)	Ctrl+Shift+K
Create a new task request	Ctrl+Shift+U
Open selected item	Ctrl+O
Print selected item	Ctrl+P
Select all items	Ctrl+A
Delete selected item	Ctrl+D
Forward a task as an attachment	Ctrl+F
Switch between the Navigation Pane, Tasks list, and To-Do Bar	Shift+Tab
Open selected item as a journal item	Ctrl+J
Undo last action	Ctrl+Z
Flag an item or mark complete	Insert

Table AA-9: Text Formatting Operations

Action	Keyboard Command
Display the Format menu	Alt+O
Display the Font dialog box	Ctrl+Shift+P
Switch case (with text selected)	Shift+F3

Action	Keyboard Command
Format letters as small capitals	Ctrl+Shift+K
Make letters bold	Ctrl+B
Add bullets	Ctrl+Shift+L
Make letters italic	Ctrl+I
Increase indent	Ctrl+T
Decrease indent	Ctrl+Shift+T
Left align	Ctrl+L
Center	Ctrl+E
Underline	Ctrl+U
Increase font size	Ctrl+] or Ctrl+Shift+>
Decrease font size	Ctrl+[or Ctrl+Shift+<
Cut	Ctrl+X or Shift+Delete
Copy	Ctrl+C or Ctrl+Insert
Paste	Ctrl+V or Shift+Insert
Clear formatting	Ctrl+Shift+Z or Ctrl+spacebar
Delete the next word	Ctrl+Shift+H
Stretch a paragraph to fit between the margins	Ctrl+Shift+J
Apply styles	Ctrl+Shift+S
Create a hanging indent	Ctrl+T
Insert a hyperlink	Ctrl+K
Left align a paragraph	Ctrl+L
Right align a paragraph	Ctrl+R
Reduce a hanging indent	Ctrl+Shift+T
Remove paragraph formatting	Ctrl+Q

Table AA-10: Print Preview Operations

Action	Keyboard Command
Open Print Preview	Ctrl+F2
Print a print preview	Alt+P
Open Page Setup from Print Preview	Alt+S or Alt+U
Zoom	Alt+Z
Close Print Preview	Alt+C

Table AA-11: Send/Receive Operations

Action	Keyboard Command
Start a send/receive for all defined Send/Receive groups that Include this group in Send/Receive (F9) selected	F9
Start a send/receive for the current folder, retrieving full items	Shift+F9
Start a send/receive	Ctrl+M
Define Send/Receive groups	Ctrl+Alt+S

Recommended Reading

An incredible amount of additional reading is available to help you learn more about Outlook. I recently searched Amazon.com for "Microsoft Outlook" and found 3,080 book results. In addition to books, you can turn to many online resources, which is the subject of Appendix C.

The books I've listed here were chosen less for their value as references about Outlook and more for their discussions of how to put Outlook to work. Two are specifically about Outlook and two are more general in nature but completely applicable to Outlook as the central dashboard from which you run your day. I have no doubt that you will learn much about time and task management, managing e-mail overload, and feeling more in control of your information after reading any (or all) of them.

Getting Things Done: The Art of Stress-Free Productivity

Getting Things Done: The Art of Stress-Free Productivity, David Allen. Viking Adult, 2001.

I cannot recommend this book too highly: It has been a life-changer for me. David Allen's approach to personal productivity has been adopted by people all over the world and by organizations of all sizes. In typical self-deprecating fashion, Allen claims he has a degree in "advanced common sense" and after reading the book you may agree.

It's not so much that GTD (as fans refer to it) contains brand new, never before seen or heard ideas. It's the way so many ideas and techniques you may have encountered are assembled into a methodology that is easy to get started with and to refine and adapt to your individual needs as you master the basics.

I've gotten to know David Allen over the years I've been practicing GTD and have gone to his well-attended seminars twice. Each time, I have walked away with new insights into how to get more done each day and reduce the amount of stress my workload creates.

Total Workday Control Using Microsoft Outlook: The Eight Best Practices of Task and E-Mail Management

Total Workday Control Using Microsoft Outlook: The Eight Best Practices of Task and E-Mail Management, Michael Linenberger. New Academy Publishers, 2006.

Total Workday Control is an Outlook-specific approach to getting your Inbox empty on a regular basis by moving every actionable e-mail message to your calendar or task list. Built on a number of time and task management ideas borrowed from David Allen and Steven Covey, TWC shows you in step-by-step instructions, how to take advantage of the power made available by Outlook's customizable views to create a powerful system for managing your work (and play).

I was honored when Michael asked me to contribute the Foreword to this book, and I recommend it all the time. I can tell you that no one has ever complained about this recommendation! Michael's techniques have recently been incorporated into a template for the ClearContext Inbox Management System I describe in Chapter 17.

Take Back Your Life! Special Edition: Using Microsoft Outlook to Get Organized and Stay Organized

Take Back Your Life! Special Edition: Using Microsoft Outlook to Get Organized and Stay Organized, Sally McGhee. Microsoft Press; Book & CD-ROM edition, 2005.

Sally McGhee and David Allen (*Getting Things Done*) were early collaborators, so it's no surprise that *Take Back Your Life* and GTD have so much in common. There are differences in the approach each author takes, but the common elements make *Take Back Your Life* a great companion to *Getting Things Done.* Unlike GTD, which remains agnostic about the tools and technology used to implement its practices, McGhee's approach is all about Outlook, and the most recent edition of the book has been updated to address some of the new features in Outlook 2007 and includes a CD with resource and reference material.

The Simplicity Survival Handbook: 32 Ways to Do Less and Accomplish More

The Simplicity Survival Handbook: 32 Ways to Do Less and Accomplish More, Bill Jensen. Basic Books, 2003.

Bill Jensen's *Simplicity Survival Handbook* has absolutely nothing to do with Outlook. That in no way takes away the value in reading the book, which provides a number of recipes for simplifying your workday and helping you focus on what's really important. Jensen has a wicked sense of humor — one of the suggestions in the book is to rip a single chapter out and throw the rest of the book away.

Jensen has written a number of books, but I think this is the single best volume for people looking for simple changes they can make to their approach to work that pay back big dividends. My favorite idea from the book is the idea that the most important number in your life is 1440. That is the number of minutes each of you gets in a day. No one gets more. No one gets less. How you decide to spend those minutes has everything to do with how much and what you get accomplished each day.

Online Resources

An overwhelming amount of information is available online about Microsoft Outlook. Conduct a search in your favorite search engine, and you can find millions of results. With so much information available, finding the best resources for answers to your questions about using Outlook can be challenging.

I've put together the following list of online resources to help you get started. It is in no way intended to be exhaustive (millions of search results, remember?), but it does represent the sites that I visit most frequently and the blogs that have found a permanent spot in my RSS subscription list.

Microsoft Office Online

This is the official 2007 Microsoft Office system Web site found at `http://office.microsoft.com`.

This site should be the first bookmark you should add to your Web browser. It has a wealth of information, training materials, templates, clip art, and other resources to extend and enhance your experience using the Office suite. The Outlook section provides access to an amazing quantity of information that can help you become a power Outlook user.

Microsoft Learning

The 2007 Microsoft Office system Learning Portal, located at www.microsoft.com/learning/office2007/default.mspx, provides a variety of learning tools for users of the company's technologies. The company publishes books, training courses, and other materials to assist individuals and organizations in enhancing their skills and knowledge. The Learning Portal is a section of the Microsoft Learning site devoted entirely to education materials focused on the new version of Office.

Microsoft Small Business Center

Found at www.microsoft.com/smallbusiness/hub.mspx, the Small Business Center is another Microsoft resource site that is the best place to start when looking for information about using Business Contact Manager, Small Business Accounting, the Dynamics CRM system, and other tools in conjunction with Outlook 2007 to support your small business.

Office Zealot.com

The Office Zealot community site (http://officezealot.com/Office2007) is where I began my blogging career and is one of the best collections of information about Microsoft Office. The Office Zealot site aggregates the blogs of nearly 100 Microsoft and third-party developers who blog about every conceivable aspect of the Office system and related technologies. The URL provided here takes you to everything on the site related to Office 2007.

Slipstick Systems

Slipstick Systems (www.slipstick.com) is a site devoted entirely to Outlook and Exchange Server. Founded by Sue Mosher, a well-known Microsoft MVP for Outlook, the site was sold to another Outlook MVP, Diane Poremsky, who continues to provide up-to-date information about extending Outlook with add-ins and utility applications as well as providing a steady stream of news about Outlook and Exchange Server. The site offers free e-mail newsletter and RSS subscriptions.

Sperry Systems

I recommend Sperry Systems in Chapter 17 as an excellent one-stop shop for Outlook add-ins. All the company's products are high-quality tools that can extend and enhance Outlook to better support the type of work you do. Find them at www.sperrysoftware.com/Outlook/default.asp.

The Office UI Bible (online)

Located at http://blogs.msdn.com/jensenh/archive/2006/11/10/the-office-2007-ui-bible.aspx, Jensen Harris, who is a member of the Office team at Microsoft, has been chronicling the evolution of the new user interface in Office 2007. Since beginning work on the project, Jensen has written more than 200 articles on his blog that describe the thoughts and decision-making behind what is inarguably the single biggest overhaul of the Office suite since it was first released 11 versions ago. A Microsoft MVP for OneNote named Patrick Schmid assembled all of Jensen's posts into a nicely organized Office UI Bible, which is a great reference when you're wondering why things work the way they do in Office 2007.

Time and Task Management in Outlook blog

Melissa Macbeth's Time and Task Management in Outlook blog (http://blogs.msdn.com/melissamacbeth/) is one of my favorite sources of great ideas for using Outlook to maximum effect. Melissa is a Program Manager in the Outlook group at Microsoft.

Time and Task Management using Microsoft Outlook

This is a Microsoft e-Learning course that I co-authored with fellow blogger Jeremy Wright in 2005. Find it at www.microsoft.com/learning/syllabi/en-us/4006Afinal.mspx.

Although it was written for Outlook 2003 users, all the advice, techniques, and procedures for maximizing Outlook by creating custom views is just as applicable to Outlook 2007.

address book Contains information about individuals and groups including name, physical and network addresses, phone numbers, and more. Your address book may be provided by Microsoft Outlook, Microsoft Exchange Server, Microsoft SharePoint Server, or a directory service, depending on how Outlook has been configured.

address card A layout option in Outlook that displays contact information in a format similar to a conventional business card.

All Mail Folders The list that displays all the folders available in your mailbox(es). If the Folder List is not visible, click the Folder List icon or button on the Navigation Pane.

appointment An item in your Calendar that does not include invitations to or from other people.

archiving Moving old or expired items out of your primary PST file to a separate PST file or other location for storage.

attachment A file that is delivered with an e-mail message, meeting request, or assigned task.

AutoArchive A feature in Outlook that archives messages automatically at scheduled intervals. AutoArchive is active by default on all folders in your Outlook PST file. Each folder can have its own settings.

AutoPreview An option in the Message List that displays the first three lines of each message in your Inbox or other message folders.

Cached Exchange Mode An Exchange Server option that provides the option in Outlook to create local copies of your mailbox and address book and keep them synchronized with the server. Cached Exchange Mode monitors your connection status and speed. When you are not connected to the server, you can perform almost all operations except sending and receiving new e-mail. When you are connected, Cached Exchange Mode optimizes data transfer based on the speed of your connection.

Calendar The time management view in Outlook.

category A keyword or phrase that you can assign to Outlook items to allow for filtering, organizing, and viewing related items. In Outlook 2007, categories use color and can be attached to every information object in the application.

contact A record in your Contacts folder in which information — such as street and e-mail addresses, telephone and fax numbers, and Web page URLs — related to an individual or organization is stored.

Date Navigator The thumbnail calendar that appears next to the appointment area in the Outlook Calendar and in the new To-Do Bar in all views. You can jump to any date by selecting it in the Date Navigator.

desktop alert A small window that appears on your desktop when a new e-mail message arrives in your Inbox.

distribution list A grouping of individual e-mail addresses combined into a single name in your Contacts list. When you send an e-mail message to the list name, everyone included receives a copy of the message.

draft A message that has not been sent. Draft messages are stored in their own folder.

e-mail address A unique text string, including a person's user name and domain name separated by the @ sign — for example, someone@company.com.

e-mail server A computer that handles sending, receiving, and storing of e-mail messages.

encrypting A method used to protect information in transit. An encrypted message is unreadable by anyone except the recipient, who uses a public key provided by the sender to decrypt it.

event An Outlook Calendar entry for an activity that lasts 24 hours or longer. Also called an all-day event.

Folder List The Navigation Pane view that displays the folders available in your mailbox. The Folder List can be displayed by selecting the Folder List from the View menu or by clicking the Folder List icon at the bottom of the Navigation Pane.

Follow-Up Flag A flag that can be applied to an e-mail message to indicate that an action needs to be taken. Outlook and OneNote can synchronize follow-up flag information in tasks and meeting notes.

Global Address List An address book served from a Microsoft Exchange Server that contains all the e-mail addresses in your organization.

HTML Stands for Hypertext Markup Language, a tag-based language used to create Web pages and format e-mail messages.

HTML format The default format used by Outlook to compose e-mail messages with rich content including images, colors, multiple fonts, tables, and other enhancements.

HTTP Stands for HyperText Transfer Protocol, a protocol used to access Web pages and Webmail services like HotMail.

IMAP Stands for Internet Message Access Protocol, an e-mail protocol that stores messages on a server and provides you with the option to choose which messages to download by viewing their headers.

importance A tag that can be applied to reflect the urgency of an e-mail message. Messages can be tagged High, Normal, or Low importance in Outlook.

Inbox The default message folder in Outlook where incoming messages arrive.

instant messaging An internet application that allows you to conduct text-based, voice, or video conversations in real time over the Internet.

Internet mail An e-mail account that you connect to over the Internet. POP3, IMAP, and HTTP are the protocols used to access Internet mail accounts.

meeting request A specially formatted e-mail message used to invite recipients to a meeting.

message header Summary information that can be downloaded to your computer and used to decide whether to download, copy, or delete an entire message from the server.

Microsoft Exchange Server An e-mail and collaboration server used in many mid-sized and large organizations.

Navigation Pane A customizable panel on the left side of Outlook's application window that allows you to navigate between views, invoke layouts, and access mail folders.

news server A computer that hosts newsgroups.

newsgroup A collection of messages, grouped together and arranged by date, that relate to a particular topic posted to a news server.

newsreader A program that is used to read messages posted to a newsgroup. Windows XP includes Outlook Express to read and participate in newsgroups. Windows Vista includes Windows Live Mail Desktop to provide this capability. Web-based newsgroup readers are also available from Google and other providers.

Outlook Rich Text Format (RTF) A format for Outlook e-mail messages that supports a number of formatting options. RTF is supported by some Microsoft e-mail clients including recent versions of Outlook (97 and newer).

plain text A format for e-mail messages that does not include any text formatting. Plain text is supported by all e-mail programs.

POP3 (Post Office Protocol) The most common protocol used to retrieve e-mail messages from an Internet e-mail server.

print style A predefined set of paper and page settings that defines the way Outlook items are printed.

private A setting that can be applied to appointments or meetings so that other users cannot see the details, even if they have permission to view your calendar.

Reading Pane An area of the main Mail view in Outlook that displays e-mail messages without having to open them.

recurring A setting that can be applied to any appointment or task that occurs on a regular basis.

reminder A message that appears at a specified interval before an appointment, meeting, or task announcing when the activity is set to occur. Reminders appear anytime Outlook is running, even if it isn't your active program.

Ribbon A replacement for conventional toolbars used in Outlook 2007 content forms and in Word, Excel, and PowerPoint 2007.

rules An Outlook feature that combines conditions, actions, and exceptions to automatically process and organize messages.

Search Folder A virtual folder that contains a view of all e-mail items matching specific search criteria. Items deleted while viewing a Search Folder are actually deleted, but deleting a Search Folder only deletes the virtual folder, not its contents.

Secure Multipurpose Internet Mail Extensions (S/MIME) A standard for generating authenticated and encrypted e-mail.

sensitivity A security setting applied to an e-mail message to indicate whether a message should be treated as normal, personal, private, or confidential.

signature Text and/or pictures that can be manually or automatically appended to the end of an outgoing or forwarded e-mail message.

spam Junk e-mail, sometimes euphemistically called Unsolicited Commercial E-mail.

stationery A pre-designed layout for e-mail messages that specifies fonts, images, and other design elements.

synchronizing Copying changed items between a server and a corresponding folder on a PC so that both are up to date.

Task Input Panel Tasks that appear in the To-Do Bar.

Tasks list Tasks that appear in the Tasks folder and in the Task Input Panel in the To-Do Bar.

theme A set of unified design elements and color schemes used to automatically format e-mail messages. Outlook 2007 includes a gallery of themes.

Uniform Resource Locator (URL) A text string that defines the address of Web pages and other resources available on the Internet.

vCard A standard format for storing and sharing contact information.

virtual folders Similar to shortcuts on the Windows desktop. Virtual folders link to an original folder without requiring the contents of the actual folder be copied. Search Folders are one type of virtual folder.

Windows SharePoint Services A Microsoft server product used to create and publish team Web sites used for information sharing and document collaboration.

work week A designation in the Outlook Calendar of the days you are available for work-related appointments and meetings. The days outside your selected work week are shaded to indicate that you typically are not available on those days.

A

S

Safe Lists Only setting, 487, 488

Safe Recipients tab, 488–489, 490–491

Safe Senders tab, 488–489, 490–491

sales activities, 369

Save & New control, 150, 151

Save As command, 127

Save command, 449

SCANPST

backup files created by, 454–455

running on Outlook PST files, 322

scanning PST files, 38–39

using, 464

verifying integrity, 60

Schedule+ 7.x, 35

Scheduling Assistant, 391

Scheduling control, 176, 179

Scheduling view, 179

script kiddies, 501

scripting language, 348

Search and Link control, 381

Search box, 83–86, 145–146

search capabilities, 21–22

Search Folder Criteria dialog box, 140, 249, 250

Search Folders

creating a river of news, 139–141

creating custom, 249–251

default, 244–246

described, 72–73, 243–244

finding large files, 471–472

modifying, 251

predefined, 247–249

Search Options dialog box, 85–86, 302

Search Options menu, 299

search parameters, 300

search results, presentation of, 84

searches, 84, 85, 299

searching

linked contacts, 163

in the Notes view, 219

security in Outlook, 486–487, 488, 489, 492–503

Security Properties dialog box, 495, 496

Select Attendees and Resources dialog box, 180

Select control, 110

Select Folder(s) dialog box, 140, 250–251

Send a Calendar via E-mail dialog box, 117, 187–188

Send button, 127

Send command, 150

Send e-mail command, 344

Send/Receive Groups dialog box, 53, 55

Send/Receive Settings dialog box, 55–56

Sent Items, archiving, 469

Sent Items folder, 468–469, 470

server storage, 452

Service Properties dialog box, 363, 364

service providers for Exchange Server, 389

shapes, 92–93, 100

Shapes gallery, 100, 102

Shared Notebook templates, 406, 407

SharePoint

accessing group calendars, 190

described, 28–29

discussion boards, 501

environment, 429

Outlook and, 486–487, 488, 489, 492–503

Shortcuts display, 80–81

Show As control, 176

Show Fields dialog box, 212, 260–261

Show group, 151–152, 176, 201

Show in Groups command, 209, 246

side-by-side mode for calendars, 191–192

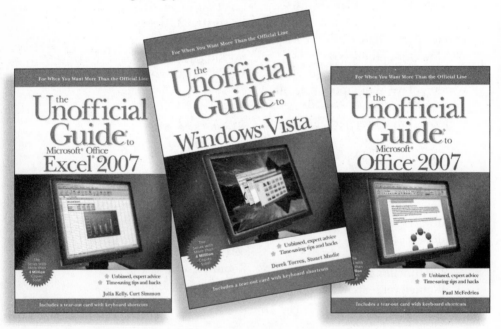
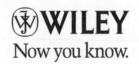